J. B. LIGHTFOOT

The Acts of the Apostles
A Newly Discovered Commentary

THE LIGHTFOOT LEGACY SET

◆

Volume 1

Edited by
BEN WITHERINGTON III
and **TODD D. STILL**

IVP Academic

An imprint of InterVarsity Press
Downers Grove, Illinois

InterVarsity Press
P.O. Box 1400, Downers Grove, IL 60515-1426
World Wide Web: www.ivpress.com
Email: email@ivpress.com

InterVarsity Press® is the book-publishing division of InterVarsity Christian Fellowship/USA®, a movement of students and faculty active on campus at hundreds of universities, colleges and schools of nursing in the United States of America, and a member movement of the International Fellowship of Evangelical Students. For information about local and regional activities, write Public Relations Dept., InterVarsity Christian Fellowship/USA, 6400 Schroeder Rd., P.O. Box 7895, Madison, WI 53707-7895, or visit the IVCF website at www.intervarsity.org.

Cover design: David Fassett
Interior design: Beth McGill
Images: Joseph Lightfoot, English theologian and Bishop of Durham, Lock and Whitfield (19th century) / Private Collection / © Look and Learn / Elgar Collection / Bridgeman Images
recycled paper: © tomograf/iStockphoto
glossy insert page images courtesy of Durham Cathedral Library / © Chapter of Durham Cathedral

ISBN 978-0-8308-2944-6 (print)
ISBN 978-0-8308-9673-8 (digital)

Printed in the United States of America ∞

Library of Congress Cataloging-in-Publication Data
Lightfoot, Joseph Barber, 1828-1889.
 The Acts of the Apostles : a new commentary / by J.B. Lightfoot ;
edited and annotated by Ben Witherington III and Todd D. Still ;
assisted by Jeanette M. Hagen.
  pages cm.—(The Lightfoot legacy ; Volume One)
 Includes bibliographical references and index.
 ISBN 978-0-8308-2944-6 (hardcover : alk. paper)
 1. Bible. Acts—Commentaries. I. Witherington, Ben, III, 1951-
editor. II. Title.
 BS2625.53.L54 2014
 226.6'07—dc23

                                                                    2014024728

P	23	22	21	20	19	18	17	16	15	14	13	12	11	10	9	8	7	6	5	4	3	2	1
Y	33	32	31	30	29	28	27	26	25	24	23	22	21	20	19	18	17	16	15	14			

Figure 1. J. B. Lightfoot

Quotations Regarding
J. B. Lightfoot and His Work
(On Acts)

"Lightfoot had looked forward to writing a commentary on the Acts."[1]
F. J. A. Hort

"His editions and commentaries . . . as well as his critical dissertations have an imperishable value, and even where it is impossible to agree with his results, his grounds are never to be neglected. The respect for his opponent which distinguished him . . . has brought him the highest respect of all parties. . . . There never has been an apologist who was less of an advocate than Lightfoot. . . . He [was] an independent, free scholar . . . in the absolute sense of the words. He has never defended a tradition for the tradition's sake. But how many times, when the tradition was previously defended inadequtely and so threatened to lose its reputation, has he saved the tradition with sweeping reasons!"[2]
Adolf von Harnack

"In the great bulk of his literary work Bishop Lightfoot depended entirely on his own labours. He never employed an amanuensis; he rarely allowed anyone else even to verify his references. The only relief which he would accept was the almost mechanical correction of the proof/sheets of the new editions, as they were called for, of his Epistles of St Paul."[3]
H. E. Savage

"His lectures on the Greek New Testament were distinguished not only by their ability but also by their spiritual power. A pupil who attended one of the earliest

---

[1] F. J. A. Hort, "Lightfoot, Joseph Barber," in *The Dictionary of National Biography*, ed. L. Stephen (London: Smith, Elder and Co., 1885), 33:238. Hort wrote the biographical entry on Lightfoot.
[2] Adolf von Harnack, review of *Essays in Biblical Greek* by Edwin Hatch, *Theologische Literaturzeitung* 15, no. 12 (1890): 298. Cf Hort, "Lightfoot," pp. 239-40.
[3] G. R. Eden and F. C. Macdonald, eds., *Lightfoot of Durham* (Cambridge: Cambridge University Press, 1932), p. 110.

courses remarks: 'I remember well how much the class was impressed, when, after giving us the usual introductory matter, Lightfoot closed the book and said, "After all is said and done, the only way to know the Greek Testament properly is by prayer" and dwelt further on this thought."[4]

The Cambridge Review

"We are glad to be able to hope, from hints which have from time to time reached the public ear, that a large portion of the whole field was covered by Dr. Lightfoot's labours, and that some of the MSS. which are in the care of his literary executors will in due course be published; for even if they are only posthumous fragments, the student . . . will thankfully welcome them."

Anonymous obituary to Lightfoot in the *Contemporary Review,* 1890

---

[4]Cited by Eden and Macdonald, *Lightfoot of Durham,* p. 13.

To the two most recent Lightfoot Professors of Divinity at

Durham University, J. D. G. Dunn and John M. G. Barclay,

as well as to C. K. Barrett, another University of Durham

professor of divinity of blessed memory.

CONTENTS

Abbreviations

ANCIENT AUTHORS AND WORKS

Achilles Tat.	Achilles Tatius, *Leucippe et Clitophon*
Aelian	
Var. Hist.	*Varia historia*
Aeschylus	
Eum.	*Eumenides*
Pers.	*Persae*
Sept. C. Theb.	*Septem contra Thebas*
Ambrose	
Exp. Evang. Luc.	*Expositio Evangelii secundum Lucam*
Ammon. Macel./Amm. Marc./	Ammaianus Marcellinus
Apostl. Const.	*Apostolic Constitutions*
Arastus/Ar. Ach.	
Phenom.	*Phaenomena*
Arch.	Archilochus
Arist.	Aristotle or Aristophanes
Aristotle	
De Mund.	*De Mundo*
Polit.	*Politics*
Rhet.	*Rhetoric*
Aristophanes	
Av.	*Aves*
Nub.	*Nubes*
Ran.	*Ranae*
Arrian	
Hist.	*History of Alexander's Expedition* (= *Anabasis*)
Athanasius	
Ep. Ad Dracont.	*Letter to Dracontius*
Auctor, Ab Catapha.	Author, *Of Cataphaticism*
Augustine	
Op.	*De opera monachorum*
B.T.	Babylonian Talmud
Sanhed.	*Sanhedrin*
Chrystost.	John Chrysostom
Ap./ap. Aeg./Comm. in Acts Apostl.	*Homiliae in Acta apostolorum*
Cicero	
ad Att.	*Epistulae ad Atticum*
de Leg.	*De legibus*
Pro Bal.	*Pro Balbo*

Pro Flacc.	*Pro Flacco*
Pro Aui.	*Pro Quinctio*
Pro Rabri.	*Pro Rabirio Postumo*
Verr.	*In Verrem*
Cleanthes	*Clementine Recognitions*
Hymn	*Hymn to Zeus*
Clem Recogn	*Clementine Recognitions*
Clem. of Rom.	Clement of Rome
Clemen. *Hom.*	*The Clementine Homilies*
Clement of Alexandria	
Strom.	*Stromata*
Corpus Inscrip.	Corpus Inscription
Cyril of Jerusalem	
Catech.	*Catecheses*
D(iog). L(aertius)	Diogenes Laertius
Pythag.	*Life of Pythagoras*
Demosthenes	
Panton.	*Contra Pantaenetum*
Diod(orus) Sic(culus)	Diodorus Sicculus
Dionysius of Hal.	Dionysius of Halicarnassus
Epiph.	Epiphanius
Haer.	*Adversus haereses*
Pan.	*Panarion*
Epist. Barnab.	*Epistle of Barnabas*
Euripides	
Iph./Iph. Taur.	*Iphigenia taurica*
Eury. *Ion*	Euripides, *Ion*
Eus.	Eusebius of Caesarea
H.E.	*Historia ecclesiastica*
Praep. Evang.	*Praeparatio evangelica*
Galen	
Anat./deAnat.Admin.	*De Anatomicis Administrationibus*
Herod.	Herodotus
Hier.	Hieronymus (*see* Jerome)
Hilar.	Hilary of Poitiers
Horace	
Epod.	*Epodi*
Ig.	Ignatius
Ephes.	*Epistle to the Ephesians*
Magn.	*Epistle to the Magnesians*

Philad.	*Epistle to the Philadelphians*
Polyc.	*Epistle to Polycarp*
Rom.	*Epistle to the Romans*
Smyrn.	*Epistle to the Smyrnaeans*
Iph. Taur.	*see* Euripides
Isidor. Pelus.	Isidore of Pelusium
Ep.	*Epistles*
Jerome	
ad. Tit.	*Commentariorum in Epistulam ad Titum liber*
De Eccles. Script.	*De Scriptoribus Ecclesiasticus*
De Ver. Illustr.	*De viris illustribus*
prof. Epistl.	*Epistulae*
Josephus	
Ant.	*Antiquitates judaicae*
Bell. Jud.	*Bellum judaicum*
c. Ap.	*Contra Apionem*
J.T.	Jerusalem Talmud
Taan. Fol.	*Ta'anit*, folio
Justin	
Apol.	*Apology*
Dial.	*Dialogue with Trypho*
Justin.	Justinian
Lac.	Lactantius
Luc.	Lucian
Calum.	*Calumniae non temere credendum*
Lex.	*Lexiphanes*
Mae.	*Muscae laudation*
Phlg.	*De morte Peregrini*
Mishnah	
Sand.	*Sanhedrin*
Origen	
contra Cels.	*Contra Celsum*
Epistl. to Alex.	*Epistle to Alexandria*
Hom. in Jerm.	*Homiliae in Jeremiam*
Hom. in Luc.	*Homiliae in Lucam*
Ovid	
Meta.	*Metamorphoses*
Pelagius	
Comm. in Philemon	*Commentary on Philemon*
Philo	
Apocryph.	Apocryphal

Fragm.	Fragments
de Munf. Op.	*De opificio mundi*
in Flacc.	*In Flaccum*
Leg. ad Gaius	*Legatio ad Gaium*
Leg. Alleg.	*Legum allegoriae*
Vit. Mos.	*De vita Mosis*
Philo of Byzantine	
de Spectacl. Mud	*On the Seven Wonders*
Philostratus	
Vita Ap.	*Vita Apollonii*
Photius	
Amphil.	*Amphilochia*
Plato	
Apol.	*Apologia*
Leg.	*Leges*
Soph.	*Sophista*
Symp.	*Symposium*
Tim.	*Timaeus*
Plautus	
Must.	*Mostellaria*
Pliny the Elder	
N.H.	*Naturalis historia*
Plutarch	
de Def. Oracl.	*De defectu oraculorum*
de Superstit.	*De superstition*
Moral. de Stoic	*Moralia*
Pomp.	*Pompeius*
Vit. Rom.	*Romulus*
Polycarp	
Phil.	*Epistle to the Philippians*
Seneca	
de ira.	*On Anger*
Epist.	*Epistulae morales*
Quest. iv. Prob./	*Naturales quaestiones*
Quaest. Nat. iv.	
Shep. Hermas	Shepherd of Hermas
Sim.	*Similitudes*
Vis.	*Visions*
Soph.	Sophocles
Aj.	*Ajax*

Od.	*Oedipus coloneus*
Statius	
Sil.	*Silvae*
Steph. Byz.	Stephanus of Byzantium
Suet.	Suetonius
Claud.	*Claudius*
Sibyl. Oracle	*Sibylline Oracles*
Tacitus	
Annal.	*Annales*
Hist	*Historiae*
Tatian	
Orat. ad Graec.	*Oratio ad Graecos*
Tertullian	
(Adv.) Marc.	*Adversus Marcionem*
de Pudic.	*De pudicitia*
de Spect.	*De spectaculis*
de Prescr. Hiret./	*De praescriptione haereticorum*
Praescr. Haer.	
Test. 12 Patriarch	*Testaments of the Twelve Patriarchs*
Theocr.	Theocritus
Theod. Mops.	Theodore Mopsuestia
Argum. in Eph.	*Commentary on Ephesians*
Theodoret	
Comm. in Phil.	*Commentary on Philippians*
Theophrastus	
Charact.	*Characteres*
Theophilus	
ad Autol.	*Ad Autolycum*
Xen. (Ephes.)	Xenophon (of Ephesus)
Anab.	*Anabasis*
Ap.	*Apologia Socratis*
Cyr.	*Cyropaedia*
De Rep. Ab.	*Respublica Lacedaemoniorum*
Hell.	*Hellenica*
Mem.	*Memorabilia*

MODERN SOURCES AND PERSONS

Alf.	Henry Alford, *The New Testament for English Readers*, 4 vols. (London: Rivingtons, 1866)
Aucher, *Armen. Gramm.*	P. Paschal Aucher and Lord Byron, *A Grammar, Armenian and English* (Venice, 1873)

Baumg./Baumgar./ Baumgart./	Michael Baumgarten, *The Acts of the Apostles*, trans. A. J. W. Morrison, 3 vols. (Edinburgh: T & T Clark, 1854)
Becker and Marquardt	W. A. Becker and J. Marquardt, *Handbuch der Römischen Alterthümer*
Bengel	Johannes Bengel
Boeckh, C.I.G.	Philipp August Boeckh, *Corpus Inscriptionum Graecarum*
Born.	F. A. Bornemann, *Acta Apostolorum ad Cod. Cantabrigiensis fidem recensuit* (Grossenhainae, 1848)
Bunsen	C. J. Bunsen, *Hippolytus and His Age* (1852)
Cesnola	L. P. d'Cesnola
Cony+H/C&H/C+H	W. J. Conybeare and J. S. Howson, *The Life and Epistles of St. Paul*, 2nd. ed., 2 vols. (London: Longman, Brown, Green, Longmans, & Roberts, 1856)
Ch. H.	J. A. W. Neander, *General History of the Christian Religion and Church*, trans. Joseph Terry, 5 vols. (Edinburgh: T & T Clark, 1847–1852)
C.I.L.	*Corpus Inscriptionum Latinarum*
Davids. Bibl. Crit.	Samuel Davidson, *A Treatise on Biblical Criticism*, 2 vols. (Edinburgh: Black, 1852)
Davidson, *Sac. Herm.*	Samuel Davidson, *Sacred Hermeneutics* (Edinburgh: T & T Clark, 1843)
de Wette	W. M. L. de Wette, *Einleitung in das Neue Testament* (1826)
Eckhel	J. H. Eckhel, *Kurzgefasste Anfangsgrunde zur alten Numismatik* (1787)
Ewald	W. H. A. Ewald, *Kritische Grammatik der hebräischen Sprache* (1827)
Gesenius	W. Gesenius, *Hebräisches u. Chaldäisches Handwörterbuch* (1812)
Gibbon	E. Gibbon, *The Decline and Fall of the Roman Empire*, 6 vols. (1776–1788)
Gloag	J. P. Gloag, *Commentary on the Acts of the Apostles*, 2 vols. (1870)
Guhl	Alope Guhl, *Ephesiaca*
Hermann, *Grech. Ant.*	C. F. Hermann, *A Manual of the Political Antiquities of Greece Historically Considered* (London: Talboys, 1836)
Hup. *Studien und Krit.*	Hermann Hupfeld, *Studien und Kritiken*
Illgen	D. C. F. Illgen, *Zeitschrift fur die Historische Theologie* (1852)
Kühner	R. Kühner, *Ausführliche Grammatik der griechischen Sprache* (1869)
Lachm./Lachmann	Karl Lachmann
Meineke, Com. Frag.	Augustus Meineke, *Fragmenta Comicorum Graecorum*, 7 vols. (Berlin, 1839–1857)
Meyer	H. A. W. Meyer
Millman	H. H. Millman, *History of Latin Christianity* (1855)
Mu.	Moulton
Ol.	Hermann Olshauson, *Biblical Commentary on the New Testament*, 6 vols. (New York: Sheldon, 1859–1862)

Paley *Evv.*	William Paley, *Evidences of the Existence and Attributes of the Deity*
Paley *H. Paul.*	William Paley, *Horae Paulina*
Realworterbuch	see Winer, Gram.
Renan	J. E. Renan, *Histoire des Origines du Christianisme* (1863–1881)
Strng.	Strong
Thrupp	J. F. Thrupp, *Ancient Jerusalem* (1855)
Tisch./Tischendorf	Constantin von Tischendorf
Tregelles	S. P. Tregelles, *Account of the Printed Text of the Greek New Testament* (1854)
Trench N.T. Syn./Synom.	R. C. Trench, *Synonyms of the New Testament*, 9th ed. (London: MacMillan, 1880)
W+H	Wescott and Hort
Wettstein	J. J. Wettstein, *Novum Testamentum Graecum editionis receptae cum lectionibus variantibus codicum manuscript* (1751)
Winer, Gram./Real.	G. B. Winer, *Grammatik des N.T. Spachidioms und Biblisches Realworterbuch*

MISCELLANEOUS

Ap.	Apud
A.U.C.	*Ab urbe condita*
Evv.	Evangelists
Ir. Alb.	Lucceius Albinus
l.c.	loco citato
sq./sqq.	the following one(s)
v.l.	varias lectiones

FOREWORD

In 1978, I (Ben) was in the Durham Cathedral cloister visiting the Monk's Dormitory that then, as now, served as a display room for important artifacts and manuscripts. It was also something of an archival library. I was a young doctoral student of Charles Kingsley Barrett and had already come across the name of J. B. Lightfoot on various occasions. Indeed, I had bought a reprint of his classic Philippians commentary while I was still in seminary in Massachusetts several years earlier. While perusing the various display cases, I came across an open notebook that displayed Lightfoot's comments on a notoriously difficult passage in Acts 15, and I wondered whether more of this sort of meticulous exegetical material existed, written in Lightfoot's own hand, somewhere else in that library.

Naturally I was interested, since there were no publications by Lightfoot that directly dealt with Acts, and certainly no commentaries by Lightfoot on Acts. I mentioned this discovery to Professor Barrett, who himself was an admirer of J. B. Lightfoot. In fact, in the early 1970s he had written a *Durham University Journal* article in which he praised Lightfoot as arguably the foremost scholar of the New Testament of his era.[1] Somehow, however, nothing more happened in regard to this matter, and in truth, I forgot about it.

I mentioned in passing seeing this material some years later to Professor J. D. G. Dunn, who was then the Lightfoot Professor of Divinity at Durham University. Still, nothing more came of it. Yes, there was a celebration of the centennial of Lightfoot's death in 1989, planned and orga-

---

[1]C. K. Barrett, "Joseph Barber Lightfoot," *Durham University Journal* 64 (1972): 193–204.

nized by the tireless efforts of Professor Dunn, that produced a fine special issue of the *Durham University Journal*, published in 1990, with various articles about the legacy of Lightfoot.[2] There was even a fine monograph done by G. R. Treloar on Lightfoot as a historian.[3] Although it was clear that Treloar had read and studied some of Lightfoot's unpublished work on Acts, the primary sources had not been completely read or studied, much less published.

On my sabbatical in the spring of 2013, when I was scholar-in-residence in St. John's College at Durham University, I decided to try to see just what Lightfoot materials might still be gathering dust in the Cathedral library. I must confess, I was not prepared for what I found. There, in the Monk's Dormitory in a tall bookcase—whose lower compartment was filled with Lightfoot files, folders, letters, pictures, inkwells and more—sat not only three brown notebooks of Lightfoot's detailed exegetical lectures on Acts numbering over 140 pages, but also a further gigantic blue box full of hundreds of pages of additional Acts materials, including a lengthy excursus on the authenticity of the Stephen speech. But even that was not all.

There was also a whole blue box full of hundreds of pages of Lightfoot's exegetical studies on the Gospel of John, lectures on 2 Corinthians, two notebooks on 1 Peter, and finally a further notebook of Lightfoot's reflections on early Judaism. All were in Lightfoot's own hand, all done in great detail and none of it, except the first four or five pages of the introduction to Galatians contained in the first Acts notebook (which Kaye and Treloar excerpted and published in a *Durham University Journal* article in 1990[4]), has ever been published—until now.[5]

---

[2]Professor Dunn edited this special edition of the journal, which includes articles by David M. Thompson on Lightfoot as a churchman, Martin Hengel on Lightfoot's interaction with the Tübingen school on the Gospel of John and the second century, C. K. Barrett on Lightfoot as a biblical commentator, and James D. G. Dunn on the contributions of Lightfoot to church and academy.

[3]G. R. Treloar, *Lightfoot the Historian: The Nature and Role of History in the Life and Thought of J. B. Lightfoot*, Wissenschaftliche Untersuchungen zum Neuen Testament 2.103 (Tübingen: Mohr Siebeck, 1998).

[4]B. N. Kaye and G. R. Treloar, "J. B. Lightfoot and New Testament Interpretation: An Unpublished Manuscript of 1855," *Durham University Journal* 82 (1990): 160–75 (on 171–75).

[5]There are a few other exceptions to this remark: (1) The appendices in this volume were previously published in periodicals and dictionaries but have long since been out of print and are in the public domain, and (2) Lightfoot's essays on the authenticity of the Gospel of John, examining both the external and internal evidence, were published, but not his exegesis of John. These

It is important to say at this juncture that this material would still be unpublished were it not for (1) the capable help of the Durham Cathedral Library staff, especially Catherine Turner (now retired) and Gabrielle Sewell; (2) the hard work of a current doctoral student at the University of Durham, Jeanette Hagen, who did much of the painstaking work of reading and transcribing this material;[6] (3) the generosity of Asbury Seminary, Baylor University (through an Arts and Humanities Faculty Development Program Grant administered by the office of the vice provost of research) and Willard J. Still, who helped to pay for the digitalization and transcription of these materials; and (4) our friends at InterVarsity Press, in particular Andy Le Peau, Jim Hoover, Dan Reid and David Congdon, who saw the value of letting this material see the light of day so it might provide valuable help for our understanding of the New Testament, help from an unexpected quarter.[7]

From where exactly did this material come? The answer is from Lightfoot's lecture notebooks. When Lightfoot served as fellow (1851), Hulsean Professor of Divinity (1861) and Lady Margaret's Professor (1875) at Cambridge University, he gave several series of lectures on Acts, the Gospel of John, 1 Peter and 2 Corinthians (among other subjects). The first Acts notebook, which also includes notes on Galatians, begins with these words—"Lenten Term, 1855." Over time, as he continued to lecture on these great New Testament texts, Lightfoot would revise his lectures, further annotate them, change his mind on a few things and add things. This in part explains why there are two sets of lecture notes on Acts, neither one of which gets all the way to Acts 28. One set of notes goes up to Acts 20, the other to Acts 21.[8]

---

essays were first published posthumously by Macmillan in 1893. Baker republished them in 1979 with a fresh introduction by Philip Edgecumbe Hughes under the title *Biblical Essays*. We have re-presented here just one of the twelve essays in that volume, the essay about Paul's fate after the events chronicled in Acts. (BW3)

[6]The editors would also like to express their gratitude to Ben Snyder of Asbury Seminary for his help in compiling the list of abbreviations and to Andy Stubblefield of Truett Seminary for creating the indices.

[7]Todd Still joined this ambitious project at the invitation of BW3 in early June 2013. (TDS)

[8]While Lightfoot's books were divided between Cambridge and Durham after his death (his actual library had been on the shelves in the library of Bishop Auckland Palace), it does not appear that any of his papers and unpublished materials went back to Cambridge. I did some digging during my most recent stint in Cambridge and found nothing there. There might be something in the

When Lightfoot became bishop of Durham in 1879, he brought all of his Cambridge work on the New Testament, and much else, with him. This is how these materials eventually came into the possession of the Durham Cathedral Library. Lightfoot had been lecturing on Acts and John and other parts of the New Testament for more than twenty years when he left Cambridge for Durham, and the impression one gets from these unpublished manuscripts is that, having already published commentaries on Galatians (1865), Philippians (1868), and Colossians and Philemon (1875), Lightfoot's views on Acts, John, 2 Corinthians and 1 Peter were mostly formed by the time he came to Durham. Indeed, one finds in these same Acts notebooks some of the materials that went into Lightfoot's Galatians commentary and his fragmentary commentaries on certain Pauline letters (namely, Romans, the Corinthian and Thessalonian correspondences, and Ephesians).[9] It is clear, however, that even after he had come to Durham, Lightfoot continued to read about and to work on Acts. In fact, he wrote a detailed introductory article on Acts in the 1880s for the second British edition of William Smith's *Dictionary of the Bible*.[10]

Instead of opting for a certain degree of redundancy in this volume, we have chosen to offer a single set of exegetical comments from Lightfoot on Acts 1–21. We have done so by combining materials from both sets of his lecture notes. We will reserve all of Lightfoot's materials on the Fourth Gospel and early Judaism on the one hand and on the other 1 Peter and 2 Corinthians for volumes two and three in this series. Our hope is that these materials will be as rewarding for you in your reading and studying as they have been for us.

To be sure, it is an honor to work on these long-lost manuscripts from a great exegete and historian who set in motion a long line of great New Testament scholars in Durham. Scholars who, like Lightfoot, left their mark in Durham include Lightfoot's contemporary and friend B. F. Westcott as well

---

Trinity College archives, but nothing so far has surfaced. Whatever it may be, if anything, it does not look like it will add to this largesse of unpublished biblical materials. (BW3)

[9]Lightfoot's comments on these Pauline letters were published posthumously as *Notes on the Epistles of St. Paul* (London: Macmillan, 1895).

[10]Happily, we have found this long-out-of-print article and have included it in this volume as appendix A. This article attests to the fact that Lightfoot was still working on Acts in the 1880s and, as Hort says, wanted to write a proper commentary on it. (BW3)

as Alfred Plummer, William Sanday, H. E. W. Turner, C. K. Barrett, C. E. B. Cranfield, J. D. G. Dunn, J. M. G. Barclay, Stephen Barton and Francis Watson. These are but a few of those who have followed in the footsteps and in the tradition of Lightfoot, *focusing on detailed historical, exegetical and theological study of the text.* This volume, and the two to follow, continue that Durham legacy and contribution to New Testament scholarship.

Ben Witherington III
St. John's College, Durham, England
Pentecost 2013

Todd D. Still
Baylor University/Truett Seminary, Waco, Texas
Advent 2013/Epiphany 2014

EDITORS' INTRODUCTION

J. B. Lightfoot
as Biblical Commentator

*No one could match Lightfoot for "exactness of scholarship,
width of erudition, scientific method, sobriety of
judgment and lucidity of style."*[1]

WILLIAM SANDAY

*"No one ever loitered so late in the Great Court that he did not see
Lightfoot's lamp burning in his study window, though not many
either was so regularly present in morning Chapel at
seven o'clock that he did not find Lightfoot
always there with him."*[2]

BISHOP HANDLEY C. G. MOULE

JOSEPH BARBER LIGHTFOOT (1828–1889) was in many ways ideally
suited to be a commentator on the New Testament. He had mastery of

---

[1]William Sanday, "Bishop Lightfoot," *The Expositor* 4 (1886): 13–29 (on 13). Sanday was also a
Durhamite, most well known for producing the International Critical Commentary on Romans
with Arthur Headlam.
[2]Lightfoot's successor (with one in between) as bishop of Durham.

numerous ancient and modern languages (German, French, Spanish, Italian, Latin, Classical Greek, Koine Greek, and the Greek of the church fathers) and a good working knowledge of many others, including Hebrew, Aramaic, Syriac, Armenian, Ethiopic and Coptic. Some of these languages he taught himself. It was clear enough from early on that Lightfoot had a gift for languages. He once asked a friend whether he did not find it to be the case that *one forgets what language one is reading* when one becomes absorbed in a text![3] There have been precious few biblical scholars over time who could have candidly made such a remark about so many different languages.

Lightfoot also had a keen interest in history and understood its importance for the study of a historical religion such as Christianity. He was a critical and perspicuous thinker and writer with few peers in any age of Christian history. Furthermore, Lightfoot was able to devote himself to the study of the New Testament in ways and to a degree that few scholars before or since his time have been able to do, not least because he never married and had no family for whom to care.[4] Yet when we look at the list of his publications, we may be somewhat surprised that there are not more works of biblical exegesis. Here is a list of his works that were first published in the nineteenth century.

- *Saint Paul's Epistle to the Galatians* (London: Macmillan, 1865)

- *Saint Paul's Epistle to the Philippians* (London: Macmillan, 1868)

- *S. Clement of Rome* (London: Macmillan, 1869)

---

[3]He made this remark to J. R. Harmer. See G. R. Eden and F. C. Macdonald, *Lightfoot of Durham: Memorials and Appreciations* (Cambridge: Cambridge University Press, 1932), 118–19. Apparently, Lightfoot also knew Arabic. It is a great pity that no proper biography has ever been written on Lightfoot. What we have in *Lightfoot of Durham* is some fond remembrances of the man by a few of the people who knew him. Only a portion of the volume discusses his academic work, and even then only very cursorily. Do see, however, pp. 105–22 and the brief discussions by H. E. Savage and Bishop J. R. Harmer (Lightfoot's chaplain, secretary and proofreader for some years, before becoming a bishop himself). Note also the essays by the dean of Wells and the bishop of Gloucester (pp. 123–41). Notice that there are *no scholars* writing essays in this volume. This speaks volumes about Lightfoot's work for and impact on the church. There is a nice anecdote in appendix D below about how as a boy at school, when someone asked how he was coming along with his German, the reply given from the school was: "Oh he's mastered German, he's moved on to Anglo-Saxon!" (BW3)

[4]If one wonders why someone like Lightfoot agreed to take a post like the episcopal seat in Durham after a thriving academic life in Cambridge and after having turned down the chance to be bishop of Litchfield, the answer in part is family connections. He had a great love for the "north" of England, as his mother was from Newcastle and his family on his father's side was from Yorkshire. He saw it, in one sense, as returning to his ancestral home. (BW3)

- *Fresh Revision of the English New Testament* (London: Macmillan, 1871)
- *Saint Paul's Epistles to the Colossians and Philemon* (London: Macmillan, 1875)
- *Primary Charge* (London: Macmillan, 1882)
- *The Apostolic Fathers, Part 2, S. Ignatius, S. Polycarp*, 3 vols. (London: Macmillan, 1885–1889)
- *Essays on Supernatural Religion* (London: Macmillan, 1889)
- *The Apostolic Fathers, Part 1, S. Clement of Rome*, 2 vols. (London: Macmillan, 1890)
- *Cambridge Sermons* (London: Macmillan, 1890)
- *Leaders in the Northern Church* (London: Macmillan, 1890)
- *Ordination Addresses* (London: Macmillan, 1890)
- *Apostolic Fathers Abridged* (London: Macmillan, 1891)
- *Sermons Preached in St. Paul's* (London: Macmillan, 1891)
- *Special Sermons* (London: Macmillan, 1891)
- *The Contemporary Pulpit Library: Sermons by Bishop Lightfoot* (London: Swan Sonnenschein, 1892)
- *Dissertations on the Apostolic Age* (London: Macmillan, 1892)
- *Biblical Essays* (London: Macmillan, 1893)
- *Historical Essays* (London: Macmillan, 1895)
- *Notes on the Epistles of St. Paul from Unpublished Commentaries* (London: Macmillan, 1895)

Compare this to the inventory created by B. N. Kaye after inspecting everything the Durham Cathedral Library had in handwritten script by Lightfoot:

- Lecture notes on Acts
- Lecture notes on Ephesians
- Script on the destination of Ephesians (published in *Biblical Essays*)
- Lecture notes on 1 Corinthians 1:1–15:54
- Lecture notes on 1 Peter

- Internal evidence for the authencity and genuineness of St. John's Gospel (printed in *Biblical Essays*)

- External evidence for the authenticity and genuineness of St. John's Gospel (printed in *Biblical Essays*)

- External testimony for St. John's Gospel (rough notes worked up in *Biblical Essays*)

- Second set of notes on internal evidence (printed in *The Expositor* [1890])

- Notes on introduction to John and John 1:1–12:2

- Notes on introduction to Romans and Romans 1:1–9:6 and a separate set of incomplete notes briefly covering Romans 4–13

- Notes on Thessalonians

- Preliminary text for William Smith's *Dictionary of the Bible* article

- Chronology of St. Paul's life and epistles

- The text of St. Paul's epistles

- St. Paul's preparation for the ministry

- Chronology of St. Paul's life and epistles (printed in *Biblical Essays*)

- The churches of Macedonia (printed in *Biblical Essays*)

- The church of Thessalonica (printed in *Biblical Essays*)

- Notes on the genuineness of 1 and 2 Thessalonians

- Unlabeled notes on the text of 1 and 2 Thessalonians

From even a cursory comparison of these two lists, several things become apparent: (1) There is a good deal of material on Acts, John, Paul and 1 Peter that never saw the light of day; and (2) Lightfoot wrote as much, and as often, for the sake of the church and its ministry and about the church and its ministry as he did on subjects of historical or exegetical interest. But where had Lightfoot gained all his knowledge and erudition? What sort of education and what teachers produced such a scholar and churchman?

THE GROOMING OF A SCHOLAR

C. K. Barrett reminds us that Lightfoot in the first instance gained his skills as a commentator on the Bible from studying at King Edward's School in

Birmingham under James Lee Prince. Such study gave him a thoroughgoing training in both Greek and Latin, with wide reading in classical literature and history. When Lightfoot went to study at Trinity College, Cambridge, he worked with B. F. Westcott, who was three years his senior. In 1851 he took the Classical Tripos and came out as a Senior Classic.[5] Barrett relates the well-known story that Lightfoot wrote his tripos exam without a single mistake, which Barrett thinks refers to his work on the language parts of the exam. Afterward, Lightfoot was elected to a fellowship at Trinity and went on to teach languages to other students at Trinity. In his "spare" time he was learning theology and reading the apostolic fathers.[6]

At the tender age of thirty-three, Lightfoot was named Hulsean Professor of Divinity and was the mainstay of the faculty there, even with the addition of Westcott and Hort. Of his lectures in Cambridge, F. J. A. Hort reports,

> They consisted chiefly, if not wholly, of expositions of parts of books of the New Testament, and especially of St. Paul's Epistles, with discussions and leading topics usually included in "Introductions" to these books. Their value and interest were soon widely recognized in the university, and before long no lecture-room then available sufficed to contain the hearers, both candidates for holy orders and older residents; so that leave had to be obtained for the use of the hall of Trinity.[7]

His commentaries on what we now call the later Pauline letters (Philippians, Colossians and Philemon) as well as on Galatians began to come out in the 1860s, but it is clear that already in the 1850s, based on his Cambridge lecture notes, which we can now inspect, that Lightfoot had already sorted out his view of Acts and its relationship to the Pauline corpus as well as Pauline chronology. He had also done extensive work on the Gospel of John and 1 Peter. Indeed, we find some of his Galatians commentary in the same notebook as his lecture notes on Acts. In other words, Lightfoot's previously unpublished work on Acts, John, 1 Peter and some of Paul's letters was produced when he was at the height of his powers and commentary-writing

---

[5] A tripos is an exam taken for the BA degree with honors at Cambridge University. (TDS)

[6] C. K. Barrett, "J. B. Lightfoot as Biblical Commentator," *Durham University Journal* (1992): 53–70 (on 54).

[7] F. J. A. Hort, "Lightfoot, Joseph Barber," *Dictionary of National Biography, 1885–1900* (London: Smith, Elder & Co), 33:232–40, on p. 233.

ability. *These heretofore unpublished notes on Acts and other subjects are often as detailed as the published commentaries and are from the same period of Lightfoot's life.*

If we ask why some of this material was not published during Lightfoot's lifetime, the answer is ready to hand—it is incomplete. None of these unpublished manuscripts were full commentaries on the books in question. But there are further reasons why Lightfoot did not publish his voluminous materials on Acts and John. As Barrett notes, Lightfoot, Westcott and Hort had agreed to divide up the New Testament among them and to write commentaries on each book.[8] Lightfoot was tasked with treating the Pauline corpus, not the Gospels, Acts or 1 Peter.[9] Furthermore, the last of his published commentaries (on Colossians and Philemon) came out less than four years before Lightfoot became bishop of Durham in 1879, a work in which he became almost totally absorbed for the rest of his life, which proved to be ten years.[10] Regarding Lightfoot's commentary work, Hort remarks:

> Technical language is as far as possible avoided and exposition, essentially scientific, is clothed in simple and transparent language. The natural meaning of each verse is set forth without polemical matter. The prevailing characteristic is . . . good sense unaccompanied by either the insight or delusion of subtlety. Introductions, which precede the commentaries, handle the subject-matter with freshness and reality, almost every section being in effect a bright

---

[8]At an earlier point in time, Lightfoot, Westcott and Hort were meant to write commentaries for the Smith's Commentary series. Although this plan did not pan out, it is of present import to note that Lightfoot was supposed to have commented on Acts for this series. (TDS)

[9]It was Alexander Macmillan who suggested to Westcott the possibility of a Cambridge commentary on the entire New Testament. Westcott in turn enlisted Lightfoot and Hort for the project, to be based on the Westcott and Hort Greek text.

Until beginning this work on Lightfoot, I had not realized that the original attempt to have a Cambridge Bible Commentary on the whole New Testament had begun with this agreement, although it never came to full fruition. In the 1960s and '70s, C. F. D. Moule, the relative of the successor of Lightfoot in the Durham episcopacy (H. G. C. Moule), revived the attempt to have a Cambridge Bible Commentary on the Greek New Testament, but it too was destined not to be completed. Indeed, it produced only a couple of notable volumes, C. E. B. Cranfield's volume on Mark and Moule's on Colossians and Philemon. This brings us to the turn of the twenty-first century when I, another Durham man, was named editor of the New Cambridge Bible Commentary series, along with my Asbury colleague Bill Arnold, who is the Old Testament editor. This third attempt has now produced volumes on both Old and New Testament books, but there is still much to be done, and more volumes are forthcoming. (BW3)

[10]For example, he became absorbed in training ordinands for the Anglican ministry, in setting up the diocese of Newcastle and in paying for churches to be built.

Photographs of cupboards in Durham Cathedral Library and of the cupboard doors behind which Ben Witheringtom III found the papers that comprise The Lightfoot Legacy

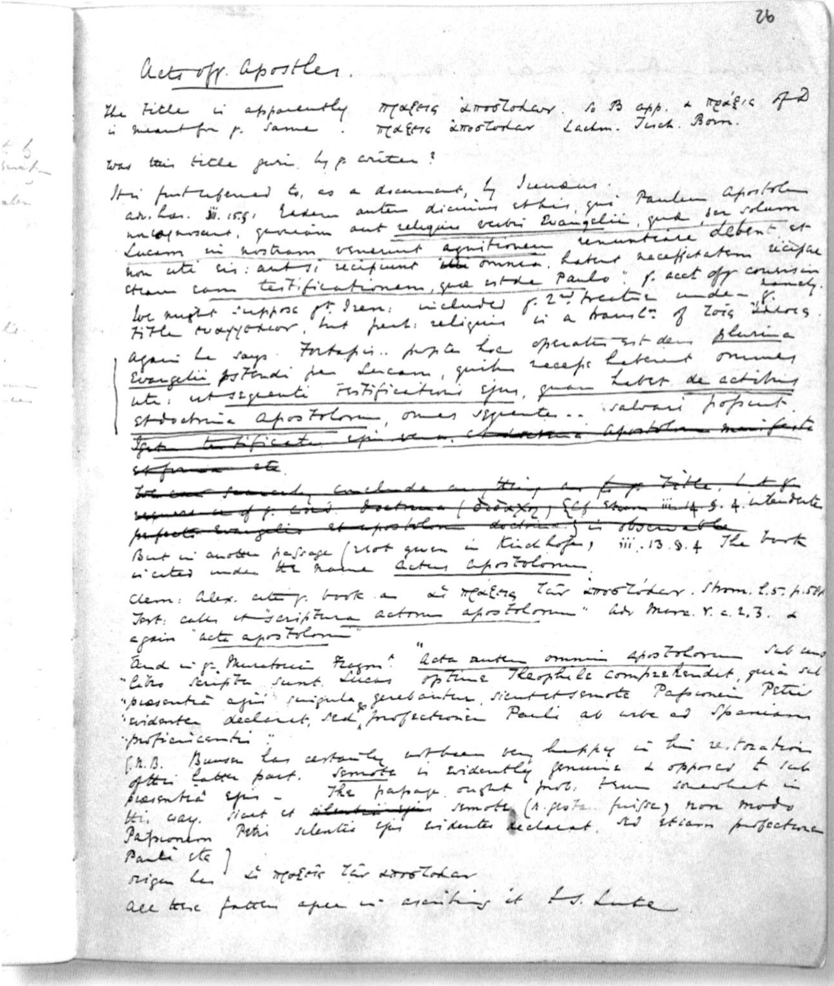
26

Acts of y^e Apostles.

The title is apparently πράξεις ἀποστόλων. So B app. & πράξις of D is meant for y^e same. πράξεις ἀποστόλων Lachm. Tisch. Born.

Was this title given by y^e writer?

It is first referred to, as a document, by Irenaeus. Paulum apostolum adv. haer. iii. 15. 1. Eadem autem dicimus etiam his, qui Paulum apostolum non cognoscunt, quoniam aut religiis verbi Evangelii, quod per solum Lucam in nostram venerunt agnitionem, renuntiare debent, et non uti eis: aut si recipiunt omnem, habent necessitatem recipere etiam eam testificationem, quae est de Paulo". ye acct of ye conversion namely.

We might suppose y^t Iren: includes ye 2nd treatise under ye title εὐαγγέλιον, but perh: religiis is a transl^n of τοῖς λόγοις.

Again he says. Fortassis.. propter hoc operatus est deus plurima Evangelii ostendi per Lucam, quibus necesse haberent omnes uti: ut sequenti testificationi ejus, quam habet de actibus et doctrina apostolorum, omnes sequentes.. salvari possint.

~~[illegible]~~

But in another passage (not given in Kirchhofer), iii. 13. §. 4 The book is cited under the name Actus Apostolorum.

Clem: Alex. cites ye book as αἱ πράξεις τῶν ἀποστόλων. Strom. l. 5. p. 58[illegible]

Tert: calls it "scriptura actorum apostolorum" adv. Marc. v. c. 2, 3. & again "acta apostolorum"

And in ye Muratorian fragm^t "Acta autem omnium apostolorum sub uno libro scripta sunt. Lucas optime Theophile comprehendit, quia sub praesentia ejus singula gerebantur, sicut et semote Passionem Petri evidenter declarat, sed & profectionem Pauli ab urbe ad Spaniam proficiscentis".

[N.B. Bunsen has certainly not been very happy in his restoration of this latter part. Semote is evidently genuine & opposed to sub praesentia ejus – The passage ought prob. to run somewhat in this way. Sicut et semote (i.e. gesta fuisse) non modo Passionem Petri silentio ejus evidenter declarat, sed etiam profectionem Pauli etc]

Origen has αἱ πράξεις τῶν ἀποστόλων

All these fathers agree in ascribing it to S. Luke

Lightfoot's treatment of the title "Acts of the Apostles"

The diaconate

This was evidently the first establishment of the office. There had hitherto been no fixed distributors of alms, but the apostles had delegated this duty now to one, now to another. The consequence of this irregularity was that the Hellenist widows either were, or imagined themselves, neglected.

If these seven had been appointed simply to confine their ministrations to the Hellenists, we should scarcely have expected to find them designated as οἱ ἑπτά, when there must have been other deacons, their brethren in office, & their equals in other respects — But indeed the whole narrative seems to imply that this class of officers did not exist before, & that the irregularities had occurred owing to there being no definite responsible persons.

This then was the first establishment of the diaconate.

The functions of the seven seem not to have been confined to ministering to the Hellenist christians — There is no restriction of the kind implied in the text. They must have attended as well to the Hebrew as Hellenist widows. But their names are all Greek. True, yet their names do not necessarily imply a Hellenistic origin — witness p. apostles Andrew & Philip — Yet it is probable that they were all or most often Hellenist. In this case we see only an exercise of that great love, which pervaded the infant church.

Their ministrations then Extended to Hebrews as well as Hellenists

Were they connected with p. later diaconate?

The word διάκονος is never used of them in p. acts. They are styled οἱ ἑπτά "the seven" — But

(1). διάκονος, διάκονια occur repeatedly in describing their ministrations

(2). Such stress is laid on p. circumstance in the narrative that the writer evidently considered he was narrating an event ... had some influence on p. subsequent organization of the church ...

See Philippians ...

A page from Lightfoot's extensive notes on St. Stephen's speech

Caesarea

Neapolis
(Sychem)

Azotus Caperaria Jerusalem

Ascalon

Eleutheropolis Bettoun

Hebron

Gaza

Lightfoot's sketch of and remarks upon three possible routes that Philip might have taken from Jerusalem to Gaza (cf. Acts 8:26)

Herod the Great

Aristobulus (put to death A.D. 6) — Philip ... Archelaus (m. Herodias ...) — Herod Philip (Tetrarch of Ituraea & Trachonitis) — Herod Antipas (Tetrarch of Galilee; Died in exile at Lyons)

Herod K g of Chalcis († A.D. 48) — Herod Agrippa I (died ... A.D. 44) — Herodias

Agrippa II — Bernice — Drusilla

Herod the Great. Massacre of the Innocents
Herod Antipas. beheads John the Baptist. takes part in the Crucifixion of our Lord
Herod Agrippa I. Persecutes the Ch. put James to death.
Agrippa II. hears St. Paul.

Lightfoot's chart of and cursory comments on Herod the Great's family tree (see further Acts 13:1)

Miletus to Cos   1 (?)
Cos to Rhodes   1   xxi. 1
Rhodes to Patara   1.
Patara to Tyre   5 d(?).
Sojourn at Tyre   7.   xxi. 4
Tyre to Ptolemais   1
Sojourn at Ptolemais   1   xxi. 7
Journey to Caesarea   1   xxi. 8

                        18.

} This reckoning
  is ample. In
  xxvii. 3 to
  Tyre from Caesarea
  is to Sidon and
  occupies one day

The reckoning of 5 days from Patara to Tyre is
taken from Chrysost. Hom. i. Act. 45 [Op. IX. p. 340].
He was acquainted with these facts.

Chrysost. reckons 34 days from Philippi to Ptolemais.

This reckoning is quite in accordance with the
other ancient voyages: e.g. on the 4th day from
Rhodes to Alexandria Diod. iii. 34.
With a favourable wind a vessel could go from 1000
to 1200 stades in the 24 hours.
See Friedländer Sittengesch. II. pp. 14, 15.

See Wesseler p. 402
Reiske (de Celte) p. 337

6 + 19 + 18 = 43
We have then 43 days.

Now, when St. Paul arrived at Caesarea, he stays
ἡμέρας πλείους (xxi. 0)

As it had been his object to arrive at Jerusalem at
Pentecost 'if it were possible', this sojourn at
Caesarea might be due to either of two causes
(1) Either he found that he could not arrive in
time to keep the feast and so object is frustrated
or (2) There was plenty of time still to spare —
The reckoning shows that the latter was the case

Δημοσθ. Philipp.
πυνθανόμενοι κατὰ τὴν ἀγοράν, εἴ τι λέγεται νεώτερον

Seneca Ep. 94 Alexander... quod cuique optimum est.
caput, Lacedaemon nisi iubet, Athenas tacere

ὡς δεισιδαιμονεστέρους   our careful & well pair'd matters.
               ?
See first 2 ch.

Ἰδία ας if St Paul had said 'I am not going to accuse
you of any irreligion: if anything, your religion is in
excess: only it is misdirected'

There is a passage in Olian Var. Hist. v. 17 on the
δεισιδαιμονία of the Athenians.

θεωρῶ. See from clear St Paul stood, he might have said
θεωρεῖν too fact
See Constable.
L.G.C. Lift on to known text he Position & Liddell
from her by whom's d. trach. (the Propylaea)

23   ἀναθεωρῶν, Diod. xii. 15 ἐξ ἐπιστολῆς τῶν θεωρομένων ...
      ἀναθεωρῆσαι δὲ καὶ μετ' ἀκριβείας ἐξετάξαντος
                                              too ...

so the world see, as he passes through the city (διερχόμενος)
he may gather from Pausanias

Ἀγνώστωι θεῶι
        to an unknown God; to an unknown God.
he aske of the Athenians

Pausan. χ χνε 1.1.4 speaks of Phalerus, mentions βωμοὶ
θεῶν ἀγνώστων ὀνομαζόμενοι
                 to which
Philost. vi. 3 σωφρονέστερον γὰρ τὸ περὶ πάντων θεῶν εὖ
λέγειν καὶ ταῦτα Ἀθήνησιν, οὗ καὶ ἀγνώστων δαιμόνων

little historical essay. To each commentary is appended a dissertation, which includes some of Lightfoot's most careful and thorough work.[11]

There was one gargantuan academic project Lightfoot continued to work on even after he became bishop—his monumental and groundbreaking studies on the apostolic fathers, though he mostly only found time to work on this project during holidays and while traveling.

> There are vivid descriptions of Lightfoot being found in a boat or railway carriage with an Armenian or Coptic grammar in hand or calmly correcting proofs while being driven down precipitous paths in Norway. . . . But above all the secret lay in his ability to switch off, giving himself totally to what was before him. As his chaplain [J. R. Harmer] put it . . . "His power of detachment and concentration was extraordinary. I have seen him break off from an incomplete sentence for a momentous interview with one of his clergy, give him his undivided and sympathetic attention followed by the wisest counsel and final decision, and almost before the door was closed upon his visitor become once more absorbed in his literary work."[12]

Lest we worry that in later life Lightfoot went off the boil as he labored away on the apostolic fathers, Stephen Neill assuages such concern. "If I had my way," Neill maintains, "at least five hundred pages of Lightfoot's *Apostolic Fathers* would be required reading for every theological student in his first year. I cannot imagine any better introduction to critical method, or a better preparation for facing some of the difficult problems of New Testament interpretation that yet remain unsolved."[13]

There was probably, however, another reason why Lightfoot never published his work on John and Acts. His friend, colleague and original Cambridge mentor B. F. Westcott *was* producing a commentary on John. Lightfoot would likely have regarded it as bad form to publish something that competed with his colleague's work, especially when they had already agreed regarding the division of labor when it came to the New Testament. Furthermore, his other colleague F. J. A. Hort was scheduled to do Acts.

Nevertheless, we may be thankful that Lightfoot continued to work and

---

[11]Hort, "Lightfoot," 237–38.
[12]John A. T. Robinson, "Joseph Barber Lightfoot" (Durham Cathedral Lecture, 1981), p. 13.
[13]Stephen C. Neill, *The Interpretation of the New Testament 1861–1961* (Oxford: Oxford University Press, 1966), p. 57.

lecture on Acts. According to John A. T. Robinson, his lectures on Acts were
so popular that 247 Cambridge students attended them in 1877.[14] So much
was Acts regularly in the forefront of Lightfoot's mind that the last real
lecture he gave in Cambridge before going to Durham was a lengthy lecture
on the authenticity of the Stephen speech. He gave this lecture in the dining
hall at Trinity just after he received the call to Durham. At long last, this
lecture appears in print as an excursus in this volume. It is a rebuttal of a
critique by an anonymous author who had called into question the historical
veracity of a fair amount of Acts (and the rest of the New Testament). In fact,
the last major academic piece that Lightfoot seems to have written on the
New Testament is his introductory article on Acts for Smith's *Dictionary of
the Bible*, written sometime in the mid-1880s (see appendix A below).

But well before that famous last lecture in the dining hall or his last article
on the New Testament, Lightfoot had been working hard on his Acts lecture
notes. G. R. Treloar tells the story this way:

> In 1854 Lightfoot was appointed Assistant Tutor at Trinity College. His new
> teaching commitments required him to lecture on the Acts of the Apostles and
> the Pauline Letters. The basis of his approach was the new text and the com-
> mentary produced for English students by Henry Alford, while he also made
> frequent reference to the recent New Testament introduction by Samuel
> Davidson. To these he added the resources furnished by German scholarship
> which he defended to the undergraduates from the abuse to which it was still
> subject: "A sweeping condemnation of everything that is German is not honest,
> it is not Christian. There is as much diversity among German writers, as there is
> among ourselves. Then and only then shall we as a nation have the right to inflict
> this undiscriminating censure, when we have spent as much time and pains over
> the sacred writings as they have, and produced results as considerable."
>
> He himself used the new philological aids, most notably the *Grammatik des
> N.T. Sprachidioms and Biblisches Realworterbuch* of G. B. Winer. For the inter-
> pretation of the text he turned to the recent commentaries of Michael
> Baumgarten and H. A. W. Meyer. For the larger historical context he drew on
> the histories of the Apostolic period by J. A. W. Neander, Chev. Bunsen, and
> Philip Schaff. Although these were acceptable as (in the main) writers of the
> "mediating school," Lightfoot did not slavishly follow the German scholars, but

---

[14]Robinson, "Lightfoot," p. 11.

critically used them to bring out the meaning and historical bearing of the text. Historical criticism of this order was also used to defend the authenticity and the veracity of Acts from its critics, most notably F. C. Baur and Eduard Zeller. From the beginning Lightfoot set himself the task of presenting and defending traditional Christianity to undergraduates through the texts set for study by the best and most up-to-date scholarly materials available, an aspiration which soon attracted the attention of the College and the wider University.[15]

Turning to another academic matter, we learn early on what kind of man Lightfoot was when it came to collegiality. Having become Hulsean Professor of Divinity at Cambridge at the remarkably young age of thirty-three, when the Regius Professorship of Divinity became open in 1870, it was assumed that he would take it. But when Lightfoot learned that Westcott would be returning to Cambridge after fulfilling an ecclesiastical assignment, he turned down the post so that it might be given to Westcott.

> Lightfoot used all his influence to induce his friend Westcott to become a candidate and resolutely declined to stand himself. After Lightfoot's death, Dr. Westcott wrote, "He called me to Cambridge to occupy a place which was his own by right; and having done this he spared no pains to secure for his colleague favorable opportunities for action, while he himself withdrew from the position which he had so long virtually occupied."[16]

This speaks volumes about the character of the man.

Instead of becoming Regius Professor, five years later Lightfoot accepted the Lady Margaret's chair. As such, Lightfoot focused on his exegetical work, work that went into his lectures. These labors remained largely unknown after he died, since they were mostly unpublished. In fact, Lightfoot never fully revised any non-Pauline materials into commentary form since there was neither time nor opportunity to do so once he became bishop of Durham. Then, he died prematurely.[17]

---

[15]G. R. Treloar, "J. B. Lightfoot and St. Paul, 1854–65: A Study of Intentions and Method," *Lucas: An Evangelical History Review* 7 (1989): 5–34 (here 7–8).

[16]Hort, "Lightfoot," p. 234.

[17]There are clear indications that Lightfoot revised his Acts notes at least three times: (1) There are two whole sets of lecture notes, one set in three brown notebooks (the earlier ones) and a second set written on loose-leaf sheets and stored in a blue box (the later ones). (2) Within the latter notes, there are two revisions, one in pen and another in pencil. When one reads through all these Acts notes it becomes evident that these are not merely notes intended to support university lectures. They are too detailed (including footnote references to secondary sources)

So it was that these invaluable Cambridge New Testament notes of Lightfoot remained unpublished. They were presumably first moved to Bishop Auckland Palace (the residence of the bishop of Durham) when Lightfoot moved to Durham. Following his death, they were transported to the Durham Cathedral Library.[18] There, they have barely seen the light of day since 1889, with only a handful of scholars and clerics even reading a small part of these materials over the last 150 years.[19] We trust that these Lightfoot volumes will remedy this regrettable neglect.

LIGHTFOOT'S METHOD

Lightfoot learned early on about the value of writing out one's thoughts about the Scriptures. He once advised: "Begin to write as soon as you possibly can. That was what Prince Lee [his headmaster at King Edward's, Birmingham] always said to us. This is the way to learn. Almost all I have learnt has come from writing books. If you write a book on a subject, you have to read everything that has been written about it."[20]

As Robinson stresses, "One turns back with relief to his patient, inductive method after so many of the pre-judgments and unexamined assumptions of form- and redaction-criticism. . . . Lightfoot would have been horrified to think that serious scholarship could by-pass the historical questions or suppose they could be settled *a priori* by the theological."[21] *This is because Lightfoot believed wholeheartedly that nothing could be theologically true that was historically false when it comes to matters involving a historical religion such as Christianity.*

---

to be just that. No, Lightfoot seems to have been preparing this material for possible future publication. However, he was never able to finish the work. (BW3)

[18]Hort ("Lightfoot," p. 237) says that Lightfoot's library was divided between the divinity school at Cambridge and the University of Durham. What he does not tell us is what happened to his papers, letters and unpublished manuscripts. We now know that they stayed in Durham in a cupboard in the Monk's Dormitory in the Cathedral close.

[19]Barrett ("Lightfoot as Biblical Commentator," p. 55) observes, "Three commentaries [i.e. Galatians, Philippians and Colossians] were published in Lightfoot's lifetime. He left lecture notes, and other notes, on other epistles which doubtless he would have used in published work had he lived, and had his interest not become absorbed in what must be regarded as his greatest work, that on the text of 1 Clement and the Epistles of Ignatius (with 2 Clement and Polycarp thrown in for full measure)—not to mention his conscientious, time-consuming work as bishop of Durham."

[20]Robinson, "Lightfoot," p. 13.

[21]Ibid., p. 16.

If we ask about Lightfoot's particular modus operandi with respect to commentary writing, his approach is basically the same inductive method: (1) Establish the text by dealing with the text-critical issues, including the textual variants. In the case of Acts, this entails two very different traditions of the text (the Alexandrian text and the so-called Western text). (2) Offer necessary grammatical and syntactical notes and discussions. (3) Proceed with exegesis proper. For Lightfoot, this sometimes entailed long excursi on special topics and more exegetically problematic matters as well as translations of key phrases into English. (4) Deal with theological issues and larger topics that might involve several New Testament documents.

Lightfoot assumed that his audience would know enough Greek and scholia to be able to figure out his elliptical references to parallels in other Greek texts and the like as well as his brief (and sometimes infrequent) footnotes referencing the work of other scholars. "The permanent value of Lightfoot's historical work depends on his sagacity in dealing with the materials out of which history has to be constructed. He was invariably faithful to a rigorous philological discipline, and was preserved by native candor from distorting influences."[22]

It may be asked at this juncture, What is the value of this material today, since many good commentaries on Acts, John, 2 Corinthians and 1 Peter have been written since the time of Lightfoot? The answer to this question is twofold. First, there is Lightfoot's encyclopedic knowledge of early Greek literature, a knowledge that is probably unequaled to this day by any subsequent commentator on the New Testament.[23] As Barrett points out, Lightfoot did not have, nor did he need, a lexicon to find parallels to New Testament Greek usage. As a close look at his Galatians commentary shows: "He knows Origen, Ephraem Syrus, Eusebius of Emesa, Chrys-

---

[22]Hort, "Lightfoot," p. 239.

[23]The only New Testament scholar I have ever met, studied with or talked to that was even close to Lightfoot in these skills was Bruce Metzger, with whom I studied the apostolic fathers in a summer course at Princeton. He too had a vast panoply of languages at his command as well as an encyclopedic knowledge of Greek and early Christian literature. It appears he had a photographic memory, and one wonders whether Lightfoot did as well. Savage (*Lightfoot of Durham*, p. 110) seems to confirm this conjecture when he speaks of Lightfoot's "remarkable accuracy of memory which enabled him to apply it readily. Page after page was written *currente calamo* with few or no books of reference at hand, and with only a 'ver.' here and there in the margin, where future verification was required." (BW3)

ostom, Severianus, Theodore of Mopsuestia, Theodoret, Euthalius, Gennadius, Photius, Victorinus, Hilary, Jerome, Augustine, Pelagius, Cassiodorus, John of Damascus," not to mention all the pagan Greek literature and later catenae of Greek and Latin sources.[24] Lightfoot was a walking lexicon of Greek literature of all sorts, and not infrequently he was able to cite definitive parallels to New Testament usage that decided the issue of the meaning of a word or a phrase.

Second, as Dunn notes, time and again Lightfoot *"clearly demonstrates the importance of reading a historical text within its historical context, that the meaning of a text does not arise out of the text alone, but out of the text read in context and that the original context and intention of the author is a determinative and controlling factor in what may be read or heard from such a text. . . . Lightfoot would certainly have approved a referential theory of meaning: that that to which the language of the text refers determines and controls the meaning of the text."*[25]

This approach is sorely needed today as commentators increasingly dismiss or ignore the importance of original-language study and of the original historical context of a document, or try to do "theological interpretation" of the text without first having done their historical homework to determine the original contextual meaning of the text, whether theological in character or not. It may be hoped that this series of volumes will revive an interest in the full gamut of subjects relevant to the study of the New Testament, not least ancient history, including social history; the classics; a precise knowledge of Greek, including its grammar and syntax and rhetoric; and, of course, the theology and ethics of the material itself. Doubtless Lightfoot himself would be pleased if this were one outcome of the publication of his long-lost exegetical studies on the New Testament.[26]

---

[24]Barrett, "Lightfoot as Biblical Commentator," p. 57.

[25]James D. G. Dunn, "Lightfoot in Retrospect," *Durham University Journal* (1992): 71–94 (here 75–76), italics added for emphasis.

[26]It is possible that he might be a bit miffed to see all this material published since it is incomplete. Lightfoot was nothing if not a perfectionist when it came to fully completing tasks to the best of his ability. The numerous little parenthical notes to himself to verify a reference or the check marks in the manuscript indicating a reference verified testify to this scholarly habit. Nevertheless, this material, even though incomplete, is extremely valuable, as even a casual reading of what follows should demonstrate. (BW3)

WHAT TO EXPECT IN READING THIS COMMENTARY

As we have already had occasion to note, this Acts commentary is incomplete. Indeed, it stops at Acts 21. There are also places along the way where verses are skipped or skimmed over lightly. Of course this is also true in other commentaries that do not try to address every single verse. In fact, most commentaries do not attempt to remark on each and every verse. If one will approach this commentary on the basis of what it is intended to accomplish, what Lightfoot meant to give us, then it can be enormously helpful, useful and interesting.

First of all, it has to be remembered that Lightfoot was first and foremost a historian. He was also an expert in Greek language and a formidable text critic. What you will find in abundance in this commentary is the following: (1) A myriad of detailed discussions of text-critical issues, with Lightfoot often arguing that the Received Text (or the Majority Text or the Authorized Version) has erred in its rendering of the original Greek and the translation of the same. This is one reason Lightfoot, Westcott and Hort set out to produce a revision of the standard English translation of their day. (2) You will also find a great deal of comment on Greek grammar, syntax, phrases and meanings of words. Lightfoot's vast knowledge of ancient Greek texts is brought to bear in figuring out the meaning of the words in this or that verse. Lightfoot had few peers and no superiors in this sort of work. His use of the inscriptional and other sorts of archaeological evidence to figure out what certain Greek words and phrases mean was groundbreaking. (3) Interest in and insight into historical matters, such as the chronology of Acts, particular historical problems like the two accounts of Judas's death, the relationship of the Paul of Acts to the Paul of the letters, what historical person actually wrote Acts and how much he knew and what his sources were, and so on. Here again Lightfoot absolutely shines, and it is a great pity that we did not have this material published much sooner, as it would hopefully have forestalled all sorts of rash judgments about Luke as a writer of Greek or as a historian and would equally have made nearly impossible the conjecture that this document was written in the second century A.D. (4) A comparison of Paul's letters to Acts and the weaving together of a coherent picture of earliest Christianity. Lightfoot was the recognized expert on Paul after his Pauline commentaries were published. Had this other material on

Acts, John and 1 Peter been published in his lifetime, it would have been seen that he was the expert in the English-speaking world on much more of the New Testament as well, despite the dismissive comments of some who suggested "he is only a historian, not a theologian." His enormous and detailed treatment of the *logos* material in John 1 would have silenced that criticism.[27]

We have left in the text Lightfoot's interaction with many of his dialogue partners of the day, or an earlier period, to give a sense of who Lightfoot was. He was a man who read widely and interacted critically as well as positively with his fellow scholars in the United Kingdom, France and Germany. He quite deliberately takes on the Tübingen school of F. C. Baur and company at numerous points, for example, in his extended treatments of the Stephen speech and in the account of the first missionary journey of Paul recounted in Acts 13–14. He does so in a manner that is not polemical. Lightfoot gives other scholars their due when they make good points. Nevertheless, he is firm in his conclusions that the sort of Hegelian thesis-antithesis analysis of James and company versus Paul and company or the Hebrews versus the Hellenists or Jewish Christianity versus Gentile Christianity *will simply not do as an analysis of the historical character of earliest Christianity.* Had we had this material even a hundred years ago, the course of New Testament studies might have been different than it turned out to be in the twentieth century. Fortunately, with the aid of J. B. Lightfoot, it is not too late to rectify some of the interpretive mistakes of the past.

Finally, this commentary shows exactly the way Lightfoot approached his study of the New Testament—carefully, prayerfully and, in his own words, with "the highest reason and the fullest faith." Not one or the other, but both. Time and again Lightfoot's intellect and his piety shine through in these lost manuscripts. He shows us repeatedly that faith and reason need not be at odds with each other, especially if it is *fides quaerens intellectum* ("faith seeking understanding"). Honesty about early Christianity and its Lord need not be feared by a person of Christian faith, whether then or now. Taken for what it is, this commentary will not merely "tease the mind into active thought" (a phrase made famous by C. H. Dodd, a Cambridge man like Lightfoot)[28] but also nourish the soul.

---

[27]Lightfoot's treatment of the *logos* in John 1 will appear in vol. 2 of this series.

[28]C. H. Dodd, *The Parables of the Kingdom*, rev. ed. (New York: Scribner's, 1961), p. 5.

Part One

Introduction to
Commenting in General

Reflections on the Necessity of a Clear and Proper View of the Inspiration of Scripture as a Presupposition for Correctly Approaching the Bible[1]

By way of preface . . . I would wish to say a few words with regard to the spirit in which we should enter into the study of the Greek New Testament and the manner in which our work should be carried out.[2] The following remarks have been hastily written down and therefore are very imperfect in point of expression, but I venture to hope that the matter is less faulty. At all events, it has been well thought over: for I should consider myself very reprehensible indeed, if I should dare to speak on such subjects without due preparation.[3]

---

[1] I have inserted this heading so that the reader will know the sort of prolegomena that follows in the next few pages. Those looking for Lightfoot's comments on introductory matters dealing with Acts may proceed to the next section. (BW3)

[2] The transcription of Lightfoot's own words begins with this sentence.

[3] The first few pages of Lightfoot's first Acts notebook were previously transcribed by B. N. Kaye and G. R. Treloar and published in the *Durham University Journal*. See B. N. Kaye and G. R. Treloar, "J. B. Lightfoot and New Testament Interpretation: An Unpublished Manuscript of 1855," *Durham University Journal* 82 (1990): 160–75 (on 171–75). The bulk of that article, however, is not a transcript. It is an analysis of Lightfoot's hermeneutical approach. After having read

First of all then, our method of study and system of interpretation must necessarily be dependent on the view we take of the inspiration of Holy Scripture. It will be so either consciously or unconsciously. This we might reasonably have supposed a priori, and the history of Biblical Criticism teaches us that such has in fact been the case.

Now in an inspired writing there are two elements, the human and the divine, or as it is sometimes expressed, the letter and the spirit, and the different views held of the doctrine of inspiration depend on the prominence given to one or the other of these elements, and the judgment formed of their mutual relations. Hence it will be seen that no conceivable shade of opinion is excluded, and every attempt at classifying these views must be more or less fallacious. But it will be sufficiently exact for our present purpose roughly to assume a threefold division—in the first of these the divine element being too exclusively considered, the second the undue prominence being assigned to the human agency, and in the third and only adequate view of inspiration, each of these elements being recognized in its proper sphere, and the two harmoniously combined. The first of these views is irrational, the second is rationalistic, the third alone is in accordance with the highest reason and the fullest faith.

The irrational view—that which loses sight of the human agency—is prior in time (I am speaking now of Modern Criticism)—to the rationalistic. It refuses to recognize any peculiarities in the individual writer, who is under the guidance of the Spirit. It is insensible to any varieties of style, any difference in the method of treatment in different books of Holy Scripture. It reduces the whole Bible to one uniform color. It is needless to say that such a view must fall at once before the assaults of criticism. If this were all, it might be borne patiently, but unhappily it has dragged down the tottering faith of not a few in its fall. It may also be said that it is derogatory to the majesty of God, that it has no support from analogy in his workings elsewhere, and no authority from Holy Scripture itself.

This theory of inspiration provokes a reaction. The rationalistic view is the natural consequence of its exaggerated form. In this the human agency

---

the handscript of Lightfoot, I made a few minor emendations to their rendering of the first four or so pages of the first brown notebook, but their transcription is largely accurate and is followed here. (BW3) is put so prominently forward that the divine is obscured. The divine agency is perhaps not actually denied, but it is so virtually. By indefinitely extending the action of inspiration, it is in fact rendered meaningless. It is allowed that Moses and David, that St. Paul and St. John, were inspired; but then it claims the same privilege for Homer and Aeschylus, for Pythagoras and Plato. Now I should be the last to deny that 'whatever is good, whatever is beautiful, whatever is true'[4] in the heathen writers derived from the primal source of all beauty, truth and goodness. I have been taught, and fully believe it, that every good gift and every perfect gift cometh from above.[5] *Nor do I care to contend strenuously that the difference is one of kind and not of degree. It is difficult in most cases to maintain the distinction when hard pressed. It is not easy to say where the one ends and the other begins. But what I would say is this: that practically there is such a vast difference between the illumination of apostle and prophet and the illumination of the philosopher and poet, that calling both by the same term 'inspiration' instead of tending to clear our conceptions, does in fact leave a very erroneous impression on our minds.*[6] Inspiration is thus emptied of its significance.

The true view of inspiration is a mean between these extremes—or rather it is a combination of the two—it recognizes the element of truth which each contains, adopting and uniting them. And it recognizes them too in all their fullness. It does not assign less power to the divine agency, nor does it ignore any of the characteristics of the human instrument. The truth is one, but it has many sides. One man is more fitted than another from natural endowments, to appreciate it from some particular point of view. No man is capable of seeing it from every side, else he becomes more than a man. The Holy Spirit has chosen its instruments, as Christ chose his apostles for their natural gifts, whether intellectual or spiritual, and has inspired them for our

---

[4]This is seemingly an allusion to Phil 4:8. (TDS)

[5]See Jas 1:17. (TDS)

[6]This is the later version of Lightfoot's sentence. The earlier version in the notes reads: "Nor again do I lay much stress on there being a difference of kind, rather than of degree in the two cases. I fear this distinction between difference in kind and difference in degree is in most cases an artificial distinction, appealing to our limited faculties and imperfect knowledge, that in the moral and spiritual as in the physical world, it will be very difficult to draw the line where the one ends and the other begins." See Kaye and Treloar, "J. B. Lightfoot and New Testament Interpretation," p. 172n3. They concur that the sentences in this note are the earlier recension of what Lightfoot wrote at this juncture. (BW3)

instruction and guidance. But it has not destroyed their individuality. One sacred writer, St. Paul, views the Gospel as the abrogation of the Law, another, St. James, as the fulfillment. They are not contradictory, but complementary the one to the other, for the Gospel is at once the abrogation and the fulfillment of the Law. One Evangelist, St. John, dwells chiefly on the eternal Sonship of the Savior; another, St. Luke, on his human tenderness and his sympathies with our infirmities. They are both true, for he is very God and very Man. It is not that the different writers of the New Testament held discordant views, but their individual temperament or the circumstances of their education led them to dwell more fully on some special point. They were therefore fit instruments under the guidance of the Holy Spirit to develop their particular truth, and we may suppose without presumption, that they had each their part assigned them according to their natural capabilities or their acquirements in penning the volume of Holy Scripture, as we know that they had in raising the fabric of the Church.[7]

I have made these remarks on what appear to be the right and wrong views of inspiration because, as I said before, the method we adopt in studying Holy Scripture and our System of Interpretation is of necessity closely connected with the theory we hold on this point. Where there is an exaggeration in the one, there is a corresponding exaggeration in the other. Where any point is lost sight of in the one, something is found to be missing also in the other.

Thus we find that when the theory of inspiration, which I have ventured to call irrational, prevailed, the interpretation of the New Testament was marked by corresponding defects. As the human element was entirely lost sight of, so criticism and grammar were alike disregarded in the interpretation. 'The spirit and not the letter' was the watchword of those who held these views—and those words of St. Paul are equally abused by many now.[8] I will not stop now to discuss the sense in which we are to discard the letter and cling to the spirit, but one thing is plain. If St. Paul used the words 'the letter killeth but the Spirit giveth life' in the sense in which he is supposed

---

[7]Kaye and Treloar have "rearing the fabric" here, but this is surely a misreading of what Lightfoot wrote, though I admit his handwriting is sometimes quite difficult to decipher. A fabric cannot be "reared" but it can be "woven" (if cloth were meant) or "raised" (as here, when material construction is meant; cf. the German *Fabrik*). (BW3)

[8]See 2 Cor 3:6. (TDS)

by such persons to use them, then he condemns himself. For you will recollect that in a passage in Galatians he bases his interpretation of a prophecy
in the Old Testament on the basis of a singular instead of a plural number
οὐ λέγει καὶ τοῖς σπέρμασιν, ὡς ἐπὶ πολλῶν, ἀλλ᾽ ὡς ἐφ᾽ ἑνός καὶ τῷ σπέρματι
σου, ὅς ἐστιν Χριστός (Gal 3:16).[9] Other instances may be multiplied, but
this will suffice. I think it will be seen from this that the minutest points of
language are worthy of our consideration in studying the New Testament,
and I think we have a right [to say and do so].[10] We have a right to appeal to
St. Paul in our defense when we are accused of over subtlety and unjustifiable refining in dwelling on grammatical forms. In fact, according to the
loose system of interpretation, which unfortunately has not yet disappeared
in England, language is a mere plaything. Words have no fixed meaning.
They are at the mercy of the interpreter. I will give you an instance from a
book which was very highly thought of—and still continues to be in some
quarters. It is a Commentary on the Epistles published about the middle of
the last century. The title of one of the preliminary essays is 'On Translating
the Greek Used by the Writers of the New Testament.' We are there told,
among other information sufficiently startling, that the indicative is often
put for the subjunctive and vice versa (ἵνα καρπὸν πολὺν φέρητε is translated 'when ye bear much fruit'), that the infinitive was used by the Hebrews
for the verb in any of its moods and tenses and therefore, it is implied, by
the New Testament writers, that the present tense is sometimes put for the
preterite, sometimes for the future, sometimes for the imperfect: we learn
that ἀλλά means 'yet certainly,' 'now indeed,' 'for because,' 'wheretofore,
therefore,' 'unless except,' 'yet however,' that γὰρ at times means 'wherefore,
therefore,' and that, as Phavorinus tells us, 'it is put for δέ, consequently it
has all the different meanings of δέ accordingly.' It is to be translated sometimes 'and now' at other times 'but yet, although.' εἰς signifies 'in, concerning,
with against, before, by, in order to, of or concerning, among, at, towards.' ἐν
means 'with, to, into, towards, for, by, of, through, concerning, on, nigh to,
instead of, among, at, after, under. . . .'[11] I have spared you some of the more

---

[9]Here as elsewhere we will be following the Westcott and Hort version of the Greek text, as is
only appropriate in a volume on Lightfoot, except where Lightfoot differs.

[10]This earlier version seems more to the point than the later substituted remark: "The passage is
a very difficult one no doubt and raises grave questions. But for my purpose it is convincing."

[11]At this juncture he continues to multiply specific grammatical examples.

egregious blunders. These instances are taken from a book, which enjoyed a considerable reputation. Interpretation based on such principles, if they can be called principles, is hopeless. It is needless to remark how unworthy, not to say irreverent (free from any such intent may have been the motives of the writer) this view becomes. It is not against this particular author that I would wish to direct the remark. He undertook a task of great labor, and discharged it, I doubt not, in a conscientious spirit. But the whole system is as bad as it can be. It is the offspring of gross indolence—there is no loving spirit here. It is not the spirit which gathers the crumbs that fall from the Master's table.[12] We cannot expect the blessing of Jacob, unless like him we wrestle with the angel until the breaking of the day.[13]

And I may remark here in passing that I see no ground whatever for supposing that the language of the Inspired Writers is careless or ungrammatical. It is true that the dialect, in which they wrote, was not the pure Greek of earlier times and that in certain cases the grammatical forms and significations of words had undergone some changes. But a language may be impure and yet exact, and so at the time of the Christian era, there was, I believe, as certainly an acknowledged standard by which language was measured, as there was in the age of Xenophon and Plato, though this standard may have been different. And it is not too much to say that on examination it will be found that Aristotle himself is not more exact—in his use of terms—than St. Paul.

I have pointed out one result of the irrational view of inspiration—the neglect of the language of the New Testament. I will allude to another. It begets an extreme jealousy of any attempt to reproduce the circumstances under which the Gospel was first preached, to enter into the character and habits of thought of the preachers themselves, to decipher the influences which directed their words and actions. This jealousy culminates in the case of St. Paul. Yet how much valuable instruction would thus be excluded! If St. Paul is indeed the model of all for all Christian missionaries, he is only so, because like them he is molded by outward circumstances, like them he is

---

[12]This allusion to Mt 15:27 is followed in the subsequent sentence with a reference to Gen 32:22-32. (TDS)

[13]It is not clear which writer from the eighteenth century Lightfoot here has in mind, though he made similar criticisms of his contemporaries A. P. Stanley and B. Jowett. (BW3)

influenced by human feelings and sympathies, like them he has his own individuality of character. And they who would study this model to most effect, must strive to enter into his struggles, to appreciate his weakness as well as his strength, to think his thoughts and to live his life. And surely, if this were not intended, it would be strange that so perfect a picture of the character and working of the great Apostle should have been presented to us, that his external actions should be so faithfully reproduced in St. Luke's narrative, that his inward feelings and motives should find such lively expression in his own letters or as it would be expressed in modern phraseology, that he should be the most subjective of all writers, that in short we should know more of him than we do of any other person of antiquity. Surely it were a cruel and irreverent thought, that these opportunities and inducements were put in our way as our temptation—not for our guidance.

But faulty as this system is, in its leading idea at least, the spirituality of mind necessary for the study of Holy Scripture, it is exalted far above the opposite extreme, which, by the general principle of reaction, it provokes. The rationalistic interpretation, as is the case with the corresponding theory of inspiration, never rises above the mere intellectual. It is the boast of this school, if school it can be called, that it approaches the study of sacred writings, free from prepossessions. It subjects the Scriptures to a dry searching criticism, as it would handle any other book. Let us examine this boast. In the first place, is it possible? In the second place is it desirable? It is not too much to say that no such freedom is attainable, and that those who profess to have it, do in fact, at least in most cases, substitute in place of these prepossessions others more questionable in their character, certain favorite dogmas and philosophical systems.

Nor indeed, even if attainable, is this freedom to be desired, in the sense in which it is professed. For under the head of prepossessions, which they wish to banish, they include two totally different classes of sentiments—those which are produced by outward circumstances, as from our education and social position—prejudices in fact—and those which result from the inward dictates of our heart—the voice of God speaking within us—the light which [enlightens][14] every man who cometh into the world[15] and which

---

[14]Lightfoot uses "lighteth," which is no longer an English word. (BW3)
[15]See Jn 1:9. (TDS)

speaking to us of the moral distinction of right and wrong, of our inherent sinfulness, of our spiritual destitution, and our dependence on a higher power, naturally disposes us to any system, which recognizes these truths and supplies these defects.

The former of these prepossessions we must indeed resign; the latter we must cling to at all hazards. Most of all we must avoid this dry heartless criticism, which professes to undertake its task in such a spirit. Wordsworth warns off from his poet's grave the mere intellectualist.[16] From these more sacred precincts we must 'warn him' off too. It is not for such as these that the truths of the Gospels are open—not for the 'reasoning self-sufficing thing, the intellectual all in all.' For, in fact, this school transfers the cause from the proper court of judicature. The human element must indeed be tried *in fons rationis*. The text must be discussed, the interpretation fixed, historical questions decided before this tribunal—but there is a higher court of appeal. The *forum conscientiae*, I use the word in its widest sense, as signifying our moral and spiritual consciousness, and in this court the verdict will often be reversed.

To this Caesar of our inward nature, the inspired writings appeal, and to Caesar they must go.[17] It may be that they would have been acquitted when tried before Festus and Agrippa, as most certainly they will, if the judges are sufficiently able and unprejudiced.[18] But there is always this rectifying power to appeal to. It takes into account elements which were before neglected. It has larger data from which to give a verdict. What then I mean is simply this—that mere human criticism cannot grasp the entire question. It is only conversant with the human element in the inspired writings, and thus though it may come to a right decision, it is almost equally liable to failure, for there is scarcely any historical fact, there is no moral or philosophical doctrine which, cannot be and has not been disputed with some plausibility. And as the importance of the fact or doctrine in question rises, in the same degree are diversities of opinions multiplied. I believe it is this reference to

---

[16]For an example of what Lightfoot might have in mind here, see William Wordsworth's 1798 poem "The Tables Turned," which among other lines includes the well-known words: "Books! 'tis a dull and endless strife: / Come, hear the woodland linnet, / How sweet his music! on my life, / There's more of wisdom in it." (TDS)

[17]See Acts 25:12.

[18]On Paul's trial before Agrippa and Festus, see Acts 26.

our inward tribunal that St. Paul means when he speaks of comparing things spiritual πνευματικοῖς πνευματικὰ συγκρίνοντες,[19] i.e. referring to doctrines which are offered to us as spiritual truths, to the standard of spiritual experiences within us. ψυχικὸς δὲ ἄνθρωπος οὐ δέχεται τὰ τοῦ πνεύματος τοῦ θεοῦ· μωρία γὰρ αὐτῷ ἐστιν. The blessing is denied not to the carnal man only . . .[20] but also to him, who may possess every intellectual endowment, but yet wants this spirituality, without which they are all in vain. This is the error of the great body of later German critics—not all of them, for there are some noble exceptions, an error far more dangerous than the former.

Still, though we deprecate their views, we are not at liberty to discard the result of their labors. They have accumulated a vast amount of useful matter. They have subjected the sacred writings to an exact and searching criticism, and they have not failed to throw considerable light on special points. All that acuteness and learning could effect, they have attained to. It is impossible that we should not find something valuable at least, where so much labor has been spent. I shall therefore avail myself from time to time of anything in these writers which may elucidate our subject. One protest I must enter in the name of charity and truth. A sweeping condemnation of everything that is German is not honest, it is not Christian. There is as much diversity among German writers, as there is among ourselves. Then and then only shall we, as a nation, have a right to inflict this undiscriminating censure, when we have spent as much time and pains over the sacred writings as they have and produced results as considerable. If the amount of evil in German criticism is to be deplored, the amount of good is at least greater, than anything we have to show on our parts.

The timidity which shrinks from the application of modern science or criticism to the interpretation of the Scripture, evinces a very unworthy view of its character. If the Scriptures are indeed true, they must be in accordance with every true principle of whatever kind. It is against the wrong application of such principles and against the presumption, which pushes them too far, that we must protest. It is not much knowledge, but little knowledge that is the dangerous thing here as elsewhere. From the full light of science

---

[19]For this Greek phrase and the ones that follows, see 1 Cor 2:13-14.
[20]Lightfoot adds in parenthesis here the term σαρκικός, but this is probably not the equivalent to the term ψυχικός.

or criticism we have nothing to fear. The glimmering of light, which rather deserves the name of darkness visible, hides and distorts the truth. I am also afraid to refer once more to lines which of late from frequent quotation have become almost hackneyed, but it appears to me that the thoughtful theologian can choose no more suitable than the words in which Tennyson has so nobly portrayed the harmony of faith and reason:

> Let knowledge grow from more and more
> That more of reverence within us dwell
> That mind and soul according well
> May make one music as before.
> ['In Memoriam,' Prologue, stanza six]

I said I should not refuse to make use of writings the main principles of which I should strenuously disown where they threw light on our subject. Whether it is advisable for young students to meddle with them is a different question. If they have not sufficient time to devote to the study, it is better that they should keep aloof. In that case they will only start objections, which they have no time to answer, and confuse rather than clearing their notions. Supposing they have time and energy, I cannot deprecate their doing so, even where I do not advise it.

For I do not feel any right to abridge for others the Christian liberty which I claim for myself, but it is with this sincere desire to learn God's will that you may act upon it. And then I have no fear of the result. I have no fear of the result because I have the most trustworthy assurances of it. You recollect the words of our Lord in St. John ἐάν τις θέλῃ τὸ θέλημα αὐτοῦ ποιεῖν (if any man is ready to do God's will, desirous of doing it) γνώσεται περὶ τῆς διδαχῆς πότερον ἐκ τοῦ θεοῦ ἐστιν.[21] There is the old maxim 'Pectus facit theologium.' Here the heart may often lead you right, where the head fails, but the head without the heart, will never make you or me a divine in the high sense of the word.

I wish I could have said better what I wanted to say to you, but if these remarks have in any way served to lead you to right views on this important subject, it is sufficient. I felt that they were not altogether unneeded. I mean that the more exact our study of Scripture becomes, up to a certain point,

---

[21]See Jn 7:17.

the more difficulties present themselves. There may be apparent discrepancies, which it is difficult to reconcile, facts narrated, which it is difficult to explain, doctrines propounded, which we cannot account for. We naturally dwell on single points. Thus a particular difficulty assumes an undue prominence and threatens to destroy the balance of our minds. But if we approach the subject in a proper frame, the poison will bring with it, its antidote, the evil will right itself. We shall find that special difficulties are multiplied, difficulties too which we are often forced to leave unexplained, the foundations on which our faith is built, are widened and strengthened at the same time. It is the aggregate of evidence by which the case must be judged. Special objections must sink in comparison with this.

Last of all, these remarks would be most defective, if I failed to remind you, as I need to be reminded myself, that above all things prayer is necessary for the right understanding of the Holy Scripture. As speaking to Christians, I might appeal at once to the authority of Scripture itself, an authority which you all recognize. But if it can be said that as a matter of argument, I am arguing in a circle, because the recognition of the duty of prayer presupposes a belief in the truth of Holy Scripture, I could put the matter in this light. If you are studying an ancient writer, a historian for instance such as Thucydides or Tacitus, you would not expect to understand him unless you endeavored to transport yourself into the time at which he wrote, to think and feel with him, and to realize all the circumstances which influenced the life and actions of men of that day. Otherwise, your study would be barren of any results. So it is with the study of Holy Scripture. These documents come before you as spiritual writings, and to appreciate them you must put yourself in communication with the Spirit. Prayer is the medium of communication. And therefore it is necessary for the right understanding of the Bible.

Part Two

Introduction to Acts—
Preliminary Matters[1]

THE QUESTION WHICH ARISES respecting any book is the genuineness
and authenticity of it. The genuineness has to do with the state of the text,
the authenticity with the person of the author. The investigation of the one
may coincide with the investigation of the other, but does not necessarily so.
The question of the *genuineness* of a book is closely connected with the
textual criticism of the various manuscripts containing the book, in part or
whole. The sources for establishing the text of any New Testament book are
fourfold: 1) manuscripts; 2) versions; 3) quotations from the Church Fathers;
and 4) conjectural emendations.

MANUSCRIPTS AND LECTIONARIES

The older or uncial manuscripts are marked by capital letters in the common

---

[1]Here and in various other places in these volumes what Lightfoot has given us is detailed notes
for lectures coupled with some fully written out paragraphs. The editors have to decide whether
to expand the notes into whole sentences or simply leave the notes as notes. Since it seemed better that there be a narrative flow to these volumes, in some places the notes have been turned into
full sentences *where it was clear what the thrust of the notes was indicating.* In other cases, where
the handwriting was rather impenetrable or the telegraphic fashion of a note made it difficult if
not impossible to decipher, I decided it would be the better part of valor to leave out anything that
was truly obscure and did not seem likely to be of major importance to Lightfoot's case. We have
decided to leave the Greek text without the breathing and accents marks where Lightfoot does so
because sometimes he follows the standard Greek text of his day in these matters and sometimes
he does not. The same applies to the Hebrew vowel pointing. Sometimes he includes it and sometimes not. (BW3)

critical editions, the later or cursive, by numbers. In the Acts of the Apostles, the manuscripts must be evaluated in respect of age. To give some account of the more ancient manuscripts these include:

A. Codex Alexandrinus (cf. Davids. Bibl. Crit. vol. ii. p. 271)

B. Codex Vaticanus (ibid., p. 275)

C. Codex C (ibid., p. 281)

D. Codex Bezae or Cantabrigensis (ibid., p. 285)

Various dates suggest that ultimately these manuscripts come from the second century. Of the revised account of Acts according to Codex D, we note the strange phenomenon exhibited by this manuscript and the re-markable character of its interpolations. These are more numerous in the Acts than elsewhere (e.g. Acts 4:32, 15; 11:2d; 12:3, 10). It may be remarked:

(a) That if these are interpolations, they are at any rate not easily ac-counted for.

(b) That the manuscript exhibits more nearly than any other Greek text, readings found in the earliest versions—e.g. all of Syriac, Coptic, Sahidic, Italian and in the early Fathers.

And therefore, granting that the passages found here are interpolations, the manuscript is still a most important authority when its readings are supported by other documents. On the whole we may agree with Tregelles (Greek Text p. 150) that B and D are the most important manuscripts. But how does one date an ancient manuscript? From what considerations is a date determined?

1) The material

2) Ink

3) Manner of writing (Davids. vol. ii p. 263sqq.)

4) Form of letters

Besides manuscripts, there are Lectionaries (εὐαγγελιστάρια . . . ibid., p. 269). Of the relative value of manuscripts and the estimate of their collective authority we must speak hereafter.

VERSIONS

Those of real importance are the Syriac, Latin, Egyptian, Ethiopic and

Gothic. [There are others, which I shall merely name—the Arabic, Perisan, Georgian, Armenian and Slavonic]. The most important of all are the *Syriac* and *Latin.*

Syriac

    i. Peshito (Davids. vol. ii. p. 151) (syr)

    ii. Philoxenian (ibid., p. 185) syr^p and syr^p mg.

    iii. Jerusalem Syriac (ibid., p. 198)

The Latin

    i. The older Latin version or versions. (ibid., p. 242)

    ii. (The Itala a recension of this mss.? Very ancient)

    iii. The version of St. Jerome. Vulgate (ibid., p. 249)

Egyptian or Coptic (p. 206)

    i. Sahidic or Thebaic Upper Egypt (probably from the 3rd century)

    ii. Memphitic. Lower Egypt (copt).

Ethiopic (p. 203)
Gothic (p. 231)

QUOTATIONS FROM THE FATHERS

Points to be considered: 1) the age; 2) country; 3) religious views; 4) accuracy, or the reverse, of the writer. Whether he argues from the text in question, or introduces it merely incidentally.

CONJECTURAL EMENDATION

This is to be altogether excluded from the domain of sacred criticism, for:

    i. It is improbable—almost impossible—that in any case the correct reading has disappeared from every existing authority (whether mss. vers. or the Fathers) and therefore conjectural emendation is unnecessary;

    ii. It is such a dangerous element in sacred criticism, that it is the safer course to exclude it entirely, rather than to retain it for the sake of some possible advantage in an individual case.

THE RULES OF TEXTUAL CRITICISM

What then are the rules to be observed in textual criticism?

(A) In estimating the preponderance of authority (i.e. external evidence) for a reading,

      a. Our first impulse is to form a numerical estimate. But this is obviously inadequate. An edition of Milton of the sixteenth century is a much better authority for the original text than twenty editions published within the present century. This [numerical estimate method] has been entirely abandoned in sacred criticism.[2]

      b. The next step is the estimate from antiquity. This again is not supportable, for a later manuscript from the hand of an accurate transcriber is in many cases far more valuable than an earlier written by a careless or dishonest scribe.

      c. Therefore intrinsic credibility must be combined with antiquity. But even this is inadequate. We may have a reading supported by twenty manuscripts of equal antiquity and general accuracy, and another only by ten and yet the verdict will be rightly given in favor of the latter. Because in the former case there are twenty manuscripts which bear marks of being derived from the same source whereas of the latter five belong to one, and five to another class. Thus we have *two independent* testimonies in favor of the later reading.

      d. Other manuscripts therefore must be sorted and arranged in classes, in order that we judge by *independent* witnesses.

(B) In subordination of the testimony of authority we must weigh the intrinsic probabilities in favor of or against a particular reading based on the *Internal Evidence*.

---

[2]This remark of course is highly ironic today in view of all the arguments used to support the so-called Majority Text in defense of the KJV English translation of the text. Lightfoot, it will be noted, was part of the team of revisers of the Authorized Version and had no interest in propping up an ancient translation, for instance the 1611 KJV, not well supported by the best textual criticism. (BW3)

a. The great rule is that enunciated by Bengel in the words 'Proclivi scriptioni praestat ardua.' This rule may be applied in many ways—but it is only applicable when attributions are nearly balanced, obscure exceptions are preferred to the more plain: unusual forms of words to the more usual, harsher constructions to more simple.

b. Readings containing apparent historical or doctrinal difficulties are to be preferred. Shorter readings are to be preferred to longer when the words added are of the nature of a gloss.

c. Readings which favor any theological or religious bias are suspicious. (I.e. especially that of the predominant party, as those which are marked by strong orthodoxy or asceticism. Davids.)

d. That reading is to be preferred which is more in character with the general style of the writer.

e. That reading is to be rejected which is unsuitable to the context.

History of Textual Criticism in Modern Times

In regards to the earliest printed Greek texts, we may list the first published to be that of Erasmus in 1516 (that of the *Complutensian Polyglot* had been printed in 1514 but not published). We must also mention Stephanus and Beza, with *Elzevir* based on Stephanus' third edition, and the *Textus Receptus* derived from *Elzevir*. As for theories of recensions, there is Griesbach (though in some degree anticipated by Bengel) 1774–7, and the following stages can be mentioned:

1) The Alexandrine Fathers and Philox. Versions B.C.F.

2) Occidental—Cyprian, Tertullian, Irenaeus, leading to later versions—Sahidic, It.

3) Constantine

As for the emancipation of the Textus Receptus, *Lachmann* 1831.

To Tischendorf (1841) we owe the enunciation of principles of reconstruction of the text. Reconstruction of text: (1) Alexandrian; (2) Latin or (1) Asiatic; (2) Byzantine.[3]

THE AUTHENTICITY AND AUTHORSHIP OF ACTS[4]

The first question to be raised is—is the narrative *credible*? This matter must be concluded from its intrinsic character, and also from its agreement with external testimony. As for the latter, external testimony may be gotten from the heretical sects on doctrinal grounds: (1) Ebionites; (2) Marcionites; and (3) Manichaeans.

(A) Intrinsic Character

(i.) The modesty of his claims. Preface to the Gospel in Lk 1:1-4

(ii.) Apparent discrepancies. These only evince credibility, where they are the exception. No argument could be drawn from them if they were habitual. But the reverse is the case. If the writer of this narrative is an imposter, he is one of no ordinary kind. He gives proof of the most consummate skill and deepest design—as we shall see. There is therefore no possible account which can be given for his apparent contradictions—or the hypothesis is of a forgery (e.g. the account of St. Paul's conversion, as given in several places Acts 9:7; 22:9; 26:13 [cf. the reason of Paul's leaving Jerusalem Acts 9:30 with Acts 22:17]).

(iii.) His admission of errors and imperfections on the part of his principal characters (e.g. the inaccuracies of St. Stephen's speech, quarrel of St. Paul and Barnabas, the presentation of St. Paul in Acts 23, also in Acts 20:25, a story of Paul which was not fulfilled).

---

[3]What is remarkable about all this is that in an age where precritical approaches to the text of the New Testament were still very common, particularly in the English-speaking world, Lightfoot was fully committed to the principle that *text determines canon*, that is, that only what was in the original inspired manuscripts should be considered and dealt with as Scripture, hence the need for textual criticism and the need for recovering the earliest possible text. (BW3)

[4]It is worth comparing this introductory material to appendix A in this volume, not least because there we find a fuller expression of Lightfoot's views on these essential matters of prolegomena.

(iv.) The incomplete nature of his records—undramatic and yet natural (e.g. St. Stephen's speech. It is the beginning of a speech. It is broken off towards the end, but though of considerable length, is a mere preface and does not arrive at any result. In short it is as unlikely a forgery as it well can be and is inexplicable, except on the supposition of it really having been spoken).

(v.) The internal consistency of his narrative (e.g. the shipwreck, Acts 27. Cf. Smith, *The Voyage and Shipwreck of St. Paul*).

(vi.) The naturalness in his delineation of characters—the probability that they could have acted under the circumstances as he has represented them acting (e.g. the letter of Claudius Lysias, Acts 23, the accusation of Tertullian and defense of St. Paul before Felix, Acts 24).

(vii.) The modification of style—Hebraic coloring in the earlier part, gradually shading off.

(B) Credibility

Confirmation by an exhaustive view is of course impossible: we must therefore select some points:

(i.) Knowledge evinced of facts

1. (Space). *Geographical.* The wide extent of country traversed over—Judah, Syria, Asia Minor, Macedonia, Greece. The Mediterranean and the islands of Italy.

2. (Time). *Historical.*

(a). Profane History. e.g. Gallio is called proconsul of Achaia (18:12) ἀνθυπάτου ὄντος τῆς Ἀχαΐας (cf. C+H *Life of St. Paul.* i.155) Tiberius had made Achaia (formerly a senatorial province) an imperial one. It was restored to the senate by Claudius (Suet. *Claud.* xxv). Claudius was emperor from A.D. 41–54.

If the writer had placed the incident only a few years later, the term could have been procurator (cf. Paley Evv. pt. ii. c. vi).

(b). *Christian History*
Obvious facts may be neglected. Incidental coincidences alone to be appraised (Paley's *H. Paul.* e.g. the contribution of alms).

(ii.) Knowledge evinced of individuals.

Their Character.

e.g. *Gallio*—cf. Acts 18:17 (καὶ οὐδὲν τούτων τῷ Γαλλίωνι ἔμελεν)

What of the character of him given in heathen records? (cf. C+H *Life of St. Paul* i. p. 449)

His own brother says that though he is loved as much as he can be, he is not loved as he deserves.

He is called '*dulcis* Gallio'; both to Seneca and to Statius.

Again Seneca, 'His conduct on those occasions is what might have been expected for such a man. The amicable good-natured friend becomes the easy indifferent governor. He is without moral indignation, however excellently disposed.'

As for St. Paul, his rule of becoming 'all things to all men' is observable in this record. Compare for instance his speeches at Lystra, at Athens and the Jews at Antioch in Pisidia. At Lystra (Acts 14), he is addressing unlettered barbarians. He appeals to the charges of pagan magic as operations of the true God. At Athens he is speaking to lettered and philosophic guests (Acts 17). He cites the language of their own poets (speaking of dependence of a deity), appeals to the existence of an altar as the evidence of this striving after higher truth. Difference in his language is notable when compared to what he says to the Jews (Acts 13). It is here to their national privileges and feelings and to their past history that he directs his speech.

It may appear as though this rule of accommodation sometimes led him too far as in the case of the disputes between the Pharisees and the Sadducees.

THE STYLE AND CONTENT OF ACTS

The author's grasp of Greek grammar, syntax and vocabulary is noteworthy, and is shown by his extensive use of synonyms. Here is a small sampling of the common ones we find just in the first couple of chapters of Acts.

1:7	χρόνοι, καιροί
7, 8	ἐξουσία, δύναμις
14	προσευχή, δέησις
2:2, 4	πνοή, πνεῦμα
45	κτῆμα, ὕπαρξις
3:10	θάμβος, ἔκστασις
4:7	τίς, ποῖος
5:15	κλινάριον, κράβαττος
7:42	σφάγιον, θυσία

In regard to the style and content of Acts, the speeches of St. Peter are Petrine in thought and in diction (Acts 15). That of James and the apostolic circular letter, those of James. Those of St. Paul, especially the farewell address to the Ephesian elders which most resembles the epistles of that period (Cor; Gal; Rom), are Pauline. What then is the result of all this?

If we conclude the writing is a forgery and the author had no certain knowledge of the facts which he narrates, we must suppose not only that he was a most consummate novelist, but that he is perfect in the delineation of the characters—though most artistic in the construction of his narrative, so skillful as to make it appear perfectly natural. Also, that he was most exactly and clearly informed in an exceedingly wide range of subjects—the complete history of his time, the geography of great parts of the known world, the character and even the style of the persons he introduces and uses this information with such art as to give the appearance of incidental and un-designed coincidence. If this is mere fabrication, he applied himself to the forgery. And for what? Why this imposture? To propagate a faith which he can scarcely have believed and to establish facts which he knew to be false?

And who was this consummate artist? How is it that we know nothing of him? One possessed of such information? One who as a writer has never been equaled? Why did he write anonymously, or even try to pass off his work in the name of another? How unselfish, and yet how dishonest. *Alter-nately*, we must suppose that the writer was well informed and the narrative is true—which is the more likely supposition? But the evidence does not end here. When we come to examining the authorship of the book, we shall find such a coherence to the phenomena which it exhibits, as to strengthen and confirm the evidence which is already mounting.

WHO IS THE AUTHOR OF THIS BOOK?

He was a companion of St. Paul's. There are unmistakable indications of this. On considering this point, it is necessary to call attention to the connection between the Gospel and the Acts. They profess to be connected and to come from the same hand. This of course is no proof. We can't enter into an ex-amination of this claim. It is sufficient to say that the language is the same; the essence of thought identical; and that there is a unity of purpose, with the summary in Lk 1:1-4 introducing the two works. We shall therefore assume the identity of authorship in the two works: at the same time, it will be seen in the course of our examination how truthful and coherent such a view is. [See Davidson II p. 226]

We will therefore consider the two, as one work, and examine its claim to having been written by a companion of St. Paul.

(a) The design and tenor of the work are Pauline.
     If we were asked to mention the characteristic of St. Paul's teaching and practice we should say that it was his view of the universality of Christ's kingdom. This is exactly what the narrative enforces—both in the Gospel and in the Acts.
     The *Gospel*—The Evangelist traces the genealogy of the Savior to

the father of mankind. After the presentation in the temple, prophecies of the child that he shall be not only a glory to God's people Israel but also a light to the Gentiles. The miracles and parables peculiar to the third Gospel bear this mark also. The miraculous catch of fish, the ten lepers cleansed, the person with the spirit of infirmity, the parable of the two debtors, the good Samaritan, the lost drachma, the Prodigal Son, the Pharisee and the Publican, etc. etc.

The Acts—Cornelius—the Apostolic Council. The whole manner of St. Paul's teaching. 'The Jew first and then the Greek.'

(b) Special facts given which are narrated aptly on the authority of St. Paul.

(1) Cf. 1 Cor 11:23 with Luke 22:19.

(2) 1 Cor 15:5 with Luke 24:34.
Again part of Paul's Gospel. The allusion in St. Luke incidental.

(3) 1 Tim 5:18 compared with Luke 10:7, where the same words are found. Whatever be the explanation of the apparent quotation in 1 Tim the result is the same as far as our purpose is concerned.

SUMMARY

What then is our evidence that the work was written by a companion of St. Paul? We will for the present lay aside external testimony. We have seen that the whole scope and tenor of the work bears the stamp of St. Paul's teaching in that respect which may be considered in his special characteristic—that the style and diction bear a resemblance to that of the great Apostle, only such a resemblance as might be looked for between the writings of a master and a favorite disciple, his religious vocabulary being more or less derived from St. Paul. And lastly that certain facts are narrated in the third Gospel which are found nowhere else in the New Testament except in the epistles of the Apostle, or are narrated in a way which is peculiar to him—and yet with such differences in arrangement and detail (some particulars being omitted and others superceded) and in such an incidental manner as to show that they did not come from the pen of a forger who had the epistles of St. Paul before him. Such is the indirect testimony, but have we any direct evidence to this connection between the writer and St. Paul?

As for mode of expression it is sufficient to establish this connection and yet so incidental and so slight as at once to preclude the notion of a fraud. A man might read the whole Gospel through and not discover that the writer was a disciple of St. Paul. Nay he probably could not discern it, though he read it again and again. There is not the slightest direct hint of it. He might continue his readings. He would have to get half through the Acts, and still have found no indication. And when he does stumble upon it, of what kind is it? Not the patent statement of the fact such as alone could have satisfied the forger—witness the acknowledged forgeries of the sub-apostolic age, and especially a forger in these simple, inartistic times. There are not many uses of the first person plural in describing certain incidents in the life of St. Paul. 'We endeavored to go to Macedonia'; 'we set sail.' Mark also how truthful this very use of the language is when closely examined. It begins at a certain point in St. Paul's travels and suddenly ceases at Philippi. Then again it is there after an interval of several chapters in the narrative. After a lapse of several years in point of time—(Acts 17:1–20:3) it recurs at the same place, Philippi. The writer has been left at that place during the interval and is taken up when St. Paul returns to the same place. But he does not tell us this directly. We might read the narrative twenty times over and not find it out.

It is worth remarking too that this direct testimony, slight in itself, is contained in an entirely different treatise—published at a different time certainly separated from it is the copies multiplied for dispersion—from the more decisive passages which point indirectly to the fact, these passages which narrate circumstances which is in the manner or language of St. Paul. Is this like a forgery? A forger leaves us doubt when he tends to be taken for the author of the work. And if the work favors anything it is the way of authority by establishing a connection between the author and some important person, he would take care to make this patent. In the Gospel this connection is not directly discernable at all. In the Acts it would easily escape notice. It appears then that this book was written by a companion of St. Paul.

Now there are three names that will suggest themselves as fitting the evidence, or at least not opposed to it Sylvanus (Silas), Timothy and Luke.

How are we to determine the probable author? Is there any reason (exclusive of external testimony) for this book to be by one more than another of these—the three most distinguished of St. Paul's companions? The indications are slight indeed.

(1) The writer is regularly speaking of diseases, the approach of a professional man (it is technical usage without being pedantic—Luke 4:38; 8:43-44; Acts 3:7; 12:23; 13:11; 28:8; cf. Col 4:14. He is also called a physician in the Muratorian Canon, in Eusebius and Jerome).

(2) There are some slight turns that would lead one to suppose that the writer was a native of Antioch.

(3) There are reasons it is unlikely to be Timothy or Silas. The writer speaks of Timothy and Silas in the third person. Were one of these men the author it would destroy the appropriating and consistency of the use of the first person plural. Further, the writer distinguishes himself from Timothy in Acts 20:5. It is not likely to be Silas because there is no evidence even from the Epistles of St. Paul that Silas accompanied Paul on his third missionary tour or went with him to Italy.

In short, the most natural conclusion is that this work was written by a sometime companion of Paul, a particular one, namely St. Luke.[5]

---

[5]Lightfoot wrote a splendid article on Acts for William Smith's second British edition of his *Dictionary of the Bible*. The original article in that dictionary, which was first published in 1863 in London by John Murray in three volumes, was deemed deficient, and Lightfoot was asked to supply a better article. We are able to provide that full article once more in this volume in appendix A. (BW3)

Part Three

The Commentary on Acts

The Superscript

The title is apparently πράξεις ἀποστόλων. So B app. and πρᾶξεις of D is meant for the same. πράξεις ἀποστόλων (Lachm., Tisch., Born.). Was the title given by the writer? It is first referred to, as a document, by Irenaeus *Adversus Haereses* iii.15. But in another passage (iii.13) the book is cited under the name *Actus Apostolorum*. Clement of Alexandria cites the book as αἱ πράξεις τῶν ἀποστόλων (*Strom.* 50.5). Tertullian calls it 'scriptura actorum Apostolorum' (*Adv. Marc.* 2.3) and again *Actus Apostolorum* and in the Muratorian Canon list, 'Acts of All the Apostles.' Origen has αἱ πράξεις τῶν ἀποστόλων. All the Fathers agree in ascribing it to St. Luke.

As for sources, they are threefold: 1) written documents (e.g. the circular letter); 2) oral information (see, e.g. Lk 1:1-4); 3) information gathered when traveling with St. Paul.[1] There is evidence of design in the selection and arrangement of material, not in the invention of material. The source criticism also does not help us much with the issue of dating. Nothing is certain, but presumably the Gospel [was written] before the destruction of Jerusalem (not after, as Meyer) and the Acts was written after the Gospel. The termination of Acts 28 is not abrupt and provides no clue to determining the date.

---

[1] Nothing is claimed about St. Luke receiving the facts by inspiration.

The Preface

THE BRIEF PREFACE IN ACTS is to be compared with both the *commencement* and *conclusion* of St. Luke's Gospel. The result is a conviction that the sacred writer had a definite plan in view, and that this plan was *not an afterthought*, nor was it clearly conceived at the time the Gospel was written. For when we come to examine the words of this preface, we find that the writer refers back to the former treatise *as the account of what Jesus began to do and to teach*. Many explanations are offered of this word ἤρξατο. But from the position of the word, it is evident that ἤρξατο is emphatic and not Ιησοῦς, and that the comparison is between the work that Jesus *began*, and that which *he carried out*.

The work that Jesus *began*, then, is given in the former treatise as we are told here, and we might expect that this could be followed by a reference to the work which He carried out. But just here the continuity of the sentence is broken, and instead of the second clause of the explanation being given, the writer runs off on a narrative of facts. In the *facts* here narrated then we are to seek the clue to the explanation.

But again, turning back to the Gospel, we find that the same facts that are here the starting point, are there (in Lk 24) the conclusion. They are narrated twice over. They thus form the link of connection between the two treatises. The facts in question are between His resurrection and ascension. The history of our Lord's discourse with the disciples, though twice narrated, is told in a different way. In the Gospel, prominence is given to that part of it which has reference to the past, in the Acts that part is given at greater length which points to the future. In the Gospel the discourses of our Lord during this interval are related with a view to the confirmation of His earlier teaching, while in the Acts those words are given more in detail which speak of our Lord's future life, of His continued presence with His followers and His operations in the founding and building up the Christian church. Compare, for example Luke 24:44 with Acts 1:3-6. In the former, Christ is seen as fulfilling past prophecy. In Acts it is about Christ influencing future history to the end of the times.

The two narratives then which we call the Gospel and the Acts are two parts of one great history, the one giving an account of the life and work of Jesus in the flesh, the other an account of the life and work of Jesus in the church for he is still living, though he was dead (μετὰ τὸ παθεῖν).[1] He is still present among us. He is still exhibiting His power and love by miracles, wonders and signs (δυνάμεσιν καὶ τέρασιν καὶ σημείοις). 'Lo I am with you always, even unto the end of the world.'[2]

And the gospel writer has not been silent about this parallelism—There is indeed more than one intimation of it. But in the reference to the Baptism of John it is brought prominently forward. As at the commencement of our Lord's ministry in the flesh, the Baptism of John was the ordained preparation, so the ministry of our Lord in the church is ushered in by the Baptism of the disciples by the Holy Spirit on the day of Pentecost.[3]

And in accordance with this view,[4] which obliges us to look upon this history as the narrative of the working of Jesus in the church, we find that throughout the body of this treatise our Lord himself is represented as the chief agent. This appears to a very remarkable degree.[5] Prayer is offered to Him in making choice of the Twelfth apostle (Acts 1:24). He it is, who poured out the Spirit on the day of Pentecost (Acts 2:33). He works miracles by the

---

[1] See Rev 1:18: καὶ ἐγενόμην νεκρὸς καὶ ἰδοὺ ζῶν εἰμι εἰς τοὺς αἰῶνας τῶν αἰώνων.

[2] Note Mt 28:20.

[3] And as our Lord refers back to John and his baptism here, so does John carry our thoughts forward to Jesus and His baptism by the Holy Spirit. "I indeed baptize you with water, but one mightier than I comes . . . He shall baptize with the Holy Ghost and with fire" (Luke 3:16 though the account is not peculiar to this evangelist)—a prophecy which has its fulfillment at least partially and that in a remarkable manner on the day of Pentecost. Observe that the baptism by fire on the day of Pentecost is represented in the Acts as the work of Jesus (cf. Acts 2:33).

[4] "Which be it observed, reminds us strongly of the language and spirit of St. Paul—I mean, that though it is assumed by all the inspired writers, it appears most prominently in the great Apostle of the Gentiles—this *personal presence* of Jesus in the church."

[5] See Baumgarten pp. 28–29.

apostles' hands (Acts 4:10; 9:34, etc.). He reveals himself to St. Stephen in his dying hour (Acts 7:55). Again He appears to Saul of Tarsus, in fact the interventions of Jesus are numerous. It is the Spirit of Jesus (the correct reading) who forbade the apostles to go to Bithynia (Acts 16:7). That Baumgarten is right in referring ὁ κύριος to 'the Lord Jesus' seems to be shown from

(1) the whole tenor of Acts which is to represent Jesus as the Head of the Church

(2) From particular passages

   a. Acts 1:2

   b. Cf. Acts 10:10, 13, 15 with Acts 5:17

(3) From a declaration of St. Peter, which seems to be intended as a key to the whole book. Acts 2:34-36. Hence such passages as Acts 2:47.

Now the history of Christ's ministry in the flesh could be given entire, and so this written by St. Luke (περὶ πάντων ὧν ἤρξατο Ἰησοῦς κ.τ.λ.), but the ministry of our Lord in the church—not being yet concluded—could not be so narrated. Hence the inspired writer has chosen a period, which, though itself only a part, yet typifies and foreshadows the whole.

It is, as it were, a microcosm of the history of the church and as preparatory following up the train of thought, we should remark on a passage which contains 'the table of contents' of the narrative: 'Ye shall be witnesses unto me both in Jerusalem and in all Judea and Samaria and unto the uttermost parts of the Earth' (Acts 1:8). This is the text on which the whole book is the commentary. And here again we have another instance of what we have seen already, and we shall have more of them hereafter—that St. Luke makes the narrative of the words and deeds of others serve, instead of an explanation of his design and object. It is from his choice and arrangement of materials—and not from any detailed exposition of his own—that we are to learn the great truths that he wishes to enforce. Consider the structure that follows this verse: 'You shall receive power by the descent of the Holy Spirit upon you and ye shall be witness unto me' (Acts 1:8). Chapter One is merely preparatory then we have: (1) Acts 2:1-3; (2) Acts 2:14-7:60; (3) 8:1-11:18; and (4) 11:19-28:31 or put another way, (1) in Jerusalem (2) and in all

Judea and (3) in Samaria and (4) unto the uttermost parts of the earth. A close examination shows that this design is closely interwoven in the whole book. As an example take the conflict of the Christian church with Judaism and Gnosticism in the persons of the Sanhedrin and of Simon Magus. We may compare this with the design of Herodotus' history.

The first two sections are complete: the fulfillment of the third is not actually, but potentially. Such an earnest of it is afforded as to leave no doubt of its final accomplishment. St. Paul takes on the far west, he preaches the new faith in Rome, and Christianity had found firm footing in the strongholds of Heathendom. The rest will follow in due course. The promise can scarcely be said to have been fulfilled even now.

We should regard this book then as narrating the History of the Whole Christian Church—the working of Christ in His mystical body. It is not the personal history of St. Peter or St. Paul that is given—it is of St. Peter as the founder and St. Paul as the builder up of the church that the writer speaks. St. Peter and the remainder of the twelve represent the organization and intended composition of the church, St. Paul, its expansion and diffusive energy. The missionary labors of St. Paul are the missionary labors of the whole church in its failures and its successes.

After then giving an abstract of the History of the Christian church—not in his own words, but by adapting his narrative—St. Luke leads our minds forward to that great and terrible day—which shall be the end of all things—when the church on earth shall give place to the church in heaven—(again not by any language of his own—it is still in the way of narrative) which St. Paul calls the manifestations of the sons of God in expectation of which all creation groaneth and awaiteth in pain—speaking of that 'only far off divine event, to which creation moves.'[6]

Jesus is the agent here too—'This same Jesus which was taken up from you into heaven, shall so come in like manner as ye have seen him go into heaven.' As this ascension from earth to heaven was real and sensible, so shall His descent from Heaven to earth be not figurative—but literal, real and sensible. This, the consummation of all things, this book presents to us

---

[6]This expansive sentence concludes with an allusion to Rom 8:22 ("creation groaneth and awaiteth in pain") and a quotation of the last line of the Lord Alfred Tennyson's famous poem *In Memoriam*. (TDS)

the History of the Christian Church from its earliest beginning, until this great event shall be brought to pass.

And now to speak of the close of the book—It has been said that it ends abruptly, and so it has been supposed that the writer was interrupted (for instance in his thought). It would have been more natural that it should have ended with the martyrdom of St. Paul. The work would then have been more finished. Now had this been the personal history of St. Paul, such argument would have had some weight. But it is not. And the epoch, with which the book closes, is much more important in the history of the church than that of the death of St. Paul, or indeed any other point of time that could have been selected. If the view given above of the book is correct, the narrative is complete. As regards the aim of the writer, we have no good reason for supposing with some that it was interrupted by some accident, or with others that there even existed, or was projected a third narrative (τρίτος λόγος) to include the whole.

The close of the second treatise is strictly analogous to the close of the first. Cf. Luke 24:44-49 with Acts 28:23-29. Also cf. Luke 24:50-53 with Acts 28:30-31. A joyful termination in both cases. Here again we discern the scope of St. Luke with his own exposition, but from the course of his narrative, as is also the method of Herodotus.

Ascension, Judas' Demise, the Filling Up of the Twelve (Acts 1)

Vs. 1 The order of the treatise is given absolutely (πρῶτον) not relatively (πρότερος). Just as we should talk of the first volume, things there might be only his.

περὶ πάντων—'all' not absolutely for that were impossible (cf. John 21:25), nor, yet subjectively—everything that was known to St. Luke for he has omitted to mention a striking saying of the Lord, which is recorded incidentally in this second treatise (Acts 20:35), but 'all' relatively to the design that he had in view.

ὦ Θεόφιλε—speculation has been busy with Theophilus: but, as nothing can be concluded from the address κράτιστε Θεόφιλε,[1] we have really no date (see Meyer, *St. Luke*, p. 198). May he not have been a Philippian? It appears from the narrative that St. Luke was left at Philippi by St. Paul on his second apostolic journey, and taken up on his third—for the first person plural is dropped on the one occasion and resumes again on the other at the same place Philippi. If we suppose that Theophilus was converted by St. Luke during this stay at Philippi, it will account for this use of the plural, not introduced by any explanation, but as if the writer were speaking to one who was acquainted with his connection with St. Paul. On the other hand, the consideration that he was writing, not for Theophilus only, but for the edi-

---

[1] Cf. Lk 1:3. (TDS)

fication of the whole church would lead him to give its due prominence to the history of St. Paul's preaching there. His design obliged him to narrate the facts while it suffered him to keep himself in the background. By addressing his narrative to Theophilus, he was enabled to do this.

ἤρξατο ὁ Ἰησοῦς. Winer makes ἄχρι ἧς ἡμέρας explain ἤρξατο which Jesus began to do (and did), till the day when etc. 'somewhat as' Luke 23:5 (Gram. § 66 p. 775).

Vs. 2 The natural order attaches διὰ πνεύματος ἁγίου to ἐντειλάμενος. Winer (Gram. § 61.p. 697) well remarks that this is more in accordance with the aim of the Acts. His note is worth reading. It is observable how the Greek Fathers have genuinely connected the words with the exchange. Language led them to the right conclusion.

οὓς ἐξελέξατο is added in accord with the design of the Acts to direct the thoughts of the readers to Jesus as the prime agent (see Baumgarten). 'Der heilige Geist war das Medium (διά), durch welches (ἐντέλλή) Jesus aussprach, in der Apostel eingang' (Meyer). This however is scarcely natural.

Vs. 3 τεκμηρίοις E.V. infallible proofs. See rightly Arist. *Rhet.* 1.c.12. ἐν πολλοῖς τεκμηρίοις recalls St. Paul to our minds (1 Cor 15:1).

δι᾽ ἡμερῶν τεσσεράκοντα 'during 40 days' not 'for 40 days continually.' See Chrystost. *ap. Aeg.* ἐφίστατο γὰρ καὶ ἀφίστατο πάλιν. A period of 10 days is thus left between the Ascension and the day of Pentecost. διά with genitive is a temporal usage but has a different sense in Gal 2:1 'after an interval of.'

ὀπτανόμενος 1 Kings 3:8

λέγων τὰ περὶ τῆς βασιλείας τοῦ θεοῦ· Baumgarten (p. 14) is scarcely convincing in his application of this. βασιλείας τοῦ θεοῦ must refer to the future (cf. v. 6).

Vs. 4 συναλιζόμενος. An interesting word.

ἀπὸ Ἱεροσολύμων μὴ χωρίζεσθαι. Luke 24:49 (cf. Baumgarten, p. 15). The Acts commences with this command not to leave Jerusalem, it closes with St. Paul's conflict with the Jews at Rome. On every occasion the Gospel is offered to them first. 'The Jew first and then the Gentile.'[2]

ἡ ἐπαγγελία 'the gracious offer.' τοῦ πατρός cf. John 14:18, 26.

---

[2]See, e.g., Rom 1:16. (TDS)

ἣν ἠκούσατε The instance of this usage of the oblique to the direct narrative in the N.T. are found apparently solely in St. Luke (cf. Luke 5:14; Acts 23:22). The cognate form is found in St. Luke (Acts 23:23-24). As the account here refers to the same discourse as St. Luke 24:49, the words ἣν ἠκούσατέ μου must allude to some promise not recorded in St. Luke: such as that which St. John refers to—the promise of 'the Paraclete.' This verse goes some way in showing that where St. Luke omits a fact, this is no evidence that he was not acquainted with it. This accounts too for the abrupt change from the oblique to the direct narrative that could have left the sense ambiguous. The fact that St. Luke had not narrated the incident in the gospel obliges him to say something on it here.

Vs. 5 The opening of this second period is thus paralleled with the first period or preface (cf. St. Luke 3:16-17 where the Baptist says: ἐγὼ μὲν ὕδατι βαπτίζω ὑμᾶς· αὐτὸς ὑμᾶς βαπτίσει ἐν πνεύματι ἁγίῳ καὶ πυρί [Mark 1:8 omits καὶ πυρί; cf. its ommission in Mt 3:12]). Though the expression καὶ πυρί may have a much wider application, the idea received at least a partial and literal fulfillment on the day of Pentecost (cf. John 1:33).

Vss. 6-7 Οἱ μὲν οὖν συνελθόντες. This verse is better translated (not as E.V.) 'They then who were gathered together.' Meyer supposes that the Lord repeated his warning about the promise of the Father on several occasions in order to reconcile the account here with St. Luke's Gospel.

ἐν τῷ χρόνῳ τούτῳ not the more restricted (with Meyer) ἡ μετὰ πολλ. τάυτ. ἡ.

'Chronos,' quantitative, a duration or measure of time, but 'kairos' qualitative, a season of, possibly an opportune time? (cf. 2 Tim 3:1, καιροὶ χαλεποί).

χρόνους ἢ καιροὺς Luke here and also St. Paul separate the two by repeating the article. εἰ ἐν τῷ χρόνῳ a diffident way of interrogating—a hesitating interrogative doubtful of reply. It is remarkable that St. Paul, speaking of the same event, uses the same words. 1 Thess 5:1. περὶ δὲ τῶν χρόνων καὶ τῶν καιρῶν, ἀδ. κ.τ.λ. (cf. Mark 13:32; Mt 24:36).

ἔθετο 'fixed . . .' Not as the E.V. has it.

ἐν τῇ ἰδίᾳ ἐξουσίᾳ in the exercise of His own—Mt 21:23 [Luke 20:2].

Both in the question of the apostles, and in the answer of our Lord, it seems to be taken for granted that the kingdom could be restored. The question of the disciples might have been prompted by the command of the

Lord that they should not leave Jerusalem. And also, as Meyer truly remarks, by the promise of the outpouring of the Holy Ghost, which the words of the prophet Joel connect with Messiah's reign cf. Joel 3:1; Acts 2:16. It is not the expectations of the disciples but their impatience to which the answer is directed.

Vss. 8-9 ἀλλά. 'This knowledge is withheld from you because it is not necessary for you, but such powers, as shall enable you to spread my Gospel, shall be given.'

ἐξουσία. Freedom from control likely of action, authority—δύναμις power, the ability to do.

ὑπέλαβεν 'caught him up.'

Vss. 10-11 καὶ ὡς . . . καὶ ἰδοὺ cf. Acts 10:17; Luke 7:12. There is an anacoluthon in the sentence, the sentence is framed as if there had been more. ὡς is Greek protasis (Meyer cf. p. 516). ὡς ἀτενίζοντες ἦσαν εἰς τὸν οὐρανὸν. ἀτενίζοντες peculiar to St. Luke and St. Paul? See ἀτενίζειν.

ἄνδρες Γαλιλαῖοι. cf. John 7:52; Mark 14:70. ἀληθῶς ἐξ αὐτῶν εἶ, καὶ γὰρ Γαλιλαῖος εἶ. Καὶ ἡ λαλία σου . . . So Julius the apostate styled the Christian 'Galileans.'

οὕτως ἐλεύσεται. cf. Daniel 7:13.

Vs. 12 Ἐλαιῶνος only found here. In Luke 19:29; 21:37 we have εἰς τὸ ὄρος τὸ καλούμενον Ἐλαιῶν—so we read as here, and not ἐλαίαν, as the word cannot be rendered, and we should require Ἐλαιῶνος. Josephus *Antiq.* vii.9.2. has διὰ τοῦ Ἐλαιῶνος ὄρους.

Chrysostom's hint is unnecessary. A Sabbath day's journey is a measure of length—very natural in describing the position of a place not that distant from the mother city. Josephus calls the distance of the Mt. of Olives in one place 5, in another 6 stadia. Epiphanius reckons a Sabbath day's journey at 6 stadia. The Peshitta probably by an error, translates it here '7 stadia.' It is rather probable that the Syriac translates the exact distance and so inserted it in place of strictly translating the original. The coming of Christ and judgment is connected with the Mount of Olives, cf. Zech 14:4.

Vs. 13 εἰσῆλθον so [i.e.] εἰς τὴν πόλιν.

τὸ ὑπερῷον See Winer Real. § 6 'Haüser.' There would be one flight of steps leading direct to the street (possibly the house of Mary the mother of John, Mark 12:12). Nothing towards the temple. E.V. is wrong here. Luke

24:53 does not imply this. (The order of D, E etc. ἀνέβησαν εἰς τὸ ὑπερῷον is much more natural).

ὅ τε Πέτρος 'Petro, primo, articulus pro ceteris' (Bengel).

Ἰωάννης καὶ Ἰάκωβος So A, B, C, D, al., vulg., Tisch. James was the elder brother and in the Gospels is always mentioned first (except in Luke 8:51; 9:28, in the latter of which perhaps one rightly transposes the words). In the Gospels, John is the brother of James; in the Acts (12:2), James is the brother of John. Henceforth John's importance as an apostle gives him precedence over his brother. James is never mentioned in the gospel of St. John (οἱ τοῦ Ζεβεδαίου John 21:2, but they are not placed in the usual order, after Peter).

In the list of the apostles in Luke 6:14, the order is Peter, Andrew, James, John—the brothers being pairs; here they are separated for the same reason that John is put before James. The same as Luke 6:14 (exc. Judas) with the exception of some slight differences in order. The other lists are Matthew 10:2. Mark 3:18, in both of which Σίμων ὁ καλούμενος ζηλωτής is called Σίμων ὁ Καναναῖος (the one being the Greek and the other the Hebrew for the same thing).

Ἰούδας Ἰακώβου is called in Matth. Ζεβεδίος or (Θαδδαῖος or Λ. ὁ ἐπικληθείς θ. or ὁ ἐπικλ. Λ.). But these seem to be attempts to harmonize (though the first is read by B, al, vg, it, cdd, al). Observe the text runs Ἰάκωβος ὁ τοῦ Ἀλφαίου καὶ Λεββαῖος and St. Mark Θαδδαῖον, though there again have been some attempts at harmonizing. The names of the apostles are given here and qualify the general expression and to show that it was not all those mentioned in v. 6 who abode together.

Luke places the scene of the ascension at Bethany (24:50: Ἐξήγαγεν δὲ αὐτοὺς ἕως πρὸς/εἰς Βηθανίαν).[3] This was about 15 stadia from Jerusalem (John 11:18 ὡς ἀπὸ σταδίων δεκαπέντε, which is not exact). There must always be a great deal of uncertainty in any common reckoning of distance, as there will be practically no established point from which to calculate (from a large town). It is certain that Bethany is somewhere in the immediate neighborhood of the Mount of Olives. Luke 19:29 ὡς ἤγγισεν εἰς Βηθφαγὴ καὶ Βηθανία[ν] πρὸς τὸ ὄρος τὸ καλούμενον Ἐλαιῶν (refer to Philo Apocryph. i.619.)

---

[3] The GNT says πρὸς, but Lightfoot notes εἰς. (TDS)

Vs. 14 σὺν γυναιξὶν cf. Luke 24:10

καὶ Μαριὰμ for the idea of sister wives cf. 1 Cor 9:5. The last mention of the Lord's mother in the New Testament.

καὶ τοῖς ἀδελφοῖς αὐτοῦ Apparently not apostles at least not of the 12. When we last heard of the Lord's brothers, they are unbelievers (John 7:3ff.). Now we find them associated with the apostles. Whence this change? The Lord appeared to James after His resurrection. 1 Cor 15:7. Tradition is unanimous in holding that this James, mentioned by St. Paul, is the Lord's brother.

Vss. 15-17 It is not ὁ ὄχλος τῶν ὀνομάτων which even then would not necessarily imply that the whole body of believers were there but ὄχλος ὀνομάτων. There was a number of persons, gathered together.

Πέτρος the first exercise of his primacy.

Vs. 16 ἔδει πληρωθῆναι In what sense fulfilled?

Vs. 17 ὅτι 'for' and therefore the prophecy implied this.

Vss. 18-19 There is a difficulty of reconciling the two accounts of Judas' demise.

Whatever may be the real amount of the difficulty, even if we suppose that the accounts of the two writers are irreconcilable, as we shall hope to show they are not, what is the conclusion? Not surely that the writers are in the main unworthy of credit, not surely that the facts are untrue. This must depend on the general trustworthiness of the narrative, not on any special difficulties, at all events it is not so that we judge of ordinary writings, or of facts in history. In the case of the former, we judge of the credibility or the whole mass of evidence and of the latter, we accept as much as is free from discrepancies, what is stated by all the writers, rejecting that on which they disagree.

EXCURSUS—ON THE HISTORICAL PROBLEM OF THE VARYING ACCOUNTS OF JUDAS' DEMISE

Consider a parallel instance in dealing with the death of another famous person. The accounts of Thucydides (viii.92) and Lycurgus seem utterly irreconcilable, though Lycurgus appeals to a public document. Thucydides has ἐν τη ἀγορά πληθαση, Lycurgus . . . παρα την κεννην εν τοις σισθιοις. Thucydides ὁ μὲν πατάξας διεφυγεν, ὁ δὲ ευγεργος. αργειος ανθρ. ληφθτις και βασανζομενος, etc. Lycurgus—Τατων (αποδδοδοις και φρανβαλα the murderer) ληφθεντων καὶ εἰς τὸ δεομωτηριον αποτεθεντων, etc. Besides, there are other particulars that cannot be reconciled. Again we have a third account from Lysius, which fits neither with the one nor the other (e.g. He calls Thrasyl[lus] . . . a Calcydonian and Apollodorus something else). Thucydides says the latter was caught. Lysius' words are . . . χορτο φτυγοντες. Lysius tells us that they were both caught and imprisoned. Observe that this man was a leading statesman and a notorious character and that his murder was the turning point in the political history of Athens. Might we not have expected greater uniformity in the accounts?

At all events the accounts of the death of Judas force upon us one of two conclusions—either St. Luke had seen St. Matthew's account, and felt that there was nothing irreconcilable in his own statement, or he had not, in which case we must view this testimony on points in which they do agree, as independent. In attempting to solve the difficulty we must observe that St. Matthew professes to give the history of Judas' death, while in St. Luke it is introduced by way of allusions—either by St. Peter in his speech or by St. Luke in explanation of it. Is the account St. Peter's, or is it the writer's own? The explanation of St. Luke cannot begin with οὗτος μὲν οὖν, for the particular μὲν οὖν evidently implies a continuity in the narrative, nor yet with καὶ γνωστὸν ἐγένετο for these words are too closely connected with what precedes to allow of their being separated. All then that St. Luke can have added is ἐν τῇ ἰδίᾳ διαλέκτῳ αὐτῶν and τοῦτ' ἔστιν χωρίον αἵματος. Are these words added by the writer? On this point only three suppositions can be made. Either:

(1) They were actually used by St. Peter. This seems to be out of the question. For although those present were mostly Galileans, they can scarcely have been all so, and though the Galileans' dialect was different, the difference was probably one of accent, and at all events cannot have rendered such an explanation necessary.

(2) They are simply attributed to St. Peter, regardless of all historical propriety (so De Wette). But this is quite alien to the character of the writer, who is either an honest writer, narrating instances of which he is well informed, or if a forger, is a most consummate artist. De Wette would attribute to him a blunder, which the most stupid bungler would not have fallen into.

(3)   St. Luke intended the words for his own explanation—though he
      has not made this clear from the form of expression. This is the
      most probable of the three suppositions. There are other instances
      where the sacred writers attach their own explanation or reflec-
      tions to the narrative of the language of another without giving any
      notice: so that it is difficult to discover the exact point where the
      writer begins to speak (e.g. St. Paul narrating the conference with
      St. Peter at Antioch [Gal 2:14] or St. John narrating the testimony
      of the Baptist in John).

Bearing in mind then that St. Matthew's is the narrative, and St. Peter's a
passing allusion, we must seek for the key to the difficulty in the character
and point of this allusion. St. Matthew distinctly states that Judas is in a fit
of remorse. Attend to some particulars, namely:

(1)   ἀπήγξατο 'hanged himself'—for the word, independent of any
      modification of sense which it may derive for a context, can
      scarcely mean anything else.

(2)   that the chief priests after consultation purchased a field with the
      money, which Judas had returned, which was called Akeldama.

With regard to (1) there is a church tradition that Judas lived on after his
attempt at suicide, and that the account in the Acts has reference to his
subsequent death, but this is evidently an attempt to reconcile the two accounts. At all events St. Matthew can have had no knowledge of any such
fact: else he could not have written simply ἀπήγξατο. And on this, see what
Bengel says about Judas. This latter supposition is not unlikely, if Judas had
bargained for the ground and then seized with remorse, returned the money
to the chief priests. They, after consultation agreeing that the money could
not be put in the treasury, and being obliged therefore to lay it out, would
naturally conclude the bargain that Judas commenced.

Turning to St. Luke's account then, we remark that St. Peter evidently
supposes his hearers to be acquainted with the main facts, and therefore
feels it unnecessary to give the detailed narrative he selects those facts *only*
that have a bearing on his immediate purpose. In fact he does not give an
account of Judas' death at all. It is on his connection with this parcel of
ground that he dwells. He contrasts the lot that Judas abandoned for that

which he found—the unsearchable riches of Christ that he rejected—with the material wealth which he coveted and which he obtained. But real wealth has a far different sense from that which he had sought—the place in the Heavenly Kingdom, which he lost with the place of earthly degradation which he found, betokening too the torments which awaited him in the world to come. He contrasts his Christian office with the shocking spectacle of his violent death—the ministry of reconciliation with the field of blood. How is this contrast brought out? ἔλαχεν τὸν κλῆρον τῆς διακονίας—ἐκτήσατο χωρίον ἐκ μισθοῦ τῆς ἀδικίας. And the intended spirit of St. Peter is caught by those present.

Let us view the allusion to Judas (Acts 1:18-19) in this light. He obtained the lot in this ministry. He betrayed this and he lost it. He obtained for himself a parcel of ground purchased by the reward of his iniquity—with the very money for which he had sold and betrayed his Master, that field was purchased which was destined to be the scene of his ignominy—so it was he procured for himself a parcel of ground. He had thought to obtain an inheritance with the wages of unrighteousness. So he did, but it was one far different from that which he had expected. He obtained a few feet of ground in an unhallowed spot where his corpse was thrown out and exposed as that of a malefactor, and where it presented the shocking spectacle to which St. Peter here alludes.

If we supposed with Bengel, and as we have seen, there is nothing unnatural in the supposition, that this place, which was the scene of his ignominy, had been actually chosen by him as an inheritance to be handed down to his descendants, it adds more point to the application of the first passage from the Psalms. Then the words ἡ ἔπαυλις αὐτοῦ would find their explanation in the text itself by direct inference. ἐκτήσατο would have a fuller meaning. But this is not necessary, and, as it rests on mere conjecture, no stress should be laid on it. His habitation was left desolate by his untimely death. He obtained a parcel of ground, where his body was exposed (cf. Aeschylus *Sept. C. Theb.*).

πρηνὴς γενόμενος then may be explained of his carcass left in this place, lying with the face to the ground. A passing allusion suffices St. Peter, who presumes on the knowledge of the facts in his hearers, and the circumstances which are then given point to the work of decomposition which might have produced the result here described, especially if any weight is to be attached to that very early tradition recorded on the authority of Papias, that Judas was very obese—Μέγα ἀσεβείας ὑποδεγγμα εν τουτω κοσμω περιπατησεν Ιυδας. πρησθεις γαρ επι τουτον την σαρκα. Ωστε μη δυνασθαι διελθειν αμαξης παδιως διερχομενης. Υπο της αμαξης επιεσθη, ωστε τα εμκατα αυτω εκκενωθηνας. The reader may wish to ask several questions of these remarks:

(a) Is it truly attributed to Papias and if so, is the text free from corruption? It is certainly unintelligible as it stands at present. And Papias may have said nothing more than that he grew so large that he could not pass where a normal man could.

(b) Who was Papias?

(c) What is his testimony worth?

The parcel of ground which was purchased with the price of the blood of the betrayed and polluted with that of the traitor, might well be called Akeldama even by those who did not recognize the divine mission of Jesus but looked upon him as a misguided and dangerous enthusiast, or even as an actual imposter. St. Luke does not imply that the sole reason why the name was given was owing to the death of Judas. The words ὥστε κληθῆναι τὸ χωρίον ἐκεῖνο τῇ ἰδίᾳ διαλέκτῳ κ.τ.λ. may refer as well to ἐκτήσατο χωρίον ἐκ μισθοῦ τῆς ἀδικίας, as the later part of the sentence.

There is a sort of irony in the ἐκτήσατο. This after all was the inheritance—which agrees well with the rhetorical character of the whole passage. It is not an historical account of the event, but a rhetorical allusion to it (cf. *Sept. C. Theb.* 881. Εμορασαντο δ᾽οδθκαρδιοι κτημαθ ωστε ισον λαχειν).

Akeldama is here spoken of as an accursed place, and the type of the world of torments. Just as the valley of Hinnom (Gehenna), the place where the impious sacrifices had been offered to Molech, and the common place of burial, suggested the same notion to the mind of a Jew. Though St. Peter speaks here of the external and invisible, his mind is dwelling on the invisible and spiritual. The traditional site of Akeldama was an exhausted clay-pit potter's field.

Vs. 20 γέγραπται γὰρ Ps 69:26. Peculiarly a messianic Psalm (cf. v. 9. The zeal of thine house etc.). τὴν ἐπισκοπὴν κ.τ.λ. Ps 109:7—The E.V. 'bishopric' is too special though derived from ἐπισκοπή.

Vs. 21 Elliptical expression.

Vs. 22 ἀπὸ τοῦ βαπτίσματος Ἰωάννου designating a portion of time. μάρτυρα τῆς ἀναστάσεως—the crowning miracle—1 Cor 9:1. 'have I not seen the Lord Jesus Christ?' The external testimony to the resurrection formed an important part of St. Paul's teaching (1 Cor 15:3) and was evidently dwelt upon at great length.

The circumstance is a security that the apostles are not misled, that they were especially careful about their words, and not, accustomed to the language held by some in the day, careless about external testimony, unable to weigh evidence. It was not sufficient in the case of Matthias that he had an internal conviction.

Vs. 23 Ἰωσὴφ τὸν καλούμενον Βαρσαββᾶν. Not improbably a brother of that Judas Barsabbas mentioned in Acts 15:22. Especially as Barsabbas is a patronymic. Ἰοῦστος 'Justus' a common surname with the Jews. Cf. Col 4:11; Acts 18:7 and the case of St. James the Bp. Cf. Acts 18:7 εἰς οἰκίαν τινὸς ὀνόματι Τιτίου Ἰούστου σεβομένου τὸν θεόν. Justus—δίκαιος—relating to the strict observance of the Mosaic covenant.

Vs. 24 σὺ κύριε. St. Peter leads the prayer in which they join. καρδιογνῶστα (cf. Acts 15:8). St. Peter's words (προσευξάμενοι) however must imply that prayer had been made before they uttered these words.

ἐξελέξω didst choose in the eternal counsels; not has chosen since the office was vacant (cf. Acts 1:25)

Vs. 24 might well be applied to Judas. 'Let the things that should have been for their wealth etc.' The Psalm has a special fulfilment in the person of Judas, but note that its reference is far more general. And this, though it was spoken beforehand of Judas, by the Spirit has reference to all the enemies of Christ, who go in the way of Judas.

Vs. 25 λαβεῖν τὸν τόπον (the corr. reading) τῆς διακονίας ταύτης καὶ ἀποστολῆς πορευθῆναι εἰς τὸν τόπον.

λαβεῖν τὸν τόπον corr. Lect.

τόπον τὸν ἴδιον the place of the wicked—they would allude to a place of torments as implied mysteriously in the Akeldama, the accursed spot and common charnel house.

Vs. 26 ἔδωκαν κλήρους αὐτοῖς should mean 'they assigned lots *to them*' but perhaps 'put in for them' cf. Josh. 18:10.

συγκατεψηφίσθη the decision was confirmed by those present—though probably not by an actual vote.

Pentecost and Its Aftermath
(Acts 2)

Vs. 1 ἐν τῷ συμπληροῦσθαι τὴν ἡμέραν τῆς πεντηκοστῆς not as E.V. for that would require a past tense, nor yet 'drew on' nor again does the συμπληροῦσθαι refer only to the day of Pentecost for then the word would be inappropriate, 'was being brought to a close or completion' as it was early in the day. Note: συμπληροῦσθαι implies that it made up the complement of days between the Passover and the Feast of Weeks. ὁμοθυμαδόν never = αὐτό. Here however there is some doubt about the reading. A, B, C* having αὐτό. ἐπὶ τὸ αὐτό had gathered together to the same place and were there.

Vs. 2 On πνοή/πνεῦμα, cf. Philo *Leg. Alleg.* i.§.13. πνοή is a passing breath or blast or breeze and may be violent or not, πνεῦμα on the other hand is more general. The πνοή therefore is more applicable here and more appropriate to the suddenness and transitionary character of the blast ἄφνω, φερομένης, βιαίας.

Vs. 3 διαμεριζόμεναι being distributed, divided, and apportioned out. The word has always this meaning (cf. Acts 4:7). This meaning too is indicated due to the symbolism of the passage.

ὡσεὶ πυρὸς, ὥσπερ φερομένης not really fire, or really wind (cf. Luke 3:22, where he adds σωματικῷ εἴδει).

ἐκάθισεν i.e. γλῶσσαι. ἑτέραις γλώσσαις i.e. other than this ordinary (or natural) language (cf. Mark 16:17). The writer of the last paragraph attached to St. Mark's Gospel evidently had the Gospel of St. Luke and the Acts before him. The particulars he gives are almost entirely taken from the one or the other.

Vs. 5 ἄνδρες εὐλαβεῖς like σεβόμενοι τὸν θεόν.

Vs. 6 φωνῆς i.e. of the speakers. It (. . . as one sound) reached the people (cf. Acts 19:34, and cf. Rev 5:11). φωνή could scarcely = ἦχος except in a highly poetical passage.

Vs. 8 διάλεκτος in vs. 8 does not mean 'a dialect' and therefore a distinction between γλῶσσας and διάλεκτος will not hold.

Vss. 9-28 Here in a geographical arrangement is the list of names, not an exhaustive geographical list but those countries only are mentioned in which Jews were found in great numbers. Κρῆτες καὶ Ἄραβες the struggle picked up (see Tacitus *Hist.* v.2 and the Epistle of Titus). The geographical order then is marking the Mediterranean point of reference: 1) East of Mediterranean—Parthians, Medes, etc.; 2) North of Mediterranean—Cappadocia, etc.; 3) South of Mediterranean—Libya, Cyrene; 4) West of Mediterranean—Rome (Jews and proselytes). Note that Ιουδαῖοί καὶ προσήλυτοι refers solely to Ῥωμαῖοι.

To fully understand this crucial passage one must note many particulars:

    (A) The Time

        (1) Pentecostal Feast: Passover: Crucifixion: Pentecost: Note the dependence in point of time of Pentecost on the Passover narrative and here of the Spirit's leaving in the time of crucifixion and returning here. Hence Pentecost, for a further reason, becomes a solemn festival to Christians (cf. Acts 20:16; Deut. 23:16). Bear in mind the elements of Leaven (Mt 13:33), the first fruits, the wave offering.

        (2) Giving of the Law. cf. Ex 12:2. with Ex 19:1. The Pentecostal feast had come to be associated with the giving of Law, though it may be objected that the Jews themselves did not know that this was the time of the giving of the Law. This, if true, does not matter: it is a question of fact, not of opinion. On the contrast of the giving of law and gospel (Sinai & Zion), see Hebrews 12:18.

    (B) The Symbols

        (1) The wind. John 3:8

(2) The tongues of fire

    (a). natural aptness of the image

    (b). moral aptness

        the tongue: power and eloquence
        the fire: purification. In this respect the
        baptism of the spirit differs from baptism
        of John, and of the opposite kind. See
        James 3:6; cf. Is 4:4.

    (c). διαμεριζόμεναι cf. 1 Cor 12:2.

(C) The Speaking with Tongues

What is meant by the writer here? Clearly the attendance of different tongues. Three opinions held:

(1) Baur. Teller: the writer lived much after the event, and therefore it is idle to enquire what foundation of truth there is for the narrative. A consistent view.

(2) That it happened as St. Luke narrated. Likewise consistent.

(3) That it happened in a different way from what St. Luke recorded. That it was really the utterance of ecstatic language and that St. Luke mistook it for the speaking of diverse tongues. This latter view is utterly inconsistent with the view that the narrative was written by a companion of St. Paul and a contemporary.

    (a). This was one of the most remarkable events in the history of the church and could scarcely have been or mistaken by anyone in so prominent a position as St. Luke.

    (b). The gift of tongues still continued in the church. St. Paul had it in a preeminent degree (1 Cor 14:18). The abuse of it was one of the evils he had to combat in the Corinthian church. St. Paul being constantly with St. Luke must have known what it was. Yes, but it could be argued that the gift of tongues was something different from what is represented happening on the day of Pentecost. Suppose it were. It would be the more unlikely that St. Luke should step out of his way to invent a different gift of tongues. He could not then have misunderstood the miracle of Pentecost.

The nature of the Pentecostal miracle then is clear and was so taken by the early Christian writers (e.g. Irenaeus). But was the gift of tongues as St. Paul speaks of it the same? YES because:

1. The a priori improbability that a different gift should be so called.

2. The continuity in the history. [Acts] 10:46., 11:15., 19:6, which brings us to the period of which St. Paul speaks.

3. The language of St. Paul respecting it. γένη γλ. [1 Cor] 12:28. γλ. ἀνθ. καὶ ἀγγ. 1 Cor 13:1. διαφθοράν 1 Cor 14:4. esp. 1 Cor 14:11, 21, 22.

4. The effect it produced on those present. 1 Cor 14:23.

The gift, however transitory and ecstatic, was a symbol. We may ask about its relation to the composition of languages, about the relationship of Babel and the Day of Pentecost. This gift however was not available for purposes of preaching the gospel. Quote Euseb. *H.E.* v.7. Cf. Iren. v.6.1.

Two Questions:

(1) Are the tongues of Pentecost and the tongues of 1 Cor 14 different?

(2) Are they foreign languages? Prima facie Yes—probably not to these people alone.

Vss. 29-47

Vs. 29 ἐξὸν i.e. ἔστε (not ἔστε which would scarcely be understood). 'The facts of the case are such that I can boldly say.'

Vs. 32 οὖ

Vs. 33 τῇ δεξιᾷ οὖν τοῦ θεοῦ ὑψωθείς = ὑψωθείς καὶ τῇ δεξιᾷ σταθεὶς.

Exalted on the right hand of God. It is not the dative dependent on a verb of motion. The context absolutely requires this interpretation of τῇ δεξιᾷ cf. vv. 25, 34. Though in vs. 31 it might well be taken otherwise ἐπαγγελίαν (not ὑπόσχεσιν) cf. John.

Vs. 34 Ps 110:1, cited also in Matthew 22:44 (where the best manuscripts have ὑποκάτω for ὑποπόδιον). With this exception in all 3 passages the verb agrees with LXX & Hebrews. It is evident both from this passage and that in St. Matthew that the Psalm was regarded by the Jews of that time as written by David himself. They therefore saw no inappropriateness in the supposition. At all events our Lord's authority is beyond appeal. The Psalm was probably in the first instance a prophetic declaration of a coming triumph, written to be sung on the occasion of David's going forth to battle—written by David himself, but speaking of himself in the third person inasmuch as it would be sung by others. Under the influence of the Spirit however David pitched the key so high that the language could apply to himself and found its real fulfillment in that Messiah of which the king himself was only a mere type.

Vs. 38 μετανοήσατε, βαπτισθήτω (cf. vs. 6). Let it be done at once—there is no time for delay. μετανοήσατε καὶ βαπτισθήτω ἕκαστος ὑμῶν. εἰς ἄφεσιν τῶν ἁμαρτιῶν ὑμῶν καὶ λήμψεσθε τὴν δωρεὰν τοῦ ἁγίου πνεύματος. In Mark 1:4 of John's Baptism κηρύσσων βάπτισμα μετανοίας εἰς ἄφεσιν ἁμαρτιῶν (cf. Luke 3:3). This text raises the question about the relationship of Christian Baptism to the gift of the Spirit. On δωρεά cf. James 1:17 (see *Journal of Philol.* iii. p.113).

Vs. 39 τοῖς εἰς μακράν i.e. probably the Gentiles cf. Eph 2:13. νυνὶ δὲ ἐν Χριστῷ Ἰησοῦ ὑμεῖς οἵ ποτε ὄντες μακρὰν ἐγενήθητε ἐγγὺς ἐν τῷ αἵματι τοῦ Χριστοῦ. Also Is 57:19 where however the meaning is not so clear. ὅσους ἂν προσκαλέσηται cf. Acts 2:21 (Joel 5:5). Beza understood τοῖς εἰς μακράν of time 'future generations.'

Vss. 40-41 τῆς γενεᾶς τῆς σκολιᾶς Phil 2:15. μέσον γενεᾶς σκολιᾶς καὶ διεστραμμένης. σώθητε—Not as E.V. but 'be ye saved.' It was not their own act, but the act of God.

Vs. 41 refers to baptism by immersion.

Vss. 42-47 Here we have a picture of the infant church in which the idea of a church is realized to a very high degree and which is evidently portrayed here, to point out the essential character of the church. The unity of the church then consists in:

(1) Inward conformity τῇ διδαχῇ τῶν ἀποστόλων—the apostolic doctrine

(2) Outward conformity ἡ κοινωνία (τῶν ἀποστόλων)

    a. τῇ κλάσει τοῦ ἄρτου—The Holy Sacrament

    b. ταῖς προσευχαῖς—Public prayer

καὶ is to be omitted after κοινωνία. The best authorities are unanimous. τῇ κλάσει τοῦ ἄρτου καὶ ταῖς προσευχαῖς is in apposition with, and an explanation of, τῇ κοινωνίᾳ. Vulg. 'communicatione fractionis panis' is wrong in saying that the adoption of the right reading renders this interpretation untenable. The Romanist argument drawn from the mention of the bread alone is of course untenable.

And however impracticable a community of property may be, still it realizes the idea of a Christian brotherhood more completely than the existence of separate interests in this respect admits. It is not essential to the existence of a church, but the nearer a church approaches to perfection, the more nearly will this community of goods be realized.

τῇ κλάσει τοῦ ἄρτου—the article τοῦ ἄρτου seems to point to the Eucharist not κλάσει τοῦ ἄρτου and so St. Paul distinctly 1 Cor 10:16—τὸ ποτήριον κ.τ.λ. τὸν ἄρτον ὃν κλῶμεν, οὐχὶ κοινωνία τοῦ σώματος τοῦ Χριστοῦ ἐστιν; ὅτι εἷς ἄρτος, ἓν σῶμα οἱ πολλοί ἐσμεν, οἱ γὰρ πάντες ἐκ τοῦ ἑνὸς ἄρτου μετέχομεν (the bread then should be broken when distributed, else its symbolical meaning is destroyed). The expression κλάσις ἄρτου however need not necessarily refer to the Eucharistic bread. It occurs in St. Luke 24:35; Acts 2:46; 20:7, 11; 27:35.

For the phrase in v. 46 κατ᾽ οἶκον ἄρτον ἐν τῷ ἱερῷ cf. v. 42.

In v. 47 τοὺς σῳζομένους is correct, τῇ ἐκκλησίᾳ is rightly rejected as a reading here. ἐπὶ τὸ αὐτό is to be attached to καθ᾽ ἡμέραν, and Chapter 3 begins Πέτρος δὲ καὶ Ἰωάννης.

THE BEGINNINGS AND TRIALS
OF THE CHURCH IN JERUSALEM
(ACTS 3–6)

CHAPTER 3

Vss. 1-2 ἀνέβαινον, ἐβαστάζετο.

αἰτεῖν, ἐρωτεῖν See Trench N.T. Syn. xl. p. 158.

ἡ ὥρα τῆς προσευχῆς ἡ ἐνάτη the hour of prayer being the third, sixth, and ninth ἐπὶ τὴν ὥραν.

ἡ θύρα ἡ ὡραία probably Nicanor gate. cf. Thrupp's *Jerusalem* p. 329.

Vs. 4 ἀτενίσας . . . (Meyer)

Vs. 5 ἐπεῖχεν

Vs. 6 τοῦ Ναζωραίου i.e. the despised and the friend of such. cf. Mt 2:23

ἀργύριτις, χρυσίον, ἀργύριον

Vs. 7 αἱ βάσεις αὐτοῦ καὶ τὰ σφυδρά 'the soles of his feet and his ankles.' Luke the physician speaks. See Bengel.

Vs. 10 ἐπεγίνωσκον

πρὸς τὴν ἐλεημοσύνην for our alms. cf. v. 3

θάμβους in affectu, seat of θάμβος, in the feelings, astonishment

ἔκστασις in intellectu, seat of ἔκστασις, the mind, amazement (Bengel).

Vs. 11 αὐτοῦ A, B, C, E. Received Text reads τοῦ ἰαθέντος χωλοῦ.

Vs. 12 ἐπὶ τούτῳ probably neutral—the introduction of αὐτόν without any word to refer to it, is natural enough.

ἡμῖν τί ἀτενίζετε—emphatic.

τοῦ περιπατεῖν.

Vs. 13 τὸν παῖδα cf. Mt 12:18 (where it is rightly translated), cited from Isaiah 42:1. cf. Acts 4:25 with Acts 4:27.

Punctuation in Alford bad.

κρίναντος ἐκείνου ὑμεῖς δὲ—ἀπεκτείνατε

ὑμεῖς μὲν παρεδώκατε is not answered by δὲ; the antithetical clause assumes another form ὃν ὁ θεὸς ἤγειρεν.

Vss. 14-15 ἄνδρα φονέα . . . τὸν δὲ ἀρχηγὸν τῆς ζωῆς Bengel called attention to this. Meyer says 'bildet einen doppelten contrast, natürlich zu ἄνδρα φονέα und zu ἀπεκτείνατε.'

Vs. 16 ἐπὶ τῇ πίστει τοῦ ὀνόματος.

ἡ πίστις ἡ δι᾿ αὐτοῦ Cf. 1 Pet 1:21 ὑμᾶς τοὺς δι᾿ αὐτοῦ πιστοὺς εἰς θεὸν.

i.e. the faith of those who wrought the miracle (Alford).

Vs. 17 καὶ νῦν—'formula transcendi a pretiru ad preseus' (Bengel).

Vss. 19-20 μετανοήσατε

ὅπως ἂν ἔλθωσιν καιροὶ ἀναψύξεως 'that they may come'

The hastening of God's kingdom depends on the conversion of sinners.

The world must first be converted, then the power of evil must show itself in open opposition to the gospel. The distinction of good and evil will be clearly exposed. The rebellion of Satan will be brought to a head, and then he shall be crushed and the end of all things shall come.

This time (the καιροὶ ἀναψύξεως) depends on the success of the gospel and the alacrity with which it is received by men: but it is also predetermined in the counsel of God. The apparent contradiction is inexplicable. It is only the old difficulty of reconciling God's foreknowledge with man's free will—a difficulty which was not introduced by revelation and the solution of which is therefore not to be sought from revelation. Cf. 2 Pet 3:12— προσδοκῶντας καὶ σπεύδοντας τὴν παρουσίαν τῆς τοῦ θ. ἡμέρας. Mistranslated in the E.V.

Vs. 20 προκεχειρισμένον, prepared. Textus Receptus (cf. Acts 22:14) προκεχηρυγμένον.

Vs. 21 οὐρανὸν μὲν δέξασθαι. οὐρανὸν doubtless the subj. And not the object of δέξασθαι. δέξασθαι is not an adequate word to express Christ's dwelling in heaven till he should come again in judgment. Cf. Pl. Theod. P.177A cited by Meyer.

μέν is not followed by δέ.

The clause referring to His second coming is suppressed because it is already implied in χρόνων ἀποκαταστάσεως πάντων.

ἄχρι—Baumg. cites Acts 20:6. Heb 3:13 as instances of ἄχρι signifying the conclusion of a period of time. This is true, but it seems scarcely applicable to this case. Perhaps we should state it thus. ἄχρι does not signify duration, it denotes a limit—either limit, the beginning or the end—but never the end unless there is something in the context to fix this meaning. e.g. πέντε in Acts, and καθ᾽ ἑκάστην ἡμέραν in Heb.

ἐλάλησεν διὰ στόματος τῶν ἁγίων ἀπ᾽ αἰῶνος προφητῶν Exactly the same words found cf. Luke 1:70.

I cannot believe with Baumg. that the antecedent of ὧν is πάντων—this limitation of ἀποκαταστάσεως πάντων—seems to weaken the passage. (Alford's note satisfactory). Cf. esp. St. Mt 17:11 which shows that πάντων is not generalized as Alford remarks. The grammatical difficulty of ὧν (on which Baumg. lays some stress) must be allowed.

Are not the words ἀπ᾽ αἰῶνος found here from Luke? (l[oc].c[it].)? They are marked in D and other respectable authorities and are found in different positions in others.

Vs. 22 Deut 18:15, 19, cited freely from LXX and is partly abridged.

(See Davidson, *Sac. Herm.* p. 392). Wherein Christ resembled Moses and where he differed cf. Heb 3:2

Vs. 24 καὶ κατήγγειλαν Begins the apodosis, as E.V.

τὰς ἡμέρας ταύτας See Alford, i.e. this new dispensation which is to end the ἀποκαταστάσεως πάντων.

Vs. 25 agrees with the LXX (though not verbatim) and Hebrews. E.g. LXX has ἔθνος for πατέρας. It seems in fact to be an independent translation of the Hebrew and not as Alford implies.

Vs. 26 ὑμῖν πρῶτον Alford wrong in saying 'implying the offer to the gentiles.'

Rather cf. Heb 1:1. to which this passage is a parallel πάλαι λαλήσας ὁ θεὸς τοῖς πατράσιν ἐν τοῖς προφήταις ἐπ᾽ ἐσχάτου τῶν ἡμερῶν τούτων ἐλάλησεν ἡμῖν ἐν υἱῷ.

πρῶτον 'first' in reference to what has gone before, not to what comes after ἀναστήσας. cf. v. 22.

εὐλογοῦντα (not εὐλογήσαντα) i.e. the operation was still going on. (Baumg.) ἀποστρέφειν active.

And in St. Peter's first epistle it is found in exactly the same connection. ἐξηραύνησαν προφῆται οἱ περὶ τῆς εἰς ὑμᾶς χάριτος προφητεύσαντες . . . οἷς ἀπεκαλύφθη ὅτι οὐχ ἑαυτοῖς ὑμῖν δὲ διηκόνουν αὐτά, ἃ νῦν ἀνηγγέλη ὑμῖν κ.τ.λ. (1 Pet 1:10, 12) cf. Mt 13:17.

ACTS 4: THE CONTROVERSY BEGINS

Vs. 1 οἱ ἱερεῖς for they would view the acts of the apostles as a denial of their authority in doctrinal matters.

ὁ στρατηγὸς τοῦ ἱεροῦ who would consider it a breach of order

οἱ Σαδδουκαῖοι to whom the doctrine taught were unpalatable. Bengel: Cum unlieribus ego et liberius multo major.

Vs. 2 ἐν τῷ Ἰησοῦ τὴν ἀνάστασιν τὴν ἐκ νεκρῶν Alford confines the sense too narrowly. The resurrection of the dead as exhibited in the case of Jesus whose resurrection was not only an instance, but also an earnest of that which would be wrought in others. Cf. the doctrine as taught by St. Paul in 1 Cor 15.

Vs. 3 There seems to be no authority for taking τήρησιν . . . as local prison, though the analogy of the synonyms might seem to sanction this. cf. Thucydides vi.86.

ἔθεντο εἰς τήρησιν put them under confinement: unless Acts 5:18 should seem to require the sense of 'prison.'

Vs. 4 τῶν ἀνδρῶν is probably used because the number of women who belonged to the church was hitherto small and might be neglected in reckoning up the numbers.

Vs. 5 ἐπὶ τὴν αὔριον ἐπί with the accusative cannot be simply a designation of time: it must denote a purpose for the morrow. cf. Acts 3:1, E.V. 'on the morrow' is wrong.

αὐτῶν of the Jews (as Alford). There is not a single antecedent, to which it can be referred, but it is determined by v. 4. [For] αὐτῶν . . . [see] D, al, syr, cop, celt, arr.

ἐν Ἰερουσαλήμ is undoubtedly the right reading. But Alford's explanation will not stand. No one would think of saying 'in London' to denote that the event did not take place at St. Paul's. If it had been ἐν τῇ πόδει, Alford's interpretation would have been more tenable. ἐν Ἰερουσαλήμ they may have lived, many of them, outside the city. Tradition points out the country-house of Caiaphas. cf. Thrupp's *Jerusalem* p. 241.

Vs. 7 ἐν ποίᾳ δυνάμει

ποῖος is never exactly equivalent to τίς in the New Testament cf. 1 Pet 1:11 ποῖος interrogative where it has not the signification 'of what sort,' implies incredulity, or perplexity on the part of the enquirer and is almost = τὶς ποτέ. In the classical writers we find it in the state of transition to this meaning.

Vss. 8-10 ἐν τίνι misc: Alford is wrong. A Person is implied in ἐν ποίᾳ δυνάμει ἢ ἐν ποίῳ ὀνόματι. cf. v. 12 in which there is an apparent reference to this.

In vs. 10 ἐν τούτῳ probably masc. as Alford suggests.

Vs. 11 ὁ λίθος ὁ γενόμενος εἰς κεφαλὴν γωνίας i.e. ἀκρογωνιαῖος (Eph 2:20; 1 Pet 1:6). St. Paul's words are the best commentary on the meaning of this metaphor. ὄντος ἀκρογωνιαίου αὐτοῦ Χριστοῦ Ἰησοῦ, ἐν ᾧ πᾶσα οἰκοδομὴ συναρμολογουμένη αὔξει εἰς ναὸν ἅγιον ἐν κυρίῳ.[1] The 'keystone' of an arch serves the same purpose.

It is observable in how many cases the texts and traditions from the Old Testament brought forward by St. Peter have been applied before by our Lord.

For instance, in this passage. Cf. Matthew 22:42, and St. Peter repeats it again in his epistle. l[oc].c[it.]. Wherever this passage (from Ps. 117:22-23) is cited in the New Testament i.e. in the three synoptic Evangelists (St. Luke has only the first part) and in St. Peter's Epistle it agrees verbatim with the LXX. St. Peter's words here, which do not profess to be direct quotation, point to the same version.

Vs. 12 ὄνομά ἐστιν ἔτερον . . . τὸ δεδομένον Alford's Latin rendering does not account for the article τὸ δεδομένον. cf. Gal 3:21.

Vs. 13 ἐθαύμαζον a commentary on the words of the Psalmist: παρὰ κυρίου ἐγένετο αὔτη καὶ ἔστι θαυμαστὴ ἐν οφθαλμοῖς ἡμῶν.[2] See Alford on Mt l[oc] c[it.].

ἰδιώτης used [of] . . . (1) the state, or refers (2) to a public functionary, or (3) to a person of rank, or (4) to an 'individual' officer in the army, or (5) to a professed gymnast or (6) to an artisan or (7) to a poet (prose writer) and (8) more generally to the stupid, ignorant.

ἐπεγίνωσκόν they recognized. 'Ihre Verwunderung schärfte jetzt ihre Reminiscenz.' (Meyer)

---

[1] See Eph 2:20-21. (TDS)
[2] A citation of Ps 118:23 (LXX). (TDS)

Vs. 17 ἐπὶ τῷ ὀνόματι

διανεμηθῇ Totum pro gangrona habent. Ea emi sic descributa. 2 Tim 2:17. Bengel.

Vs. 20 cf. 1 John 1:3

Vs. 22 τὸ σημεῖον τοῦτο τῆς ἰάσεως. And so St. Peter himself had employed it as a σημεῖον. (cf. vv. 9, 12) ἐν τίνι οὗτος σέσωται with οὐκ ἔστιν ἐν ἄλλῳ οὐδενὶ ἡ σωτηρία. cf. ἡ πίστις σου σέσωκέν σε (St. Mk 10:52) of Bartimaeus. Σώζειν both there and here being too strong a word to apply to the healing of the body.

Vs. 23 τοὺς ἰδίους i.e. their own. It is useless to attempt to define its meaning.

Vs. 24 'Petrus etain hic verba videtur proivisse: sed coteri quoque voce sunt soi' (?—check Bengel).

Vs. 25 The reading of A, B, E etc. though very ancient, cannot be right—Is. 51 verbatim with LXX & Heb. It is certainly without sense. Alford under-estimates the case in saying the construction is harsh. It is an impossible construction. Moreover would God Himself be said to speak διὰ πνεύματος ἁγίου? Nothing but the absolute proof of this reading would justify us in disregarding such a mass of authority, as I think Tisch. has rightly done. Probably the original text had διὰ στόματος Δ.π.σ. and some pious copyist corrected it to πνεύματος ἁγίου wishing for some phrase which contained a more express declaration of the implication of Scripture. If this correction was written over the original text, the original words not being erased, it would be inserted in future copies. It is difficult to say whether τοῦ πατρὸς ἡμῶν is a gloss or not.

St. Luke seems to interpret ἔθνη of the Romans, λαός of the Jews, οἱ βασιλεῖς τῆς γῆς of Herod, and οἱ ἄρχοντες of Pilate. See the order in which they are given. The part which Herod bore in the transaction is narrated by St. Luke alone of the Evangelists Luke 23:7. (Meyer here is difficult but then the explanation which I find in Bengel is indisputably right.) This depends on the peculiar significance of λαός. See Acts 15:14.

φρυάσσειν ... 'to snort'/not to whinny which is χρεμετίζειν cf. Lac. *Serm.* x

Vs. 27 συνήχθησαν ποιῆσαι

Vs. 28 ὅσα ἡ χείρ σου καὶ ἡ βουλή etc. see Alford.

Vs. 30 Not as Alford, but take ἐν τῷ–γίνεσθαι together as Bengel.

Vs. 32 πιστευ<u>σάν</u>των. Not πιστευόντων. 'Those who had accepted the faith.'
τι τῶν ὑπαρχόντων αὐτῷ ἔλεγεν See Alford.

ἡ καρδία καὶ ἡ ψυχὴ 'in credendis et agendis' (Bengel).

Vs. 33 ἀπεδίδουν (reddebant). For this testimony was a trust in their hand.
χάρις the grace of God, prompting the rich to these deeds of charity and
thus providing for the relief of the poor.

Vs. 34 χωρίων estates.

τῶν πιπρασκομένων (not loosely for πραθένταν as Alford), implying that
the sales were constantly going on.

Vs. 35 See Alford. Διεδίδετο. As E.V. 'distribution was made'

Vs. 36 Barnabas רב נבואה υἱὸς προφητείας so that υἱὸς παρακλήσεως is
'son of exhortation.' Cf. Acts 11:23. Where he asserts his claim to the name.
Baumg. refers to 1 Cor 14:3. ὁ δὲ προφητεύων ἀνθρώποις λαλεῖ οἰκοδομὴν
καὶ παράκλησιν καὶ παραμυθίαν. Barnabas one of the 70 acc. to Clement
Alexandr. in his Epistles.

Κύπριος τῷ γένει The formidable insurrection of the Jews in Cyprus in
the reign of Trajan is an evidence of their concerns. (cf. C+H *Life of St. Paul*
i.p. 152) (p. 172. ed. 2)

Vs. 37 τὸ χρῆμα

Acts 5: Internal and External Trials

Vs. 5 ἀκούων not ἀκούσας
ἐπὶ πάντας τοὺς ἀκούοντας

Vs. 6 οἱ νεώτεροι See below on the subject of deacons.

Vs. 7 Ἐγένετο δὲ—καὶ—μὴ εἰδυῖα

Vs. 8 ἀπεκρίθη. Pertaining to some expression of enquiry, or astonishment—
not necessarily to any spoken words. See Acts 3:12. The word only betokens
that something is expected of the speaker and so regularly ἀποκρίνεσθαι = to
say in explanation τοσούτου. Naming and summarizing, cf. Ezra 4:11, 17, E.V.

Vs. 11 ἐπὶ πάντας

Excursus: The Sanhedrin and the High Priests

συνέδριον *(Sanhedrin, corrupted from* סַנְהֶדְרִין*).* Composed of 70
members. The High Priest being thought of as the leader, not necessarily the
president. It took charge of all religious matters and certain cases of state

trials. It was not only a court of judication, but also in ecclesiastical matters, the legislative court. Said by the Talmudist to have been founded by Moses. (cf. Num. 11:16). The council of 70 however, established by Moses, seems to have been merely temporary, and to have ceased to exist when the Israelites settled in Canaan. However the precedent may have determined the number of the later Tribunal.

It is called in Greek βουλή and a member of it βουλευτής. Cf. Mark 15:43 ἀρχιερεύς. The chief priest καί ἐξοχήν is called such in LXX (cf. Lev. 4:3 ἀρχιερεύς ... ὁ ἱερεὺς ὁ μέγας). In Apocrypha and New Testament ἀρχιερεύς. The name ἀρχιερεύς however is given to those who had once held the office and had been deposed so that we find the plur. ἀρχιερεῖς of persons living at the same time—Joseph. *Bell. Jud.* iv.5.2.

γένος ἀρχιερατικόν—i.e. the descendants of either Eleazar or the two sons of Aaron—though Herod admitted some of the ordinary priests to the high priesthood. Cf. Joseph. *Ant.* xx.10.

ὁ στρατηγός τοῦ ἱεροῦ cf. Joseph. *Ant.* xx.6.2.

περὶ ἄνανιαν τὸν ἀρχιερέα καὶ τὸν στρατηγον ἄνανον—showing that he was a Jew and therefore not captain of the Roman garrison of Antonia as some suppose. Cf. *Bell. Jud.* vi.5.3. where the στρατηγός is spoken of in connection with this. He is generally called simply ὁ στρατηγός in Josephus. The head of the temple police.

Annas and Caiaphas. In Matthew 26:57 (Mark and Luke do not mention the name) Jesus is led before Caiaphas the High Priest. In John 11:49; 18:13, Caiaphas is styled High Priest τοῦ ἐνιαυτοῦ ἐκείνου. And Annas is mentioned in πενθερὸς τοῦ Καϊάφα, ὃς ἦν ἀρχ. τ. ἐν. ἐκ. Here we have 'the high priest and those with him.' In Acts 4:6 we read of Ἄννας ὁ ἀρχιερεὺς καὶ Καϊάφας. And in Luke 3:2 the year is dated ἐπὶ ἀρχιερέως Ἄννα καὶ Καϊάφα. It seems clear from this that the title ἀρχιερεύς is implied to both these persons in a higher and special sense. The view which Alford takes (Luke 3:2) is at least plausible.

Annas (cf. Lucas, Lucanus, Silas, Sylvanus) the high priest has been deposed by Valerius Eratus a few years before (a.u.c. 779. cf Joseph. *Ant.* xviii.2.2) and after some changes, Caiaphas obtained the office (A.D. 25) and was deposed by Vitellius (A.D. 37) being succeeded by a son of Annas or Ananas Joseph. *Ant.* xviii.4.3.

Thus Annas would be High Priest *de jure* and Caiaphas *de facto*. The Jews would especially recognize the title of Annas and to this point see the singular ἐπὶ ἀρχιερέως Ἄννας καὶ . . . as though Caiaphas had no right to the title. Josephus the historian (l.c.) calls Caiaphas Ἰωσήτος ὁ καὶ Καϊάφας. Vitellius substituted the son of Annas in place of Caiaphas apparently to gratify the people. Hence perhaps we may conclude that the people acknowledged the validity of the title of Annas so long as he lived.

Vs. 12 Some difficulty in ascertaining the connection of the sentences. στοᾷ Σολομῶντος. Acts 3:2; John 10:23.

Vs. 13 The construction is probably very simple. Οἱ λοιποί those without the Gospel. cf. 1 Thess 4:13; Eph 2:3.

κολλᾶσθαι 'to meddle with.' 'Man sich in respektvolles Entfernung im ihnen hielt.' (Meyer) Or particularly it may have a more directly bad sense = to persecute. Cf. Aquila's version of 1 Sam 31:2; 2 Sam 1:6.

Vs. 14 The nominative plus προσετίθεντο and some substantive which is in apposition to πλήθη not πιστεύοντες. πιστεύοντες cannot signify 'believers'—the nomnt. προσετίθεντο is to λαός προσετίθεντο τῷ κυρίῳ together 'were added to the Lord, as believing.'

Vs. 15 κλιναρίων καὶ κραβάττων Pet: 'couches and pallets.' The second term is certainly used of a portable piece of furniture and one easily moved. Bengel (who reads κλίνων) says, 'Lectus sumptuosen grabatus tenuir.'

Vs. 17 Ἀναστὰς rose up in anger

ἡ οὖσα αἵρεσις τῶν Σαδδουκαίων See Josephus *Ant.* xx.9.1.1 who distinctly states this of Ananus or Annas the then appointed High Priest in the reign of Nero and that αἵρεσιν μετήει τῶν Σαδδουκαίων. Thus we see that the family of the high priest here mentioned (whether Annas or Caiaphas) was connected with the sect of the Sadducees (for the younger Ananus was son of the one and in-law of the other). He is not improbably one of the οἱ σὺν αὐτῷ.

Vs. 20 τῆς ζωῆς ταύτης. ζωή, βίος cf. Trench. N.T. Synon. p. 100. 'ζωή vita qu . . . vivimus'—life absolutely, the essence of life. 'βίος vita qua . . . vivimus'—life as partaking of certain characteristics, generally ethical. From this it will be seen that βίος will maintain pretty nearly the same level, while ζωή will vary according to the opinion of the writer as to that in which life consists. ζωή will accordingly rank either above or below βίος. Aristotle is said to have defined βίος thus: βίος ἐστὶ λογικὴ ζωή—'rational life', and thus to a heathen βίος ranks above ζωή, for he considers ζωή to be nothing more than the life which we have in common with irrational animals.

In the Greek New Testament the case is different. βίος is still life as possessing certain ethical characteristics, good or bad, a sort of neutral word, dependent on the context for its intepretation, but ζωή has been exalted. Death is connected with sin, and life therefore with holiness. 'Life' is no longer the life physical. It is the realization of the end of our being—the Life in God. This life is coincident with the acceptance of the Gospel. It is of this new life (τῆς ζωῆς ταύτης) that the apostles are bidden to preach, so that it is an exact parallel to Acts 13:26 ὁ λόγος τῆς σωτηρίας ταύτης. The expression seems to have no reference to the resurrection from physical death, except incidentally. As our Lord says of himself (John 14:6) ἐγώ εἰμι ἡ ὁδὸς καὶ ἡ ἀλήθεια καὶ ἡ ζωή, so the Gospel is styled ἡ ὁδός (Acts 9:2, etc.), ἡ ἀλήθεια (Eph 1:13) and ἡ ζωή (here Acts 5:20).

Vs. 21 ὑπὸ τὸν ὄρθρον 'Close upon day-break'

Παραγενόμενος

πᾶσαν τὴν γερουσίαν τῶν υἱῶν Ἰσραὴλ

Vs. 22 οἱ δὲ παραγενόμενοι ὑπηρέται

Vs. 24 omit ὅ τε ἱερεὺς καὶ on authority of A, B, D, vulg, copt, sah, arm.

οἱ τε ἀρχιερεῖς καὶ would be added for Acts 4:1 and ἀρχιερεῖς may have been omitted from some ms. by mistake and the errors have been multiplied.

τί ἂν γένοιτο τοῦτο 'What this might be which had happened.' And not as Alford.

Vs. 25 ἑστῶτες cf. σταθέντες v. 20.

Vs. 27 The High Priest uses the same guarded language as before (cf. Bengel on Acts 4:7). See Chrysostom *Ap.*, Alf., & Ol.

Vs. 28 ἐπὶ τῷ ὀνόματι τούτῳ

ἐπαγαγεῖν ἐφ' ἡμᾶς τὸ αἷμα (not as Alford) simply 'to charge us with the murder of this man—for murder it was, if he was not a malefactor.'

Vs. 29 Here πειθαρχεῖν δεῖ θεῷ μᾶλλον ἢ ἀνθρώποις in Acts 4:19 ὑμῶν ἀκούειν μᾶλλον ἢ τοῦ θεοῦ.

Vs. 31 on his right hand. See Acts 2:33

μετάνοιαν answers to ἀρχηγόν

ἄφεσιν ἁμαρτιῶν to σωτῆρα (as Bengel)

Vs. 33 διεπρίοντο i.e. with indignation—the full phrase Acts 7:54.

Vs. 34 Gamaliel. See Alford. τίμιος παντὶ τῷ λαῷ. He was called 'the teacher of the law.' See C&H hence νομοδιδάσκαλος τίμιος ought probably to be taken together.

Vss. 36-37 For the point of these two instances—that of Theudas and that of Judas. See Lightfoot, *Comm. on Acts*, ad. loc.[3]

Theudas. As to the possibility of their being two of the same name under similar circumstances, see a parallel instance in the case of Sergius Paulus. Cony. & How. i.p.177, second edition. And of Θευδᾶς = Θεύδοτος or Θεύδωρος it was a name not unlikely to be assumed by a religious impostor or enthusiast. Theudas was a religious leader, Judas a political rebel.

Judas the Galilean ἐν ταῖς ἡμέραις τῆς ἀπογραφῆς of Quirinius (Κυρήνιος) cf. Luke 2:2. Whatever may be the difference in the account of the gospel, it is quite clear from this passage that St. Luke was acquainted with the correct epoch of the taxing. And with regard to the reference in his Gospel, if the sentence had run αὕτη ἀπογραφὴ πρώτη ἐγένετο ἡγεμονεύοντος, without πρώτη, there would have been a real historical difficulty, but the insertion of πρώτη removes the difficulty from the domain of history to that of interpretation. Evidence shows Quirinius in office from A.D. 6, and another term in office from B.C. 4–1.

Vs. 38-39 ἐὰν ᾖ ἐξ ἀνθρώπων, εἰ ἐκ θεοῦ ἐστιν seems certainly to show that Gamaliel was disposed to think it no human imposture. The other explanation of Alford is absurd.

καταλῦσαι Supply the ellipses 'And therefore do not try' or 'and therefore leave them alone.'

Vs. 42 κατ' οἶκον not 'in every home' as E.V.

τὸν χριστόν Ἰησοῦν

EXCURSUS: THE PRIMACY OF PETER

The prominent position held by St. Peter in these earliest days of the church leads naturally to the question: What is meant by the primacy of St. Peter, and how far are the Romanists justified in the views which they hold? It seems both futile and dangerous to deny this primacy altogether, for it is clearly enunciated in Holy Scripture and this in two ways. Directly and in-

---

[3]This is a reference to John Lightfoot's much earlier work, not to J. B. Lightfoot's. (BW3)

directly—or in other words dogmatically and historically—in the account of the promises given to Peter, and in the narrative of his subsequent Acts. Peter is one of the favored three. This however is, of course, inconclusive.

Consider the special prominence given to Peter, and commands addressed to him.

(1) Mt 16:13-19. σὺ εἶ Πέτρος. Πέτρα is certainly to be referred to Πέτρος. The change of gender being easily accounted for (cf. Stanley p. 120), and so not an allusion to a spot or building. An allusion to which Ruskin says, speaking of what he calls the 'accursed architecture, that mighty place where the seven hills slope to the Tiber, that marks by its dome the central spot where Rome has reversed the words of Christ and as he vivified the stone of the apostleship, she petrifies the apostleship into the stumbling stone' (Lectures p. 138).

(2) John 21:15-23

(3) Luke 5:1-10; 22:31-32

Allowing then the primacy of St. Peter, we may challenge the Romanist to show that the Bishop of Rome, or the Roman church has a real title to this inheritance. May we go further?

(1) These promises to Peter are exactly of the same character as those to other apostles. ἐπὶ τῆδε τῇ πέτρα. cf. Eph 2:13[4] the church is said to be built ἐπὶ τῷ θεμελίῳ τῶν ἀποστόλων καὶ προφητῶν. cf. John 21:22-23

(2) That these promises are made to depend on the personal character of St. Peter, and therefore may be expected to be the inheritance of those who represent him in this respect (πάντα ὅστις ἄν Πετρὸς). Origen.

(3) That, as history shows us the fulfillment of these promises, so does it show us that as regarding St. Peter personally they were only intended to be temporary. St. Peter disappears from the scene and St. Paul takes his place. St. Paul knows of no such supremacy as the Roman church attaches to St. Peter. And it is St. Peter himself who utters the caution against lording it over God's heritage (κατακυριεύοντες) 1 Pet 5:3.

---

[4]It is actually Eph 2:20.

ACTS 6

On the widows—'χῆραι quarum etium in sancta societete facilis obscuro'
(Bengel).

Vs. 1 πληθυνόντων intrans. Here only.

Ἑλληνισταί (Grecians E.V.) . . . Ἑβραῖοι

Ἕλληνες (Greeks E.V.) . . . Ἰουδαῖοι

Vs. 2 οὐκ ἀρεστόν ἐστιν 'it seems not fit'

διακονεῖν τραπέζαις i.e. probably the distribution of food, as the plural
τραπέζαις seems to require.

Vs. 3 χρεία necessary business.

Vs. 5 Observe the names are all Greek.

προσήλυτον Ἀντιοχέα St. Luke himself being according to early tradition
a native of Antioch and therefore likely to dwell on the fact (cf. Smith,
Voyage and Shipwreck of St. Paul).

Φίλιππος cf. Acts 8:5, 26, 40; 21:8. (living at Caesarea) In Eusebius Eccles.
History we are told that he was buried at Hierapolis with two of his daughters,
the third lying at Ephesus (*H.E.* iii.31), from Polycrates, who seems only to
know of 3 daughters (the Acts says 4). Caius says that the 4 daughters and
the father were buried at Hierapolis. Both Polycrates and Eusebius make this
Philip one of the apostles plainly contrary to the Acts (Acts 8:1, 14). Whether
Clement and Papias made the mistake is not so clear. Clement probably did.
He represents Philip the apostle as giving his daughters in marriage (Euseb.
iii.30). Of Papias nothing can be concluded. Note Eusebius' Silence (iii.39).
See especially Route, *Rell. Sch.* vol. 1.p. 379, who however will not allow the
evidence, but thinks that the daughters of the two Philips were different.

Of the Nicolaitans, cf. Rev 2:6, 15. It is at least certain that the sect of the
Nicolaitans was connected with this Nicolas by a very early tradition (see
Irenaeus i.27 and Clem. Alex. Ap. Euseb. *H.E.* iii.29). And one which is not
likely to have originated simply in the name as it is improbable that without
good ground a tradition should have been obtained which asserted the
falling away of he who held such a high position in the early church. Whether
he was really the founder of the sect or whether some of his acts or words
were perverted and misapplied by the Nicolaitans, it is impossible to say. But
the former supposition is not impossible. If there was a traitor among the
twelve there may well have been a heretic among the seven. The latter view

seems to be taken by Clement of Alexandria. The supposition that Νικολαϊτῶν is a Greek name from Balaam בלעם is very unlikely. It is at least a very indifferent translation. Tertullian does not mention Nicolas, only the Nicolaitans *De. Prescr. Hiret.* 33.

EXCURSUS: THE DIACONATE

This was evidently the first establishment of the office: there had hitherto been no fixed distributors of alms, but the apostles had delegated this duty now to one, now to another. The consequence of this irregularity was that the Hellenist widows often were neglected. If these seven had been appointed to confine their contributions to the Hellenists, we should scarcely have expected to find them designated as οἱ ἑπτά when there must have been other deacons, their colleagues in office, and their equals in other respects. But indeed the whole narrative seems to imply that this clash of offices did not exist before, and that the irregularities had occurred owing to there being no definite responsible persons. This then was the first establishment of the diaconate.

The functions of the seven seems not to have been confined to ministering to the Hellenist Christians. There is no restriction of this kind implied in the text. They must have attended as well to Hebrew as Hellenist Christians. *But you will say—'But their names are all Greek.'* True: yet this does not necessarily imply a Hellenistic origin—witness the apostles Andrew and Philip—yet it is probable that they were all, or most of them, Hellenists. In this waiving of claims on the part of the Hebrews, we see only an exercise of that Christian love which pervaded the infant church.

Their ministrations then extended to Hebrews as well as Hellenists.

Were they connected with the later diaconate? The word διάκονοι is never used of them in the Acts. They are styled οἱ ἑπτά, 'the seven,' but:

(1) διακονεῖν, διακονία occur repeatedly in describing their ministrations.

(2) Such stress is laid on the circumstances in the narrative, that the writer evidently considered he was narrating an event that had some influence on the subsequent organization of the Church.[5]

---

[5]It is a mistake to suppose that the diaconate arose from the synagogue. See further Lightfoot's *Philippians*.

(3) Their functions are *mutatis mutandis*, the same as those of the later
     diaconate—that is to say—the changes are only such as the altered
     requirements of the church would naturally bring about. We find
     the office of the diaconate not only formally established somewhat
     later (Phil 1:1; 1 Tim 3:8), but also extended to women (Rom 16:1;
     1 Tim 3:11).[6]

(4) Universal tradition—and tradition in such a case is valuable (the
     chance use of the word διάκονος in this narrative only makes it more
     valuable): connects the establishment of the 7 with the diaconate of
     later times, e.g. the diaconate at Rome where the number of deacons
     was limited to 7 though the priests were much more numerous.
     (Cornelius of Rome; Euseb. *H.E.* vi.43; Irenaeus i.26.3; Nicolaum
     unum ex septum qui primi ad deaconium, ab apostolic ordinati sunt.
     iii.12.10; Stephanus . . . qui electus est ab apostolis primus diaconus.
     And so again iv.15.1. cf. Jerome quoted in Greek i.p. See my *Philip-
     pians*, p. 186). This tradition is preserved in the 7 cardinal deacons.
     Creation of subdeacons was necessitated by the limitation.

Whence were the three orders of the Christian church derived? From the
synagogue? The ministers/priests (כֹהֵן) ὑπηρέτης, the elders (זָקֵן)
πρεσβύτεροι, and the ἀρχισυνάγωγος (רֹאשׁ הַכְּנֶסֶת)? Yes—according to the
anti-hierarchical view. Or from the Jewish priesthood—the High Priest, the
priests and the Levites? According to the hierarchical view. From neither—
this threefold organization seems to have been gradually developed by the
growing needs of the church.

We first meet with the διάκονοι here (Acts 6), with πρεσβύτεροι Acts 11:1,
with a bishop, though not by name, in James the brother of the Lord—at
Jerusalem Acts 12:17. For there is very good reason for believing that this
James was not an apostle: and if so, his prominence in the mother church is
the more striking.[7]

Vs. 6 προσευξάμενοι i.e. οἱ ἀποστ.

Vs. 7 πολύς a larger number i.e. relative to the whole number of priests,
see however Alford.

---

[6]cf. Junia s.v. 870.1.
[7]This subject is well treated by Thiersch. *Kirchem Geschichte* i. p. 73 sqq.

Vs. 8 Before he was πλήρης πνεύματος καὶ σοφίας.[8] Now he is πλήρης χάριτος καὶ δυνάμεως.

Vs. 9 Λιβερτίνων is the gen. after τῆς συναγωγῆς τῆς λεγομένης. See Winer Gram. Κυρηναίων καὶ Ἀλεξανδρέων are genitives with τῶν. As there were 480 synagogues in the city it is extremely unlikely that one should serve for so many nationalities as Bengel supposes.[9]

Ἀσίας the whole of Proconsula Asia.

τῶν ἀπὸ Κιλικίας Paul would be one of these.

Λιβερτίνων Libertas, Liberturum.

None of Meyer's quotations (from Josephus) substantiates his assertion 'in Alexandria waren von den fünf Theilen der Stadt zur von ihnen verwohnt' (Wordsworth says three of the five districts). Neither is his assertion 'In Kyrene bestand der vierte Theil. Den einwohner aus Juden' borne out by his quotations. Josephus *Ant.* xiv.7.2 says that one of the four classes in Cyrene was composed of Jews, but this is the nearest approach to it. The passage about Alexandria is in Philo, *Flaccum* § 8 p. 525. Philo says that two out of the 5 quarters are called Jewish: διὰ τὸ πλείστους Ἰουδίους ἐν ταύταις κατοικεῖν—οἴκσοι δὲ καὶ ἐν ταῖς ἄλλαις οὐκ ἀλίγοι σποραίδες. A very different statement. Wordsworth and Alford copy Meyer's statement and references without suspicion.

Vs. 13 ῥήματα The insertion βλάσφημα into the text not well supported. κατὰ τοῦ τόπου τοῦ ἁγίου cf. Acts 7.

Vs. 14 not as E.V. which would require that οὗτος should be earlier in the sentence. Jesus, this Nazarene, i.e. this contemptible fellow.

Vs. 15 ὡσεὶ πρόσωπον ἀγγέλου. An expression which might well be used of the heavenly radiance (though not miraculous) which lighted up the face of Stephen at the moment. The effect on the High Priest is very evident. 'Is this indeed so?'

---

[8]Acts 6:5 states that Stephen was "a man full of faith and the Holy Spirit" (ἄνδρα πλήρης πίστεως καὶ πνεύματος ἁγίου).

[9]Would that Lightfoot had told us how he knew this! (TDS)

The First Martyr for Christ
(Acts 7)

Vs. 1 The speech is prompted by the high priest asking if the charges against St. Stephen are true.

Vs. 2 Ἄνδρες ἀδελφοὶ καὶ πατέρες so St. Stephen is addressing the Jews—Acts 13:1.

Ὁ θεὸς τῆς δόξης

πρὶν ἢ κατοικῆσαι. The account in Genesis does not give this appearance of the Lord previously to Abraham's leaving Mesopotamia (unless the E.V. is correct in translating וַיֹּאמֶר in Gen 12:1 as a pluperfect). Philo distinctly negates the appearance, but mentions an oracle. Though neither is mentioned in the narrative in Genesis, yet some divine injunction seems to be implied in Gen 15:7; Neh 9:7.

The words of v. 3 are the words given in Genesis, as spoken to Abraham in Haran (supposing the pluperfect is untenable). Philo lays great stress on these two misquotations, as symbolizing two different steps of intellectual advancement.

Vs. 3 It is remarkable, in connection with v. 4 (μετὰ τὸ ἀποθανεῖν τὸν πατέρα) that St. Stephen here omits the clause καὶ ἐκ τοῦ οἴκου τοῦ πατρός σου found in both LXX and Heb. The quotation is otherwise verbatim from the LXX.

Vs. 4 Χαρράν

μετὰ τὸ ἀποθανεῖν τὸν πατέρα αὐτοῦ (on the chronological difficulty see Alford).

If the text of Genesis is not corrupt, the difficulty is certainly beyond clearing up: but the boasted purity of the Hebrew text has reasonably been questioned, and in Numbers especially: there is room for error. In fact a comparison of the Hebrew and the LXX in Genesis 12 gives a variation in at least half the numbers which occur there. When as here, the LXX and Hebrew agree, there is less likely to be an error: but still it is very possible— only it must have crept in very early.

Vs. 5 κληρονομίαν ἐν αὐτῇ οὐδὲ βῆμα ποδὸς

The expression οὐδὲ βῆμα ποδός from LXX Deut 2:5.

καὶ ἐπηγγείλατο the correct reading

Vss. 6-7 A compendium of the prophecies with regard to their sojourning in Egypt. The main prophecy is in Gen 15:13 from which these words are taken, with the exception of καὶ λατρεύσετε τῷ θεῷ ἐν τῷ ὄρει τούτῳ which comes from Ex 3:12

ἔτη τετρακόσια See Gal 3:17.

Vs. 8 διαθήκην περιτομῆς. To be connected with ἔτη τετρακόσια in verses 6-7.

The argument in St. Stephen's mind being probably similar to that of St. Paul in Gal 3:17. See Gen 15:13-14. πάροικον ἔσται τὸ σπέρμα σου ἐν γῇ οὐκ ἰδίᾳ καὶ δουλώσουσιν αὐτοὺς ... καὶ ταπεινώσουσιν αὐτοὺς τετρακόσια ἔτη. τὸ δὲ ἔθνος ᾧ ἐὰν δουλεύσωσιν κρινῶ ἐγώ μετὰ δὲ ταῦτα ἐξελεύσονται ὧδε μετὰ ἀποσκευῆς πολλῆς, but ὧδε is not represented in the original. And also Ex 3:12 (to Moses in Horeb) καὶ λατρεύσετε τῷ θεῷ ἐν τῷ ὄρει τούτῳ (Horeb).

Vs. 11 χορτάσματα See notes Phil 4:12. χορτάζεσθαι

Vs. 12 εἰς Αἴγυπτον Winer § 7 p. 576sq (Moulton). Comp. Acts 8:40; this is not an exact parallel. Note the emphatic position of εἰς Αἴγυπτον. Man purposes, but God disposes. It was in God's providence that they should sojourn in Egypt. Ver. 9. Ver. 10, v. 11, here v. 12 (15) ver. 17, ver. 18 (omitted in Text. Receptus etc.) More probable than the Text. Receptus. ἐν Αιγυπτῳ is best taken with ἐξαπέστειλεν.

σιτία, more general than σῖτα or σῖτον, σιτία probably farm foods of any kind.

Vs. 14 ψυχαῖς ἑβδομήκοντα The ἐν is from LXX. Gen. This number is from the LXX, the Hebrew having '70.' The additional five are made up from the descendants of Joseph—a son and grandson of Manasseh, two sons and a grandson of Ephraim—their names are given in the LXX. Basis is Ex 1:5 the LXX has 75, here the Heb has 70. In Deut 10:22, seventy is undisturbed (cf. Bengel). Gen 46:27. πᾶσαι ψυχαὶ οἴκου Ιακωβ αἱ εἰσελθοῦσαι (μετὰ Ιακωβ) εἰς Αἴγυπτον (ψυχαὶ) ἑβδομήκοντα (κοντα)πέντε.[1] Though so expressed the context is quite explicit, but it includes Joseph's descendants in Egypt. For it is before stated that those who came with Jacob were 66 in number (ver. 26) and the sons of Joseph born in Egypt 9. Some texts (e.g. A) omit μετὰ Ιακωβ. An Egyptian Hebrew may have had some Egyptian sources of information.

Vs. 16 As for the textual variants here (1) ἐν Συχέμ אּ*, B, C, Heb. (2) τοῦ ἐν Συχέμ A אּᶜ E. (3) τοῦ Συχέμ D Vulg. The A.V. has the father of Shechem, but not the Greek.

Vs. 19 τοῦ denoting a purpose as usual, and dependant on κατασοφισάμενος. Ex 2:2 ἀστεῖος simply (cf. Heb. טוֹב). κατασοφισάμενος from lxx Ex 1:10. To deal out by craft.

ζωογονεῖσθαι Ex 1:17 καὶ ἐζωογόνουν τὰ ἄρρενα and v. 18. Cf. 1:22. ζωογονεῖν means preserve alive. Judges 8:19 εἰ ἐζωογονήκειτε αὐτούς οὐκ ἂν ἀπέκτεινα ὑμᾶς. Perhaps it comes to be rendered 'grant life to them'—they being regarded as dead-men. Luke 17:33 ζῳογονήσει αὐτήν is not conclusive. In 1 Tim 6:13 ζῳογονοῦντος is the right reading.

Vs. 20 ἀστεῖος τῷ θεῷ Cf. lxx Jonah 3:3. πόλις μεγάλη τῷ θεῷ. Bengel 'an exceeding great city'; E.V. Josephus *Ant.* ii. 9.6. (See Smith's Dict. p. 428 and 2 Cor 10:4 δυνατὰ τῷ θεῷ). Cf. Also Gen 10:9. before the Lord לִפְנֵי יְהוָה.

Vs. 22 πάσῃ σοφίᾳ Αἰγυπτίων (See Stanley in Smith's Dict. p. 426). Philo *Vit. Mos.* i.5; Josephus *c. Ap.* i.26, 28, 31; (Artapanus, Eupolemas) *Praep. Evang.* ix. 26, 27; Clement Alex i. p. 363. See Lightfoot, II 670. Parallels in R. Jochanan ben Zacchai and R. Akibah. Doubtless these are suggested by the parallel.

Vs. 23 τεσσερακονταετὴς Xl. Comp. v. 30.

ἐπληροῦτο Imp: See Bengel.

Ex 2:11 μέγας γενόμενος

Irenaeus ii.22.4.

Vs. 26 αὐτοῖς συνήλλασσεν could have . . . How can Alford read συνήλλασεν? On συνήλλασσνεν cf. Bereshita Rabba . . . 115.3. Moses lived in Pharaoh's palace 40 years, in Judea 40 years and journeying to Israel 40

---

[1]The words in parenthesis here are not in the current lxx.

years. See also Ha. p. 771 ref. cf. Ex 7:40; Deut 31:1. who divided the first 80 years into 2.

ἄνδρες, ἀδελφοί ἐστε· ἵνα τί ἀδικεῖτε ἀλλήλους E.V. correctly. Not as Alford. Not a quotation. The words given in Ex 2:13 are quite diff. διὰ τί σὺ τύπτεις τὸν πλησίον.

Vss. 27-28 from Ex 2:14 word for word LXX, except the phrase ἐχθές (v. l.).

Vs. 30 ἄγγελος see Exodus 3:2. The Angel of the Lord. Ex 3:4. 'The Lord'

Vss. 33-34 from Ex 3:5, 7, 8, 10. Agreeing almost verbatim with the LXX. But here again the passage is directly or fully quoted, the intention of the speaker being only to give those parts which elucidated some new stage in God's dealings with His people. As the narrative is a compendium, so are the quotations also. He does not give the prophecies in full. He gives only the heads. In vs. 34 ἀποστείλω is the correct reading—as in LXX.

Vs. 35 ἀπέσταλκεν Where the effects are permanent. Especially the typical character. e.g. Gal 4:23 γεγέννηται; 1 Tim 2:14 γέγονεν; Heb 7:6 δεδεκάτωκεν.

ἄρχοντα καὶ λυτρωτὴν cf. Acts 7:31. cf. Acts 2:36; 3:13sq.

Vs. 38 Moses regards as a μεσίτης comp. Gal 3:19, 20; Heb 8:6; 9:15; 12:24.

Vs. 40 Almost verbatim with LXX.

Vs. 41 ἐμοσχοποίησαν Images or symbols of idolatry. The calf is the clearest. The calf of Jeroboam. Jeroboam's connection with Egypt. But ἐμοσχοποεῖν is not in the LXX. Ex 32:4, 8; Deut 9:16; Ps 105:10, nor elsewhere. A contemptuous word. See references in Sophocles, *Lex.,* Justin. *Oral.,* Ig. Comp. μοσχοποιία ibid., 6, 7.

Vs. 42 Comp. St. Paul Romans 1:24, 26, 28.

ἐν βίβλῳ τῶν προφητῶν Amos 5:25. The Old Testament is conveniently referred to under two heads ὁ νομος καὶ οἱ πρ-. Thus twofold division being used as exhaustive. Cf. Luke 16:16, 29, 31; John 1:46 etc. But sometimes a triple division is adopted. Luke 24:44 ἐν τῷ νόμῳ Μωϋσέως καὶ τοῖς προφήταις καὶ ψαλμοῖς.

ἐν βίβλῳ. The article omitted because βίβλῳ τῶν προφητῶν is regarded as a title e.g. Mt 1:1. Βίβλος γενέσεως; Luke 3:4 ἐν βίβλῳ λόγων Ἡσαΐου τοῦ προφήτου; Luke 20:42 ἐν βίβλῳ ψαλμῶν. St. Luke's usual way of quotation. It's more precise than in the other Evv. But it's βιβλίον in Luke 4:17.

Vss. 42-43 Some considerable variations from the Hebrew but agreeing very exactly with LXX. The LXX μή brings out the emphasis, the Hebrew is simply the interrogative particle הֲ.

Vs. 43 This verse from Amos 5:26 refers to the idolatrous worship of the Phoenician counterpart to Saturn. Heb. סִכּוּת מַלְכְּכֶם as here; LXX τὴν σκηνὴν τοῦ Μόλοχ. (Luther Bible—einen König).

The Heb. signifies the tabernacle of your king—But inasmuch as the word Molech serves as a name, though in Heb. always with the art. הַמֹּלֶך which signifies 'the king,' the LXX translators were justified in translating it 'Molech,' esp. as the context clearly shows that the reference is to the worship of this Phoenician Saturn. The remaining part of the verse in the Hebrew runs: וְאֵת כִּיּוּן צַלְמֵיכֶם כּוֹכַב אֱלֹהֵכֶם.

'And your images, the star of your god' (E.V.). The LXX has here καὶ τὸ ἄστρον τοῦ θεοῦ ὑμῶν Ραιφαν τοὺς τύπους αὐτῶν οὓς κ.τ.λ.- ('Ρεμφαν is not so well supported) where the translation has slightly reversed the order and translated כִּיּוּן Ραιφαν or Ρεφαν. (N.B. Ρεφαν would seem to be the accusative and not the genitive: at least this could bring it more closely in accordance with the Heb). The star of your god, namely Rephan. The Hebrew Chuin is the Arabic name, the LXX Rephan is the Coptic for the same, the planet Saturn, the symbol of the god Molech—the LXX interpreters preferred translating not its Egyptian equivalent, the word Chiun, which would have had no meaning for their fellow countrymen. It is to be observed that the Syriac translation of the O.T. takes כִּיּוּן to represent the Arabic for the planet and so also several Jewish commentators.

Speaking of the Carthaginians, Diod. Sic. xx.14 (ap. Winer Realus. ii. p. 101) says ἦν παρ αὐτοῖς ἀνδριας κρόνου καλκοῦς, ἐκτετακαις τας χείρας ὑπτιας, εγκελιμενας ἐπὶ τὴν γῆν. ἐστε τὸν ἐπιτεθέντα τῶν παίδων ἀποκυλὶεσθαι καὶ πιπτειν ἒις τι χάσμα πληρος πυρος. And in another passage xx.25 he also mentions a ιερα σκηνη as being carried about with the Carthaginian camp (E.V. in Amos 'of your Molech').

Of the symbolical meaning of this use of Molech and of the corresponding Greek legend regarding Amos, see Mac . . . i.p. Winer. Is the planet Saturn chosen as the representative of time because his periodic time was the greatest of all the known planets and therefore the best representative of time absolutely? On Ρεφαν or Ραιφαν see Winer Real. s.v. Saturn ii. p. 386.

כִּיּוֹן is interpreted by Gesenius and others 'of the frame or carriage.' See his Lexicon s.v.

ἐπέκεινα Βαβυλῶνος. In Amos it is Δαμασκοῦ both in LXX and Heb. The quotation is here again adapted to the after event. We must not expect any more exactness in the quotation, than the occasion demands. St. Stephen's motive was to give a compendium narrative of Jewish history and the manner of his quotation is subordinated to this purpose. He abbreviates and curtails. He combines different passages. He at times, as here, substitutes words, a way of interpretation which enables him to include the narrative with much greater brevity.

The words of the prophet τὴν σκηνὴν τοὺς τύπους serve as a link of connection between the two parts of the speech. St. Stephen had hitherto been speaking chiefly of the Mosaic dispensation (τὰ ἔθη τοῦ Μωϋσέως): he now turns directly to the other topic (ὁ τόπος ὁ ἅγιος). We have the history of the Holy Place. The quotation from Amos allowed him to make this transition naturally.

Vs. 44 Ἡ σκηνὴ τοῦ μαρτυρίου, Cf. Heb 8:5. The construction of this ark is described Ex 25–27. It is prefaced with the words let them make me a sanctuary that I may dwell among them. According to all that I show them after the pattern of the tabernacle etc. (Ex 25:8-9) and again Ex 25:40 LXX (and so Heb). ὅρα ποιήσεις κατὰ τὸν τύπον τὸν δεδειγμένον σοι ἐν τῷ ὄρει.[2]

The phrase Ἡ σκηνὴ τοῦ μαρτυρίου is devised from the LXX translation of Num 16:18-19 and elsewhere מוֹעֵד אֹהֶל. Note the word מוֹעֵד is generally interpreted 'congregation,' or better 'meeting.' Ex 25:22; Num 17:19; Heb. But A.V. Num 17:4. See Gesenius s.v. p. 606. Alford should have mentioned that the phrase the ark of the testimony is found Ex 25:22. τῆς κιβωτοῦ τοῦ μαρτυρίου. LXX. Cf. Ex 25:16, 21. So that the phrase Ἡ σκηνὴ τοῦ μαρτυρίου is in some manner justified, even if it could be shown, as it cannot, that the LXX is wrong. Winer accepts the LXX translation as adequate.

EXCURSUS: THE TABERNACLE

    (1) The semblance of the tabernacle of the seventy returns.

    (2) The difference. It was this which constituted its testimony.

---

[2]Ex 25:40 (LXX); cf. Heb 8:5. (TDS)

ἦν τοῖς πατράσιν The correct reading, and the sure expression. They had this other σκηνή.

LXX has κατὰ πάντα ὅσα σοι δεικνύω ἐν τῷ ὄρει.[3]

עוד (Hiph העד ועיד [Impt ויעד]). The other expression אהל העדת is rightly translated tabernacle of the testimony ἡ σκηνὴ τοῦ μαρτυρίου Num 17:17; 18:2, etc. (See Smith's Dict. s.v. Tabernacle p. 1414). The force of μαρτυρίου here must not be overlooked. The tabernacle which was a testimony to God and a testimony against false gods. Num 17:19: ἐν τῇ σκηνῇ τοῦ μαρτυρίου κατέναντι τοῦ μαρτυρίου.

Vs. 45 διαδεξάμενοι not rec. αὐτὴν. I do not see on what ground Alford condemned the sense of 'in succession' as ungrammatical.

ἐν τῇ κατασχέσει in the taking possession of the nations, i.e. their territory.

ἕως τῶν ἡμερῶν An abridged expression. And this in the time of David.

Vs. 46 Ps. 132:5 (131:5) ἕως οὗ εὕρω τόπον τῷ κυρίῳ σκήνωμα τῷ θεῷ Ἰακώβ.[4]

. . . τῷ οἴκῳ ℵ*, B, D, H . . .

Vs. 48 χειροποιήτοις om. ναοίς. A temple made with hands—depreciating.

Vs. 49 The quotation agrees in the main with the LXX and Heb. The variations being quite unimportant. Isaiah 66:1

Vs. 51 In spite of Alford's note, if we suppose that St. Stephen's hearers manifested some signs of impatience at the application of these words of the prophets—as they naturally would—we shall be much better able to appreciate the turn that his speech takes.

On ἀπερίτμητοι καρδίαις Ezek 44:7, 9 where the expression is used of the foreigner. See Jer 9:25 from which it is more directly taken πάντα τὰ ἔθνη ἀπερίτμητα σαρκί καὶ πᾶς οἶκος Ισραηλ ἀπερίτμητοι καρδίας αὐτῶν. This recommends the reading of B καρδίος. Comp. Jer 6:10 ἰδοὺ ἀπερίτμητα τὰ ὦτα αὐτῶν καὶ οὐ δύνανται ἀκούειν where again it applies to the Israelites. Also comp. Deut. 10:16; Jer 4:4. Bengel's note is good. His 'in dispositiones angelorum' is the correct rendering and well explained.

Vs. 52 comp. Mt 23:35; Luke 11:51.

τοῦ δικαίου Is 3:10 (LXX) δήσωμεν τὸν δίκαιον ὅτι δύσχρηστος ἡμῖν ἐστιν to which as found in LXX for the Heb is quite different, pertaining to what

---

[3]See Ex 25:8 (LXX). (TDS)
[4]The text reads Ἰακώβ but Lightfoot writes Ἰσραήλ. (BW3)

St. Stephen refers. Strangely enough Hegesippus refers it to James the Just Ap. Eus. *H.E.* ii.23.

νῦν in late days. ἐγένεσθε likely to be preferred to γεγένησθε.

Jerome ad. loc. says of the LXX reading 'per spiare de Christi dictum passiare' (IV. p. 57). It is so applied in Barnabas *Ep.* 6 . . . δήσωμεν.

The LXX has got hold of the verb אסר for אמר.

אמרו צדיק כי־תוב

Justin *Dial.* 17, 133, 136, 137. In § 137 he mentioned . . . Ἄρωμεν, δήσωμεν.

Vs. 53 εἰς διαταγὰς ἀγγέλων Διαταγή means more than an injunction, disposition. In N.T. it is found only here and Rom 13:2. And its meaning here is explained by Gal 3:19.

εἰς two ways of explaining: (1) 'On' or 'at' of angels. See Winer § 49 p. 496, Mt 12:41; Rom 4:20. (2) For i.e. as in Acts 13:22, and above Acts 7:21. See Winer § 32 p. 288.

Vs. 55 δόξαν θεοῦ Not θεός himself for no man hath seen God at any time. Therefore it was the symbol of His presence which was revealed—pertaining to a bright light—like the shekinah or glory which betokened His presence on the mercy seat.

ἑστῶτα On Ἰησοῦν ἑστῶτα. See Chrysostom.

This was a fit revelation to be made to him, to strengthen him in his hour of trial—for St. Stephen had declared the dispensation of the 'God of Glory' and connected it with the coming of 'Jesus.'

Vs. 56 υἱὸν θεοῦ See Alford. *Clem. Recogn.* ii.37. Aures continuo obcludens, velut ne blasphemia polluantur.

τὸν υἱὸν τοῦ ἀνθρώπου The taking up of humanity with God through the incarnation and resurrection of Christ. The central truth of Christianity. He is τὸν υἱὸν τοῦ ἀνθρώπου. See Eph 2:5-6. This is the fit conclusion of the historical narrative, commencing with the appearance of the God of Revelation to Abraham in Mesopotamia and at the first setting apart of a church. A fulfillment of Mt 26:64 (as Alford sees) is significant in itself.

Vs. 57 κράξαντες δὲ κ.τ.λ. Compare the similar expression in Mt 26:65? Isa. Eph 4.

βύσαντες τὰ ὦτα. συνέσχον τὰ ὦτα

On the taking away of the power of inflicting capital punishment taken away from the Sanhedrin before the fall of Jerusalem—See B.T. *Sanhed.* 26a, 24a. cf. John 18:31.

The facts seem to be:

(1) That the Sanhedrin had not the powers of capital punishment.

(2) That they occasionally exercised this power anyway, e.g. Ananas in the case of James the Just. Josephus *Ant.* xx.9.9. Ir. Alb. calls him to account. Cf. Lev 24:14. Heb 13:12. οἱ μάρτυρ Deut 17:7.

(3) That Pilate had probably been recalled about this time. Pilate left about A.D. 36. That this would be a very good opportunity for any irregular usurpation: as in the case of James the Just.

(4) That the narrative describes the proceedings as tumultuous. There is no reference to the verdict that found condemnation.

Vs. 60 μὴ στήσῃς The objection of De Wette & Meyer (which Alford adopts) to the sense 'weight' is surely without force—surely the language of our liturgy 'not weighing our merits, but pardoning our offences' is felt to be just as adequate (as the punishment is proportionate to the sin. The sin must be weighed first.) But 'weigh' is not the sense for στήσῃς which is naturally the one in such a context, and therefore should be discarded. στήσῃς 'set up, give it a standing place'—and so 'reckon.' Rom 10:3. Of the stoning of St. Stephen considered in its bearing on the functions of the Sanhedrin. See Winer. Real. s.v. Synedrium. (1 Cor 1:2. See Rom 10; 2 Tim 2:22)

Vs. 59 ἐπικαλούμενον See Acts 9:14, 21. (pert. Acts 2:21 comp. Jer 36)

Summary

The speech of St. Stephen appears at first sight to contain merely a compendious narrative of the early history of God's dealings with His chosen people—concluding with an outburst of indignation—at which point the speaker is interrupted and not allowed to proceed.

This is evidently an inadequate view: (1) Such a narrative would have served no purpose as regards his hearers inasmuch as the facts narrated were known to all and (2) with regard to himself, though they [i.e. the facts] might serve as a confession of his faith. Still this was not the point of the accusation. He was not charged with unbelief, but with *maintaining the tran-*

sitory nature of the Mosaic dispensation and the temple worship.

The speech is certainly interrupted—more than this—there are manifestations, as it advances, of the impatience of the hearers. The narrative, which is given in greater detail at first, becomes more abbreviated as if the speaker saw that he would not be allowed to proceed much further, he cuts short the whole of the period subsequent to the time of Solomon by a quotation from the prophet, modified in form (Βαβυλῶνος substituted for Δαμασκοῦ), so as to lead him on this second point. Then comes the outburst of indignation—and this consummates the impatience of his hearers.

We must seek for the interpretation of the speech (1) in the accusation made against him, (2) in his choice and arrangement of the facts of his narrative, and hints contained in it, (3) lastly in the manner in which these and similar facts are treated as regards their bearing on the New Testament dispensation, in other parts of the New Testament—especially in St. Paul.

For St. Stephen was justly regarded as the forerunner of St. Paul. It is as the dawn to the full shining of daylight—St. Stephen first enunciates the fact of the transitory nature of the Mosaic dispensation, and that the worship of God is not to be confined to particular places, on which St. Paul dwells with his characteristic energy—in St. Paul therefore (and in the Epistle to the Hebrews by consequence) we are to look for suggestions as to the interpretation of the speech.

As to the effects of the Stephen Speech on St. Paul we may conjecture from what source the historian derived his account of this speech. There was a young man standing by while the speech was delivered, of the same age probably with the speaker with some natural gifts, educated perhaps under the same influences and no less zealous than this Stephen, BUT with very different feelings. He viewed the speaker with all the rancor of religious hatred. He would drink in every word which was uttered, seeking how he might find in it some matter of accusation. The very language and expression of the speaker would dwell on his mind. The heavenly radiance which lit up his countenance as he spoke, the manly and fearless tones of the speaker, the burst of holy indignation, a sign more of love than of anger—his exclamation, 'I see the heavens opened,' his commending his spirit to Christ and his prayer for his murderers, all those would make a deep impression on the mind of Saul. One so thoughtful as he was, would during his journey to

Damascus be naturally meditating on the event of the previous days. It would seem strange to him that one rather like him should have arrived at such different results—that Stephen should be the sufferer, Saul the persecutor. He must have had some misgivings as to the uprightness of his actions. He would read the words of the martyr again and again. And after his miraculous conversion, by which the whole tenor of his life was changed, during that period of blindness [all the moreso], while he had not yet learnt what he must do to be saved, and duly knew that henceforth he must be a servant of that Jesus whom he had persecuted—when his eye could not rest on any objects, and he was left to the reflections of his own deeds—what more natural than that he should turn again and again to the speech of Stephen which seemed to contain the only solution to his present perplexity? It is the one thing, which would have dwelt especially on his memory—the one passage in his life that he would remember most minutely.

And indeed we have ample evidence that it did so dwell on his mind. We are constantly meeting in the writings of the apostle passages that remind us most forcibly of the defense of that first martyr. Standing out: Areopagus, and pleading the cause of Christ before the Athenians, his position was similar to that of Stephen. And St. Stephen's words are on his lips. And seeing that He is the Lord of heaven and earth, dwelling not in temples made by hands (Acts 17:24). Of the older covenant St. Paul says that act was διαταγεὶς ὑπ' ἀγγέλων.[5] St. Stephen before had told the Jews that they received it εἰς διαταγὰς ἀγγέλων.[6] Other parallel passages might be adduced—to say nothing of the whole tenor of St. Paul's teaching. As the historian then was a companion of St. Paul, we cannot doubt who was his informant, nor can we be surprised at the exactness of his information.

Now the key points of the accusation against St. Stephen are two. That he maintained (1) that Jesus could destroy the temple, (2) that He would change the Mosaic institutions. Two main threads run through his narrative, turning to them in reverse order corresponding to these two heads. The first one is prominent in the earlier; the other is the latter part of the speech.

1. Mosaic Dispensation Acts 7:2-43

---

[5]Lightfoot is alluding here to Gal 3:19, which reads in Westcott and Hort διαταγεὶς δι' ἀγγέλων. (TDS)
[6]See Acts 7:53. (TDS)

2. The Holy Place Acts 7:44-50. (But at the same time the one is more or less implied in the other.)

The quotation from Amos with which the former division closes enables him to turn without any abruptness to the second branch of his subject. Cf. ἀνελάβετε τὴν σκηνὴν τοῦ Μόλοχ . . . τοὺς τύπους οὓς ἐποιήσατε with Ἡ σκηνὴ τοῦ μαρτυρίου . . . ποιῆσαι αὐτὴν κατὰ τὸν τύπον ὃν ἑωράκει i.e. not of their own caprice, but the type of God's ordaining.[7]

How then are we to suppose that St. Stephen would have applied this narrative if he had not been interrupted? A. Historically. B. Symbolically or Typically, showing in both these ways that the older dispensation and the temple worship pointed to the mediator of a new covenant.

(A) Historical Application. i.e. by tracing the gradual development of God's purpose in His dealings with men. Showing that His dealings are always progressive and do not take a stereotyped form—and that therefore the Mosaic dispensation—consisting of fixed ordinances and the Temple worship—confined to a single spot can only be regarded as temporary—as leading to something higher than the Mosaic dispensation. We can scarcely doubt that St. Stephen would have made such an application of the narrative as St. Paul afterwards does of the same facts—in Gal 3:4—that the promise was prior to the law and therefore the covenant that was confirmed before of God in Christ. The law which was 430 years after cannot annul the promise, or make it of more effect, that the law was added because of transgressions—'ordained by angels.' It served a temporary purpose—'It was the servant which was to lead us to the school of Christ' (παιδαγωγὸς εἰς Χριστόν). Nay that at the very time it was given, Moses led the people to look forward to a future dispensation. 'A prophet shall the Lord God raise up like unto me.'[8] 'Unto him shall ye hearken.' This part of the narrative can be outlined as follows:

A. History of the Mosaic Dispensation:

1. The Preparation of the Patriarchs
   Acts 7:2-16: This period is dwelt upon to show that God's covenant with His people inaugurates the dispensation of the Law of Moses.

---

[7]This comparison is between Acts 7:43 and 7:44. (TDS)
[8]Cf. Acts 3:22 with Deut 18:15, 18. (TDS)

2. The Fulfillment

Acts 7:17-37

3. The Rebellion and Punishment

4. The Catastrophe

Acts 7:38-43. Cf. Acts 7:6 ἔτη τετρακόσια v. 8 ἔδωκεν αὐτῷ διαθήκην περιτομῆς

Here are the elements of such an interpretation. In verse 38 the word ἐκκλησίᾳ is purposely closer to show the historical continuity. Note the λόγια ζῶντα [in the same verse]. The oracles had been the sign of growth, progress. They were not a dead letter but a quickening spirit; not a stereotypical form, not a new code of ordinance, but a principle of life and therefore of development. Heb 4:12.

B. The Temple Worship (Thus we are brought to the period which relates especially to the second point, the local sanctuary.) (cf. Baumgarten p. 157sqq)

As the promise to Abraham preceded the giving of the law, so the tabernacle preceded the temple. The tabernacle was confined to no fixed locality—it moved about from place to place. It was not till the time of Solomon that the temple had been built—that David had designed it and not been permitted to accomplish it due to the sovereignty of Yahweh—and a proof not only of His ability, but also of His will to remove the seat of His worship according to His good pleasure.

(B) The Typical or Symbolical. We may view any person or event not only with regard to his or its place in history, i.e. in the progressive development of God's dealing with men, as one link in a chain—but also as a symbol or type, of that which will recur again and again. Such an application may be made with more or less exactness in ordinary History, but in Sacred History we are taught especially to look for these analogies and as the Life of Christ and the Foundation of the Church are the turning point of the world's History—the events of this epoch bring of incalculably greater importance than those of any other—so we may consider them as the antitype to which all the minor repetitions of similar circumstances stand in the relation of types—they're the substance, the others the shadow.[9] This is one application of the great principle of analogy. The higher principle that dispenses with fixed sanctuaries, with localized religion, has been shown to him through the history of the race.

Abraham the father of the faithful chosen of God—received his call in Mesopotamia (Acts 7:2). He did not go to the land of promise (Acts 7:6). When he reached Palestine he had not really settled, not given even a footing there (ver. 6). It was foretold to him that his descendants should live for centuries in a foreign land under a foreign tyrant (Acts 7:7). This did come to pass. God's grace was (Acts 7:42) then removal from the land of promise (Ex 9–15). The patriarch died in Egypt. His bones were removed to Palestine indeed. But they were deposited not in Jerusalem, but in the capitol of the Samaritans, at the Mount of Gerazim.

Now there may be great danger in its application in individual cases owing to the latitude which it allows but still we have sufficient authority for applying it to the interpretation of Scripture—not only in the broader facts, but also in the minor details—as the following instances will show. St. Paul treats the history of Hagar and Sarah (Gal 4:22) as an allegory (ἅτινά ἐστιν ἀλληγορούμενα) typifying the two covenants. He views the passing of the Israelites under the cloud and through the seas as prefiguring Christian baptism, and the eating of the manna and drinking of the water which flowed from the rock (1 Cor 10:1-3) as symbolizing the other sacrament—the partaking of the body and blood of Christ.

St. Peter views the deluge as signifying Christian Baptism, and the preservation of Noah and his family in the ark as betokening the salvation of the faithful in the ark of the church (1 Pet 4:21). The argument of the Epistle to the Hebrews is entirely built on this method of interpretation. The rebellion in the wilderness denotes the rejection of the gospel, the rest in Canaan the peace which in the consequence of the reception of it—Abraham giving tithe to Melchizedek represents the inferiority of the Mosaic to the Christian dispensation (Cf. Heb 11:8 'By faith Abraham when he was called to go out into a place which he should receive after for an inheritance [εἰς κληρονομίαν] obeyed and he went out not knowing whither he went.')

---

[9]Cf. Col 2:17. (TDS)

The ordinances of the law, the sacrifices, the very furniture of the Holy Place had all this meaning: they were all foreshadowings of Christianity. Cf. esp. Heb 9:1-5, where after describing the construction and furniture of the holy place, the inspired writer says περὶ ὧν οὐκ ἔστιν νῦν λέγειν κατὰ μέρος [note v. 5] implying that each of these had a distinct Christian significance. Thus we are at liberty to apply this system of symbolical interpretation to this speech of St. Stephen if the phenomena exhibited by the speech itself justifies us in doing so. And there are good reasons for doing so. For:

(1)   Let us consider the character of the speaker and the hearers. Stephen was in all probability a Hellenist. His accusers and therefore a large number of his hearers certainly belonged to this class (cf. Acts 6:9). The Alexandrians are especially mentioned. Now the allegorical interpretation, though allowed in the mother country, found especial favor with the Hellenists, and particularly the Alexandrians (witness Philo and the Alexandrian Fathers Origen and Clement). This treatment of Scripture could appeal at once to their peculiar bend of mind, and is therefore not unlikely to have been employed. The Epistle to the Hebrews exhibits this mode of treatment most thoroughly—and as it not improbably was penned by a Hellenist, it may serve in some degree, as a clue to the interpretation of St. Stephen's speech.

(2)   There are unmistakable hints (of which hereafter) that St. Stephen did select the events of his narrative with a view to something more than this historical bearing—in fact their allegorical meaning, e.g. vs. 37 προφήτην ὑμῖν ἀναστήσει ὁ θεὸς ἐκ τῶν ἀδελφῶν ὑμῶν ὡς ἐμε or vs. 44 κατὰ τὸν τύπον ὃν ἑωράκει.

(3)   There are certain minor details to which it is scarcely possible to assign any historical meaning—and therefore taking into account the manifest brevity which St. Stephen aimed at—we must suppose that they had a typical significance.

It is not always possible to fix this significance. In many cases I shall not attempt to do so. But the only way of accounting for their presence in the narrative appears to me to be by supposing that they had such a bearing— and the instances above given from other parts of the New Testament (esp.

the Epistle to the Hebrews) show that there is nothing unjustifiable in the supposition. The test of this view will be in the success of its application. Let us then apply it to the two parts of the narrative.

1. The History of the Dispensation.[10] Joseph—As Joseph was sold and delivered over to the heathen by his brethren, so was Christ also betrayed into the hands of the Gentiles by his brethren after the flesh—the Jewish people. He was betrayed not in his own person but also in the person of His church—but God was with Him. This persecution ended in His triumph. His own received Him not,[11] but He became ruler over the Gentiles—God has given Him the heathen for His inheritance: But there is a famine in the land of Egypt and Canaan. The superstitions of heathendom and the lifeless formalism of Judaism are alike unable to satisfy the spiritual wants of men. The Jews are at length conscious of the shortcomings. It is from the granaries of Egypt—the storehouses that have been filled by the providence of Joseph—that the Jews themselves—Joseph's brethren, must seek their food and this is exactly the view, as Thiersch remarks, which St. Paul presents (Rom 10:25 sqq) of the final restoration of Israel. 'Blindness in part is happened to Israel until the fullness of the Gentiles be come in.' 'And so all Israel shall be saved.' These (the Jews) have also now not believed that through your (the Gentiles) mercy, they also may obtain mercy—Thus then as the family of Jacob were rescued from famine by Joseph's influence in Egypt, so shall the Jewish race be finally restored through the power of Christ and the spread of the Gospel among the Gentiles.

The parallel between Moses and Christ is even more complete: and St. Stephen leaves no doubt on our minds that this parallel was intended by clenching his narrative (the facts of which are evidently chosen as having their counterparts in the Christian dispensation) with the prophecy of Moses in which distinct reference is made to it—v. 37 προφήτην . . . ἐκ τῶν ἀδελφῶν ὑμῶν ὡς ἐμέ (Compare Acts 3:22).

As Moses was cast out to perils and providentially delivered, so was Jesus rescued when a child from the massacre of Herod. As Moses was ἀστεῖος τῷ θεῷ and instructed in all the wisdom of the Egyptians, so Jesus increased in wisdom, as in stature and in form with God and man, like Moses when

---

[10]N.B.: there is quite a lot in this section that is crossed out with pencil.
[11]Cf. Jn 1:11. (TDS)

He was come to mature manhood.[12] It came into His heart to visit His brethren the children of Israel—He began the work of restoration—He sought to deliver them from their bondage. He supposed His brethren would have understood how that God by his hand would deliver them, but they understood not. He came to His own and His own received Him not.[13] When He would have taught them, they considered His interference and who made him a judge over us? We have no king but Caesar (John 19:15. Chrysostom). Yet, He was commissioned by God in a special manner to deliver His people—from the bondage of the spiritual Egypt. St. Stephen says of Moses v. 35, this Moses whom they refused saying, 'Who made thee a ruler and a judge?' The same did God send to be a redeemer as well as a ruler (καὶ ἄρχοντα καὶ λυτρωτὴν). He was the mediator of the Old Covenant. Acts 2:36; 3:13sq. St. Peter had said of Jesus (Acts 5:31): 'The God of our fathers raised up Jesus, whom ye hanged on a tree. Him both God exalted to be a prince and a savior.'[14]

As Moses wrought many miracles in the land of Egypt and in the Red Sea and in the wilderness, so also does Christ. In the land of Egypt—the place of bondage, while we are still under the dominion of sin, for Egypt is the prophetic type of sin. In the Red Sea, in the passage from the bondage of our natural state to the freedom in the gospel—whereunto we pass by baptism— the antitype of that deliverance of the Israelites when they crossed the sea (as St. Paul himself tells us).[15] As they were baptized unto Moses in the Red Sea, so are we also unto Christ—and lastly in the wilderness—no more in the land of bondage—at length in the church—but in the church militant, downcast and afflicted. Here He works many miracles for us. He gives us a spiritual food and spiritual drink—in His other sacrament. Corresponding to the manna sent down from heaven and the water that miraculously flowed from the rock (which rock is Christ).

I am not here indulging in my own fancies: it is St. Paul again who teaches us so to read the miracles of Moses. And in interpreting the wilderness to be the militant Church we are only following in the footsteps of the un-

---

[12]Note Lk 2:52. (TDS)
[13]Another reference to Jn 1:11. (TDS)
[14]The rest of this page, which expands the allegory or typology, is crossed out.
[15]So 1 Cor 10:2-4. (TDS)

known writer of the Epistle to the Hebrews. He draws out this parallel at some length (e.g. Heb 3:11–4:11), comparing the temptations or trials which befell the Israelites to those which await us who have been called to a knowledge of the Gospel and exhorting us not to follow their disobedience if we would pass from the wilderness to the land of rest—in Canaan—from the Church militant to the Church triumphant. And St. Stephen himself calls attention to this parallel by employing the word ἐν τῇ ἐκκλησίᾳ ἐν τῇ ἐρήμῳ.[16]

But as the Jews were disobedient to Moses, then so are they disobedient to Christ now: They turn him from them and in their hearts, turn back again into Egypt. Aaron headed the rebellion then: and now it is headed by Aaron's successors, the high priest and the spiritual rulers. And so they will go from bad to worse, and God will give them over to their own idolatries and the end of all this will be: that they will be carried away beyond Babylon. They have only left one bondage to submit to another—Rahab (Egypt) and Babylon are frequently coupled together in the prophetic writings.

2. In coming to the Second Part of this Defense—that which regards the Holy Place—we observe that St. Stephen intimates that the very form of the tabernacle did symbolize something future. διετάξατο ὁ λαλῶν τῷ Μωϋσῇ ποιῆσαι αὐτὴν κατὰ τὸν τύπον ὃν ἑωράκει.[17] The pattern of it was revealed by God. It would not perhaps be unjustifiable to presume that the fact of the tabernacle being constructed after a divine pattern did in itself imply that it was the type of something higher. But the language of the Epistle to the Hebrews leaves us no longer in any doubt on this point. The tabernacle is there referred to in language exactly parallel to this (Heb 8:5) only more definite, so as to serve as a community of our text—of the Jewish priests it is there said οἵτινες ὑποδείγματι καὶ σκιᾷ λατρεύουσιν τῶν ἐπουρανίων, καθὼς κεχρημάτισται Μωϋσῆς μέλλων ἐπιτελεῖν τὴν σκηνήν· ὅρα γάρ φησιν, ποιήσεις πάντα κατὰ τὸν τύπον τὸν δειχθέντα σοι ἐν τῷ ὄρει.

And subsequently (Heb 9:2sqq) the writer describes the fashion of this tabernacle somewhat minutely and explains its typical significance. Can we doubt that St. Stephen could have made a similar application if he had not been interrupted?

---

[16]See Acts 7:38. (TDS)

[17]Note Acts 7:44. (TDS)

If any of these analogies here given seem to be strained, they ought not to be allowed to be dismissed due to prejudices about our belief in the allegorical or typical bearing of the speech. It seems to exist beyond question—and it must be remembered that of the parallels which I have attempted to draw—the symbolical interpretation based thereon, a large proportion have not been arbitrarily assumed but are actually drawn from other parts of the New Testament. In many cases this is true of those analogies which perhaps *a priori* we should be disposed to consider somewhat fanciful. The principal point on which St. Stephen may have dwelt is the moral allegory of the tabernacle.

Excursus: The Authenticity of the Speech of St. Stephen[18]

[N.B. in what follows the reference to S.R. is not to the initials of a person but to the book titled *Supernatural Religion*,[19] first published in 1874, of which Lightfoot mentions page numbers from time to time. This book became a cause célèbre in its own day when published, and Lightfoot went so far as to write a full published rebuttal of it, much of which appeared in the periodical *Contemporary Review* between 1874 and May 1877 in installments, and then in full in the year of his death (1889) under the heading *Essays on Supernatural Religion*. It is clear how exercised he was by the book in what he says in this excursus/final Cambridge lecture given in 1879. The reason it is uppermost in his mind in 1879 is that a third volume had been added to the aforementioned provocation, and the third edition of *Supernatural Religion* was published in 1879. Lightfoot was continuing to respond.]

Firstly, here are the arguments of S.R. against the historical character of the narrative in Acts 7 and the authenticity of the Stephen speech in particular:

(1) The silence of St. Paul. Paul doesn't mention Stephen ever or this event

---

[18]This lecture was the last Lightfoot was to give in Cambridge. It was given in 1879 in the dining room in Trinity Hall before a hastily assembled multitude of faculty and students. The occasion was that Lightfoot had just accepted the appointment to become bishop of Durham. When one compares the handwriting of this piece with that of the Acts notebooks, it seems clear that this was written with some speed. Nevertheless, it shows Lightfoot as a master of the detailed excursus. (BW3)

[19]*Supernatural Religion* was published anonymously but ascribed to one Walter Richard Cassells (though he never admitted to writing it). Subsequent responses to Lightfoot's rebuttals were also published anonymously. Speculation that Cassells was the author really began after Lightfoot's death, when in 1895 Cassells published a series of theological articles that seemed to resonate with the themes of that book. (BW3)

(p. 149). *Response—No he doesn't, nor does he mention any other person he was connected with prior to his conversion. If there had been any detached account of St. Paul's earlier life or any direct notices of persons and events he was previously connected with, this silence might have required explanation. As it is, this observation is absolutely worthless.*

(2) But S.R. continues, protesting the phrase τὴν ἐκκλησίαν κατὰ τοὺς οἴκους. *Response—This reflects a singular inability to appreciate the city in which Saul and these Christians lived and moved. Saul moved rather like a machine, steadily, continuously in one particular direction.*

(3) Then S.R. complains 'the speech and the martyrdom made so little impression.' He also complains that the characterization seems not to comport with real life. *Response—That which is recorded as happening here has happened again and again in the life of this or that man. It is a matter of common physiological experience—the noble patience of the victim, the powerful arguments of the antagonist only seem to have made the man more ruthless, more implacable, but they lodge in the man's heart a question there. Then suddenly comes some crisis, some upheaval in the man's soul, which sets in motion some hidden elements of past experiences. Then in new circumstances things are seen in a new light. This is exactly how St. Paul represents his conduct in the passage quoted—Gal 1:11-17. Yes, Paul's conversion was through a revelation of Jesus Christ, but is it to be supposed that Jesus Christ, himself a sufferer, made no use of the instrumentality of the Christian sufferers whom St. Paul had taken and whom were put to death? They were the text through which the Spirit preached and the Spirit interposed in St. Paul's life. Does S.R. suppose that St. Paul had received every single fact about the life of Christ by direct revelation from heaven and not through narrative of eyewitnesses (see e.g. 1 Cor 15:1sq.)? These appearances are mentioned as part of the Gospel that he preached and yet obviously the accounts are received directly from eyewitnesses and indirectly from others who had heard from them. At all events, either way, the information came from human narratives.*

(4) But incidentally S.R. finds an objection in the very narrative (p. 150 note 2). His argument is twofold: (a) there is no reason to suppose that St. Paul intended his lot to be decisive; (b) the appearance to St. Stephen was not of the kind which St. Paul could have seen or adduced. It was entirely a subjective revelation. It would therefore be no proof to any of the bystanders.

Stephen's speech is regarded as blasphemy, so little do they see.

(5) A major objection to both the event and the speech of St. Stephen comes from S.R.'s reading of the historical circumstances. He finds them improbable the council meeting and the speech itself he finds historically highly improbable (p. 151). *Response—But it is this singular character of the story, which nonetheless has some elements in common with what we know has happened in Jewish history from time to time. History is constantly defying our declamations about what may or may not be historically probable. S.R.'s judgment is caused by assumptions that on closer inspection collapse. For example, there is the supposition that Jews did not have the power of capital punishment at the time. S.R. quotes St. John 18:31, but it is strange to find S.R. quoting John as an authority on historical matters (cf. Farrar, Life of Christ II, p. 368). According to the survey of the relevant forty years, capital punishment had only recently been taken from the Jews when our Lord suffered (see Josephus xx.9.1). S.R. dismisses contemptuously the supposition that it was during one of the intervals between procurators that St. Stephen was executed. But Pilate's reign ended in A.D. 35 or latest 36 and it was about this time when this incident transpired.*

(6) A further major objection of S.R. is based on the correspondences or parallels between the account in St. Luke's Gospel of our Lord's death, and the account in Acts 7 (p. 153). *Response—Many of these elements in the accounts are due to similarities of place, time, and semi-judicial or judicial procedures (e.g. same police, officers etc.). Those parts that are especially similar are dwelt on by S.R. (e.g. Acts 7:56 comp. to Luke 22:69, sayings ascribed to St. Stephen and Jesus). But this saying of Jesus is not confined to St. Luke—it is found also in Mt 26:64; Mk 14:62 and the latter are in a form nearer to St. Stephen's words. For instance comp. Mt 26:64 ὄψεσθε τὸν υἱὸν τοῦ ἀνθρώπου καθήμενον ἐκ δεξιῶν τῆς δυνάμεως to Acts 7:56 θεωρῶ. . . . τὸν υἱόν.*

His second example is Acts 7:59 comp. Lk 23:46. Response—S.R. does not take into account that the words of the Lord are taken from Ps (30) 31:6 εἰς χεῖρας σου παραθήσομαι τὸ πνεῦμά μου. . . .

His third example is Acts 7:60 comp. Luke 23:34. Response—S.R. does not tell us that in St. Luke these words are wanting in the most important authorities B, D* and are obelisked or deleted by a contemporary or near contem-

porary corrector of A. W+H[20] regard these words [in St. Luke] as not a part of the book as originally written but as retaining a high historical though not canonical authority (see pp. xxv, xxvii in W+H). In fact, the result is, that such resemblance as there is [between Acts 7 and Luke 23] is easily explicable on two grounds: 1) St. Stephen was likely placed in similar circumstances to Christ, and reflected the same mindset as Christ [in response]; 2) St. Luke reflects a special affection for such traits as prayer and forgiveness. But S.R. is the last man who should press such resemblances. The last words of dying men are often to commend their souls to God and Christ. Martyrs have often prayed such prayers, but in the specific language of the prayer of Jesus in Luke and that of Stephen there really is no resemblance (comp. Justin, Dialogue 105: 'Father into thy hands . . . ' word for word). These words of Jesus were probably reported in a wide variety of Christian accounts that are no longer extant. Notice that it is also present in Marcion's Gospel as reported by Tertullian Adv. iv.41. S.R. maintains that Marcion's Gospel was not dependent on St. Luke but rather on a much earlier source. Notice that Hegisippus puts exactly the same words into the mouth of James the Just. Moreover this saying is credited as the Lord's in the Clementine Homilies ix.20. If you read right through the argument in S.R. the author supplies his own refutation.

Now I believe that [S.R.] says at the moment what he believes to be true. But he is clearly a special pleader and he asks himself on each occasion not 'what is the probable inference from this fact,' but rather 'what inference can I get out of this fact that suits my purpose'? Hence he is constantly contradicting himself in various parts of his volume (e.g. the angel at the pool of Bethesda—Vol. I p. 103 [p. 133 in ed. 2]). In edition 1 he says it was certainly a later interpolation, in edition 2 he says probably. Or in Vol. II p. 421: 'the passage did originally belong to the text but has from an early period been omitted from the mss. on account of the difficulties it presents'—and then he gives reasons.

(7) Improbability of Historicity based on Overpressing St. Luke's verbage (S.R. p. 155). This is an inference drawn by S.R. from what is said in Acts 6:12. *Response—The incidents must have taken some time, and may have taken*

---

[20]Here and elsewhere W+H is always the abbreviation for Lightfoot's two colleagues Westcott and Hort, and their then-new critical edition of the Greek New Testament. In this manuscript we employ the W+H text of the Greek NT that Lightfoot used, except at these points where he corrected their text because he thought them to be mistaken.

some considerable amount of time. The false interpretations silenced, the tumult excited among the people, the worry of the elders and scribes, the summoning of the council from all parts of Jerusalem under the presidency of the high priest. Indeed the text suggests a current of apprehension was implied. Further, the council meets as a regular meeting of the Sanhedrin, and the accused is asked if he pleads guilty and thus he makes his defense.

But S.R. asks, How came the record to be preserved? *Response—Feats of memory are not uncommon, especially among the Jews. The Talmud speaks of traditions [orally] preserved for centuries, especially materials from the sacred books. The same could be said of the materials in the Gospels. But we need not rely just on that. Notes would have been taken at such a meeting and kept. Public notes certainly, private notes probably. There is evidence of scribes using shorthand in this era (see Meyer, Latin Literature, p. 175, referring to some of Cicero's speeches, Galen, Hippolytus, comp. Justin, Apolog. I.35).*

(8) It is complained that there are inaccuracies, more specifically 'glaring contradictions of the statements in the Old Testament' (S.R. p. 157). *Response—The real particulars of these inaccuracies I will speak to hereafter, but they show, so far as they bear on the argument at all, they in fact speak to the genuineness of the speech, much more natural in the hurry of a spoken address or of a shorthand report, than in a rhetorical effort composed in the calm of the study. Indeed some of these errors are quite improbable on the thesis that this speech is a later fiction. Just in proportion as these errors are 'glaring' so they are unlikely to be contrived.*

(9) The Resemblances between the Stephen Speech and the later Speeches of Peter and Paul (pp. 159-60). He suggests that the author has perhaps inserted here some passages out of the Pauline epistles—Rom 1:24; 2:29; Gal 3:19. *Response—But St. Paul may well have been influenced by St. Stephen.*

S.R. derives some narrative from the Gospel of St. Luke, thus it is made to do double duty. Of the rest some is taken from other speeches in Acts—Acts 22:1; 27:24; 22:14. Then there are resemblances to the speech of St. Peter—vs. 5 an allusion to the covenant given to Abraham, vs. 32 'the God of Abraham, Isaac, and Jacob.' *Response—But these are all most familiar expressions to the ear of a Jew, they occur again and again in Jewish prayers. We should rather expect some of these sorts of expressions in a Jewish speech of any length.*

He points to vs. 37—a quotation from Deut 18:15. It is quoted in a different way in the two passages. Scribes have seen this and sought to make them conform [to each other]. It is quoted for instance in Clemen. Hom. iii.53. And yet he says (p. 21) 'no use pretending that the Clemen. Hom. provide any evidence of the use or existence of the Acts.' *Response—The fact is that this was a recognized text among the Jews and a commonplace of the earliest Christian preachers. And this same remark applies to the text of vs. 52. The fact is that Justin Dial. 16 is much nearer to this passage, yet S.R. doesn't even give it a place among the 'more distant analogies.'*

He further points to the speech of St. Paul at Antioch, the opening address with the mention of the choice of the Fathers, the sojourn in Egypt, the driving out of the Canaanites, the raising up of David—Acts 18:17-19. *Response—This is all the similarity there is even though St. Stephen's speech occupies 52 verses, whereas St. Paul's 25-26 verses. Do these resemblances really need any explanation? If anything, the similarities are rather less than one might have expected. Stephen preached to Jews (cf. Paul at Antioch), but take Paul's speech at the Areopagus or to the Ephesian elders at Miletus, and things appear in a different light. When the speakers are in the same position, addressing the same audience, on the same topics, coincidences are to be expected. When addressing Jews appeals [are made] to their past history, to the past glories of the race (cf. Ps 44:1; 78; 89; 105; 106; 114; 135). We may compare similar appeals to past history, past glories in speeches to Athenians, for example before the battle of Salamis.*

(10) But the Author's Chief Argument has to do with the Language. On this score he goes into an elaborate analysis (pp. 164ff.). The point of it is that the speech betrays all the peculiarities of Luke's diction, and that therefore it was not taken from some previous report, but rather composed and inserted by the author (see especially p. 177). *Response—Now it does not appear to have occurred to this author to ask himself one preliminary question—Is it not possible that the speech, in the main, is the speech of St. Stephen, and yet still here and there the author (St. Luke) put together the rough report so that some indications of his own diction should appear? Is this not only possible, but even probable? At least when he only half asks the question and then turns away from answering it? (p. 177) The fact is lost on him that a detailed accurate report of a long speech is not to be looked for, is improbable. Not only are [his*

*accounts of things] purely arbitrary, and incapable of proof, they are opposed
to the facts of the case. In regard especially to the facts of the case [when we
are dealing with facts] they have coincidences [with other facts] and they shall
coincide.*

*Detailed attention to the speech brings even more to light, for example the
speech's deep indebtedness to the* LXX *in places. For example consider the quote
of Ex 2:14 or the use of Ex 3:3. Or in Acts 7:40 the use of Ex 32:1 and the quote
from Amos 5:26.* εἰσάγειν *is the common word in the* LXX *for bringing into the
promised land. In this one section of the speech we have twenty words from
direct quotation, four more from the larger OT context. Out of a total of 83
words here, only 37 are not accounted for as coming from the* LXX *citation or
paraphrase. Close scrutiny of the linguistic usage in Acts 7 here shows: 1) deep
indebtedness to the OT, particularly the* LXX, *though there is a freedom to
paraphrase or even use some words in a different way, and 2) no real possibility
that it was constructed out of Pauline snippets here and there, contra S.R. So
for instance . . . as to words used in a different way: 1)* βῆμα *already cited,
always elsewhere 'tribunal'; 2)* ἐκτιθέναι *'to expose' of children comp. Ex 18:5
but elsewhere* ἐκτιθέναι *to expose but* ἐκτίθεσθαι *'to expand' Acts 11:4; 18:26;
28:23; 2) words not used for any special purposes in the Acts compared to the
other parts of the NT. e.g. Paul's epistles, where we could come up with 86
words just from the four capital Paulines, and 139 from the whole. Of the total
of 156 words in the Stephen speech, only four are really used in ways in Paul
that comport with their use here, though there are broader parallels: Here are
a few examples: a)* δυνατός *appears in Acts but is more common in Paul;
b)* ἀπωθεῖν *much more common in St. Paul; c)* εὐφραίνειν *only Acts 2:26 from
the* LXX, *only six times in St. Luke's Gospel (four in the prodigal son story),
three times in St. Paul, three times in Revelation, but 220 times in the* LXX;
d)* ἐξαποστέλλειν *used some six times in Acts (one in St. Paul's speech), three
times in Luke's Gospel, nine in St. Paul (Gal 4:4, 6) but some 250 times in the
LXX, often used of the journeys to and from Egypt (Gen 44:3; 45:24); e)* βρέφος,
*not used at all elsewhere in Acts, five times in Luke (mostly of our Lord's in-
fancy), 2 Tim 3:15; 1 Pet 2:2; f) if we turn to phrases like 'the most high'
(ὁ ὑψίστος) in the absolute Luke 1:32, 35, 76; 6:35, four times in Acts, or 'God most
high' (ὁ θεός ὁ ὑψίστος Acts 16:17; Mark 5:7; Heb 7:1) this phrase occurs 23 times
in the Psalms alone, always with the phrase 'most high' applied to the Biblical*

God, except once, and 14 times (counting vocatives) in the absolute. When one surveys the parallels to every single word in the Stephen speech, it is a remarkable list. **Not a single word which is not a common word, and not a single word unique to this speech and St. Luke's writings.**[21] *Of S.R.'s. list of forty five words which betray the hand of St. Luke (pp. 172sq.), eleven are not in this speech at all, of the other thirty four, most can clearly be accounted for out of the* LXX *(see the parallels in vss. 7-42), or as common words in Greek, including in the Greek New Testament.* But what about Luke's use of ἀνήρ, at the beginning of speeches, here and at Acts 22:1 in this particular manner (addressed to the same audience)? In Acts 11:32 and Acts 17:22 we also have the use of ἀνήρ but with the ethnic extraction of the audience. The fact is we have nothing to compare these examples to in the Gospels or in the Epistles because there are no set addresses there. But this may be based on a Hebraism (see Gen 13:8).[22]

In sum, the arguments against the genuineness of the speech entirely failed. Are there any arguments in its favor? The strongest. Firstly, there is the strong presumption from the known character of the author. There is his approach in the Gospel [to his source material], which we can test. Does his account turn from being a narration of facts which actually occurred and words which were actually spoken suddenly to becoming a narration of lies?

S.R. presents us with the old dilemma—'He [Luke] has an uncritical eye, and the Christian circle was an especially uncritical circle. They would receive or believe anything.' This argument is urged by no one more strongly

---

[21]The pattern here is clear enough, and Lightfoot's point is—*there is nothing in the Stephen speech that could not have come from reflection on the OT by Stephen himself, particularly reflection on the* LXX, *nothing that requires the theory that it was derived from elsewhere in the NT, and nothing that requires the thesis that it was an invention of the author of Acts.* This is the conclusion to which Lightfoot is driving by providing this vast amount of linguistic data to refute S.R.'s arguments. As the lecture goes on, in places in the original the handwriting became very difficult to read, in some places impenetrable, but the overall thrust and direction of providing all this linguistic data, and the examples cited above, illustrate his argument clearly enough. For those who want to puzzle out some of the additional examples, there are digital images of the Lightfoot pages, now housed in Asbury Seminary Library. Fortunately, the handwriting is clearer as he concludes his lecture by turning around and providing argument in favor of the genuineness of the speech, to which we now turn. (BW3)

[22]In other words, Lightfoot's point is that the lack of parallels is due to the differences in types of material. It does not necessarily provide evidence that the "author" was freely inventing and composing this material out of whole cloth. (BW3)

than the author of *Supernatural Religion*. Now this statement is exaggerated, but there is a substantial amount of truth at the bottom of it. But what then? This is a double-edged weapon and the other edge is quite as keen, perhaps even keener than the one S.R. wields. The age which is too uncritical to detect [fraud] is *a fortiori* too uncritical to *insert* any narrative, more especially, any long and varied narrative (like the Acts of the Apostles), that might bear any slight resemblance to verisimilitude. As for the Acts of the Apostles, there is no book in the New Testament like it, and hardly any contemporary book like it. The various localities, the various persons (Jewish, Christian, heathen), the multitude of occurrences—we have geography, history, archaeology (Jewish, Christian, Greek, Roman) and yet how readily in keeping with these settings and persons—Athens—we see Athenian life as it was, Ephesus—Ephesian ideas and customs abound, Jerusalem—everything in keeping.

Or look at it from another point of view—not from its relationship to external facts but as to its internal character: 1) half-telling an incident or speech; 2) the list of names (e.g. of deacons) is incomplete; 3) the growth and change reported and seen in the narrative. Consider the authenticity of the Semitic character of the early part of the narrative, the freedom and expansion of the later parts when the Gospel enters into the world of Greece. Or consider these very speeches in Acts—the similarity of speeches spoken under similar circumstances is an argument in favor of their genuineness, if (but not otherwise) the speeches spoken under different circumstances differ. *And this is the case.*

Consider the speech to the Ephesian elders, replete with Pauline expressions and turns of thought, or take the speech at the Areopagus and the very presence of a philosophical audience.[23] While there is similarity in the speeches there is also dissimilarity—the Pauline ideas only show up first in a Pauline speech (13:38-39). There is nothing like this in the earlier speeches in Acts.

In fact S.R. comes up with a totally impossible character for the writer of Acts. At one moment he is the stupidest of the stupid. At the next moment he is Shakespeare and a Mommsen in one. If he made St. Peter, and St.

---

[23]He means a philosophically sophisticated audience. (BW3)

Stephen, and St. Paul at Antioch refer to the same topics because he had not wits enough to vary the speeches, he must be considered to be the acme of stupidity. And yet this is the same man who presents us with the speech of this same Paul at Miletus and the believably authentic report of his sojourn in Ephesus. We are presented with an utter improbability—that Luke had a worse critical eye than we find in The Clementine Homilies, the Apocryphal Gospels, and the Greek Romances.

Now to turn to the speech in itself, I say it never could have been created by a fraud. It could not because: 1) it serves no purpose! There is no doctrine (Petrine or Pauline) enunciated, there is no aim served, and it is, in places, unintelligible, such that critics in this century are debating eagerly what it means. It serves no literary purpose either, it is incongruous and out of place. Least of all would it have served any purpose in the second century (the supposed time when S.R. suggests it was composed—comp. p. 159), as it makes no appeal to any subject that would have interested [the church then]. It is one thing to point to the arguments in the speech [as a sign of invention] but *not to the contradictions*. Take for instance the reference to the burial of the patriarchs in vs. 15 or the quote from Amos in vs. 43. There is a stubborn residuum in this speech that will not allow the explanation on these grounds, this theory of free composition. 2) It would not. This sort of speech could have only arisen out of the circumstances of the case. A close examination shows that while the incidences in the speech are applicable to the situation, yet they are never applied. The purport then is buried deep below the surface. It has to be unearthed by the careful examination of criticism. The fact is, that the speech is hurried towards the end. There are signs of a brewing tumult. The systematic application is never made, but indignant remonstrance takes its place, yet there is no explanation of all this. The consequent result of this is the apparent purpose is left in the dark. *Certainly invention never indulges in such vagary.* If this is artifice, it is the most consummate artifice. But supposing it is an actual speech then everything is explained, more specifically the errors in the speech. They could arise out of the haste of speaking or more likely the haste of the report. Errors crop up in part due to compression. I close with an example of what the full evidence looks like before compression.

In regard to the error about the burial of the patriarchs, the facts in the

Old Testament are these: 1) Abraham purchased Machpelah—Gen 23:8 sq.; 2) Jacob purchased a field at Schechem from the children of Hamor, the father of Schechem Gen 33:19; 3) Jacob was buried at Machpelah where Abraham and Isaac lay Gen 47:30; 49:30 sq.; 4) Joseph was buried at Schechem Ex 13:19; Gen 1:26; Josh 24:32. 5) of the burial of Joseph's brothers nothing is said in the Old Testament. Note that compression of multiple pieces of data seems to have happened in the report of the call of Abraham as well.

It seems to have been a formal belief of the Jews that the bodies were brought up from Egypt, see Josephus *Ant.* ii.8.2 i.e. that their bodies were transferred to Palestine while their children were still living, and long before the Exodus. Though the tradition is worth very little as historical evidence, yet it is far from improbable in itself. The body of Joseph would be kept back, as he was an Egyptian prince. See *Bell. Jud.* iv.9.7, on this account of the patriarchs, the Egyptians had no claims. If they were relocated then, there bodies would most naturally be buried at Hebron in the hereditary sanctuary where Abraham and Sarah, Isaac and Rebecca, Jacob and Leah lay. On the other hand some rabbinical writers speak as though they were translated at the Exodus. In this case, they would have naturally been buried at Schechem for the same reason for which Joseph was buried there. It was the 'first fruit' of the conquest as the Israelites emerged from the desert. Stanley's *Sinai and Palestine*, p. 233. See Lightfoot, *Apostolic Fathers* II, p. 668.

Simon, the Samaritans, and Philip
(Acts 8)

Vs. 1 Σαῦλος, the name. Saul, the son of Kish, a Benjaminite, not only used of St. Paul in Acts (see Acts 13:21). St. Paul belongs to the tribe of Benjamin (Rom 11:1; Phil 3:5). But it is a name not confined to Benjaminites. It occurs among the descendents of Levi (1 Chron 6:24) and of a son of Simeon (Gen 46:10; Ex 6:15) and a Canaanite, hence the Saulites (Num 26:13; 1 Chron 4:29). It is even an Edomite name (Gen 36:37; 1 Chron 1:48-49). There has been a conjecture that Saul/Shaul derives from the Hebrew for Sheol. When not referring to the son of Kish it is always spelled Shaul in the A.V. except Gen 36:37. In *Antiquities* 20.9.4 Josephus mentions one Σαῦλος a member of the royal Herodian house. In *Bell. Jud.* ii.10.4, ii.20.1 one who gained a certain notoriety in the Jewish War. Mishnah *Sand.* xi.1 we have one Abba Shaul. Always in St. Luke it is Σαῦλος. St. Luke continues to call him by his Jewish name (though not by the Jewish form of the name) until Acts 13:9.

As for his age, Acts 7:58—νεανίας. Hippocrates in Philo *de Munf. Op.* 25M says παίδιον ages 1-7, παῖς 8-14, μειράκιον 15-21, νεανίσκος to 28, ἀνήρ to 49, πρεσβύτης to 56. Dion Cassius calls Caesar a νεανίσκος when he is about forty. Galen xvii.2 says νεανίσκος = 25-35 while μειράκιον = 18-24. D. Laertius, *Pythag.* viii.10—παῖς = 1-20, νεανίσκος = 21-40, γενικής = 41-60, γέρων = 61-80. Galen ix defines the limit of νεανίσκος as 35. Paul's sister's son is called νεανίας—Acts 23:17sq. in the year A.D. 58. This again does not advance our understanding of Paul's age. But in Philemon vs. 9, Paul calls himself πρεσβύτης in about A.D. 62. But, for example, Basil dies at fifty and he calls himself an 'old man.' πρεσβύτης in fact = πρεσβευτής comp. Eph 6:20.

ἦν συνευδοκῶν (stronger than συνευδόκει) expressing permanence. See Baumg. p. 174. There is nothing in the narrative here that suggests he was a member of the Sanhedrin. On the contrary he is only introduced afterwards. In Acts 26:10 ἀναιρουμένων τε αὐτῶν κατήνεγκα ψῆφον might seem to imply this, and though not precise (for this might be meant figuratively here), this seems to be the more probable interpretation. If so νεανίας cannot be taken to mean early youth. He must be at least twenty. Could Saul be a married man? Compare 1 Cor 7:7 and the statement of Clement of Alexandria (in Eusebius *H.E.* iii.30) rests on a false interpretation of two passages—Phil 4:3 and 1 Cor 9:5. It is not a tradition.

χώρας country or district see Luke 21:21 (comp. John 4:35; James 5:4; Acts 26:11).

τῶν ἀποστόλων See the tradition of Apollonius (in Eusebius *H.E.* v.18; comp. Clement of Alex. *Strom.* vi.).

ἐν τῇ ἡμέρᾳ ἐκείνῃ[1] 'at that time' i.e. it began on that day. I have found no instance in which the phrase has a final sense, although it is once used in the Gospel of the last day, but this is no parousia reference here.

πάντες not literally.

Vs. 2 συνεκόμισαν—a pregnant expression (comp. Soph. *Aj.* 1067).

ἄνδρες εὐλαβεῖς i.e. probably Jews not Christians as the circumstances seem to suggest (comp. Luke 2:25; Acts 2:5; 22:12; See Baumg. p. 172). For the opposition—implied in δέ (v. 2) and the second δέ (v. 3) points to this sense.

As for the scene of the martyrdom, on the gate of St. Stephen (comp. Robinson, I p. 321sq.). From an early period in church history unto the 15th century, a gate to the north of the city (probably Damascus gate). From the 15th century on, an east gate leading to the valley of Jehoshephat, in particular the more southern of the east gates of the city. Even the earlier tradition is too late to be of any value (com. C+H I p. 89sq.). On the legend of what happened to Stephen's body (A.D. 415) see Augustine *Op.* vii. 2sq. On the tradition that the body was buried by Lucien, priest of Caphar-Gamala. Appearances of Gamaliel to Lucien (and also to a monk), searching the place of the bodies by himself (of Absalom, Nicodemus, Stephen). The bodies

---

[1]Note that Lightfoot uses a different word order than that used in Westcott and Hort and Nestle-Aland 27/28. (TDS)

found, the name Celiel = Στέφανος. Moved later to Jerusalem. The story was apparently believed by Augustine.

Vs. 4 Οἱ μὲν οὖν The work of Stephen is taken up by Philip: 1) preacher to the Samaritans; 2) preacher to the barbarian proselyte.[2]

EXCURSUS: SIMON MAGUS[3]

We shall see presently, that there is very good reason for subscribing to that view of early Church writers which represented Simon Magus as the father of Gnosticism. If this be the case, we shall be at no loss to understand the position, which this account of the Apostles' collision with Simon Magus occupies, in the narrative of St. Luke. We have just been reading the account of the conflict of the church with Judaism (as represented by the Sanhedrin, the spiritual leaders of the Jews), and we now are directed to its conflict with Gnosticism in the person of Simon Magus. These two forms of error, Judaism and Gnosticism, being the Scylla and Charybdis of the Christian Church, the two precipices between which her paths lay, and between which it still lies, for Judaism and Gnosticism are constantly recurring under different names but with the same characteristics in the main—the one a heartless formalism tied down to ritual observances, a religion material and unspiritual, the other a spirit of lawless and unbridled speculation not infrequently accompanied by moral depravity, the natural deduction of its unjustifiable premises.

Thus then this part of the narrative, the contact of the Apostles with Simon Magus, is not only important in itself, but also as representing the

---

[2]See Lightfoot, *Galatians*, p. 298 5th ed.

[3]It is perhaps here in this excursus, and to some degree in the one on Stephen's speech, that we find Lightfoot could have most benefited from this last century of careful study of early Judaism and Gnosticism, for to a considerable degree he is wrong on both counts. Gnosticism probably did not exist in the first century A.D. and probably cannot be traced back to Simon the Magician (and Luke does not suggest it can) and perhaps more importantly the caricature of early Judaism as essentially a religion of heartless and unspiritual formalism and mere ritual is in no way a fair representation of the great diversity and variety we find in early Judaism, as has been shown by, among others, two later Lightfoot Professors at Durham—J. D. G. Dunn and John M. G. Barclay. One can also say that what we now know about first-century Samaritanism does not suggest it was riddled with Gnostic mysticism whatever may have been the case with Simon. To the contrary it seems to have been another temple-centered form of early Judaism with messianic expectations, and its sacred texts were just the books of the Pentateuch, not unlike Sadducean thinking. On this see Ben Witherington III, *John's Wisdom* (Louisville: Westminster John Knox, 1995). (BW3)

struggles which accosts the church from time to time. And thus it is, as we have seen to be the case, with most if not all the circumstances hitherto narrated in Acts—that we have here another *representative fact*.

Simon Magus was a native of Ghita in Samaria. We have this on the authority of Justin Martyr, his fellow countryman. Josephus mentions one Simon who was an accomplice of the procurator, Felix, and aided him in his suit with Druscilla, by his sorceries (see Neander, Pfl. I, p. 108). Josephus however says that Simon is a Cyprian. In this he is probably in error, confusing Ghita with Citium (see Alford). The account of Justin Martyr is more trustworthy as coming from a fellow countryman, and as being more precise (giving the exact place of his birth).[4]

The story of his worship at Rome is founded on an error of Justin Martyr, the discovery of the famous stone with the inscription in the exact spot described by Justin Martyr *Apol. I* 69D [or Chapter 26] is sufficient proof of this—(ἀνδριὰς ἀνεγήγερται ἐν τῷ τίβερι ποταμαῷ μεταξὺ τῶν δυὸ γεφυρῶν). 'There was a Samaritan, Simon, a native of the village called Gitto, who in the reign of Claudius Caesar, and in your royal city of Rome, did mighty acts of magic, by virtue of the art of the devils operating in him. He was considered a god, and as a god was honoured by you with a statue, which statue was erected on the river Tiber, between the two bridges, and bore this inscription, in the language of Rome—Simoni Deo Sancto, To Simon the holy God. And almost all the Samaritans, and a few even of other nations, worship him, and acknowledge him as the first god.'

Though in itself the fact is not improbable, when we consider the elasticity of Roman mythology and remember the story that Tiberius offered a place in the Pantheon for a statue of Christ, it becomes improbable. It is remarkable as well that whereas Irenaeus and others repeated Justin's story uncritically, Hippolytus who certainly had the treatise of Irenaeus before him, when writing about Simon, passes over the story in silence. He was Bishop of Pontus and resided in Rome in the very neighborhood and therefore had the means of knowing the falsehood of the story (see Bunsen, *Hippolytus* second edition, vol. I, p. 354).

There seems to have been great religious activity among the Samaritans

---

[4]On this place see Illgen, Zeitschrift, 1841, Fasc. 3, p. 18sq. and Otto.

at this time. They were susceptible in their impressions and easily imposed upon by the sorceries of pretended magicians and by the fancies of Oriental mysticism. Their name had become a byword among the Jews—'you are a Samaritan and have a demon' i.e. dealers in magical arts and witchcraft and evidences of demonical possession (see Thes. i. p. 89). They, at the same time, were looking forward to the coming of the Messiah, which they expected under the name of 'the Restorer.' This indiscriminating superstition will easily account for the relation in which they are exhibited in the narrative both to Simon and to the Apostles. No less than three early founders of heretical sects in the first century are Samaritans—Doscitheus, Simon, and Menander (Simon's disciple—on him see Justin *Apol. I* 69E, 91b). Christianity seems to have faired no better in Samaria than in Judea (see Justin I 99B [or Chapter 56]—'demons put forward other men, the Samaritans Simon and Menander, who did many mighty works by magic, and deceived many, and still keep them deceived. For even among yourselves, as we said before, Simon was in the royal city Rome in the reign of Claudius Cæsar, and so greatly astonished the sacred senate and people of the Romans, that he was considered a god, and honoured, like the others whom you honour as gods, with a statue').

While Simonism which had more in it to satisfy their tastes for the marvelous and their love of mysticism, flowing through there luxuriantly (nearly the whole nation was Simonians—see the quote above), Origen says that in his own day, he might be overstating the case in reckoning them at 30. Probably the superstition had nearly died in the rest of the world, but it is probable that in the land of its birth, it still prevailed to an extent, about which Origen was not aware.

It is difficult to ascertain the exact doctrines taught by Simon Magus. A book called 'the Great Announcement' was the Bible of the Simonians and was reputed to have been written by Simon himself. It is referred to by name, and large extracts of it are given in Hippolytus and it was apparently in the hands of Irenaeus. This book was probably written at the close of the first century, by a disciple of Simon (probably Menander) and would stand in the same relationship to its teachings as the writings of Plato to that of Socrates. In the broad lines then, we may recognize the doctrines inculcated by Simon himself, and in fact it agrees with the allusions in the Acts. Simon seems to have held all the characteristic opinions of Gnosticism, for 1) he maintained the doctrine of emanations and their incarnation, 2) he was a dualist (if we may judge from the opinions associated with him), i.e. he held that the creator of the world, the Demiurge, was inferior to God, the absolute Being, and 3) he seems (unless he is maligned by orthodox writers) to have turned his own mystical doctrines to account in justifying his own sensuality and impurity. This was an excess which characterized the more degraded form of Gnosticism.

Οὗτός ἐστιν ἡ δύναμις τοῦ Θεοῦ ἡ καλουμένη μεγάλη (Acts 8:10). There is no doubt that δύναμις here means an emanation. ἡ μεγάλη δύναμις is frequently used in 'the Great Announcement' for the primary emanation (not an 'angel' as De Wette and Alford are disposed to take it). There is no necessity of supposing any immediate connection with the Alexandrian logos doctrine, for this doctrine was held in other forms by Oriental mystics. But even such a connection with Alexandria is not out of the question. We have no need to presume any knowledge behind and in Samaritan hearers or anything more than a susceptibility for such mystical speculations. Simon himself may have learned it from the Alexandrian school and imported it into Samaria. And the language in the Acts seems to show that the doctrine was new to his hearers. At least so I conclude from the word ἡ καλουμένη. It would seem that Simon had been harassing them, and explaining what was meant by this 'greatest emanation'—*the emanation* and how it came to be embodied in him. The people catch up the notion and as newly instructed they style it 'the power which is called Great.' If it had been a familiar notion to them they would not have used the word ἡ καλουμένη.

Was Simon a Christian in any sense of the term? Consider the judgment of Irenaeus, l.c. xxiii. no.1 [Book I, Chapter 33]—'This man, then, was glorified by many as if he were a god; and he taught that it was himself who appeared among the Jews as the Son, but descended in Samaria as the Father while he came to other nations in the character of the Holy Spirit. He represented himself, in a word, as being the loftiest of all powers, that is, the Being who is the Father over all, and he allowed himself to be called by whatsoever title men were pleased to address him.'

But Hippolytus (vi.19, p. 66) seems to refer this to someone else—εἰς ἐπανόρθωσιν ἐληδυθεναι αὐτόν (who? For there is no antecedent) ἔφη (σε ὁ Σίμων) μεταμορφούμενον καί ἐξομοιδουμενος . . . We cannot refer αὐτόν to the same person. As for ἔφη, this would require αὐτός. Yet there is no antecedent given. Ireneaus (or his editor) attributes it to Simon himself. Bunsen suppresses the use of αὐτόν in Hippolytus and refers to Christ, but there is nothing in the Greek text to lead us to this conclusion. Ought we to read ἑαυτόν in Hippolytus or does αὐτόν refer to 'God' or 'the Logos'? At all events, Bunsen appears to be wrong in saying that it does not refer at all to Simon himself. The words in Irenaeus are explicit and point this explanation . . . i.e. that ἡ μεγάλη δύναμις which was now incarnate in him (i.e. Simon) was the same that had assumed a bodily form in Jesus who seemed to have suffered in Judaea. This ἡ μεγάλη δύναμις manifested itself in Jesus in Judaea as *the Son*, it was now manifesting itself in a higher form (such was his blasphemy) in Simon himself in Samaria *as the Father* and among other nations as *the Holy Spirit*.

This conclusion is both in accord with the Gnostic doctrine of successive incarnations of the same δύναμις and also agrees with Simon's (or Simonism's) teaching in regard to Helen, assuming her to be the same as Helen of Troy etc. If this be true we can understand how on the one hand Simon should be regarded as the father of Gnostic Christian heretics, and on the other hand Origen should say (see Alford) λανθάνει τὸν κέλσον etc. If this heresy was grafted on to Christianity, we can account more easily for its spread in Samaria.

This highest emanation, which Simon identified with himself, is called (μεγάλη ἀπόφασις), ἡ ἀπέραντος δύναμις. ἡ ῥίζα τῶν ὅλαν, τὸπυες. ὁ ἑστώς, στάς, στησομενος . . . phrases using either δύναμις or μεγάλη, from which is said to proceed six other emanations in three pairs—ἐν δὶ τουτοις ἅπασιν ἐμμέμικτας καὶ κέκραται, ὡς ἔφην, ἡ μεγάλη δύναμις ἡ ἀπέραντος, ὁ ἑστώς. And he turned the Mosaic cosmology to account in support of his views.

Vs. 5 εἰς πόλιν τῆς Σαμαρείας 'to a city of Samaria' probably Shechem— but Alford's note is grammatically as bad as it can be. For in the first place in the parallel passage John 4:5 πόλιν τῆς Σαμαρείας, evidently means 'a city,' as the addition λεγομένην Συχὰρ should (if it has been that city which is called it would have been τὴν π.τ.Σ. τὴν λεγ. Ζ). Secondly, in 2 Pet 2:6 the names of the cities are given and therefore the definite article is unnecessary. Thirdly, though εἰς πόλιν by itself might mean to 'town' viewing the metropolis as the 'town' or 'city' par excellence, εἰς πόλιν τῆς Σ. certainly cannot mean to *the* (chief) town of Samaria. Fourthly instead of ἐν τῇ πὸλει ἐκείνη we should have had some other phrase.

vs. 9 τὸ ἔθνος not τὸν λαόν

Vs. 10 ἡ καλουμένη μεγάλη These words are certainly part of the original text. It is strange that they should have been ignored by Neander, Bunsen, Schaff and others, as they certainly aid in explaining the pretensions of something.

Vs. 13 ἐπίστευσεν in a low sense—His belief is evidenced by his offering money for the gift of the Spirit.

Vs. 17 See Baumg. Vol. i.p. 190 sqq. who seems to take the correct view of this circumstance.

Vs. 18—'Simony' misapplied in common usage.

Vs. 23 ὄντα εἰς χ.

χολὴν πικρίας καὶ σύνδεσμον ἀδικίας. χολὴν πικρίας—bitter gall. cf. Deut 29:10; Heb 12:15. Referring chiefly to his influence on others (cf. Heb l.c.).

σύνδεσμον ἀδικίας—LXX. lviii.8 referring to his own spiritual state.

Vs. 25 Εὐαγγελίζειν and εὐαγγελίζεσθαι are very frequent in St. Luke's Gospel and the Acts. There is one instance only in the other Evangelists—Mt 11:51. These verbs occur frequently in St. Paul.

εὐηγγ. governs an accusative, either of the tidings themselves or of the recipients of them.

κώμας villages, see Alford.

Vs. 26 The narrative leads us to suppose that St. Philip did not return to Jerusalem with the Apostles. We left him in the neighborhood of Sychar, and the mention of ἀπὸ Ἰερουσαλήμ would be unnecessary if Philip were at Jerusalem.

ἐπὶ τὴν ὁδὸν—αὔτη—i.e. 'the road'—not contrasting it with any other road to Gaza. The words are clear so far, but with other roads which he might have taken.

Vs. 32 ἡ δὲ περιοχὴ 'the passage' called in Hebrew פרשיות. On the sections of the Old Testament see Davidson, *Bible Comm.* I p. 56. Isaiah 53:7-8—cited almost verbatim from the LXX, as indeed we might have expected the Ethiopian to read it out of this version. In vs. 7 the Hebrew and Greek agree, in vs. 8, some difference. For Ἐν τῇ ταπεινώσει ἡ κρίσις αὐτοῦ ἤρθη the Hebrew has words which in the E.V. are translated 'he was taken from prison and from judgment' but in the margin 'he was taken away by distress and judgment, but' and this is rendered by Bishop Jowett 'by an opportune judgment.' The lxx seems to mean (so Meyer) 'His trial ended abruptly in his humiliation.'

ἤχθη—he was done away with. Either the reading of the lxx translators was different or they have mistranslated.

Vs. 33 τὴν γενεὰν αὐτοῦ τίς διηγήσεται—γενεάν, Hebrew דּוֹרוֹ (fr. דּוֹר) 'to move in a circle.' Bishop Jowett's translation 'his manner of living' makes admirable sense, but the Hebrew דּוֹר seems scarcely to bear that meaning (did Rab. Loewe so interpret it?), and still less can γενεάν take that translation. Nor does the interpretation which Meyer and Alford adopt—'the wickedness of his contemporaries' seem at all natural, requiring as it does, so much to be supplied. May it not be 'yet who shall declare (what tongue can tell of) the character of his times (the wonders of messiah's days),' so that the words would be parenthetical? What a contrast to the humiliation he underwent. [ἡ γενεὰ is otherwise interpreted of His eternal sonship.] In this case ὅτι will attach the sentence following to ἡ κρίσις αὐτοῦ ἤρθη.

There are three ways at least from Jerusalem to Gaza. 1) That of the itineraries: Ceperaria, Eleutheropolis, Ascalon, Gaza—This seems to have been the ordinary 'post-road'; 2) Going South, on the main Southern road as far as Hebron and then branching off; 3) That of Robinson. We might be disposed to think that the road in question was that of the itineraries, as it is described as ἡ ὁδὸς ἡ καταβαίνουσα ἀπὸ Ἰερουσαλὴμ εἰς Γάζαν. But:

(1) The other road seems to be more direct, though not so good a road—and the road of the itineraries deserves rather to be called ἡ ὁδὸς ἡ καταβαίνουσα εἰς Ασκαλαν—as Ascalon was the point at which their road touched the coast and to which therefore it would probably be said καταβαίνειν.

(2) The words κατὰ μεσημβρίαν seem to imply that Philip was to continue his direction southward from Jerusalem whereas the road of the itineraries branches off nearly due west (See Baumg. i. l.c.).

(3) Philip is directed to take the road because it is infrequented (αὕτη ἐστὶν ἔρημος). The road of the itineraries being the main thoroughfare to the coast must have had considerable traffic on it—observe the words too: not ἔρημος γὰρ ἐστί, but αὕτη ἐστὶν ἔρημος.

Tradition points out a pool on the road between Jerusalem to Hebron, as the scene of the Eunuch's baptism. To this it may be objected: First, that this is not strictly speaking on the road leading from Jerusalem to Gaza; second, that this part of the road (being a thoroughfare) was very much frequented. In any case, we must place the scene of the baptism between Hebron and Gaza.

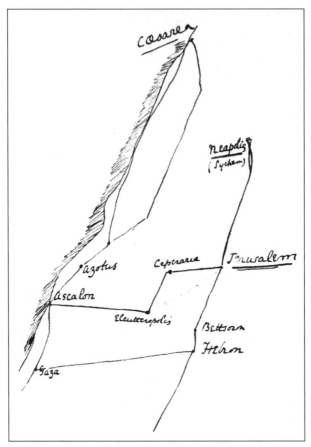

Figure 2. Lightfoot's map of the journey to Gaza and the possible routes

Excursus: Conversion of the Ethiopian

Vs. 34 The word εὐνοῦχος by etymology signifies 'chamberlain,' and though it is sometimes used generally to signify 'an officer of the court,' yet it most frequently implies a physical defect, and as this chamberlain was in the court of Candace, we may suppose that this is the case here. He was evidently a member of a congregation. His knowledge of the Scripture proves this. Besides, the object of his errand to Jerusalem implies it. He would then be a proselyte of the covenant, admitted by circumcision. The Mosaic law however excludes eunuchs from the congregation (Deut 23:1). But from Isaiah 56:3 and from the position of Ebedmelech in the court of Zedekiah (Jer 39:15-17), it would seem that this prohibition had been relaxed. Still the admission of such a person was only a sufferance. The prohibition still stood on the statute-book.

We are therefore to consider the baptism of the Ethiopian Chamberlain as an annulling of all physical disabilities, as that of Cornelius is of all national distinctions. And then Isaiah 56:3, which had a partial fulfillment in the relaxation of the prohibitions, is fully accomplished in Messiah's kingdom.

Observe here, that the case of the Ethiopian, and that of Cornelius are placed in juxtaposition in the prophecy (v. 3)—the Son of the stranger and the Eunuch. We may observe also that the native land of this convert is that same district of upper Egypt (Merve), which is called in the Old Testament Sheba—so that prophecies such as Ps 72:15 receive this accomplishment by this event (see Baumg.).

If we suppose with Meyer and Alford that the Ethiopian was a proselyte of the gate like Cornelius, then we are at a loss to understand the prominence given to the narrative of Cornelius' conversion—and the vision of St. Peter is emptied of its meaning. Evidently the baptism of Cornelius was the *first fruits of its kind.*

Vs. 37 To be omitted.

The Conversion of Saul
(Acts 9)

In Acts 9:1-30 we have the account of Saul's conversion and of his first preaching among the Jews. In Acts 9:31-43 we have the last account of the state of the Jewish churches. Acts 10:1-18 provides the account of the first fruits of the Gentiles—Cornelius and his household. There is an obvious design in the order in which these events occurred and in which they are narrated. The time was drawing near when the Gentiles should be admitted, an apostle was raised up to preach to them. He was a Jew and his conversion is given as a part of the history of the Jewish Church, but it is an immediate preparation for the extension of Christ's Church.

Before arriving at that point however, we have to take our farewell of the Jewish Churches (i.e. the churches of the circumcision—in Judaea and Samaria). The prospect is cheering. Internally, there is the picture of unanimity and trust in God, externally they enjoy peace (cf. Acts 9:31—'the church had rest'). Internally there is the greatest faith and hope and the most godly practice (vs. 26). And the power of the church is exhibited by miracles wrought for others, besides members of the church (Aeneas as well as Dorcas). The scene closes with the crowning miracle of apostolic agency—the raising of the dead to life. This was a fit culmination for the history of the churches of the circumcision. Wherever we come in contact with the churches in Jerusalem and Judaea again, it is in reference to the Gentile heathens, not in regard to its own internal history. With the conversion of Cornelius, we make, as it were, a fresh start.

Vs. 1 ἔτι looks back to Acts 8:3.

ἐμπνέων seems to mean to 'inhale,' 'breathe,' 'draw in breath,' but not 'to breath upon' hence: 1) to inspire, 2) to breathe. Live. American English translation, 'breathing out' thus seems wide of the mark, though 'breathing' would be better. Comp. Ps 17:16: ἀπὸ ἐμπνεύσεως πνεύματος ὀργῆς σου 'from the breathing of the spirit of wrath' cf. Ps.; John 20:22. Meyer is wrong here about this verb, Josh 10:40 does not support him. The preposition of course has some meaning, but not that which Meyer assigns to it. Josh 10–11 some seven times including absolutely 'everything that hath breath.' Comp. Arist. *Ran.* 341, Theocr. xxix.20 (cf. Kühner II p. 307). The word is not found elsewhere in the New Testament.

ἀπειλῆς No ordinary sort of speech, it seems to carry with it the idea of an ardor, not simply the idea of 'communication'?

τῷ ἀρχιερεῖ Caiaphas if before A.D. 37. Thereafter displaced by the son of Annas (Josephus *Ant.* xviii.4.3), who in turn was succeeded by his own brother Theophilus by Pentecost 37 (*Ant.* xviii.5.3). He was high priest from 37–41. See Alford. γένους ἀρχιερατικοῦ (Acts 4:6 explained by Josephus *Ant* xx.9.1—that he had five sons who were high priests).

Vs. 2 ἐπιστολάς comp. Acts 28:21; 2 Cor 3:1. cf. Is 18:1-2 and Lightfoot, *Gal.* p. 93 5th ed.

εἰς Δαμασκὸν πρὸς τὰς συναγωγάς and cf. vs. 20; Josephus *Bell. Jud.* ii.20.2, xix.9.23 speaking of the Jews in Damascus. Comp. 24: 22, 14. On traditional sites comp. Lewin I, p. 49.

τῆς ὁδοῦ John 14:5, 6. So John 10:9: 'I am the door.' On the demand made to James comp. Hegisippus (in Eusebius *H.E.* ii.23). Just as in Acts 1 we have an allusion to the promise of the Comforter, so here to the Johannine notion of Jesus as the door.

Vs. 3 φῶς It was midday Acts 22:6; 26:13. This is presented as fact. There would be no illusion. See Alford.

Vs. 4 φωνὴν In Hebrew [in] Acts 26:14, probably means Aramaic comp. Acts 21:40; 20:2.

Here 'a light shone about him' and 'he fell to the earth and heard a voice saying . . . '

Those with him however had a different experience—οἱ δὲ ἄνδρες οἱ συνοδεύοντες αὐτῷ εἰστήκεισαν ἐνεοί, ἀκούοντες μὲν τῆς φωνῆς, μηδένα δὲ θεωροῦντες (vs. 7).

Vs. 5 Interpolations reflect harmonizing tendency. κύριος εἶπεν from Acts 26:15, ὁ Ναζωραῖος from Acts 22:8. See different manuscript authorities. The readings vary considerably, words having been inserted and altered from the two accounts of the same event from later in Acts, just as we find the text of the Gospel parallels corrupted from the same cause. Erasmus handled them on the basis of the Latin. On the Graeco codicils see Tregelles, *Printed Text*, p. 23.

Examples:

κύριος εἶπεν in the Textus Receptus but should be omitted.

σκληρόν σοι πρὸς κέντρα λακτίζειν found in the Textus Receptus should be omitted. It is very poorly supported and brought in from Acts 22 and Acts 26.

Points of difference in the three narratives:

1) the sight—'They' saw only the light, he also saw the person. Acts 22:9—τὸ μὲν φῶς ἐθεάσαντο; Acts 26:13—περιλάμψαν με φῶς καὶ τοὺς σὺν ἐμοὶ πορευομένους.

2) the sound—'They' only heard the sound, he heard the articulate speech comp. John 12:28-29 which is exactly parallel. On φωνή see Rev 24:2; 19:6. φωνή as voice only, λόγος as intelligible speech. See Ignatius, *Rom.* The accusative is a little more direct than the genitive but no stress can be laid on the change of case. See Kuh. Vol. II p. 309sq.

3) the attitude of the bystanders—Here in Acts 9:7—εἱστήκεισαν ἐνεοί—stood speechless, i.e. are arrested in the moment, all fell to the ground—the after effects πάντων τε καταπεσόντων ἡμῶν, Acts 26:14.

4) the commission—Acts 26:16-18, given at the time of the event. Either: a) it was repeated or b) the account in Acts 26 is comprehensive.

Now the evidential value of these differences is that they suggest: 1) the material is obtained from different documents, and 2) the recorder is trustworthy.

On the apparent discrepancies between the three accounts of the conversion see Baumgar. Vol. I p. 216sq.

St. Paul's Account of the Conversion

1) An interactive objective appearance—1 Cor 9:1; 15:8 cf. Gal 1:1. 2 Cor 12:2 refers to something rather different as the date shows— πρὸ ἐτῶν δεκατεσσάρων (if 2 Cor written in A.D. 58 then this event is in A.D. 45 or 46).

2) No preparation implied—Gal 1:11. A 'miracle' Apostle from a reaction to the lightning flash. Vs. 5 τίς εἰ κύριε, translated συ— see John 4:11, 15, 19; Acts 16:30, but elsewhere in the Acts συ = ἄνδρες Acts 7:26, and in the shipwreck story Acts 27:10, 21, 25.

3) Not at the point recognizing *who* it is, though recognizing it is a person. Indeed the question implies an uncertainty if not an ignorance. Vs. 10—μαθητὴς, Acts 22:12 he is designated a εὐλαβὴς κατὰ τὸν νόμον. This placed him as a mediator between Saul and his countrymen.

Vs. 6 σκληρόν σοι from Acts 26:14 and a bit modified from Acts 22:10.

Vs. 8 αὐτοῦ οὐδὲν ἔβλεπεν as one who could not see, in a state of blindness.

Vs. 10 See Alford's note on Ananias and C+H I, pp. 102, 115 in second edition.

Vs. 11 ἀναστάς or ἀνάστα

Εὐθεῖαν See Conybeare and Howson I, p. 113; Lewin, *St. Paul,* I pp. 53, 69 and the map, Sultan's or Queen St. Traditional house of Judas, Stanley, *Palestine*, p. 109, street of the bazaar. See Rob. *Palestine*, p. 455, various names, reported remains of a colonnade.

Vs. 12 This exactly corresponds to the double miracle involving Peter and Cornelius—Acts 10:3, 10.

Vs. 14 and Acts 9:21; 22:30 ἀρχιερέως; cf. Acts 26:16. See my 'Internal Evidence of St. John' p. 53.

Vs. 15 σκεῦος ἐκλογῆς, i.e. by the will of God to use his own familiar phrase. In the Gospel Mt 22:14 ἐκλεκτος, Mt 24:22, 24, 31 and so also in St. Mark and St. Luke. This may be suggested in the expression in Rom 9:21sq. But in St. Peter 1 Pet 1:1; 2 Pet 1:10 ἐκλεκτός and ἐκλογή respectively and so St. Paul. Col 3:12; 1 Thess 1:4; Rom 9:20. *It denotes God's gracious purpose, but does not necessarily imply God selects.*

υἱῶν τε Ἰσραήλ This was not his special commission, therefore it is added.

Vs. 18 ὡσεὶ λεπίδες comp. Tobit 11:13. On the use of ὡσεί comp. Luke 22:44; Acts 3:24. An analogy is involved, but something tactile. See also Acts 9:8 above.

Vs. 20 εὐθέως κ.τ.λ. comp. Acts 26:20. For ὁ υἱὸς τοῦ θεοῦ = ὁ χριστός see Acts 9:22 below. Comp. Mt 16:16; 26:63; Luke 4:41 on the connecting of the two titles and Luke 22:6; comp. John 1:34; 10:35; 11:27; 20:31.

τὸν Ἰησοῦν with the best manuscripts as the sense requires.

Vs. 21 ὁ πορθήσας He adopts the expression himself in Gal 1:13, but the author of Acts had evidently not seen the Epistle to the Galatians. Comp. Acts 8:3—ἐλυμαίνετο Paley compares 1 Kings 2:38.

ἐληλύθει 'had come' 'was come.' v. l. ἐληλύθεν not so good.

Vs. 22 συμβιβάζων to make to go together, to put together, reconcile, conclude.

Here we must find a place for the journey to Arabia (Gal 1:17).

Vs. 23 ἡμέραι ἱκαναί He went to Arabia. What Arabia? See Lightfoot, *Gal.* p. 89, Lewin, I. p. 55sq. Contrast S.R. III, p. 207. His account falls to the ground if it is remembered: 1) I nowhere said that St. Luke was aware of this visit to Arabia but suggested the contrary; and 2) ἡμέραι ἱκαναί can mean after a considerable period of time, but is it a phrase of sufficient latitude to allow for the journey? We do not know how long St. Paul stayed in Arabia. What we know is that the whole period from the conversion to the trip to Jerusalem was three years. The visit to Arabia was probably unknown to St. Luke, he passes it over as he does St. Paul's second visit to Corinth (during the stay at Ephesus). If we consider the region meant by 'Arabia' this will not seem improbable. See C+H vol I, p. 104. It is our common, modern imprecision in using the word 'Arabia' that causes the difficulty.

It would have been more to the point if S.R. had compared closely the account in Galatians. I perceive that S.R. overlooked the rest of the note. On the relationship between Damascus and Arabia see Justin Mart. *Dial. with Trypho* 305A, yet see Stanley, p. 50.

Vs. 24 καὶ τὰς πύλας is the right reading.

Vs. 25 The incident alluded to in 2 Cor 11:32-33. διὰ τοῦ τείχους here but in 2 Cor 11:33 διὰ θυρίδος. Joshua 2:15; 1 Sam 19:12.

Here ἐν σπυρίδι but in 2 Cor 11:33 ἐν σαργάνῃ. The latter was used especially for fish. σπυρίς is used similarly, especially of fish baskets. σπυρίς, κοφίνος (Mt 16:9-10; Mark 8:19-20) an ordinary loose weave basket of the country.

The reference in 2 Cor 11:32-33 supports several considerations: 1) the motive of the allusion there, the apparent incongruity. The notice, the degradation, the weakness being smuggled away in a basket; 2) the historical circumstances. Difficulties regarding the incident, connected more with the statement in 2 Corinthians than with the account in Acts. Recent discoveries and investigations of inscriptions have shed some light on the subject. Firstly Aretas and Malchus seem to alternate as names of kings of Nabatea. For an earlier Aretas reference see 2 Macc 5:8. Corpus Inscriptiones evidence discussed in de Vogue and Waddington, in *Recovery of Palestine*, p. 110 sq.; de Vogue *Revue d' Archaeolog.* Avril 1864, p. 288. The evidence shows that the dominion of Aretas stretched to the neighborhood of Damascus. Much of the data however dates to the time of the Roman conquest of A.D. 165 under Trajan. There is an Aretas coin with its own dating of 101, but this seems to be equivalent to 37/38 (end of Pilate's reign) or 52/53 Caesarean era. It has Aretas, Philodemus (Oneas) but how is this particular one connected to Damascus? Josephus, *Ant.* xviii.5.1 says Aretas is the father in law to Herod Antipas, tetrarch of Galilee. Herod repudiates his wife for Herodias. There is thus a quarrel between Aretas and Antipas about boundaries, and Antipas is entirely defeated. Tiberius, a friend of Antipas, orders Vitellius to attack Aretas, expedition sets out to Petra, but halts at Jerusalem. News comes of Tiberius' death (March A.D. 37) and Vitellius' campaign is stopped, Vitellius returns to Antioch. We also learn he had a grudge against Antipas (*Ant.* xviii.4.5) and wanted his opportunity to avenge himself. This all occurred therefore shortly before the time [referred to in Acts and 2 Corinthians] of which we are speaking. In former times, Damascus had belonged to the Nabatean kings (*Ant.* xiii.15.2). But for some time before this Damascus had been a free municipality under the Roman governor of Syria. See Boeckh., III, p. 183sq.; Lewin, I, p. 67. But now there are two more important facts: 1) Caesar (A.D. 38) makes a new redistribution of the Eastern provinces in these parts; 2) the heads of Augustus, Tiberius, and Nero and his successors are on the coins of Damascus, BUT not those of Gaius and Claudius (see Eckhel, *Numis.* III, p. 330; Duoment V, p. 285sq.). Therefore, it seems that

Gaius restored to Aretas the city of Damascus that had belonged to his predecessors. This solution is more probable than a temporary seizure of the
city by Aretas. The idea of an ethnarch is of one appointed by a foreign
emperor to rule over his own country (Lucian, *Mae.* 17), see Josephus *Ant.*
xiv.7.2, cf. the edict of Claudius to the Alexandrians (*Ant.* xix.5.2) cf. Strabo
xvii.1.13, Origen *Epistl. To Alex.* 14, 1 Macc 14:4. In any case, St. Paul as a Jew
would be under the Jewish ethnarch. On the comparison with Acts 22:17sq.
see Lightfoot, *Gal.* p. 125.

Vs. 26 On comparison with the narrative in Galatians, see Lightfoot, *Gal.*
p. 91.

Vs. 27 Βαρναβᾶς is the primary person of interest cf. Acts 11:22, 30; 13:2.
Coincident with the change of the name Σαῦλος δὲ ὁ καὶ Παυλος (Acts 13:9)
is the reversal of this practice. Immediately after 13:9 we hear in Acts 13:13 οἱ
περὶ Παῦλον and where the two are again mentioned together (Acts 13:43)
and thenceforth it is Paul and Barnabas (the exception for an exceptional
reason being Acts 14:12, 15). Note the truthfulness of this and the impossibility of creating such a natural effect in an artificial narrative. See C+H vol.
I, p. 113.

πρὸς τοὺς ἀποστόλους See Gal 1:18.

αὐτὸν probably with ἐπιλαβόμενος. The same ambiguity as in Acts 16:19
(see references in *Shep. Hermas* s.v. p. 1668 and Winer no. 37, p. 252; also
Moulton), but in Luke 23:26 Σίμωνα is undoubtedly the reference there with
no ambiguity of construction.

πρὸς τοὺς ἀποστόλους—i.e. Cephas. Gal 1:19 does not necessarily imply
James was an apostle at all, still less that he was one of the Twelve, but see
Gal 1:17.

Vs. 28 εἰς Ἰερουσαλήμ connected with the former verb. On the various
spellings of the city name see my note at Gal 4:26 and my excursus in *Galatians* p. 92. This stay of St. Paul's was only fifteen days duration (Gal 1:19).

Vs. 29 Ἑλληνιστάς He takes up the work of Stephen Acts 6:8. Some few
read Ἑλληνάς but the preferred reading is obviously correct. The internal
and external evidence are at one. On the term for the land, see Acts 11:20
where Ἑλληνάς is correct.

Vs. 30 For ἐπιγνόντες δὲ κ.τ.λ. comp. Acts 22:17sq. and see my *Galatians*,
p. 124. See also my notes on Gal 1:20-21. Vs. 21 there says ἔπειτα ἦλθον εἰς

τὰ κλίματα τῆς Συρίας καὶ τῆς Κιλικίας. He appears to have visited Syria on the way to Tarsus in Cilicia. Probably he would take a ship at Caesarea (Maritima is meant here),[1] and sail to Seleucia and then go on to Antioch (see however C+H I, p. 115). This hurried departure accounts for the fact narrated in Gal 1:22-23—ἤμην δὲ ἀγνοούμενος τῷ προσώπῳ ταῖς ἐκκλησίαις τῆς Ἰουδαίας ταῖς ἐν Χριστῷ, μόνον δὲ ἀκούοντες ἦσαν . . . i.e. out of Jerusalem as he was obliged to very rapidly leave Judaea and go to Caesarea.

κατήγαγον comp. κατελθεῖν Acts 12:19; 25:6, but in Acts 27:22 κατελθεῖν is of the sea voyage. Thus it can mean down from the mountain country (e.g 12:19) or down from the high seas (as in 27:22). And conversely ἀνέβη in Acts 25:1, 'to go up.'[2] A direct revelation from God (see Acts 27:17-21) effected what personal fear alone could not do and he left Jerusalem.

THE CHURCHES OF JUDAEA—FINAL PROSPECTS

THE SECTION Acts 9:30-11:19: 1) the last picture of the Jewish churches (Acts 9:31-43) and 2) Acts 10:1-11:18 the conversion of Cornelius and the principle of extension is established. This ends with ἄρα καὶ τοῖς ἔθνεσιν ὁ θεὸς (Acts 11:18). Thus the principle having been sanctioned by divine action and acquiesced to by the eldest of the apostles, the way is clear for the missionary work of St. Paul. The critical part of the narrative has now arrived. To Acts 11:19 we must compare Acts 8:4. The widening of the mission [begun by Stephen, then Peter].

Vs. 31 The inner life, and vss. 32-43 and the direct mission to the Jews.

καθ' ὅλης On the construction see Winer, p. 457, with a notion of 'covering the whole . . .' (see Alford).

Vs. 32 διὰ πάντων κατελθεῖν with the neuter. It is perhaps not absolutely impossible on grammatical grounds that the phrase διὰ πάντων τῶν ἁγίων might stand but the simple phrase διὰ πάντων with the neuter is much more unusual.

Vs. 34 Ἰησοῦς ὁ Χριστός The article here seems to imply that Aeneas was not one of the saints (Alford strongly makes this point and draws that con-

---

[1] Here is one of the rare places where Lightfoot requires correction, having written Caesarea Philippi by mistake. But in his later notes he does correct himself, saying it is absolutely not Caesarea Philippi, but rather Caesarea Stratonis and cites C+H 1:114n4.

[2] I have noted in these lecture notes a little check mark over a reference from time to time. What this means is that while Lightfoot wrote all of this out from memory, he went back in some cases and double-checked references. (BW3)

clusion). We may add the apparent intended opposition in vs. 36. Ἐν Ἰόππῃ
δέ τις ἦν μαθήτρια.

Vs. 35 τὸν Σαρῶνα See Stanley, p. 255, 499 on the definite article.

Vs. 36 Δορκάς = צְבִי

Vs. 37 ἐν ὑπερῴῳ Not as Alford has it.

Vs. 43 παρά τινι Σίμωνι βυρσεῖ

The Surprising Story of Cornelius
(Acts 10)

We have here the commencement of a new era in the church's history with the conversion of Cornelius. Cornelius is the 'earnest' of the admission of the Gentiles. Consequently we find that great prominence is given to it in the narrative, like was given to the conversion of St. Paul, which was the preparation for this great event. Peter's vision (Acts 10:10, 16-28; 11:5-10) and the vision of Cornelius (10:3-6, 30-32; 11:13-14) are each narrated *three times* (see Bengel). Moreover, as Cornelius' house was the first fruit of the Gentiles, as the Jewish converts of the day of Pentecost were of the Jews, we find the two events brought into parallelism. The outpouring of the Spirit (with the external token of the gift of tongues) is declared by St. Peter to be the same as that manifested on the day of Pentecost. See Acts 10:44 ἐπέπεσεν τὸ Πνεῦμα τὸ Ἅγιον ἐπὶ πάντας τοὺς ἀκούοντας τὸν λόγον and Acts 10:45-46, of which Peter says in Acts 10:47 τούτους, οἵτινες τὸ Πνεῦμα τὸ Ἅγιον ἔλαβον ὡς καὶ ἡμεῖς, and in narrating the event to his countrymen, not what he says in Acts 11:15-17.

And this parallelism is still further enforced by a reference to John the Baptist—the baptism of water as contrasted with the baptism of the Spirit, just as the same reference had been made in the contrast brought out with regard to the day of Pentecost (Acts 1:5). Baumgarten (vol. i. p. 280) however supposes that the form which the gift of tongues here takes is intermediate between that of the day of Pentecost and that of the later Apostolic times. Why did the outpouring of the Holy Spirit precede baptism in this case? (cf.

Schaff, vol. I, p. 263). In any case, the importance of the outward rite is enforced here, as in the case of St. Paul.

Vs. 1 Καισαρίᾳ The capital of Judaea and the seat of the procurators. Cornelius would be one of the Italian bodyguard of the procurator.

Σπεῖρα generally a maniple, but here perhaps a detached cohort. See Baumg. I, p. 263.

Vs. 2 εὐσεβὴς καὶ φοβούμενος τὸν Θεὸν At all events a genuine presentation of the Gospel to the centurion and notice the eagerness he shares with others to hear it (cf. Luke 7:4). Cf. Baumg. I, p. 265. IG 266. This man was a person of rank and importance and already a God-fearer.

τῷ λαῷ i.e. the Jews. When St. Luke speaks of the people of Caesarea generally he uses the term δῆμος, Acts 12:22.

Vs. 10 ἔκστασις ὅραμα Alford's distinction seems to be out of place, see Acts 10:17, 19.

Vs. 11 ἀρχαῖς corners. Cf. Acts 11:5—it simply means the extremities. Perhaps the E.V. is right in translating this 'ends' (as there is no article).

Vs. 12 πάντα τὰ τετράποδα καὶ ἑρπετὰ τῆς γῆς all of the animal kingdoms of the earth.

Vs. 29 Τίνι λόγῳ means 'on what account.' See Iph. *Taur.* no. 1358.

Vs. 30 Ἀπὸ τετάρτης ἡμέρας Alford's references do not support his rendering, for in these passages Ἀπό implies some continuance, and it does not merely mark a point of time.

Vs. 34 προσωπολήμπτης See Baumg. I, p. 273sq.

Vs. 36 ἀπέστειλεν τοῖς υἱοῖς Ἰσραὴλ εὐαγγελιζόμενος εἰρήνην διὰ Ἰησοῦ Χριστοῦ This is the speaker's own view, he does not necessarily attribute it to the hearers.

Vs. 37 ὑμεῖς οἴδατε here and elsewhere means 'as you ought to know.'

Vs. 38 ὁ Θεὸς ἦν μετ' αὐτοῦ He was the Immanuel prophesied.

Vs. 48 See Alford's note.

Trouble in Zion—Peter Explains
(Acts 11)

Vs. 17 ἐγὼ δὲ τίς ἤμην Why take the τίς as interrogative at all?

Vs. 19 The earliest preaching in the Gentile Churches, though we have no reason to believe that there was any formal admission of the Gentiles before Cornelius.

Acts 11:20ff: The Widening of the Mission

[Acts 11:19, with its reference back to the effect of the persecution of Stephen, indicates that those who fled travelled as far as Phoenica, Cyprus, and Antioch, and note that they confined themselves to speaking only to Jews.]

Vs. 20 Κύπριοι καὶ Κυρηναῖοι Of Cyrenians cf. Acts 6:9; Mark 15:21; Acts 2:10. One of these is mentioned below, Acts 13:1. Cyprus = Kittim = Citium. Of the Jews there see 1 Macc 15:21 and especially Josephus, *Ant.* xv.10.1 where he quotes Strabo xvii.12.2. Jews were sent to Cyprus by Cleopatra. Mentioned also as an important Jewish colony by Philo, *Leg. Ad Gaius* sec. 36. See also J. T. *Sukkah* v.1—'and they . . . went on the sea as far as Cyprus of the Messiah of Jews under Trajan.' Cf. Dion. L. xviii.32. There was an insurrection under Trajan. They are numbered at 240,000.

Cyprian Christians mentioned: 1) Barnabas Acts 4:36; 2) Mnason 21:16—ἀρχαίῳ μαθητῇ, perhaps one of these included here.

καὶ πρὸς τοὺς Ἑλληνιστὰς The right reading here? See B, D*, E. καὶ πρὸς τοὺς Ἑλληνάς A, Aleph, D. The verses preceding here are of no account as they make no difference of the two readings. The external evidence therefore, very dubious. This is not however the case with the Peshitto in Acts 9:29

where Ἑλληνιστάς refers to Jews who know Greek and in Acts 6:1 where the Greek disciples are simply 'the Greeks.' The reasons for preferring Ἕλληνάς: 1) the καί seems to be part of the text and yet it has no meaning unless an extension is spoken of; 2) the opposition in 6:1 is τῶν Ἑλληνιστῶν πρὸς τοὺς Ἑβραίους, not Ἕλλην vs. Ἰουδαῖος; 3) the sequence and context of the narrative requires it. Otherwise there would be no eventuality which would lead to the mission of Barnabas and the subsequent events. But if so, can this be before or after the conversion of Cornelius?

It is impossible to say. On the one hand there are the distinct headings in St. Luke's narrative. But he is said to drop them and resume them alternately so as to keep them parallel. See Acts 11:30; 12:1-23; 12:24. There is reference to the internal unity of the apostles and the Jerusalem church [earlier], but here we are focusing on the external movement that I have been following.[1] These events may have followed a little after, or come a little before, the conversion of Cornelius. Roughly speaking we may say that it synchronizes. But at all events it should be seen not as a consequence of the conversion of Cornelius, but rather an independent movement in the same direction. *We are told nothing of the success of those who preached among the Jews, only of those who carry the Gospel to the Greeks.*

Vs. 22 περὶ αὐτῶν Barnabas, 'the son of consolation/exhortation,' is sent by Jerusalem Church to check on things at Antioch. διελθεῖν [see Acts 11:19] seems to imply they went by land. Whether this came before or after the conversion of Cornelius is not clear. The mission of Barnabas must have been after.

Vs. 23 παρεκάλει True to his name Acts 4:36. παράκλησις = προφητεία. For προφητεία is not 'prediction' but rather inspired preaching and παράκλησις is not 'consolation' but rather 'exhortation' so that the two meet. Philo, iv, p. 116, προφήτης γὰρ ἴδιον. . . . Comp. 1 Cor 14:3 ὁ δὲ προφητεύων ἀνθρώποις λαλεῖ οἰκοδομὴν καὶ παράκλησιν καὶ παραμυθίαν and 1 Cor 14:31 δύνασθε γὰρ καθ᾿ ἕνα πάντες προφητεύειν, ἵνα πάντες μανθάνωσιν καὶ πάντες παρακαλῶνται. So also Acts 15:32 προφῆται ὄντες διὰ λόγου πόλλου παρεκάλεσαν. . . . Cf. Ps 119:171—'my lips speak with paeans . . . ' (*nabi for*

---

[1] I.e., in these lectures. But clearly Lightfoot has given himself far more material than the lectures needed here and elsewhere in the manuscript, material he had hoped to form into a commentary. (BW3)

naba . . . in the Syriac). Barnabas appears as a προφήτης later at Acts 13:1.

Προθέσει purpose, determination, 2 Tim 3:10.

Vs. 24 ἀνὴρ ἀγαθὸς καὶ πλήρης Πνεύματος Ἁγίου—See Baumg.

Vs. 25 See the strange reading of D—καὶ εὑρὼν αὐτὸν ἤγαγεν αὐτὸν εἰς Ἀντιόχειαν, similarly Tischendorf (8th ed.).

Vs. 26 αὐτοῖς

χρηματίσαι 1) in a special sense 'to determine an oracle' but comp. Heb 12:25; 'directed' Acts 10:22; 2) to play a part; 3) 'to be considered,' 'taken for,' 'called' in later classical Greek. In the New Testament Rom 7:3.

πρώτως Aleph, B, D* is not 'first,' but rather 'primarily,' 'especially.' πρώτως is the right reading because 1) superior authorities Aleph, B, D* vs. A, Dx and the rest; 2) a rare word was unlikely to be substituted for a common word, whereas the reverse was frequently the case. On the usage in Greek comp. Sophocles, Thucydides, Plato, Aristotle, Galen etc.

ἐν Ἀντιοχείᾳ Philostratus, *Vita Ap.* iii.58; Hadrian *Vita* 14; Marcus Aurelius *Vita* 25.

Χριστιανούς a Gentile appellation for Christians used here by the Antiochenes, in Acts 26:28 by Agrippa. In 1 Pet 4:16 it is a term appropriated, having come from without. They called themselves οἱ ἅγιοι, οἱ ἀδελφοί, οἱ πιστοί, μαθηταί. They were called by Jews Ναζωραῖοι Acts 24:5. They would have preferred to be designated 'followers of the Christ.'

Therefore, varied. Not necessarily following the account of the name by Renan, II. p. 234. He mentions by name Ἡρῳδιανοί, Σιμῳνιανοί as analogous though on no good grounds, for why should Latin names be given to all the sects when the church was emphatically Greek? Winer no. 16, p. 119, speaks in the same way, though more cautiously calling it a Latinizing formation. Renan also considers Ἀσιανοί a Latinism, but Σαρδιανοί etc. are quite beyond the reach of objection. See Kühner, para. 334.7 (Vol. I, p. 720sq.). The New Testament confirms our view, namely that it was a heathen appellation (cf. Acts 26:28; 1 Pet 4:16). In Ignatius we find Χριστιανισμούς (*Magn.* 10, *Rom.* 3). As early as Ignatius it had lost all its heathen tinge, which it still exhibits in the New Testament. On Tacitus' later confusion of Chrestus with Christos see Lightfoot, *Phil.* p. 16.

Vss. 27-30 Here we have evidence of friendly feeling between the Jewish and Gentile Christians, as represented by Jerusalem and Antioch, which was renewed in the circular letter issued at the apostolic conclave. Cf. 1 Cor 9:11 'If we have shared with you spiritual things, is it a great thing if we reap your carnal things'?

Vs. 27 προφῆται See Alford.

Vs. 28 Ἅγαβος He is mentioned again at Acts 21:10, there as though introduced for the first time, probably because taken from a different document. On prophetic sign acts comp. e.g. 1 Kings 22:11; Isaiah 20:3, Ezek 5.

διὰ τοῦ πνεύματος so Acts 21:11.

λιμὸν μεγάλην On famine see Luke 15:14 but not Luke 4:25. See Winer no. 9, p. 73 (Moulton). Famine at Sparta was represented in a picture, Altem. x.75. On the date, the first famine in Judaea mentioned by Josephus, *Ant.* xx.2.6 and xx.5.2, occurred during the proconsulships of Fadus (A.D. 44–46) and Tiberius Alexander (A.D. 46–48). It seems it was spread over a considerable time—two or three years. Josephus relates the providential visit of Queen Helena of Adiabene who visited Jerusalem during the famine and ordered grain and figs from Egypt when she saw the conditions there. This was not the one that transpired under Claudius for that took place earlier. The accession of Claudius was in Jan. 24th A.D. 41. Agabus' prophecy may have been uttered about A.D. 43–44 but hardly earlier (i.e. just before the famine broke out). The death of Herod Agrippa was nearly synchronous, but whether before or after we cannot say.

ἐφ' ὅλην τὴν οἰκουμένην During the reign of Claudius there were several famines in various parts of the Empire, but no synchronous universal famine. Cf. Dion lx.11 referring to something going on about A.D. 51; cf. Tacitus *Annal.* xii.43; Suetonius, *Claudius*, 18. On one in Greece see Schone, p. 152 and see Baumg. vol I, p. 303.

The term οἰκουμένην in Greek times meant Greece and its surroundings (see *Shep. Hermas* s.v. p. 1777). In Roman times it refers to the Roman Empire (cf. Luke 2:1; Herodian. v.2.5), 'under the Roman oikemene.'

Vs. 29 διακονίαν See below on Acts 12:25. The ministry of service cf. 1 Cor 16:15; 2 Cor 8:4; 9:1, 12, 13 but in Rom 15:31 the reading may be δωροφορία. This famine explains the request (in A.D. 51) in Gal 2:10. On a later occasion (A.D. 58) we find Paul again the bearer (Acts 24:17). It is the latter occasion to which the mentions in Cor and Rom refer. The Christians at Antioch are able to collect money and send it before the famine begins.

Vs. 30 πρὸς τοὺς πρεσβυτέρους the first mention of the elders. On the other hand, the apostles are not mentioned. Are the two connected? The next chapter describes a persecution—James beheaded, Peter imprisoned and escaped, apparently leaves Jerusalem (vs. 17). This would, not improbably, be the signal for the dispersion of the apostles on this wider mission. Here therefore (comp. Acts 12:17) the local authorities in Jerusalem were the elders, James and the elders. It seems not improbable then that while the first persecution was connected with the establishment of the diaconate; the second one is connected with the establishment of the presbytery. The πρεσβύτεροι formed on the model of the synagogue (thus differing from the diaconate). See Lightfoot, *Phil.* pp. 199sq. On the order of the names 'Barnabas and Saul' in various places in the Acts, see below.

THE PERSECUTED CHURCH
AND THE DAWN OF THE
MISSION OF THE PERSECUTOR
(ACTS 12)

IN ACTS 12 WE FIND THE FOLLOWING SCHEMA: 1) Acts 12:1-19 the persecution of Herod, death of James, imprisonment of Peter; 2) Acts 12:20-23 the fate of the persecutor; 3) Acts 12:24 the fate of the persecuted church. The purpose of the narrative is to exhibit the condition of the church in Jerusalem when St. Paul arrives. This persecution must have happened before St. Paul arrived. But, one could say, not necessarily so, what about the death of Herod? Well, this is simply added to show how God disposes events and how futile is the opposition to Him and his divine purposes. The persecutor is disposed of miraculously because he allows himself to be clothed in divine ways; the persecuted church meantime grows and flourishes. Still it may have transpired before St. Paul's arrival. At all events it was nearly synchronous. Josephus places the death of Herod Agrippa at about A.D. 44. This agrees with the other notice of time, in Acts 11:28, respecting the famine.

Vs. 1 ἐπέβαλεν Ἡρῴδης ὁ βασιλεὺς τὰς χεῖρας Herod persecutes the church.

Vs. 2 Ἰάκωβον Perhaps he was singled out for some bold act, the son of thunder, an act that would be likely to provoke persecution. See the moving story of Clement which however is reproduced e.g. in the case of St. Hippolytus.

Vss. 3-4 Herod's compliance with Jewish feeling in respecting the festival is in accordance with his character as given by Josephus. See also ἰδὼν δὲ ὅτι ἀρεστόν ἐστιν τοῖς Ἰουδαίοις. He had not the natural cruelty of Herod the Great or Herod Antipas. As to his demise, he invites comparison with what St. Paul says in 2 Thess 2:3—'the man of sin, the son of perdition who exalts himself over all that is called god, or that is worshipped, so that he as god sits in the Temple showing himself to be god.'

Vs. 10 See the strange addition of D.

Vs. 12 Ἰωάνου τοῦ ἐπικαλουμένου Μάρκου

Vs. 13 ὑπακοῦσαι 'to answer the knock.' On the probable classical term see Plato *Phaedo* 59E.

Vs. 17 Ἰακώβῳ as the permanent resident authority in Jerusalem, probably not an apostle. The view of Baumg. (Vol. I, p. 322) with regard to 'and he went to another place' (i.e. Peter) seems to have some truth to it. And the conduct of Peter here is similar to that of Paul in Acts 9:31. External persecution is the signal that they are called to a wider mission field.

Vs. 20 θυμομαχῶν having an angry quarrel.

Vs. 24 Ὁ δὲ λόγος τοῦ κυρίου ηὔξανεν καὶ ἐπληθύνετο. For the contrast comp. 1 Peter 1:24-25. On the object of the account of Herod's demise see Baumg. Vol. I, p. 328.

Vs. 25 No allusion to this event in the Epistle to the Galatians, see Lightfoot, *Galatians*, p. 126.

Ἰωάνην He has been mentioned before (Acts 12:12). How they came to select him is explained. Here we have one of the 'undesigned coincidences' comp. Col 4:10—ὁ ἀνεψιὸς Βαρναβᾶ. On this, his first appearing, he is mentioned with both St. Peter (Acts 12:12) and St. Paul (here). So it is to the latest period of their lives. Of St. Paul see 2 Tim 4:11, and of St. Peter 1 Pet 5:13.

The First Missionary Journey
(Acts 13–14)

Acts 13–14 contain the account of the setting apart of Paul and Barnabas for the apostleship and their first missionary journey. The events extend over a period of six years A.D. 44–50, or rather they are all that are recorded during that period. The missionary journey itself comprises Cyprus (the native place of Barnabas), and the southeastern district of the province of Asia Minor, Pamphylia, Pisidia, and Lycaonia. The three towns in which a somewhat detached account of their preaching is given are Antioch (Pisidian), Lystra and Iconium. This first missionary venture is marked not only by great successes but by great perils. St. Paul refers to the difficulties with marked emphasis at the end of his life (2 Tim 3:11). There is a possibility that the account of this journey was once a separate document. The opening presentation of the account reads like the commencement of a long narrative. Here it will be good to give an overview of the three missionary journeys.

Excursus: St. Paul's Apostolic Journeys
(N.B.—Antioch the Starting Point of all the Journeys)

First Missionary Journey—Acts 13–14 (accompanied by Barnabas). (Seleucia), Cyprus (Salamis and Paphos), Pamphylia (Perga), Pisidia (Antioch), ὁ λόγος τοῦ Κυρίου δι' ὅλης τῆς χώρας (Iconium), Lycaonia (Lystra, Derbe) (and again visiting the same places in reverse order) (Lystra, Iconium, Antioch, Perga), (Attalia), Antioch. 15.1 Controversy at Antioch, visit to Jerusalem, (Apostolic Conclave) return to Antioch.

Second Missionary Journey—Acts 15:35–18:22 (accompanied by Silas).
Passes through Syria and Cilicia confirming the churches Derbe, Lystra
(Timothy joins them Acts 16:3). Διῆλθον δὲ τὴν Φρυγίαν καὶ Γαλατικὴν
χώραν, κωλυθέντες ὑπὸ τοῦ Ἁγίου Πνεύματος λαλῆσαι τὸν λόγον ἐν τῇ
Ἀσίᾳ· ἐλθόντες δὲ κατὰ τὴν Μυσίαν . . . παρελθόντες δὲ τὴν Μυσίαν
κατέβησαν εἰς Τρῳάδα (Acts 16:6-8). Macedonia (Philippi, Amphipolis,
Apollonis, Thessalonike, Berea). Silas and Timothy remain there. By sea to
Athens (sends the summons to Silas and Timothy to get to Athens with all
speed, but nothing said of their arrival). Corinth (Silas and Timothy
arrive), sails with Aquila and Priscilla (nothing said of Silas and Timothy)
to Syria by way of Ephesus, Caesarea, Jerusalem (ἀναβὰς Acts 18:22),
κατέβη εἰς Ἀντιόχειαν.

Third Missionary Journey (Acts 18:23–27:44). Galatia, Phrygia (Apollos
in Ephesus, commended to the church at Corinth), διελθόντα τὰ
ἀνωτερικὰ μέρη (Acts 19:1), Ephesus (ἔθετο ὁ Παῦλος ἐν τῷ πνεύματι
διελθὼν τὴν Μακεδονίαν καὶ Ἀχαΐαν πορεύεσθαι εἰς Ἱεροσόλυμα εἰπὼν ὅτι
μετὰ τὸ γενέσθαι με ἐκεῖ δεῖ με καὶ Ῥώμην ἰδεῖν [Acts 19:21], and sends off
the others and Erastus to Macedonia himself staying in Asia for some
time—Acts 19:21-22), Ephesus (uproar of Demetrius), Macedonia, Hellas.
Stays three months (γενομένης ἐπιβουλῆς αὐτῷ ὑπὸ τῶν Ἰουδαίων
μέλλοντι ἀνάγεσθαι εἰς τὴν Συρίαν, ἐγένετο γνώμης τοῦ ὑποστρέφειν
διὰ Μακεδονίας—Acts 20:3). Sopater, Aristarchus, Secundus accompany
him. Troas, Assos, Mitylene, Cos, Rhodes, Patara, Tyre, Ptolemais, Caesarea, Rome.

ANTIOCH TAKES CENTRE STAGE

13.1 ἐν Ἀντιοχείᾳ Notice that coincidentally with the beginning of Paul's
apostleship, Antioch displaces Jerusalem as the missionary centre of Christianity. From Antioch they receive their commission, from Antioch they
set out, and to Antioch they return and report their experiences (Acts
14:26-27).

τὴν οὖσαν ἐκκλησίαν Not the church that was *there*, but rather the church
that was *then*. Comp. Rom 13:1 on the construction οὖσαι ὑπὸ θεοῦ
τεταγμέναι εἰσίν. The passages cited by Alford for the other meaning do not
bear it out (e.g. Mark 8:1).

προφῆται καὶ διδάσκαλοι These were the second and third orders in the church, the first being the apostles. 1 Cor 12:28—ἔθετο ὁ θεὸς ἐν τῇ ἐκκλησίᾳ πρῶτον ἀποστόλους, δεύτερον προφήτας, τρίτον διδασκάλους. . . . Which were prophets and which teachers in the list probably we cannot say. There is no point in the list at which a line can be drawn. On the charism of teaching see Schaff, ii. p. 154.

ὁ τε Βαρναβᾶς The definite article on account of his preeminence, in vs. 2 as well.

καὶ Συμεὼν ὁ καλούμενος Νίγερ Comp. Josephus Bell. Jud. ii.20.4, ii.19.2, iii.2.2 etc. on Niger. See Q. Coeclus Niger, a questor of Jewish extraction Renan III. p. 512. See also, Plutarch, Cicero, 7. The name was common among the Romans.

Λούκιος ὁ Κυρηναῖος Perhaps one of those mentioned in Acts 2:10. The name is far too common to suggest an identity with the Lucius of Rom 16:21 though the one commonality is he is a Jew (Acts 2:18). The identification with St. Luke is improbable. As the names are different it goes for nothing that the Cyrenians were famous physicians (Herod. iii.31). This Lucius is one of the 70 in the Apostolic Constitutions vii.46. Lucius is made bishop of Cenchreae.

Μαναήν A Hebrew name (Menahem) meaning 'to console.' On Menahem the usurper of the throne—2 Kings 15:14. In the LXX Μαναήμ (B) but A has it as here. In Josephus, Ant. xv.10.5 a certain Manaen is said to have procured his future by hailing as King of the Jews, Herod when he was young. There is an allusion to this same man in the J.T. Haggigah 16.2 (see Lightfoot II. p. 685) where his defection is severely censured. (See Tholuck's Glaubwürdigkeit, p. 167). This cannot be the same Manaen for one is the contemporary of Herod the Great, the other of Herod's son, but the repetition of the name in the courts of the Herods is a significant fact, but our Manaen may well be a relative of these persons. While the elder Manaen was brought up with Herod the Great, the younger Manaen, whether son or nephew, would not unnaturally be brought up with the younger Herod. A little later there is yet another Manaen, a son of Judas the Galilean, who took a prominent part in the war with the Romans (Bell. Jud. ii.17.8, 9; Vit. 5). There is also a second-century heretic mentioned by Hippolytus (viii. 12; ix.17).

Table 1. The Herods

	Herod the Great	
Aristobolus Archelaeus (put to death A.D. 6)	**Herod Philip** (married Herodias; ruler of Ituraea and Trachontis)	**Herod Agrippa I** (son of Aristob. died about A.D. 44)
Herod Antipas (tetrarch of Gal., died in exile in Lyons)	**Herod King of Chalcis** (son of Aristob., died A.D. 48)	**Herodias**
Agrippa II	**Berenice** (the three children of Agrippa I)	**Druscilla**

Herod the Great—massacre of the innocents

Herod Antipas—beheaded John the Baptizer, takes part in the examination of Christ

Herod Agrippa I—persecuted the church, executed James Zebedee

Herod Agrippa II—hears St. Paul at trial

σύντροφος 'foster-brother,' or more generally 'companion' in later life, and more literally 'being in the same land with.' The passages in Polybius (e.g. v.9.4) are exactly parallel and point to the former meaning, cf. 2 Macc 9:29. In the court of kings, some are seen as 'companions' or even 'playmates' of the children of the king. Here, as Wordsworth says, we have a striking example of 'the one taken, and the other left.'[1] Archalaeus and Antipas were brought up in Rome (*Ant.* xii.1.3). Whether it was before or after their return to Israel that Manaen was the playmate of Antipas we cannot say.

Ἡρῴδου τοῦ τετραάρχου Herod Antipas, tetrarch of Galilee and Peraea, Luke 3:1; Josephus *Ant.* xvii.8.1. They were strictly speaking, tetrarchies of the whole, and Archelaeus held two (*Ant.* xvii.2.4). Hence Herod Antipas is strictly designated 'the tetrarch' as he had one (Luke 3:19; 9:7; Mt 14:1; Josephus *Ant.* xviii.5.1). Mark 6:14, with less precision, calls him ὁ βασιλεὺς

---

[1]The Wordsworth of whom Lightfoot speaks here is not William Wordsworth the poet but John Twycoss Christopher Wordsworth, the minister (canon of Westminister). See J. T. C. Wordsworth, *The New Testament of Our Lord and Saviour in the Original Greek: With Notes*, part 2, *The Acts of the Apostles* (London: Rivingston, Waterloo Place, 1857), p. 63. (TDS)

Ἡρῴδης, not 'Herod THE king' which would have been misleading as it would have made the term 'king' a distinctive appellation of this particular Herod. There was a special reason why the title 'the tetrarch' should be added, for when he dies it makes clear what territory specifically he had occupied. In Mt 14:1 he is introduced as Ἡρῴδης ὁ τετραάρχης, but after this he is simply called 'king,' which illustrates Mark 6:14. Herod Antipas was still living when we arrive at this point in our narrative, but he had been banished to Lyons in A.D. 39 by the machinations of his nephew Herod Agrippa I (Josephus *Ant.* xviii.7.2), and his dominion added to those of Agrippa I. This Manaen may not have been around at the time of Antipas' banishing.

For some reason or other, St. Luke evinces a particular knowledge of Herod's household (e.g. Luke 8:3: καὶ Ἰωάννα γυνὴ Χουζᾶ ἐπιτρόπου Ἡρῴδου). And he alone records the audience of our Lord before Antipas (Lk 23:7sq.; Acts 4:27). And here the mention of Manaen, and the mention of the death of Herod Agrippa I (Acts 12, see Prof. Plumptre's *Biblical Studies*, p. 377 on Manaen). The mention of Joanna, the wife of Herod's estate manager, and Manaen here illustrate each other. It is clear that a hearing of John's teaching had been authorized in the royal household. The hearings began when it says that Herod himself heard John gladly (καὶ ἡδέως αὐτοῦ ἤκουεν—Mark 6:20). His hearing continued when he examined our Lord. There is obviously much talk in Herod's household about the new movement of John and then Jesus, e.g Mt 14:2—καὶ εἶπεν τοῖς παισὶν αὐτοῦ . . . which includes the servants, and also this might have included his steward and Manaen his foster-brother (see especially Luke 9:7, 9—διηπόρει διὰ τὸ λέγεσθαι ὑπὸ τινων . . . and ἐζήτει ἰδεῖν αὐτόν). Indeed, his own kingdom was the headquarters of the movement! It was natural that the royal household would not escape the news of this. See especially Luke 23:8—Ὁ δὲ Ἡρῴδης ἰδὼν τὸν Ἰησοῦν ἐχάρη λίαν, ἦν γὰρ ἐξ ἱκανῶν χρόνων θέλων ἰδεῖν αὐτὸν διὰ τὸ ἀκούειν περὶ αὐτοῦ καὶ ἤλπιζεν τι σημεῖον ἰδεῖν ὑπ' αὐτοῦ γινόμενον.

Σαῦλος mentioned last, perhaps because he was the least prominent in rank of the persons mentioned. If so, it is remarkable that the first and last on the list are chosen, and also that they speedily change places.

The τίνες is inserted in The Textus Receptus to make the sentence more smooth.

Vs. 2 εἰς τὸ ἔργον. τὸ ἔργον used absolutely of the Gospel. See Acts 15:38;

Phil 2:30, So Ignatius *Ephes.* 14, γὰρ ἐπαγγελίας τὸ ἔργον and in his *Rom.* 3 τὸ ἔργον. Probably the reference is to *the* work here, since they have been called together for this.

ἀφορίσατε comp. Rom 1:1 (not quite the same as Gal 1:15).

δή 'verily' Acts 15:36 and Luke 2:15.

The call of the Spirit and the outward and visible action.

Vs. 4 εἰς Σελεύκειαν The port of Antioch. It is reckoned to be forty-one miles from there by water, sixteen and a half by land. It is called Seleucia Plena, and Seleucia ad Mare (C+H i. p. 167). A very common name (cf. Antiochia, Apamea, Laodicea) see Strabo, xvi. p. 751.

κατῆλθον It has a double use. To come down from the higher land to the coast as here, or to put into port from the high seas (see Acts 27:5).

Κύπρον about one hundred miles from Seleucia, but by sea the journey is about one hundred fifty miles to Salamis and once there one hundred miles from Salamis to Paphos being at opposite ends of the island. Both figure in the *Sybilline Oracles* iv. 125 on Salamis, v.449 on Paphos. The home place of Barnabas and other early disciples. A Jewish colony.

Vs. 5 ἐν Σαλαμῖνι Salamis, afterwards Constantia. Large Jewish population. I cannot verify the statements of e.g. Milman II. p. 421 but Salamis was made a desert by the insurrection of the Jews under Hadrian. See Dio lxviii.32 cited in Eusebius iv.6. He says a word about it.

ἐν ταῖς συναγωγαῖς As at Damascus Acts 9:20.

καὶ Ἰωάννην ὑπηρέτην *comp.* Acts 19:22, especially on the baptizing see 1 Cor 1:14-17.

Vs. 6 ὅλην τὴν νῆσον ἄχρι Πάφου A distance of about one hundred miles. Comp. Tacitus Hist. ii.iii (see Lewin I. p. 122). In the inscriptions Paphos is called Sebaste Claudia Flavia or more simply called Sebaste (A.U.C. 739 see Dion liv.23). In Greek the abbreviation was σλ. Κλ. Φλ. Paphos was the metropolitan residence of the proconsul C.I.L. iii.218 (which contains a good deal of information about Cyprus). See Cesnola, *Cyprus* 29, p. 425 where he says that 'the proconsul Paulus may be the Sergius Paulus of Acts xiii. Instances of the suppression of one of the names is not rare' (see Sergius Secundus Paulus in Lightfoot, *Colossians*, p. 63).[2]

---

[2] It is detailed references like these, including cross references to Lightfoot's own commentaries, that strongly suggest Lightfoot was not just writing up lecture notes. We may also have a clue

Μάγον A neutral word, or at least not necessarily pejorative (see Mt 2:1). Hence the addition of the prefix ψευδο, comp. Acts 19:19. See the article on Magi in Smith's Dictionary. Magic, the outcome of a yearning after the supernatural when not satisfied in a legitimate way. Religion is a necessity of the human heart. The producing of systems of abstract philosophy, hence the phenomenon of the civilized world at this time—Chaldee, holy men, worship of Isis, etc. The struggle of the church against magic, and its adoption by the Neo-Platonists. What is characteristic of magic, sorcery etc. is it is religion divorced from morality.

Βαριησοῦς A patronymic like Bar-Timaeus, Bar-tholomew, Bar-Sabas, Bar-abbas etc. He must have had some other name as well. The variation in the mss. here reflects the shrinking from allowing the sacred name of Jesus to be used in such cases. See on Mt 27:23—Meyer, III. p. 918.

Ἰουδαῖον of Jews involved in the magical arts see Acts 19:19.

Vs. 7 σὺν τῷ ἀνθυπάτῳ the proconsul. Distinctive of the senatorial provinces. In A.D. 27, after the battle of Actium, Cyprus had been made an imperial province (see Dio liii.11). A few years later (A.D. 32) it was handed over to the Senate. See Dion Cass. liv.4. See also Strabo xvii p. 840 for the mention of the senatorial province. There was an inscription record about this time of the proconsuls of Cyprus (e.g. L. Annius Bassus A.D. 52 and his predecessor Q. Julius Cardus mentioned in the inscription—see Boeckh. nos. 2631, 2632). The name of at least four proconsuls during the reign of Claudius occur. These two plus Cominius Proculus and Quadratus on the coins. See Ackeman's *Numismatic Illustrations*, p. 39sq. See references in Becker and Marquardt, iii. p. 173. Hence the objections of some earlier commentators that St. Luke is inaccurate here fall to the ground. They had observed the earlier passage in Dio, and overlooked the latter. We find the same accuracy by St. Luke when it comes to Gallio the proconsul of Achaia. Provinces constantly changed [from imperial to senatorial or vice versa]. On a procurator of Cyprus see C.I.L. iii.6072, for a proconsul iii.218 (about A.D. 190) and also ix.433.

On the temple of Paphian Aphrodite see Eckhel, III, p. 84.

Σεργίῳ Παύλῳ A person of the same name is mentioned by Pliny

---

here to a terminus a quo for when he last worked on these notes, for the Colossians commentary came out in 1875 and this reference here suggests it is already in print. (BW3)

(*Elenchos ab. Lab.* ii, xviii) and perhaps a descendant of our man is mentioned by Galen (*Anat.* i.2 Kühner, Vol. II. p. 218), more than a century later. He too was a man of rank (about A.D. 160).

ἀνδρὶ συνετῷ here called a prudent man. Curiously enough, he is introduced in one passage as Σεργίος τε ὁ καὶ Παῦλος, for so it must be read, but in the vast majority of the papyri he is simply called Παῦλος. The alliance of such a man with a sorcerer and imposter like Elymas is a significant fact. The same dissatisfaction with the religion of his world and the philosophies of his day that had brought him into contact with Elymas led him also to communicate with Barnabas and Saul.

Vs. 8 Ἐλύμας—alama, alim. On the name Freytas, III, p. 213. Hence the name Eulema with which we are familiar. I cannot find that the root occurs in this sense in the cognate languages Hebrew and Aramaic, hence this man's name points to the same extra-Judaic source as his magical practices. Indeed, his circumstances themselves would suggest as much. We would naturally have looked to Phoenica and Syria, but the evidence does not encourage us to seek the affinities here.

Ἐλύμας ὁ μάγος οὕτως γὰρ μεθερμηνεύεται τὸ ὄνομα αὐτοῦ The word μάγος seems not to be Semitic but rather Aryan, that is, Persian in its origin. See Gesenius s.v. μάγος. Connected with the Persian 'malat', Greek μέγας, Latin magus, but it was adopted into the Chaldean (Babylonian), see Jer 39:3, 13, the 'rabmag', a title of Nergalshalrezer. See the article by Prof. Rawlinson on 'rabmag' in Smith's Dictionary (cf. rabsani, rabslakeh).

Vs. 9 ὁ καὶ Παῦλος The first mention of his name, Paul. It is impossible not to connect this with the mention of Sergius Paulus. The coincidence forces us to this conclusion. So Jerome, *Epist. To Philem.* See Chapter 5 and the reference in Coneybeare and H. As for other suggestions: 1) a reference to his stature, being short—cf. 2 Cor 10:10, *Acts of Paul and Thecla* 3—the reference to Paul being μικρόν (see C+H I, p. 70 and the references in Stanley, the traditional account of Paul); 2) a reference to his humility, 1 Cor 15:9 (cf. 1 Cor 3:8). So Augustine (ref. to in C+H I p. 186). 3) the resemblance in sound, i.e. Saul, Paul, like Jose, Jason, Silas, Silvanus (see C+H I, p. 185). 1), 2), 3) may have assisted to recommend the name, but the coincidence in time with the conversion of Sergius Paulus was the occasion and motive.

ἀτενίσας So too Acts 14:9; 23:1. Also of St. Paul. No ground [here] for the theory of weak eyes, for used e.g. of Peter Acts 3:4; 10:4. See Lightfoot, *Galatians*, p. 189.

Vs. 10 ῥᾳδιουργίας The older sense of the word seems to have been indolence, carelessness, or an easy-going disposition e.g. Xenephon *Mem.* ii.1.20. But later, in Polybius and onwards it is 'want of principle,' unscrupulousness, guile, imposture, e.g. Lucian, *Calum.* 20. Comp. Acts 18:14 ῥαδιούργημα.

υἱὲ διαβόλου In striking contrast to his name, as Meyer says, 'son of Jesus,' 'son of the Savior.'

διαστρέφων τὰς ὁδοὺς τοῦ κυρίου τὰς εὐθείας Comp. Micah 3:9 LXX on διαστρέφων.

Vs. 11 ἀχλὺς καὶ σκότος Luke the Physician. In Galen (in Wettstein) ἀχλύς, ὀφθαλμός πάθος, multiple references.

χειραγωγούς Plutarch, *de Stoicorum* 1063B.

Vs. 13 οἱ περὶ Παῦλον Paul is now the prominent person. When they started, it would have been Barnabas' company?

Πέργην See Lewin, I, p. 234. About 60 stadia = seven miles up from the coast to the city. See Strabo xiv.4, p. 667. St. Paul would probably land at Attalia (see his return Acts 14:25) and go by road the few miles to Perga. On the temple of Artemis (Strabo l.c. and see Lewin, p. 135). St. Paul does not appear to have stayed and preached here on this occasion. This is different from his return, see Acts 14:25. It is not ἐπιστηρίζοντες τὰς ψυχὰς (as in Acts 14:22) but καὶ λαλήσαντες . . . τὸν λόγον as if it were for the first time.

Παμφυλίας (Πασα φυλη) Strabo, xiv, p. 668.

Ἰωάννης δὲ Probably from timidity or lack of zeal. This was after having arrived in Pamphylia and having been deterred by the people. See Acts 15:37 where Paul regards it as a sort of apostasy. The κινδύνοις ποταμῶν, κινδύνοις λῃστῶν, κινδύνοις ἐκ γένους, κινδύνοις ἐξ ἐθνῶν (2 Cor 11:26) may have occurred here at this time (see C+H, I p. 197). Strabo xii, p. 571 describes the country as rugged, with raging rivers and he has a few choice words about the Pamphlians (p. 570).

Vs. 14 Αὐτοὶ δὲ διελθόντες But they themselves passing through the country.

τὴν Πισιδίαν, the correct reading (A, B, Aleph, C). On the use of the term see Strabo, xii. p. 577. I have not found another instance of 'Pisdian' used as an adjective. Comp. however Acts 16:6; Mark 1:5; John 3:22. All these names of places are properly adjectives.

Ἀντιόχεια On inscriptions chiefly Latin, C.I.L. iii.209sq. This was a Roman colony city—a Caesarea and was the capital of Pisidia (see Pliny *N.H.* v.24), hence Antiocheia Caesarea or Caesarea Antiochus almost due north of Perga.

τῇ ἡμέρα τῶν σαββάτων See Col 2:16. On the reading of the Law see Acts 15:21; 2 Cor 3:14. On the reading of the prophets Luke 4:17. The expositor was sometimes the reader himself, see Philo, Fragm. II.580sq. but sometimes it was a different person (*Quod Omni* 12, i.e. II b 458). After the reading from the prophets came the sermon, or exposition, or exhortation. See, again, Luke 4:17. Now it so happens that in the then extant arrangement of lessons, the beginning of Deut 1:1–3:21 and the beginning of Is 1:1–27, are read on the same day. See Justin Martyr *Apol.* i.67 (p. 98C), and *Second Epistle of Clement* Appendix p. 303sq. Bengel has pointed out parallels to both lessons in vss. 17-19. See especially Deut 1:31, 38, and from Isaiah 1:2, 26. I do not think that the idea is to be lightly rejected. If the reference to Isaiah were not here distinct, it would still deserve great consideration. And indeed this reference would explain what otherwise would need explanation, especially in light of what is mentioned in vs. 20. On the later date for the lectionary see Hup. *Studien und Krit.* 1837, p. 843. This does not seem to be a formidable argument. It is plain that some lectionary or other existed at the time, and the later one based along the lines of the earlier one.

Vs. 15 ἀρχισυνάγωγοι normally plural cf. Mark 5:22; Luke 8:41; Acts 18:8, 17. Luke 13:17 presents us with an example. This apparent zealous leader who was present is the 'ruler of the synagogue' and can make pronouncement at the time.

παρακλήσεως See Acts 4:36.

κατασείσας See Acts 12:17—it procures silence.

The Speech of St. Paul. Representative of this sort of preaching to the Jews as at Lystra to the barbarians, and as at Athens to the cultivated Greeks, and at Miletus to the disciples. His rule—'to the Jew first' (Rom 1:16; 15:8). Probably not a full report of the sort of preaching to the Jews here. It can be discussed under two headings: its resemblances and its peculiarities.

1) Its long historical preface is like the Stephen speech that serves as a) an explanation, and b) an introduction of the Gospel.

2) A similar audience under similar circumstances. There are no such resemblances to the speech at Areopagus or the speech at Miletus. In both there is an implicit argument with both Jew and Judaizing Christian. Notice as well the double argument concerning the resurrection with: a) an appeal to the eyewitnesses, as well as b) the testimony of Scripture. As with the Stephen speech we have the combination of quotations in vs. 21 comp. Rom 3:10 (Ps, Prov, Is) or 1 Cor 15:54 (Is 25:8; Hos 13:4). Like the Stephen speech, this is not a speech that any later Christian fiction writer would have invented.

3) Introduction of the Pauline doctrine (Acts 13:38, 39, 41 and cf. Acts 13:23 to Gal 3:29). He does here at Psidian Antioch exactly what he himself would later say and do at Corinth (see 1 Cor 15:3).

Vs. 16 οἱ φοβούμενοι τὸν θεὸν So again at vs. 26. Cf. Acts 10:2, 22. Elsewhere σεβομένοι Acts 13:43, 50; 17:17. Proselytes and other worshippers. As to their number and importance, Josephus, *Ant.* xx.8.11 tells of a prominent Jewish woman who interceded on behalf of the Jewish in Jerusalem.

Vs. 17 ὕψωσεν 1) by the marvelous increase in numbers, and 2) by the miracles wrought on their behalf. However ὕψωσεν in Is 1:2 means brought up, reared, and so it should probably be taken here.

Vs. 18 ἐτροποφόρησεν This was arguably from the LXX of Deut 1:31 cf. 2 Macc 7:27 of a mother rearing a child. There is therefore an a priori probability that St. Paul meant this here. Origen however (*Hom. on Jerm.* xviii, III, p. 248) explains the term in Deut 1:31 at great length, explaining that the term τροποφόρησεν was appropriate to express the Hebrew and so also *contra Cels.* iv.71 (I, p. 556). Hence the reading also occurred in the LXX earlier on, and it is so read now in the *Apostolic Constitutions* vii.36, but there is nothing in the immediate context to determine the issue. ἐτροποφόρησεν is read in Aleph, B, C2, D, Harclean and is not an unsuitable reading. See Cicero *ad Att.* xiii.29, *Ar. Ran* 1481. In any case, St. Paul might well have had a copy of the LXX with τροποφόρησει in it and have adopted that reading as suitably expressive.

Vs. 19 κατεκληρονόμησεν The right reading. Sometimes to distribute as a lot or an inheritance see Deut 1:38; 1 Sam 2:8; Jer 3:18.

Vs. 20 ὡς ἔτεσιν τετρακοσίοις καὶ πεντήκοντα. καὶ μετὰ ταῦτα ἔδωκεν κριτὰς ἕως Σαμουὴλ προφήτου.[3] Unquestionably the correct reading. For the dative, John 2:20 and Rom 16:25. See Winer, no. xxxi p. 271 (Moulton). Here it denotes the period, indicating the period of fulfillment. In other words it was close on 450 years before the Israelites settled in Canaan. Alford's note here must be altogether set aside. The reading of the uncial text makes no difference. 1 Kings 6:1 however gives the time span from the Exodus to the building of the Temple in the fourth year of Solomon as only 480 years. Our text would agree almost precisely with the chronology of Josephus in *Ant.* viii.3.1 which reckons it as 592 years after the Exodus (reckoned as follows—592 minus 40 years of wandering, minus 25 years Joshua, 40 years Saul, 40 years David = 443, allowing for seven years of coming or going [or rounding up to 450]). And the reckoning of years agrees with the notices in the book of Judges.

Σαμουὴλ The first of the continuous succession of prophets as in Acts 3:24. Especially known as 'Samuel *the* prophet.' Stanley I, p. 403, 419. With him, *nabi* first comes into usage 1 Sam 9:9. 'It is at the close of the period of the judges that prophets first become not merely an occasional occurrence but a fixed institution in the Jewish [community]' (Stanley p. 419).[4] And on the end of one dispensation (the judges) and the commencement of the next (the kings), see Stanley, Vol. I, p. 398. The prophetic dispensation was parallel with the monarchy. On the institution of the 'school of the prophets,' 1 Sam 10:5, 10; 19:20. See Stanley's Lectures I, p. 395sq. Samuel is not ὁ προφήτης but rather just προφήτης here, the right reading i.e. not 'until Samuel the prophet' but rather 'until Samuel was prophet.' Comp. Mark 2:26 where there is a similar v.l. referring to Abiathar where the issue is whether there is a definite article before 'high priest' or not.

Vs. 21 ἐκ φυλῆς Βενιαμίν Comp. Rom 9:1; Phil 3:5.

ἔτη τεσσεράκοντα The Biblical account says nothing about this, though the notices are consistent with it. E.G. 2 Sam 2:10 Ishbosheth, Saul's son, is forty years old at his death and Saul was a young man when he was anointed king

---

[3]Westcott and Hort reads ἔτεσι instead of ἔτεσιν. (TDS)

[4]Stanley actually calls it "the Jewish Church," but I have altered this for obvious reasons. (BW3)

(1 Sam 9:2). Josephus, *Ant.* vi.14.9 suggests exactly 40 years in all, but this is not reconcilable with what the narrative itself says (1 Sam 19:18; 2 Sam 5:4).

Vs. 22 μεταστήσας αὐτὸν Did a typological application to himself go through Paul's mind, the second Saul? The removal of Saul the persecutor, and the substitution of a servant of God?

εὗρον This echoes the language of the Psalms. See Ps 88:21 (89:21); cf. 1 Sam 13:14; Is 44:28.

Vs. 23 ἤγαγεν

Vs. 24 πρὸ προσώπου A Hebraism.

Vs. 25 Τί ἐμὲ ὑπονοεῖτε εἶναι; οὐκ εἰμὶ ἐγώ. Comp. John 3:28 and John 1:20. On the rest of the passage Luke 3:15sq. John 1:20, 26, 27. But the motive? Comp. Acts 1:5; 11:16; 19:4. Directed against the so-called disciples of John and the heno-baptists? Consider the interplay only a few years later (Acts 18:25; 19:4). Again in the Gospel of John, it seems clear he has this sect in view. Comp. John 1:15sq; 3:23sq.; 5:33sq.; 10:40sq. (see Lightfoot, *Col.* p. 402sq.).

Vs. 26 ὑμῖν The you is the Jews of the Diaspora and the proselytes as well as οἱ . . . κατοικοῦντες ἐν Ἰερουσαλὴμ (vs. 27) and so . . . ἐξαπεστάλη. Having travelled with Barnabas, the Gospel is preached to the Dispersion, and when it fails with the Dispersion it is offered to the Gentiles (Acts 13:46).

Vs. 27 κρίναντες ('judging' not condemning, this is a system problem) ἐπλήρωσαν. αὐτον goes with 'judging', 'fulfilling' with αὐτας.

Vs. 29 St. Paul had no object in separating those who crucified Jesus and took him down, from those who buried him. In fact the main point is that he was buried.

Vs. 30 ὃς ὤφθη ἐπὶ ἡμέρας πλείους See Acts 1:3. ὤφθη is also the Pauline word for the appearances, 1 Cor 15:5sq. This is a very unsure inference, but St. Paul was acquainted with the appearances in Galilee related by St. Matthew and St. John. Indeed the appearance to more than 500 brethren (1 Cor 15:6) is most naturally placed in Galilee. St. Paul is thinking of the apostles and immediate disciples who just happened to be Galileans. These were least likely to be deceived, and those who were his chief disciples.

Vs. 33 τοῖς τέκνοις ἡμῶν[5] Not intended to exclude themselves. Comp.

---

[5]He is following Westcott and Hort here, cf. the Nestle-Aland GNT.

Acts 2:39. But this is more expressive that the Textus Receptus. One solution is to take one half of the Textus Receptus reading, ἡμῖν for ἡμῶν, but external authority will not allow it. To all of them—see Acts 13:36.

External Evidence:

For δευτέρῳ A, B, Aleph, C, E, L, P, H, 1361. And also the versions—Memph., Theb., Vulg., Syr., Peshit., Syr. Harcl., Ethiop., Ambrosiaster *de fed.* v.1 (I. p. 555).

For πρώτῳ D, Hilar. Tractate on the Ps. II, p. 31, Origen, II, p. 537sq. So too same variable mss. in Bede. Then there are a number of mss. that omit the reference to the Psalms—46 Latin mss.

Conclusion: While there is overwhelming support for the 'second Psalm' reading, rarely is the consenus so great for a controverted reading. The authority for πρώτῳ is all of one kind. It is just that some authorities deny or reject this fact. But the alteration is exactly the same as the sort of corrections we find in D, and it allowed some authorities excuses. Moreover, a comparison of the case for the two readings is in favor of 'Second' rather than 'First.' The testimonies for the reading 'Second' requires a different ordering of the Greek words (ἐν τῷ πρώτῳ ψαλμῷ), and we find that it has been altered, for the reference to 'second' comes after the mention of the Psalm.

Importantly, it is difficult to imagine, if the 'first' reading were original that one could arrive by correction at the word order we find in the 'second' reading. All this not withstanding, the chief editors, Tischendorf (8th ed.), Tregelles, Lachmann, Griesbach etc. have the reading ἐν τῷ πρώτῳ ψαλμῷ. Lachmann apparently feels so strongly about this that he takes the A.V. word order and the πρώτῳ reading from D and creates a reading that is not found in any authority! The sole argument on the other side is the probability that πρώτῳ would be altered to 'second.' If the manuscript authorities were fairly evenly balanced, the argument could have weight, but with this preponderance of authorities, it doesn't.

In our time the tendency to want to argue for the 'first' reading is in part because this is the numbering system with which we are familiar. But in the early centuries might there not be a tendency in the other direction? What are the facts?[6]

---

[6]If you are wondering why Lightfoot belabors this particular text-critical point it is because: (1) he is on the A.V. revision committee and is arguing against the traditionalists who want to

Talmud *Berachot* Folio 9—(quote at length in Scholt. p. 455). The context is a discussion of why Ps 18 (19) should be repeated after the Eighteen Benedictions. R. Jehuda the son of R. Simon . . . said 'because David put it after the Eighteen Psalms.' But he ought to have said 19. Answer: the two pericopae make one psalm. In support of this, appeal is made to a teaching of R. Samuel . . . who relates that R. Johana that David began each favorite Psalm with 'Blessed' and so he commences the first psalm with 'Blessed is the man' and ends it with 'Blessed are all they. . . .'

Similarly an obscure passage from J.T. *Taan.* Fol. 65 (quoted in Lightfoot II, p. 690), 'R. Joshua ben Levi says It was according to the Eighteen Psalms from the beginning of the Psalms, the Lord hears these in the day of trouble (xx.1), but if any were to say unto there are nineteen, they say unto him that "why do the heathen rage" (Ps.ii) is not reckoned among them.' Niper II, p. 337sq. l.c. says that of two Hebrew copies that were followed in his land, the two psalms were attached together. . . .

Justin Martyr, *Apol.* 140 quotes Ps 1; 2 continuously as though they form one unit, prefacing them with a summary of contents in the prophets and writings. Again, Tertullian, *adv. Marc.* iv.22 refers to the discussion of 'the Son' in Ps 2:7 as in the 'primo psalmo.' Cyprian i.13 speaking of the same matter refers to the 'primo psalmo' as well, in some mss. though the best supported reading is 'secundo.'

There are other church fathers as well whose conception of the relationship of Psalm 1 and Psalm 2 is the same as Justin's, namely that they are one psalm. See again Apollonianus in Tischendorf.

Thus it is plain that for the Christian church in the early centuries, this arrangement was by no means uncommon. In fact, it is defended by both rabbinical and early Christian authority. Some saw in this arrangement a special meaning and adopted the text accordingly. Thus in fact, the character of the alteration in D, which are frequently made to suit a certain tradition, and generally some problematic tradition.[7]

---

strongly support D, and for that matter the "Majority Text," at numerous points. This should sound familiar to those who even in the twenty-first century hear arguments for the Greek text that is the basis of the KJV; (2) he is quite convinced such arguing on behalf of the Western text of Acts is historically wrong. It does not represent the original text of Acts. (BW3)

[7]It is worth pointing out that it was Archbishop Stephen Langton (1150–1228) who first divided the Bible into chapters and verses, a very long time after the New Testament era. (BW3)

υἱός μου εἶ σύ Heb 1:5; 5:5, and a v.l. in Luke 3:22 in D and Latin authorities (the same class of authorities as in the 'first,' 'second' variants). See *Clement of Rome* 36. On the double reference of the Psalm, the primary and secondary reference. Secondary is the messianic reference, but it is already seen among the rabbis see B.T. *Sukkah* Folio 52 (see Lightfoot, II, p. 690).

Γεγέννηκα does not refer to eternal sonship, but rather to the manifestation of the sonship in time, as the adverb σήμερον shows. The secondary reference is to be compared to the primary one. Here it is manifested by the resurrection comp. Rom 1:4—ἐξ ἀναστάσεως νεκρῶν, not that his nature was changed by the resurrection but that his permanent form was defined.

What parts of the Psalm were treated as messianic? Ps 2:1-2 see Acts 4:25-26, and Ps 2:10 ('kings') a general consensus (such as one rarely finds) among the rabbis about this, and they made challenging critiques. How the prophetic spirit exhorts us here. How the psalm predicts the demise of Pilate and Herod, rulers of Jews and Gentiles. How Christ was to be believed on by persons of every race. How God calls him Son and promises to subject every race to him. How the foolish attempt to escape from his power. How God calls all unto repentance before the day of judgment. (At the same time he has the LXX reading of vs. 10).

Vs. 34 ἀνέστησεν αὐτὸν ἐκ νεκρῶν

Δώσω See Is 55:3 where the LXX agrees with the Hebrew. The mercies he promised to David. But all the promises made to David are only partially fulfilled in David himself, their true fulfillment was in David's greater son, the messiah, of which David was a type. Thus, the promise of universal dominion, thus again the promise of freedom from corruption which we hear of here in the next verse. See Is 55:3-5 and the whole context, especially illustrated by Ps 89:20, 24, 27, 29, 34-35, 37 and 2 Sam 7:8, 13, 15-16. David lives still, as present in his descendants and the covenant with David as a continuous application. See Delitzsch Is. l.c.

ὅσια A pious man. See 2 Chron 6:42 Comp. *Clement of Rome*, I p. 187.

τὰ πιστά trustworthy, sure, assured.

Vs. 35 διότι The right reading. Not διό. The resurrection is a fulfillment of a promise, but God could not completely fulfill his merciful plan to David himself, because it had been promised to David 'thou wilt not leave my soul in hell.'

λέγει Best taken impersonally—the place 'it is said' as e.g. in Eph 5:14.

How he proposes here to understand ὁ θεός, supposing that God speaks here what David speaks to God, but this is not necessary and therefore to be avoided. Notice the Pauline character of all this.

Ps 16:10 comp. Acts 2:27. Resemblance to St. Peter, and why not? The application of the passage is most natural in itself. Consider the communication with Peter in Gal 1:18.

Vs. 40 τὸ εἰρημένον ἐν τοῖς προφήταις Comp. Mt 2:23 διὰ τῶν προφητῶν ὅτι Ναζωραῖος (Mark 1:2—a false reading), John 6:45; Is 54:13, but comp. Jer 31:34; Micah 4:2; Acts 7:42 citing Amos, Acts 15:15 citing Amos as well. The 'book of the prophets' = the Twelve as most commonly where there is a special quotation see Acts 7:42; 15:15.

Vs. 41 ἴδετε, οἱ καταφρονηταί Hab 1:5 the Chaldean invasion, so Hab 2:5 applies in Gal 3:11. There is probably also an allusion to this latter passage in Gal 3:29 (see Lightfoot, *Gal.* p. 138, notes). Yes, we see the Pauline character of what is said in this speech in Acts 13. The LXX must have read בָּכוֹדָם for בַּגּוֹים here see Hab 1:13; 2:5 and is so translated καταφρονηταί and so also the Peshitta. Note the LXX also has ἀφανίσθητε.

Vs. 42 Ἐξιόντων δὲ αὐτῶν i.e. Paul and Barnabas.

παρεκάλουν i.e. the worshippers in the synagogue. The grouping in the Authorized Text is unwarranted. The separation of Jews and Gentiles came later.

μεταξὺ on which see *Clement of Rome 64, Epist. Barnab. 13.*

Vs. 43 σεβομένων προσηλύτων The former term refers to the devout, A.V. has 'religious,' see Acts 13:50; 17:4, 17. Comp. Josephus, *Ant.* xvii.7.2. προσηλύτος means a newcomer, even a stranger, an alien. See Ex 12:48-49 LXX, and so frequently in the LXX e.g. Is 54:15. It is an LXX word not appearing in classical sources. It = גֵּר, a sojourner, so that it signifies one who comes and takes up his abode temporarily or permanently with the Israelites. In the other Hexaplanic (?) sources but not in the LXX προσηλύτος and cognates is the equivalent of ἐπηλύς and its cognates (e.g. in *Barnabas, Soph. Leg.*).

τῇ χάριτι τοῦ θεοῦ Pauline doctrine = τῷ εὐαγγελλίῳ see 2 Cor 6:1; 8:9 cf. Rom 3:29; 5:15; 6:15sq. Eph 2:5-7, 8. See Lightfoot notes on Col 1:6 (p. 136). On this comp. John 1:17 ὁ νόμος διὰ Μωϋσέως ἐδόθη, ἡ χάρις καὶ ἡ ἀλήθεια διὰ Ἰησοῦ Χριστοῦ ἐγένετο. Cf. Gal 5:4; Acts 15:11; 20:24.

Vs. 44 σχεδόν comp. Acts 19:26. A natural hyperbole.

τὸν λόγον τοῦ κυρίου i.e. Jesus Christ, see vss. 48, 49 and frequently in Acts. But the question is—is the genitive subjective or objective?

Vs. 46 ὁ Παῦλος First, the chief speaker.

ἀπωθεῖσθε thrust away *from yourselves*.

ἀξίους κρίνετε ἑαυτοὺς as evinced by their acts.

τῆς αἰωνίου ζωῆς the knowledge of the Gospel is this.

πρῶτον Rom 1:16; 2:9-10. The first in privilege or the first in responsibility. So e.g. the end of Acts in Rome see Acts 28.

Vs. 47 τέθεικά Is 49:6 from the LXX word for word and substantially agreeing with the Hebrew with minor differences. Comp. Luke 2:32.

Vs. 48 ὅσοι ἦσαν τεταγμένοι appointed.

εἰς ζωὴν αἰώνιον See John 5:24; 17:23. This belief *in* eternal life involves he who partakes of it has eternal life just as he who partakes of food and sacrament etc. has temporal life. Comp. σωτηρία and its cognates.

Vs. 50 τὰς σεβομένας γυναῖκας The women especially affected, as e.g. at Damascus. See Josephus, *Bell. Jud.* ii.20.2 on devout women. The A.V. is strange here 'decent and honorable women' but these are moral epithets prompting moral approval whereas the Greek terms treat in one case religion and in the other case social position.

εὐσχήμονας gentle folk. Acts 17:12; comp. Mark 15:43.

Vs. 51 ἐκτιναξάμενοι A direct reference to one of our Lord's sayings. Luke 9:5 cf. Luke 10:2; Mt 10:14. This perhaps explains vs. 47 οὕτως γὰρ ἐντέταλται ἡμῖν ὁ κύριος and see Luke 9:5 ἐπ' αὐτούς ('against them').

Acts 14—Barnabas and Saul = Zeus and Hermes?

Vs. 1 Ἰκονίῳ about sixty miles east, or a little south of east, of Pisidian Antioch. Noted by different contours to Phyrgia and Lycaonia and Pisidia. It was apt to get high snow, if traveling to Asia Minor from Syrian Antioch through Tarsus and Sardis to Ephesus (the road through Pisidian Antioch). An important place in medieval times, and home to the Seljuk sultans. Mentioned by Xenephon in the Anabasis, no houses so doubtless not yet what it afterwards became. See Strabo xii.6, p. 568.

κατὰ τὸ αὐτὸ Only here in the New Testament (but comp. ἐπὶ τὸ αὐτὸ) but it occurs several times in the LXX 1 Sam 11:11; 30:24; 31:6 etc. It means not in the same way, but together as the LXX shows.

Ἰουδαῖοι As always throughout Apostolic history and afterwards e.g. *Martyrdom of Polycarp.*

Vs. 3 διδόντι with the following καί. Thus it explains μαρτυροῦντι [how the Lord bore witness by giving . . .].

Vs. 5 ὁρμὴ a mad impulse, here mental rather than physical as the context shows. Comp. James 3:4.

τῶν ἐθνῶν τε καὶ Ἰουδαίων here as forming one body.

Hence σὺν τοῖς ἄρχουσιν αὐτῶν should refer to both Gentile and Jewish leaders, the magistrates of the former and the synagogue rulers of the latter. Comp. Acts 4:26-27.

ὑβρίσαι καὶ λιθοβολῆσαι αὐτούς comp. 1 Thess 2:2. προπαθόντες καὶ ὑβρισθέντες.

Comp. Acts 14:19; 2 Cor 11:5, the discussion in Paley's *Horae Paulinae;* cf. The Legend of Paul and Thecla, the story about Demos, Hermogenes and the stoning.

Vs. 6 τὰς πόλεις τῆς Λυκαονίας thus implying that Iconium was not Lycaonian but 1) geographically and ethnographically doubtful. See Xenophon, *Anab.* i.2.19; 2) politically, Pliny *N.H.* v.27. Pliny distinguishes where the tetrarchy is, and 'ipsa Lycaonia,' i.e. Lycaonia proper. Strabo xii.6 (p. 568) also speaks of the separate government.

This explains two things: 1) Lycaonia is limited to Lystra and Derbe; and 2) κατέφυγον they would be under a different government. This leads to an important point—this part of Lycaonia had passed through different hands. It had belonged to Amnytas, king of Galatia. On his death in 25 B.C. it was bestowed on Archelaeus king of Capadoccia. In A.D. 17 it was attached to the Roman province of Galatia and in A.D. 37 it was assigned to Antiochus king of Comagene. The historians only say that part of Cilicia was given to him. Dion lix.6-8 i.e. Cilicia Asperca as appears from other notices (see Lewin, *Fast. Sac.* p. 250), BUT, the coins show that Lycaonia was also assigned to him. See Eckhel, III, p. 255 sq. He was deposed by Caligula, restored by Claudius in A.D. 41, and reigned until A.D. 71. Josephus *Bell. Jud.* vii.7.1. Therefore, at this time, this portion of Lycaonia was under him.

Λύστραν comp. vs. 8 ἐν Λύστροις. Comp. Acts 16:1-2 where there is the same variation (Λύστροις in 16:2). About 30-40 miles south and somewhat east of Iconium. Later said to be 1,001 churches in the vicinity (see Hamilton, II, p. 319 on Kara Dagh, and see Lewin, I, p. 148).

Λύστραν καὶ Δέρβην The geographical order. On a later trip he approaches from the east (16:2) and takes them in a different order.

Vs. 9 ἤκουεν Probably the right reading here. B, C, Harclean Syr. More expressive. 'Was listening to' when the occurrence happens.

Vs. 10 μεγάλῃ φωνῇ so we must read (not μεγάλῃ τῇ φωνῇ raising his voice, contrast Acts 26:24 where it is the undisputed reading).

ἥλατο The right reading, not ἤλλετο. The initial account. Means 'leapt up.' See Acts 3:8 ἐξαλλόμενος ἔστη καὶ περιεπάτει, whereas ἤλλετο would comport with that passage.

Vs. 11 Λυκαονιστὶ: 1) the language meant. Steph. Byz. says in Derbe they spoke this language. See Strabo xiv.4 (p. 631); 2) Relation to the narrative here; 3) bearing on the gift of tongues.

Vs. 12 Δία . . . Ἑρμῆν Appearance 1) to Lycan, the mythical founder of Lycaonia, see Ovid, *Meta.* i.237, and 2) to Baucis and Philemon, Ovid, *Meta.* viiii.626. See Lightfoot, *Colossians*, p. 304.

Δία More imposing in physical appearance.

Ἑρμῆν The constant attendant of Zeus (see Euripides, *Ion* on Hermes) and the one gifted with words.

ἐπειδὴ αὐτὸς ἦν ὁ ἡγούμενος τοῦ λόγου See Macrobius, *Saturnalia* i.8. See Wettstein.

Vs. 13 πρὸ τῆς πόλεως (αὐτῶν to be struck out). A position assigned to a titular deity. S.C. Teb. 152 comp. 482, 496.

For example, Artemis at Ephesus, Boeckh C.I.G. 2963C (and see Boeckh's note on 'the great deity Artemis' followed by πρὸ πόλεως. . . .). Cf. Hecate at Aphrodisias 2796, Demeter at Smyrna 3194, 3211 again πρὸ πόλεως. Comp. Wood, *Ephesus*, viii.2 p. 23 (and his note on πρὸ πόλεως).

ταύρους καὶ στέμματα

πυλῶνας porch, gatehouse, portals, A.V. 'unto the gates' in connection with 'which was before the city' is misleading. πυλῶνας here is the outer gate leading into the court where the temple stood. Highly developed in Egyptian temples. Of an outer gate to a private house see Acts 12:13 τὴν θύραν τοῦ πυλῶνος. πυλῶνος here is the outer gate. Comp. Mt 26:71.

Vs. 14 οἱ ἀπόστολοι 1) on the range of the term see Lightfoot, *Gal.* p. 92sq.

On Barnabas as an apostle see Gal 2:9; Acts 9:5-6. Personal witness to Christ. This probably is the case with Barnabas, see Acts 4:36. But 2) When did he become an apostle? Acts 13:1-2. There they are prophets, the two highest orders of the exceptional ministry (Eph 4:11 cf. Eph 2:20; 3:5; 1 Cor 12:28-29).

ἐξεπήδησαν 'rushed in'

Vs. 15 ὁμοιοπαθεῖς comp. James 1:17 whereas God is ἀπαθή. For the incident, see the case of St. Peter in Acts 10:26, of St. John in Rev 19:10.

εὐαγγελιζόμενοι ὑμᾶς

ζῶντα Pointing to the statues about them (see Raphael's cartoon of Hermes).

τῶν ματαίων An equivalent of the Hebrew הֶבֶל meaning 1) breath; 2) a vain, fleeting, empty something; 3) used especially of idols. Sometimes translated εἴδωλα see Deut 32:21, sometimes ματαία 1 Kings 16:13, so too 2 Kings 17:15; Jer 2:5. Sometimes ματαία seems to refer to a lie, see Amos 2:4. Sometimes the term seems to be used of a shaggy demon of the wood (see Lev 17:7). So 2 Chron 11:15, a fiend. The basic idea of ματαία is 'blind,' 'purposeless' so εἴδωλον, a Jewish application of the word, probably not found in classical sources. The subsidiary idea of a 'phantom' becomes prominent—1 Cor 8:4.

θεὸν ζῶντα a living God. The correct reading here. Much more expressive than the variants, for the stress is laid on the attributes not on the person. So too 1 Thess 1:9 showing how Pauline the language is here. Comp. 2 Cor 6:16 where the contrast is made with εἴδωλα, and doubtless elsewhere, where the force is not so obvious e.g. 2 Cor 3:3 where the contrast is between a dead letter and a living God.

Vs. 17 αὐτὸν, the focus, see my note on Col 1:20.

ὑετοὺς The drought in the country. Strabo xii.6 'the distance is eighteen [miles] but it [the road] is said to be now almost impossible because of the scarcity of water and provisions.'

ὑμῖν, ὑμῶν the correct readings, i.e. you Gentiles, you barbarians, but to the Jews was vouchsafed a more direct revelation of Himself.

Vs. 18 The conversion of Timothy, see the note on 16:1.

Vs. 19 λιθάσαντες, a Jewish mode of punishment, though here it was done with the aid of heathen and in a tumultuous way. The incident mentioned in 2 Cor 11:25. Doubtless this transpires on account of Paul's 'blasphemy' see Acts 9:58, 59. Comp. *Iliad* iv. 88 (and Fragm. p. 1503, Becker).

Vs. 20 The site not necessarily ascertained. See Lewin I, p. 151sq. Ruins seen by Hamilton, I p. 313sq. an acropolis not far from the lake Ak Ghieul. This is possibly Derbe because *Steph. Byz.* says φρέριον καὶ λιμήν (for which read λίμνη). Hamilton however places it at Dule, somewhat to the south, because Dule resembles Δελβετα = Δέρβη. But there is no lake there, and as there can be no λιμήν at Derbe (wherever it was) the substitution of λίμνη seems certain. See the letter of Hamilton to Horsa and C+H, I p. 228, the later version in which he seems prepared to abandon his view about Derbe.

Vs. 21 ἱκανοὺς

εἰς τὴν Λύστραν Note the definite article with this word and not with the others. The return to Lystra, where his life had so recently been in jeopardy, is emphasized. The original conception of the sentence in the author's mind seems to have ended with the mention of Lystra and καὶ εἰς Ἰκόνιον καὶ [εἰς] Ἀντιόχειαν is an after-thought or rather two after-thoughts, hence the repetition of the preposition.

Vs. 22 ἐπιστηρίζοντες Acts 15:32, 41; 18:23 (where στηρίζων is the right reading). For στηρίζειν as used by St. Paul see e.g. Rom 1:11 εἰς τὸ στηριχθῆναι ὑμᾶς.

καὶ ὅτι . . . 'and saying, we must through many afflictions enter . . .'

The tradition that St. Luke was a native of Antioch. Alford supposes, based on this passage, that his birthplace was Pisidian Antioch. This now has been refuted in *Journal of Philology* III (1856), p. 95. 'Alford . . . wrongly takes the language here as indication of the writer's presence in Antioch of Pisidia on this occasion.' And I added 'he rightly rejects the "common" explanation that ἡμᾶς is used by the writer as a Christian and of all Christians.' I pointed out that this is what is called the recitative ὅτι, i.e. it introduces the exact words of another as e.g. Acts 13:38; 15:1 and is most commonly used to indicate a quotation or indeed for the word 'saying' according to the circumstances. I went on to note that 'this abrupt shift from the oblique to the direct narrative is especially characteristic of St. Luke's style and are subsidiary proof of the unity of authorship of different parts of Acts, and between the Acts and the Third Gospel.' Comp. for instance Acts 1:4; 17:3; 23:22 and in vs. 23 there is the change from the direct [discourse] to the dialogue.

Alford's reply (Pro. p. 7 and here ad loc p. 160) . . . He says we should expect ὑμᾶς, but why? He asks, 'to what then would he have it referred'? My answer is, it is not used here by the writer, but rather by the speaker not as a Christian and [speaking] for all Christians, but rather as a Christian to the Christians he is addressing. There is an exact parallel in 1 Thess 3:2sq. where St. Paul does this same thing and uses the first person—προελέγομεν ὑμῖν ὅτι μέλλομεν . . . Observe the thoroughly Pauline character of this passage.

Vs. 23 κατ᾽ ἐκκλησίαν Is it 1) 'in every church' as κατὰ πόλιν. Acts 15:21; 20:23; Tit 1:5; 2) 'in the public assembly,' 'in church' as κατ᾽ οἶκον Acts 5:42? Though Acts 13:1 might suggest the latter, but the former is more probable in light of Tit 1:5, καταστήσῃς κατὰ πόλιν πρεσβυτέρους.

Vs. 25 λαλήσαντες ἐν Πέργῃ . . . It is not ἐπιστηρίζειν here. For though they had passed through Perga before (Acts 13:3), nothing is said of them preaching on that occasion.

Ἀττάλειαν A good harbor. The name comes from Attalus II (Philadelphus) of Pergamon, on 'Adalia' see Lewin, I. p. 154; also 'Satalia'; see C+H, I p. 242sq.

Vs. 26 ἐπλήρωσαν—'fulfilled' i.e. completed, discharged.

The Apostolic Council
and Its Aftermath
(Acts 15)

W<small>E ARE AT THE POINT IN</small> S<small>T.</small> P<small>AUL'S MISSIONARY CAREER</small> in which the first missionary journey is over, and Antioch has become the centre of the missionary work. The date is probably A.D. 50 or 51, but how is it ascertained? The removal of Felix and the arrival of Festus (Acts 24:27; 25:1), this seems to have occurred in A.D. 60. The notice of the centurions from the point of the boat departing from Caesarea. So the chronology looks like this: 1) two years in Jerusalem A.D. 58–60 (Acts 24:27); 2) return to Greece A.D. 57, 58 (Acts 20:3, 6); 3) three years at Ephesus A.D. 54–57 (Acts 19:3, 10; 20:31); 4) two years at Corinth A.D. 52–54 (Acts 18:11, 18); 5) start of second missionary journey A.D. 51.

The Importance of the Epoch. 1) In St. Paul's Life—The history now begins to have parallels with the Epistles; 2) in the history of the church, the liberation of the Gentile churches. Gentile Christendom enters upon an independent career. I will defer the comparison with the references in the Epistle to the Galatians until the passage is gone through.

On the matter of text criticism, we have various curious interpolations in the Western text here in vss. 1-5 e.g. one of D's curious additions in vs. 1 is περιπατῆτε, so also Syr. Peshit. margin. These same witnesses interpolate largely again in vs. 2 ζητήσεως. In vs. 4 C***, G, H, and others add καὶ ὅτι ἤνοιξε τοῖς ἔθνεσι. And in vs. 5 D and Syr. Peshit. margin again interpolate largely.

Vs. 1 Καί τίνες κατελθόντες ἀπὸ τῆς Ιουδαίας The same τίνες in Acts 15:24. What is their relationship to the Apostles of the circumcision? Their external connection is allowed, but their representative character in this particular matter must be denied. See vs. 24 οἷς οὐ διεστειλάμεθα. This accords with St. Paul's language in Gal 2:4 παρεισάκτους ψευδαδέλφους. A later analogous instance occurs in Gal 2:12 πρὸ τοῦ γὰρ ἐλθεῖν τινας ἀπὸ Ἰακώβου, which this passage serves to explain, the occasion being similar but not identical. Epiphanius *Pan.* xxviii.4 (p. 112) says Cerinthus was the leader of this group. This is an impossibility for Cerinthus belongs to the last days of the Apostolic Age.

What of the Conduct of the Apostles of the Circumcision? 1) There is no concurrence with the principles of these Judaizers, but 2) there is a disposition to concession in practice, for the sake of peace. This disposition occasionally degenerates into complicity, as in the case of St. Peter at Antioch. κατελθόντες (vs. 1) leads to ἀναβαίνειν (vs. 2) and Gal 1:18; 2:1 (ἀνέβην). So κατελθεῖν from Judaea to Caesarea (Acts 21:12; 12:19), κατέβαινεν from Jerusalem to Jericho (Luke 10:30). But the former of these terms can have two meanings—a journey by land or a voyage (e.g. Acts 18:22). But Antioch was not strictly a seaport. κατελθεῖν, κατέβαινεν probably refer to the high mountainous country in Judaea. Comp. κατέβαινεν in Luke 10:30 and Stanley's *Sinai and Palestine*, p. 416. κατέρχεσθαι occurs about fifteen times in Luke and Acts, always in 2nd aorist form, and in only one place besides in the New Testament—James 3:15. St. Luke is more vivid than the other Evangelists in marking out peculiarities of natural scenery? [Investigate.][1]

περιτμηθῆτε—the correct reading. Their argument is—unless you have been circumcised (circumcision being a preliminary condition to acceptance), holy living is in vain.

Vs. 2 ζητήσεως—the right reading here, and probably also in Acts 15:7. Observe the order here τῷ Παύλῳ καὶ τῷ Βαρναβᾷ . . . Παῦλον καὶ Βαρναβᾶν and also in Acts 15:22. Whenever St. Luke speaks in his own manner or from the Antiochene point of view, this is always the order. But at Jerusalem it is different. At Acts 15:12 Barnabas is mentioned first, at vs. 22 Barnabas is again mentioned first. Who can doubt the authenticity of the letter and of

---

[1]This is a note of Lightfoot to himself to investigate this matter further. He suspects this is true but wants to do more research. (BW3)

this narrative? St. Luke is evidently incorporating some earlier record.

Down to Acts 13:2 the order has consistently been 'Barnabas and Saul' but from that point at which Paul's missionary zeal appears and at which his name changes from Saul to Paul (Acts 13:9), the order is reversed. Paul is henceforth the principal person (Acts 13:13, 43) and that order is consistently maintained until here and vs. 25. Barnabas is heard first here and mentioned first in the circular letter as being better known at Jerusalem (cf. Acts 4:36). There is one other apparent exception to this rule, Acts 14:14, where it is determined by the circumstances narrated (see vs. 12).

τινας ἄλλους Comp. Gal 2:1, whether there was anyone else other than Titus, as is probable, we are not told. Certainly, Titus was there. St. Paul is only concerned with Titus (as he is the subject of the subsequent dispute) but his narrative does not exclude others. Titus was a representative of Gentile Christianity (Ἕλλην ὤν—Gal 2:3). He is especially mentioned because of the dispute. Titus is not mentioned anywhere in the Acts.

πρεσβυτέρους first mentioned at Acts 12:30.

ζητήματος question, and its cognate 'questioning.'

Vs. 3 προπεμφθέντες set on their way. Acts 20:38; 21:5 (3 times in Acts, 5 in Paul, once in 3 John and not elsewhere in the New Testament).

τήν τε Φοινίκην καὶ Σαμάρειαν treated as one region for the purposes of this narrative. Φοινίκην 'the land of palms' (see Stanley, *Sinai and Palestine*, p. 263).

τοῖς ἀδελφοῖς on the evangelizing of Samaria (Acts 8) and of Phoenica (Acts 11:19).

Vs. 4 παρεδέχθησαν corresponding to προπεμφθέντες [?]. The more normal word for this sort of reception is ἀποδέχεσθαι and so ἀπεδέχθησαν is substituted in some manuscripts. But παρεδέχθησαν is probably more appropriate here as denoting reception from the hands of another, and so thus corresponding to προπεμφθέντες. It *links together* the departure and the arrival better. See παρεδέχθησαν in Polybius, vi.2.14—'he was so warmly received.' Bengel says it corresponds to προπεμφθέντες in vs. 3.

ἀπὸ is doubtless correct here. They received a welcome 'from' the church. ἀπό is a bit more expressive than ὑπό. See Winer, no. 44, p. 463sq. (Moulton).

καὶ τῶν ἀποστόλων καὶ τῶν πρεσβυτέρων The καὶ singles out and emphasizes, but does not super-add(?). 'and more especially' in Acts 1:14;

4:5-6 see especially 1 Cor 9:5 which this passage will illustrate. Hegisippus in Eusebius *H.E.* ii.23—'the Jews, and the scribes, and the Pharisees.'

μετ᾽ αὐτῶν In vs. 12 it is δι᾽ αὐτῶν. "Cum ipsis et per ipsis" (Bengel). They are συνεργοὶ θεοῦ (1 Cor 3:9; 1 Thess 3:2). The E.V. 'done with them' is ambiguous.

Vs. 5 τινες . . . τῶν Φαρισαίων See Acts 6:7. The same party as mentioned in vs. 1. There is more to decipher in Gal 2, not that they were insincere in their profession but that their principles were inconsistent with Christianity.

πεπιστευκότες 'which believed' not 'having accepted the faith.' This verb is used frequently see e.g. Rom 13:11 ὅτε ἐπιστεύσαμεν.

δεῖ περιτέμνειν These are the words of these Pharisaic Christians. The ὅτι is recitative as frequently in St. Luke. Thus the αὐτούς becomes natural here. 'Saying it is needful to circumcise them and command them to observe. . . etc.' The deputation appears to have delivered their message previously. There are plenty of instances of the insertion of the words of others, including in Acts—Acts 14:22 and below Acts 15:38. It is obvious from the discussion here that circumcision had not hitherto been imposed on the Gentiles.

Vss. 5-7 The previous discussions which are not very accurately defined here and of which St. Luke probably had no very exact information leave ample room for the disputes we find in Gal 2. In vs. 7 there is an interpolation in D. ἐν ὑμῖν, with A, B, C, Tisch. is to be preferred, as opposed to ἐν ἡμῖν in the Received Text, E, G, H, etc.

Vs. 6 Συνήχθησάν . . . οἱ ἀπόστολοι καὶ οἱ πρεσβύτεροι That others were present appears from vss. 12, 22 comp. Acts 15:23 and Acts 15:25. This is apparent from the superscription of the circular letter.

ὑμεῖς ἐπίστασθε

Vs. 7 ἀρχαίων See Acts 21:6. Days belonging to the ἀρχῇ of the Gospel. Compare Acts 11:15—ἐν δὲ τῷ ἄρξασθαί (twelve or thirteen years before). This speech spoken in A.D. 51. How early Cornelius was converted we cannot say; but probably from the sequence of St. Luke's narrative, soon after the conversion of St. Paul. This was 14 years before the present time, allowing for the Hebrew reckoning of years (i.e. 37 or 38) i.e. but a few years after the day of Pentecost and (a reference to the present time) in the first primitive age of the Gospel.

ἐν ὑμῖν—the right reading. Thus emphasizing the appeal to their direct personal experience, and he also identifies the movement in the direction of liberty to them.

The ἐν ἡμῖν of the Received Text, besides not having such good support, is less possible though prima facie it is more natural.

ἀκοῦσαι τὰ ἔθνη St. Peter first preached to the Jews and then to the Gentiles, thus the prediction of Christ that 'on this rock I will build my church' was fulfilled. This is to be understood historically not doctrinally. The historical interpretation is as amply fulfilled in the New Testament as the doctrinal one is negated. *The primacy is historical and personal, not doctrinal and continuous. The* St. Peter as the Πέτρα idea must be refined. Πέτρος both as the chief of the Apostles, and having received the first heathen convert speaks. This is the last mention of him in Acts, but he is mentioned in Galatians and 1 Corinthians.

Vs. 8 ὁ καρδιογνώστης θεὸς Only once elsewhere in the New Testament— Acts 1:24 in a prayer where St. Peter is probably the mouthpiece for the Apostles (see Bengel). Comp. Luke 16:15—the Pharisee and the publican where there is a similar antithesis implied. The expression 'to know the heart' does not seem to appear elsewhere in the Gospels. The phrase is emphatic, here as in Luke 16. 'Qui cor, non carnem, spectat'—Bengel. See vs. 9 τὰς καρδίας αὐτῶν.

δοὺς τὸ πνεῦμα See Acts 10:44-45. See St. Peter's words Acts 11:15.

καθὼς καὶ ἡμῖν Comp. Acts 11:15.

Vs. 9 οὐθὲν or οὐδὲν here?

It is not circumcision of the flesh that cleanses the heart, but rather τῇ πίστει καθαρίσας τὰς καρδίας αὐτῶν. On the force of πίστις, it is a cleansing, purifying agent. The direct antagonism, or empirical exclusion, of faith and works would not be in the mind of the Apostles. Faith necessarily implies a godly life. It was an agent, and a more effective agent than the law for it affected not only the words and action but influenced the secret springs of action—καθαρίσας τὰς καρδίας.

Vs. 10 πειράζετε i.e. endeavor to make Him reverse his decree. I do not find the expression elsewhere in the New Testament except in the quotation from Deut 6:16 ('thou shalt not tempt the Lord your God') in the Gospels and comp. Heb 3:9 citing the LXX. See Meyer ἐπιθεῖναι marks 'das beabsichtigte Resultat zu dem πειράζετε τὸν Θεόν.' See Winer, 45.3—loosely 'imponando jugo,' or 'tempt God' to make Him reverse his decree as regards to the free acceptance of Gentiles.

On ἐπιθεῖναι see Winer, no. 44, p. 400 (Moulton).

Vs. 11 διὰ τῆς χάριτος, emphatic position, not by 'works of the law.' Comp. Eph 2:5, 8; Rom 11:6; Gal 5:4.

τοῦ κυρίου Ἰησοῦ Thus, a few words describe the difference between the old and new dispensations: 1) the revelation of the person κυρίου Ἰησοῦ; 2) the mode of working—χάρις rather than works of the law. C, D, G add Χριστοῦ after 'Lord Jesus.'

σωθῆναι not σωθήσεσθαι. But σωτηρία is a present fact.

καθ' ὃν τρόπον There is no difference between Jews and Gentiles. We are not saved by works of the law, and they by faith, for the same rule applies to all.

Vs. 12 Βαρναβᾶ καὶ Παύλου They hear Barnabas first as being the more well-known, more important, more highly esteemed, person in Jerusalem. Comp. Acts 15:25; 4:36; 9:27. There is an important interpolation in D and Syr. Peshit. here.

Vss. 13-21: Textual Issues

At vs. 17 the Byzantine (Majority) text adds πάντα after the final ταῦτα.

At vs. 18 the Byzantine text adds ἐστιν τῷ θεῷ πάντα τὰ ἔργα αὐτοῦ after αἰῶνός.

At vs. 20 D, sah, Cyprian adds καὶ ὅσα μὴ θέλουσιν ἑαυτοῖς γίνεσθαι ἑτέροις μὴ ποιεῖτε.

Vs. 13 ἀπεκρίθη Always in reference to something that has gone before. Not necessarily in reply to spoken words, but frequently to acts or expectations. Here is is a sort of judicial summing up—comp. Acts 3:12; 5:8; 8:34.

Relative positions of Peter and James. Peter is the most prominent leader in the church at large. James is the foremost person, officially, in the church at Jerusalem. Comp. Acts 12:17; 21:18. This relative position present in Galatians comp. Gal 1:18-19; 2:7 with Gal 2:9-10. Hence their respective parts here. Peter takes the initiative, he suggests the line of approach. James puts the resolution into shape, acting as a sort of chairman, διὸ ἐγὼ κρίνω.

James is the brother of the Lord, the Just, the bishop of Jerusalem. For his position in Jerusalem see Acts 12:17 (Ἀπαγγείλατε Ἰακώβῳ); Acts 21:18; Gal 1:19; 2:12. Universal tradition makes him identical with the brother of the

Lord (Mt 13:55), see especially Hegisippus in Eusebius *H.E.* ii.23, also in the apocryphal Gospels, and e.g. the Pseudo-Clementines. This is inferred also from comparing Galatians with James 1:1 and Jude 1. On Galatians, there is strong reason for believing: 1) that James was a brother of the Lord in some closer sense than cousin, probably a son of Joseph by a former wife (see Jerome); 2) that he was not one of the Twelve and therefore distinct from 'James of Alphaeus' who is probably to be identified with James son of Zebedee (Mark 15:40). He is here president of the council. He speaks authoritatively (ἀκούσατέ μου, διὸ ἐγὼ κρίνω, Acts 15:19), and his proposal is accepted. ἀκούσατέ μου A Jewish form of address? Acts 2:22; 21:1 or is it an appeal to a tumultuous audience?

Vs. 14 Συμεὼν, שִׁמְעוֹן What authority does Meyer have for preferring the rabbinical form of the name? The above form is the proper name in 1 Chron 4:20 which the LXX renders Σεμεών or Σεμών, the Hebrew form of the name. James naturally uses the strict Jewish form. Here Συμεών and elsewhere in the New Testament only at 2 Pet 1:1, and even there the use is doubtful (B and several others have Σιμών). Peter's Greek autograph would probably have been Συμεών that would easily be changed into more common Greek form, remembering the practice of substituting a Greek name that nearly resembles in sounds the Hebrew one. Note the naturalness of its occurrence here. On the meaning of the Hebrew word see Gen 29:33. Σιμών a Grecized form of the name—Simon, Simonides from the Greek σίμος. See below Acts 15:22 on Silas and above note Acts 11:8. Peter is nowhere else called simply Simon or Simeon except in the Gospels. Here it is natural enough.

ἐπεσκέψατο The ἐπισκοπή of God through some great prophet (Lk 7:46) and more especially through the coming of Messiah (Lk 1:68, 78). These words ἐπεσκέψατο, ἐπισκοπή are not found in the Gospels outside of St. Luke (comp. Lk 19:44 and here), but we do find it in 1 Pet 2:12—the day of ἐπισκοπῆς. Appropriate in the mode of St. James.

ἐξ ἐθνῶν λαὸν See Acts 4:25, 27; Rom 9:25-26 from Hos 2:1, hence λαός is a special, elect, peculiar people.[2] On the difference between λαός and ἔθνη

---

[2]There is an interesting note in the margin of the manuscript here—a note from Lightfoot to himself—'see former notes.' He is surely referring to his brown notebooks, and so this means he saw these materials as a supplement to all he had done before in preparing to lecture on Acts. This brings up an important point. If one wants to get the full picture of Lightfoot's views on Acts, it is not enough to go either just through the earlier brown notebooks or the later single

see *Clem. of Rom.* 29 (in Lightfoot p. 109). See λαός of Caesarea Acts 10:2, and δημός Acts 12:2. The language here is borrowed from the Old Testament, see especially Deut 4:34; 14:4 (quotes in *Clement of Rome* l.c.). The spiritual Israel is analogous to the actual Israel, 1 Pet 2:9-10. St. Luke especially avoids the word λαός when he is speaking of any other people (e.g. Acts 12:22). δημός used for a mixed multitude of Romans, Greeks, and others such as would be found at Caesarea (cf. Acts 17:5 at Thessalonike, Acts 19:30, 33, at Ephesus. The term only occurs these four times in the New Testament). On λαός and ὄχλος see Hegisippus in Eusebius *H.E.* ii.23. On the v.l. ἐξελέξατο here is taken from Deut 14:2.

On λαός in a special sense, 'a peculiar people,' in this sense λαός is opposed to ἔθνη, in Hebrew עַם as opposed to גּוֹיִם. Hence λαός is used: 1) of a chosen people, the people of Israel; the meaning of λαός would be as precise and definite for Jews as δημός would be for Athenians. It involved a peculiar relationship with God.[3] Cf. especially Ps 2:1-2 as interpreted in Acts 4:25-27 (cf. also Acts 19:4; 21:28; 23:4, especially 26:17, 23; 28:17 and see the note at Acts 10:2; 2) of a chosen people, the spiritual Israel, as here. Acts 18:10 cf. also Rom 9:25 from Hosea 2:1; Titus 2:14, and especially 1 Pet 2:9-10 which shows clearly, to my mind, that that Epistle was not written to Jews. Διασπορᾶς in 1 Pet 1:1 is about a spiritual dispersion, just as λαός here is a spiritual λαός. The distinction between ἔθνη and λαός to the Jew in Rev 21:3 can be illustrated by the distinction between ἔθνη and πόλις to the Greek. Cf. e.g. Aristotle *Polit.* ii.2 (also i.2). The word λαός is used about 140 times in the New Testament and probably not once without this peculiar sense [investigate more closely].[4] See Rev 5:9; 7:9; 10:11; 11:9; 14:6; 17:15. In an

---

leaf blue box materials. The latter is fundamentally *not* a revision of the former except in small ways of addition; rather it is Lightfoot going through and completing, filling in the gaps. For instance, there is nothing in these blue box pages about Philip and Simon from Acts 8. The episode is entirely skipped over. This is because he had already covered it in detail in his brown notebooks. What we have done in this manuscript is put the pieces together. One final point: I have found not a single place in all these pages where there is evidence that Lightfoot had changed his mind in some major way on some significant issues pertaining to Acts history, grammar, syntax, theology, ethics etc. between the time he began writing the notes in the brown notebooks in 1855 and when he put down his pen in the 1880s after writing some of this material. (BW3)

[3]Here, as throughout the volume, Lightfoot uses the term 'peculiar' in its older English sense of 'unique' not in the sense of 'strange' or even 'weird.' (BW3)

[4]Again, this is a note from Lightfoot to himself, wanting to make sure that he is correct about such a statement. (BW3)

exhaustive enumeration, a word would naturally be employed which involved a new idea, though the precise sense has no special bearing on the particular subject.

τῷ ὀνόματι αὐτοῦ for his name. The ἐπί of the received text is explained by the passage of Amos quoted below.

Vs. 15 τούτῳ is neuter, not masculine—'with this statement,' 'hereunto.'

Vs. 16 Amos 9:11 LXX quoted at length here. The principal variations from the LXX here are: 1) μετὰ ταῦτα for 'in those days' because of the content and the context there, there is nothing for the latter to refer; 2) κατεστραμμένα for κατεσκαμμένα. The reading κατεσκαμμένα, though very highly supported, has apparently been introduced here from the LXX. While the B text of the LXX has this reading, the A text has κατεστραμμένα; 3) the addition of τὸν κύριον (in vs. 17) to complete the sentence. Though τὸν κύριον is added in some copies of the LXX it was obviously no part of the original text; others supply the accusative with με; 4) the omission of the phrase 'just as in the days of αἰῶνος,' for in the Christian teacher's eyes, the restoration has assumed a higher significance; 5) the addition of γνωστὰ ἀπ' αἰῶνος (vs. 18), of which more presently.

The LXX differs from the Hebrew in one important point. For, לְמַעַן יִירְשׁוּ אֶת־שְׁאֵרִית אֱדוֹם 'that they may inherit (possess) the remnant of Edom,' the LXX must have read 'restore' for 'possess' (a small lexical difference from the verbal form יִירְשׁוּ with a daleth instead of the resh) and אדום ('Adam') for אֱדוֹם (Edom) and then either omitted the אֶת־ or treated it as introducing the subject of the verb. See Gesenius, 168, and arguing for his statement Ewald, *Gram.* no. 277 (pp. 600-01). On the phrase, 'the remnant of Edom' see 2 Kings 14:7. There is no case exactly analogous to this, where an active verb is followed by a noun introduced by אֶת־. If possible, its force would be 'I mean the remnant of men.' If it had preceded the verb, the difficulty would have vanished 'as for the remnant of men, they shall seek etc.'

John Lightfoot (II, p. 698) supposes that the later Jews altered this due to hostility to Edom. Evidence, and probability alike, are against this supposition. The typical significance which was given to Edom by the rabbis (see John Lightfoot l.c.) is important because the difference in general purport between the Hebrew and the Greek is reduced to a minimum. The Greek becomes a loose paraphrase of the Hebrew original. Either would fairly ex-

press St. James' meaning. If he spoke Hebrew, his Greek report might inten-
tionally introduce and substitute the familiar Greek reading. If it was in
Greek, he might not think it necessary to alter the well-known form of
words, unless there was not conformity with the original. The Hebrew says
in effect that the tabernacle of David was and held sway over all the nations;
the Greek, that all the nations should seek it, seek the Lord (see Alford).

τὴν σκηνὴν Δαυὶδ This rebuilt tabernacle of David is the church of Christ,
the abode of David's son. See especially the form of the Hosanna in St. Mk
11:10—εὐλογημένη ἡ ἐρχομένη βασιλεία τοῦ πατρὸς ἡμῶν Δαυίδ· ὡσαννὰ
ἐν τοῖς ὑψίστοις; Luke 1:32—τὸν θρόνον Δαυὶδ τοῦ πατρὸς αὐτοῦ; comp.
Acts 13:34 τὰ ὅσια Δαυὶδ. Comp. Is 16:5 where this is associated with messianic days.

Vs. 17 ἐφ' οὓς . . . comp. James 2:7, the only [other] passage in the New
Testament where the phrase occurs. Either 1) the expression is proleptic—
'they shall then be called by my name' or 2) this is a declaration of the immense Sovereignty and Fatherhood of God, as in Eph 3:15.

ἐπ' αὐτοὺς A combination only occasionally found in classical Greek, but
it is common in the LXX and the New Testament because it reproduces the
Hebrew idiom.

Vs. 18 γνωστὰ ἀπ' αἰῶνος, that this is the right reading will appear from
1) external authorities—in its favor as B, Aleph, C, 13, 61, Memph. Teb. and
others; there is no such report for any other reading. The two minor variants
are a) the addition of ἐστί after γνωστά in A, D, and the Harclean Margin,
and b) the same addition plus the adding of πάντα before 'his works' in E,
H, L, 31, Syr. Pesh. and the Harclean (txt). 2) the internal evidence, the
greater difficulty of the simple reading; a) is an addition to bring out the
meaning, and b) is a further improvement on a).

γνωστὰ ἀπ' αἰῶνος means known to God. Comp. Eph 1:4 καθὼς ἐξελέξατο
ἡμᾶς ἐν αὐτῷ πρὸ καταβολῆς κόσμου. For the γνῶσις of God see Rom 9:33;
2 Cor 10:5; and in connection with the calling of his people Rom 11:2 τὸν
λαὸν αὐτοῦ ὃν προέγνω, and 1 Pet 1:2 κατὰ πρόγνωσιν θεοῦ. The γνωστὰ
ἀπ' αἰῶνος is a comment of the speaker who has freely changed the notes of
these in the quotation. Compare Βαβυλῶνος in Acts 7:43. It might be possible to take γνωστὰ to mean 'known to men,' either a) 'who does these
things which are known,' or b) 'who makes these things to be known' (to

men). There is nothing in Amos that corresponds with this phrase, which is probably the right reading.

Vs. 19 ἐγὼ κρίνω Authoritative, but not necessarily final. The circumstances do not allow the latter.

παρενοχλεῖν to interfere or disturb, to trouble one while about something. A good classical word. The notion of παρά is of doing something *beside* the main action and so interfering with it.

Vs. 20 ἀπέχεσθαι See Winer, no. 45.4, pp. 376-77.

τῶν ἀλισγημάτων τῶν εἰδώλων, to be taken as one idea = εἰδωλόθυτον.

ἀλισγημ. must not be extended to the four words.[5] ἀλισγεῖν is a truly Alexandrian word (apparently strictly confined to Alexandrian Greek, see Mu. Strng., *De Dial.,* mcc. P. 145) and not found elsewhere in the New Testament. It means 'to pollute.' It must not be extended to the four words because: 1) a comparison of Acts 15:29 shows that τῶν ἀλισγημάτων τῶν εἰδώλων = εἰδωλόθυτον; 2) the verb ἀλισγεῖν wherever it occurs in the LXX has reference to meats. See Sirach 40:29, 33; Mal 1:7, 12; Dan 1:8. For the discussion of these prohibitions, see on vs. 21 below.

τῆς πορνείας, which was regarded as an *adiaphoron* by the heathen and was even mixed up with the heathen worship. It is worth observing that St. Paul in 1 Corinthians seems to recognize the fact that πορνεία was looked on as a matter of the same kind as the partaking of 'idol meat' by the heathen, he combats the one in 1 Cor 5, 7, and then the other in 1 Cor 8, though he is careful to enforce the differences in kind. I see that Bengel also observes this connection. This view of πορνεία as *adiaphoron* was one of the great errors that the early Christian teachers had to combat. That this sin was especially prevalent at Corinth, we know. That it should be so at Antioch is very probable, since the Syrian Orontes was a proverb for all that was impure and effeminate. It would seem to explain the insertion of πορνεία if we suppose that the question had been brought forward there, and that it had been one of the subjects of complaint.

πνικτοῦ and therefore with the blood in it. Cf. Lev 17:13-14.

---

[5]In his earlier notes he says, 'ἀλισγημάτων must be taken either with all the four words which follow or with the first only, probably the latter, for cf. Acts 15:29. The use of the term also in the LXX points to this as the probable construction.' In pencil he adds later, 'This was written before I saw Alford's note.' (BW3)

τοῦ αἵματος Gen 9:4. The injunction in this letter is referred to in Acts 21:25 in a manner which well illustrates its purpose here.[6]

Vs. 21 Μωϋσῆς γὰρ What is the connection here particularly with vs. 20? To command them to abstain for Moses? In that case, the meaning will be that the fact that the Mosaic law is constantly read would make the contradiction between precept and practice more prominent and offensive to Jews. 1) But against this, it must be said, that the prohibitions though incidentally in the Mosaic law, are only a small fraction of that law, and that the greater matters, circumcision, the Sabbath, the sacrifices, the festivals, were not touched by them. The offense therefore would remain undiminished. But the prohibitions in Moses are read every Sabbath. The subject therefore comes under notice and offense is given. γάρ assigns the reason for abstaining. This shows the 'animus' which dictated the circular letter, the wish not to give offense (so Meyers and Alford). 2) Note vs. 19, μὴ παρενοχλεῖν τοῖς ἀπὸ τῶν ἐθνῶν ἐπιστρέφουσιν ἐπὶ τὸν θεόν. . . . The majority of the law of Moses is vindicated by being read in the synagogues and being brought before the attention of the Jews, Sabbath after Sabbath. To vindicate it, there is no need to disturb the peace of the Gentiles. This seems to be the right interpretation. Of course James's speech is abridged. Several observations are offered, but the choices seem to be between the two options mentioned above.

ἐκ γενεῶν ἀρχαίων See the note on Acts 13:15. Probably from the epoch of the return. The 2nd lesson from the prophets were added later.

ἐν ταῖς συναγωγαῖς to be taken with what follows?

κηρύσσοντας αὐτὸν ἔχει specifying the place, and time, and manner in which he is preached.

Though συναγωγαῖς might mean the Christian places of meeting, most especially in the mouth of St. James (see James 2:1) and some have taken it so here, yet the statement itself would not be true at this time of the Christian assemblies (ἐκ γενεῶν ἀρχαίων κατὰ . . . κατὰ πᾶν σάββατον) and the connection as explained above is in opposition to this interpretation.

ἀναγινωσκόμενος cf. Acts 13:10-15, 26; 15:10; 2 Cor 13:15 and Alford's notes on the first passage.

κατὰ πόλιν from city to city. See Winer, p. 477.

---

[6]In a penciled note he adds, 'Examine the injunctions to the church at Thyatira (Rev 2:18) with reference to this apostolic letter.' (BW3)

With regard to these injunctions in vss. 20-21 it is to be observed 1) that they are negative. They do not enjoin the performance of any positive precepts. They lay no burden on the Gentile converts; 2) they are only given as temporary. They are not ordered as involving any principle. It is simply to avoid offense, to cement a union between the Jewish and Gentile Christians (see some good remarks of Meyer's). This is quite in the spirit of St. Paul. There is no expression in any of St. Paul's Epistles, as far as I remember, which implies that the Jewish Christians at Jerusalem did wrong in observing the rite of circumcision and other parts of the ceremonial law. See, in illustration of this, Acts 21:25; cf. 1 Cor 8:13.

Vss. 22-29: Textual Issues

Vs. 23—C, D, syr., Peshit. margin add τάδε . . . καὶ οἱ ἀδελφοὶ.

Vs. 24—The words λέγοντες περιτέμνεσθαι καὶ τηρεῖν τὸν νόμον of the Textus Receptus with C, E are not genuine.

Vs. 22 σὺν ὅλῃ τῇ ἐκκλησίᾳ The Apostles and elders originate, the laity confirms (cf. appointment of bishops in the early church). The letter is circulated, as we shall see, in the name of the Apostles and elders.

ἀποστόλοις . . . ἐκλεξαμένους . . . γράψαντες A common change of case that is not particular to Hellenistic Greek (as Alford says). It is quite impossible to take ἐκλεξαμένους, as if it were equal to ἐκλεξαμένοις. The A.V. however so takes it or has so paraphrased the passage so as to commit itself to no opinion, or to the contradiction. 'To send chosen men' and so again vs. 25. The accusative ἐκλεξαμένους is in reference to πέμψαι. The γράψαντες because ἔδοξε τοῖς ἀποστόλοις = the judgment of the apostles see Acts 20:3, ποιήσας τε μῆνας τρεῖς . . . ἐγένετο γνώμης and the reference in Winer, no. 63 pp. 709-10 (Moulton).

Ἰούδας, the name is common, hence the further qualifiers (e.g. Iscariot) and here τὸν καλούμενον Βαρσαββᾶν, a patronymic like Bar-Jesus, Barnabas etc. This is possibly a brother of Joseph Barsabbas (Acts 1:23), to be carefully distinguished from Joseph Barnabas with whom he is confused in a misprint in Alford. For speculations on the meaning of the name see John Lightfoot, I p. 745; II p. 640. The name Saba occurs several times in the Old Testament.

Σίλας i.e. Silvanus. Has connections with both St. Peter and St. Paul. See mention in 1 Thess 1:1. He is obviously a Jewish Christian (comp. Acts 16:20), but like St. Paul he is also a Roman citizen (Acts 16:37-38), hence his other name Silvanus.

Vs. 23 γράψαντες διὰ χειρὸς αὐτῶν, 'sending a letter by their hands.' Meyer remarks that the necessary multiplication of copies (κατὰ τὴν Ἀντιόχειαν καὶ Συρίαν καὶ Κιλικίαν and see Acts 16:4) would render it easy to procure a copy, so that St. Luke would be well able to give the document word for word and thus its authenticity is further evidenced by the character of the document itself, which is so framed as to require explanation by word of mouth (cf. vs. 27).

καὶ οἱ to be included?[7] Included doubtless here for: 1) οἱ πρεσβύτεροι ἀδελφοὶ seems a strange phrase in later times; 2) because others besides the Apostles are recognized in the context (Acts 15:4 and especially 22). At the same time the phrase οἱ πρεσβύτεροι ἀδελφοὶ though strange to later ears was a very natural expression at this time. The word πρεσβύτερος had hardly yet got recognized as an official designation and so the addition of the word 'brothers' was naturally made. οἱ πρεσβύτεροι unqualified might suggest 'the elders' of the Jews. As it stands here, this is an indication of authenticity. I have not yet been able to find a single instance of the use of πρεσβύτερος as an adjective in the New Testament.

τοῖς κατὰ τὴν Ἀντιόχειαν καὶ Συρίαν καὶ Κιλικίαν Note the limitation of the address.

Χαίρειν Seems in this letter to belong to the hand of St. James as the substance of it certainly suggests him. Comp. James 1:1.

Vs. 24 ἠκούσαμεν, ἐτάραξαν turns to the past time.

ἐξελθόντες should probably be omitted with Aleph and B. It was added to make the sentence more complete, perhaps suggested by 1 Jn 2:9 to obviate a difficulty. ἐξ ἡμῶν ἐξελθόντες, like those other Jews who came subsequently from James to Antioch (Gal 2:12).[8]

---

[7]Lightfoot in his notebook had earlier written: 'It is not a sufficient account of καὶ οἱ to say that these words were omitted on hierarchial grounds. The probability is they are spurious and were inserted for grammatical reasons. See Bunsen, Hippol. I, p. 15.' (BW3)

[8]Perhaps an editorial comment will be forgiven at this point. Here, Lightfoot's argument for the later date of Galatians simply falls apart. Had the Jews who insisted on Gentile circumcision and their never eating nonkosher food shown up in Antioch after the Acts 15 council and after the decree was circulated, it is impossible to understand why Paul didn't just cite the decree, whether in Antioch or to his Galatians churches, and thereby render the Judaizing argument about Gen-

ἀνασκευάζοντες a hapax here in the New Testament and not found in the LXX but it is found in classical Greek—meaning to demolish, dismantle, derange, disarrange, disturb.

λέγοντες περιτέμνεσθαι καὶ τηρεῖν τὸν νόμον This is a later gloss, not part of the original text.

Vs. 25 ὁμοθυμαδὸν The A.V. seems to combine two interpretations of the word so 'assembled into one accord.' The word does not occur in the New Testament except in the Acts where it is frequent (10 times), and in Rom 15:6. It here signifies 'together.' Elsewhere the A.V. properly renders it 'with one accord.'

The γενομένοις here, 'having come to a unanimous decision,' 'having agreed unanimously,' recognizes the existence of the Πολλῆς δὲ ζητήσεως (Acts 15:7) beforehand.

Vs. 26 ἀνθρώποις παραδεδωκόσιν and recommends them.

Vs. 27 ἀπαγγέλλοντας This present tense (as frequently) became ἀγγέλλειν and denotes not so much the final delivery of the message but rather the continuous carrying of it. See Winer no. 45, p. 429sq. Meyer speaks of both the carrying of the written document and their 'mundlichen Bericht hinzufugen.' Cf. on this verse Thucydides v, Winer p. 405.

τὰ αὐτά 'the same which we wrote.'

Vs. 28 ἔδοξεν can only mean 'to the Holy Ghost and us.' Attempts to evade the force of this are unsuccessful, as e.g. Neander 'through the Holy Ghost it seemed good to us also.' But if St. Paul said of himself solely δοκῶ δὲ κἀγὼ Πνεῦμα Θεοῦ ἔχειν (1 Cor 7:40), surely there was nothing extravagant in the assumption of the council composed of all the Apostles. If ever, on such an occasion the Holy Spirit must have guided the council of the Church.

ἐπιτίθεσθαι, if a middle comp. Acts 28:10 so e.g. Thucydides ii.24, Xenephon, *Anab.* iv.5.41, and other examples in Dad. Steph. *Thes.* s.v. p. 1845. See Kühner, II p. 96. ἐπιτίθεσθαι in the middle voice seems to denote the legislation—'the means of imposing.' Hence it is appropriate here as ἐπιθεῖναι is in Acts 15:10.

---

tiles keeping the law null and void without going through all the polemics we find in the Galatian letter. In Galatians his silence on the decree is pregnant, and he is silent because *there has been no resolution of this matter yet in Jerusalem.* Galatians dates to the earlier period before that meeting, when Paul was well and truly swimming against the Judaizing tide with no help yet from James or the Jerusalem church. (BW3)

Vs. 29 εἰδωλοθύτων = τῶν ἀλισγημάτων τῶν εἰδώλων of vs. 20, comp. Acts 21:25.

The outcome of sacrifices: 1) partly consumed at the sacrificial feasts, 2) partly sold at the slaughterhouse. See 1 Cor 8:1sq.; 10:7, 14, 19sq.

αἵματος Gen 9:4 comp. Lev 17:13-14; Deut 12:23-24

πνικτῶν Lewin l.c. The *Apostolic Constitutions* give orders that warn against one of the clergy eating this.

πορνείας Not spiritual fornication but in its literal sense. Nor again in the restricted sense of: a) marriage within forbidden degrees, or b) marriage with unbelievers. But how has this come to be enumerated among the ceremonial observances? What place has a gross breach of the moral law here? Let us examine the character of these:

1) First, as to their character, they are only negative. They impose no burden on the Gentiles, enact no rules, exact no performances. They simply say 'abstain from certain things.'

2) Their object. They are articles of peace. In themselves they are neither ceremonial nor moral. They are not ceremonial, or else πορνεία would not be included. Not moral, for even though we might see an indirect moral value in abstaining from and possibly in abstaining from 'blood' and 'things strangled' (though this is more difficult), yet their utter inadequacy seen as an elementary code of morals must be fatal to this view. They might or they might not have a moral value, but the absence or presence of the moral element is not the point of their introduction.

As articles of peace therefore, there is nothing preventing this being 'extemporaneous.' They would be dictated by two considerations: 1) on the side of the Judaic Christians who impose them, those things which would give the greatest offense are prohibited. 2) on the side of the Gentile Christians as to why they are imposed, these are offenses of which they were apt to make light. This last motive would seem to explain the introduction of πορνεία. We may talk about the difference Christianity has made in the eliminating of offenses against purity, but modern feeling is no criteria of the language and mode of thinking of the ancients. No moral man would think of justifying such sins, even though he didn't take a directly Christian point of view. Even the immoral may pay no deference to public opinion but he hides his sin. But to the average [ancient] heathen the case was different:

1) there is the social aspect. They were almost regarded as *adiaphora*; 2) their religious aspect. There was a religious sanction of immorality (see notes on 1 Thess 2:3, p. 22).[9] Antioch was a very centre of these religious immoralities (see Daphne at Antioch in Euripides v.19, Gibbon c.xxiii. II p. 546). Hence: a) this situation in Jewish countries makes this document intended for heathen reading (cf. Pseudo-Phocyclides 165sq., 177sq.); b) Paul's disclaimer in 1 Thess 4:2; and c) the constant warnings of St. Paul in writing to Gentiles. These items in the decree were not together in the history of Israel. But they are mentioned together in 1 Cor 10:7-8 with εἰδωλοθύτων and εἰδωλολάτρεια, and comp. Rev 2:14; 21:8.

ἐξ ὧν Not as generally taken 'abstaining from which,' but 'in accordance with which, if you keep yourselves' (so Meyer), but cf. John 17:15; Rev 3:10.

εὖ πράξετε 'ye shall do well' = 'ye shall fare well' not 'ye shall act well' nor 'ye shall prosper.'

Vs. 30 ἦλθον so Tisch., A, B, C, D and others which is doubtless the right reading. The κατά has reference to the point of departure, not the place of arrival. The overlooking of this has created the difficulty. An Antiochene would not understand 'coming down to Antioch.' He would not think of 'coming down from Jerusalem.' Hence probably this is why the Syriac version simply has ἦλθον.

Vs. 31 παρακλήσει may mean either: 1) comfort, consolation, which the pacific character of the letter gave them and which suits the context well, or 2) exhorting because it was less harsh than they had expected. In favor of the latter is vs. 32 παρεκάλεσαν. So Meyer.

Vs. 32 καὶ αὐτοὶ, like Paul, and Barnabas, or 'equally with Paul and Barnabas' and several others at Antioch (comp. Acts 13:1).

---

[9]Lightfoot's notes on 1-2 Thessalonians, along with 1 Corinthians 1-7, Romans 1-7 and Ephesians 1:1-14, were published as *Notes of the Epistles of St. Paul from Unpublished Commentaries* (New York: Macmillan, 1895). Upon publication of those notes, one reviewer wrote, 'One of the permanent regrets of New Testament students has been the incompleteness of Lightfoot's publications upon New Testament books. In many respects the greatest biblical scholar of his own generation in England, and preeminently the defender of the conservative view of the New Testament history and literature, his works are regarded by Christians as nearly authoritative as the work of any single scholar can be' (so C. V. W., review of J. B. Lightfoot, *Notes of the Epistles of St. Paul from Unpublished Commentaries*, *The Biblical World* 6.4 [1895]: 312-13 [on 312]). Subsequent to the publication of the three volumes constituting *The Lightfoot Legacy*, New Testament scholars (and others) will have a good bit less to regret with regard to the paucity of published commentary by Lightfoot on the New Testament. (TDS)

Παρεκάλεσαν See the notes on Acts 8:24.

Vs. 33 μετ᾽ εἰρήνης

ἀποστείλαντας αὐτούς The right reading.

Vs. 34 This verse to be struck out. The correct text has nothing, but since on the next mention of Silas we find him at Antioch, the later writer inserted a clause here to assist the narrative, namely, ἔδοξε δὲ τῷ Σίλᾳ ἐπιμεῖναι αὐτοῦ, and others add 'but only Judas went.' These sorts of variants are evidence of the incompleteness of the Acts narrative. The importance of this fact in analyzing the Acts and the Epistles [is great]. The Acts is adequate for its own purpose but it is not continuous history. Nor does it relate all that the writer knows. Thus we do not find all the visits to Corinth, or the sojourn in Achaia. And more especially the movements of Silas and Timothy within Greece and Macedonia, as implied in the first Epistle to the Thessalonians, are not all delineated here.

Thinking of Acts 15:1-33 as a whole, we note the truthfulness of the account: 1) *the propriety of the speeches* as words from these very speakers both in terms of a) sentiments (see Lightfoot, *Gal.* p. 350) and b) in terms of language, for instance St. Peter, ἐξελέξατο with the inf., ἀρχαίων (cf. Acts 11:15), διὰ τοῦ στόματος, the characteristic καθὼς καὶ ἡμῖν (Acts 10:47), and πειράζετε τὸν θεὸν (taken from Alford, more examples there). The speech is natural for the time at which it is given, but quite conventional when distance of time had diminished the point stressed. Or consider the words of St. James, such as Συμεών or ἐφ᾽ οὓς ἐπικέκληται.

2) *the letter.* Its language. The connection with St. James' [writing] χαίρειν, the archaic language οἱ ἀπόστολοι καὶ οἱ πρεσβύτεροι ἀδελφοὶ. The prohibitions listed—such a list could not have been invented at a later date. The document requires explanation, by word of mouth and persons who are made for this (vs. 27).

But how did this document come into St. Luke's hands? Copies are multiplied for distribution (Acts 16:4). In fact we seem to be able to trace exactly the way St. Luke became possessed of a copy of this letter. We find Paul and Silas (Acts 16:4) leaving copies of (or at least orally delivering) the decree. A few verses later (Acts 16:10), during the same journey, St. Luke joins St. Paul. That he was in company with St. Paul at the very time he was delivering the decree is very probable. That he was with him a few months later is almost certain. Elsewhere, even if the ecclesiastical tradition that represents him as a native of Antioch is valueless, the historical connection is established. The genuineness of the document and the truthfulness of the narrative established, we next consider its difficulties in connection with St. Paul's Epistles.

> The two accounts of his visits to Jerusalem. The answer is twofold:
> a) the one is private, the other the public conference. The one gives an account of the action on the scene, the other receives the account from him, hence the personal hurt in St. Paul['s Galatians]; b) the notice of the stress on his independence from the Apostles of the circumcision, on this the narrative is silent mentioning only the concessive spirit of Jewish and Gentile Christianity.

> 4) The subsequent conduct of the principal agents: a) St. Peter. His conduct at Antioch, directly stated by St. Paul as *inconsistent*. This is the point of the rebuke; b) St. Paul. He entirely ignores the Apostolic Decree—1) its temporary character, limited field of its operation, and 2) his independent authority.

> 5) The consistent claims about all the good intentions contradicts what goes before. Evidently Silas returns to Jerusalem with Judas, and came back afterwards to Antioch.

Vss. 35-36 Between these verses is to be inserted the incident of Peter's visit to Antioch on which St. Paul dwells in Gal 2:11sq. Silas perhaps returned with Peter or with some of those that came from James. The part that Barnabas had taken in the question at issue may have caused some angry feeling between them or some distrust in Barnabas by St. Paul.

Vs. 36 διέτριβον ἐν Ἀντιοχείᾳ ... μετὰ καὶ ἑτέρων This allows ample room for the visit of St. Peter to Antioch (Gal 2:11), the conduct of Barnabas on that occasion perhaps weakened St. Paul's confidence in him, and prepared the way for the subsequent contention and separation, so the quarrel over John Mark would follow more naturally.

ἐπιστρέψαντες δὴ see Acts 13:2; Luke 2:15. 'indeed, let us ...'

δὴ cf. Acts 13:2.

Vs. 37 Ἰωάννην τὸν καλούμενον Μάρκον His mother was a disciple—Acts 12:12. He is also a cousin of Barnabas (Col 4:10), which accounts for the part Barnabas has taken in this difference. He accompanied Paul and Barnabas on St. Paul's first missionary tour (Acts 12:25; 13:5) as their ὑπηρέτην (Acts 13:5) as far as Perga (Acts 13:13, whereas in Acts 13:5 he is simply called John), and there left them to return to Jerusalem. Hence the occasion of the difference mentioned here. Μάρκος, probably the same person, was with St. Paul in Rome when he wrote to the Colossians (Col 4:10) and to Philemon (Philem 24). He would seem to have been sent by St. Paul eastward during Paul's first imprisonment. Was it in this interval that he was with St. Peter? At all events, in writing to Timothy (2 Tim 4:11) during his last imprisonment and probably shortly before his death, he asks Timothy to take up Mark and bring him with him (ἀναλαβὼν ἄγε) 'for he is profitable to me and for the ministry.' Whether the Μάρκος 'my son' of 1 Pet 5:13 is John Mark is doubtful—of this, hereafter. Ecclesiastical tradition identifies them and this Mark is almost universally represented as the writer of the 'Gospel according to St. Mark' and in close connection with St. Peter, as his ἑρμηνευτής (Eusebius H.E. iii.39). At all events, St. Peter's Mark is probably the writer of the Gospel. On St. Mark as a preacher in Alexandria (Eusebius H.E. ii.15).

Vs. 38 Observe that this altercation happened at Antioch. Luke may have been present. But at all events the force of the expression shows that Luke is repeating St. Paul's words. We can almost hear the apostle's tones of indignant remonstrance (I had observed this before reading Alford's note). Paul speaks of τὸν ἀποστάντα. Acts 12:25; 13:5, 13. John Mark had left them at the critical moment, when their journey became dangerous. 'Paul is the righteous one, Barnabas ὁ φιλάνθρωπος' (Chrysostom, and see Alford's note). This seems to be quite Barnabas' character e.g. in introducing Paul to the Apostles at Jerusalem. It was perhaps his too great easiness of nature that led him into error that St. Paul notices (Gal 2:13). However great this παροξυσμός may have been at the time, wherever St. Paul speaks of Barnabas subsequently, it is evidently with kindness and affection. This is the case even when he is censuring his conduct as in Gal 2:13 (ὥστε καὶ Βαρνάβας), and in 1 Cor 9:6 (from which we conclude he was unmarried—see Col 4:10).

τὸ ἔργον = the Gospel in St. Paul's language. See Phil 2:30 (my note), see also the note at Acts 13:2 above. Cf. Ignatius, Ephes. 14, Rom. 3.

Vs. 39 παροξυσμὸς, here again an indication of the truthfulness of the narrative—a sharp disagreement. All the roughness of the expression has evaporated in the A.V.

1) Moreover the specifics of Paul's own ends.

2) Consistent with the character of Barnabas.

3) The undesigned coincidence is twofold: a) with Galatians—previous circumstances leading to an alienation; b) with Colossians connection later between Barnabas and Mark (Col 4:10).

4) Different terms for the Apostles, this makes for conflicts.

εἰς Κύπρον Barnabas' own country (Acts 4:36). Division of the districts, partly based on familiarity—Cyprus (Acts 13), S.W. of Asia Minor (Acts 14). Barnabas takes Cyprus as his district, Paul the continent as being more familiar with it. He would pass through his native Tarsus on his way.

A. John Mark—subsequent notices of in connection with a) St. Paul, Col 4:10 (cf. Philem 24), 2 Tim 4:14; and with b) St. Peter, 1 Pet 5:13. Barnabas and Mark in ecclesiastical tradition associated together with the church in Alexandria. There is possibly some basis in fact.[10] B. Barnabas—subsequent notices of—Gal 2:13; 1 Cor 9:6; Col 4:10.

Vs. 40 ἐπιλεξάμενος This middle form is a hapax in the New Testament. Having chosen as his companion, taken him to himself. See the same term as defined in Polybius vi.26.6 of a solider choosing his assistant, or a captain his lieutenant. How did Silas get to Antioch? Perhaps he came with Peter, perhaps with the emissaries of James. At all events, communication with Antioch was early and constant. Recognition of the church, being similar to the case of Barnabas. Barnabas has acted on rational but personal motives. Paul had recognized a public duty, and secured public recognition (see Alford's note).

Vs. 41 διήρχετο Two points to be observed about St. Paul's missionary tours: 1) he is never without a companion, Barnabas before, Silas now; the word for this συνεργῷ. The mission of the Twelve Apostles (Mark 6:1) and of the seventy disciples (Luke 10:1) even when the mission did not seem to require it, they went two by two (see Mk 11:2); 2) he first traverses the old district, *confirming* the churches. Then he breaks new ground.

ἐπιστηρίζων confirming in the widest sense.

---

[10]I have left this in the text, even though Lightfoot later crossed it out. It shows at least that he took very seriously the critical analysis of later church traditions. Apparently, he changed his mind about this tradition. (BW3)

τὴν Συρίαν καὶ Κιλικίαν On the close alliance of the two provinces, see Acts 15:23, and Lightfoot, *Galatians* on Gal 1:21 on their geographical connection. There was an ecclesiastical as well as a civic connection. Visiting again the country which had been the scene of his missionary labors during his first apostolic journey, and previously. Barnabas takes the island of Cyprus, which also they had visited in company. Cf. vs. 36. The purpose of St. Paul was accomplished between them.

The Second Missionary Journey
(Acts 16)

Acts 16:1-10: Textual Issues

Vs. 1 Lachmann reads καὶ εἰς Δέρβην καὶ εἰς Λύστραν with A, B.

Vs. 4 See a long addition of D.

Vs. 6 Omit τήν before 'Galatian.'

Vs. 7 ἐλθόντες Lachmann adds δέ with A, B, C, D, E and others, and this must be the right reading.

τὸ Πνεῦμα Ἰησοῦ The Byzantine Majority text omits Ἰησοῦ, which Lachmann and Tischendorf rightly retain with A, B, C**, D, E, various Syrian witnesses.

Vs. 10 Another curious addition of D.

Tischendorf has ὁ κύριος with D, G, H and large majority of Syrian witnesses. Lachmann has ὁ θεός with A, B, C, E.

Vs. 1 Κατήντησεν reached, arrived. Peculiar to Paul and the Acts in the New Testament. Nine times in Acts, four times in St. Paul. In St. Luke it is always used of approaching or reaching a place (except Acts 26:6 where it is in one of St. Paul's speeches) and in this passage where it is used of approach from the sea. In St. Paul it is used of 'attaining' or 'pertaining to.'

ἐκεῖ i.e. Lystra as the order naturally suggests, especially with the accusative, which is the correct reading. Lystra is separated from Derbe by a repetition of εἰς. That Timothy was a native of Lystra and not Derbe appears also from: 1) vs. 2 Λύστροις καὶ Ἰκονίῳ; 2) Acts 20:4. Not a native of

Derbe but associated with a native of Derbe. The inference from this verse
that Timothy too was a native of Derbe is not only not supported by that
passage, but by implication negated. 3) the Peshitta on Acts l.c. makes him
a native of Lystra, though this may be a critical correction. Derbe is mentioned first, then Lystra the order one would reach them traveling East to
West from Cilicia. Timothy was probably converted by St. Paul on the occasion of his former visit (Acts 14:8, 20). See also 2 Tim 3:11. At least he is
called by St. Paul his son in the faith (see 1 Tim 1:2).

γυναῖκος Ἰουδαίας πιστῆς Eunice, 2 Tim 1:5. Hence the references in
2 Tim 3:10 to these parts.

Vs. 2 καὶ Ἰκονίῳ Note at Iconium rather than at Derbe, an account of the
similarities of Lystra relative to the former place. Bin M. Kallisseh probably
the site of Lystra. Cony. and H I p. 228 (2nd edition 1856). Derbe was an
especially unimportant place (cf. Acts 14:19).

Vs. 3 διὰ τοὺς Ἰουδαίους Compare the expression in Gal 2:4. The Jews in
these quarters cf. Acts 14:19. An external source of information here?

ὅτι Ἕλλην Different procedure in the case of Timothy and Titus and the
circumstances were different: 1) in the case of Timothy, it was his duty to
become a Jew to the Jew; 2) the duty of Titus was to maintain the liberty of
the Gospel. See Gal 2:3.

Vs. 4 παρεδίδοσαν Whether orally or in writing is uncertain. Probably
the latter with the strength of the expression.

αὐτοῖς the Gentile Christians in these cities.

Vs. 6 The first mention of, and first recorded visit to Galatia. On what is
meant by Galatia see Lightfoot, *Galatians,* the Introductory remarks.[1] It is
important to observe that Phrygia at this time had no political significance.
It was an inland district bounded by Pisidia (with which it was separated by
the Taurus range) on the South, by Cara, Lydia, Bithynia on the Northwest,
and by Galatia, Cappadocia, and Lycaonia on the East. The phrase 'Phyrgia
Major' signified roughly a part of Asia Minor where the Phrygian race dwelt
(see Cony. + H I p. 291, note 1 for references), but the Phrygian race spread
widely. Phrygia Minor was on the Hellespont and the northern part of
Mysia. The greater part of Phrygia was in proconsular Asia, but some was

---

[1]Lightfoot in a parenthesis asks, 'Why is it called here and at Acts 18:23 "the Galatian and Phrygian region"?' (BW3)

in the adjacent Roman provinces. Hence, sometimes it is specified over and above Asia, sometimes not (scarcely 'distinguished from' or 'excluded'). It is so specified here and Acts 2:9. It is not in 1 Pet 1:1.

Observe the correct reading here—τὴν Φρυγίαν καὶ Γαλατικὴν χώραν with τήν omitted before Γαλατικήν. This relieves us from any geographical difficulty. If τήν were to remain, and we were to suppose (as is natural and as might be expected from St. Luke's strict accuracy) that the districts were mentioned in the order in which they were visited, we should have to send St. Paul from West to East, from Phrygia to Galatia, and back again from East to West (from Galatia to Mysia). But the right reading—'the region of Phrygia and Galatia' (Φρυγίαν is an adjective) shows that the country meant was the border country and St. Paul kept, roughly speaking, along this frontier, as we might expect from his subsequent movements. The frontier runs in Struner's map about northwest, right for the heart of Bithynia. St. Paul appears to have been detained in Galatia by sickness (Gal 4:13). The suggestion that St. Luke, 'the beloved physician' first joined Paul in a professional capacity is not to be hastily rejected. He was however probably not with St. Paul at this time.

It is important in relationship to St. Paul's epistles to both the Galatians and the Colossians. We must consider: 1) the reading; 2) the grammar (comp. Mark 1:5; Luke 3:1); 3) the meaning.

The questions Galatians raises for our discussion are: 1) is the mention of Galatia here a reference to the Roman province, or the region ruled by the Gauls? (cf. Lightfoot, *Gal.* p. 19; *Col.* p. 24). If the former, then it would include Derbe and Lystra, Antioch and Iconium and thus the evangelization of Galatia has already been described. But this is contrary to: 1) St. Luke's use of geographical terms in this passage. This explains a) the use of the phrase 'the Phrygian and Galatian region,' and b) the others terms used in the context i.e. Lycaonia and Pisidia; 2) the course of the itinerary; 3) the notices in the Epistle to the Galatians.

But what exactly does the phrase 'the Phrygian and Galatian region' in 16:6 mean? We should compare Acts 18:23 which has 'the Galatian region and Phrygia.' This difference is easily explained. St. Paul then preaches in Galatia (Gal 4:13-15). Why then did St. Luke not relate these incidents after preaching in Galatia? 1) His ignorance of the facts? 2) The subsequent defection of the Galatian churches? It is useless to speculate.

The questions Colossians raises for our discussion are: 1) in view of Col 2:1 apparently St. Paul had never been there. 2) His itinerary here in Acts would not take him in that direction. Renan said that he had been there, but had not preached.

Vs. 6 Another v.l. here, and this one is rather important—διῆλθον or διελθόντες? Important because it separates Galatia from the previous places. Nothing is said of the preaching but it is implied by Acts 18:23, and there is implied opposition in διῆλθον, between Phrygia and Galatia. The κωλυθέντες signifies as much. The verb in any case denotes thoroughness [as in going completely through something] and is generally used in relationship to the preaching (Acts 8:4, 40; 9:32; 11:19; 18:23; 19:21, 22, 25).

ἐν τῇ Ἀσίᾳ 1) naming of Asia, 2) evangelization Acts 18:22; 19:1sq. Asia in the Bible is either: 1) the Syrian Kingdom though the King of Asia's name had been transferred to the King of Pergamon (see 1 Macc 8:6-8). Cf. e.g. 1 Macc 11:13. This is the sense in which we find 'Asia' in the Apocrypha. From the Pergamene Kingdom, Asia Minor passed into the hands of the Romans whence 2) Asia = proconsular Asia. The West portion of Asia included Mysia, Lydia, Caria, and the greater part of Phrygia. This is the New Testament sense.

Vs. 7 τὸ πνεῦμα Ἰησοῦ The mission of the Spirit from Jesus. Comp. Acts 2:33; Phil 1:19.

κατά in the borders of, in the neighborhood of (in this case Mysia). Mysia is a part of Asia (Howson being wrong that it is excluded from Asia, p. 209). The apostle seems to have had a series of revelations that drove him westward to Troas, and from Troas to Macedonia. He kept on the borders of proconsular Asia until he arrived at Mysia, hoping that sooner or later the hindrance might be withdrawn, and he might preach in Asia. Finding that he was prevented there also, he attempted to penetrate into Bithynia. Here too he was prevented and his only course was to pass through Mysia to the coast.

εἰς τὴν Βιθυνίαν Bithynia did however, before long, come to the Gospel. Cf. 1 Pet 1:1 and Pliny's letter 10.97.

Vs. 8 παρελθόντες 'having passed by' i.e. not preached in, for they must have passed through it.

Vs. 9 Τρῳάδα Obviously, St. Paul does not preach on this occasion. This accords with 2 Cor 2:12. 'Alexandria Troas was a recollection of the city of Priam, and a prophecy of the city of Constantine' C+H I p. 330. TRANSIENS ADIUVA NOS—the motto of S.P.G.

τῷ Παύλῳ noting the emphatic position of these words. This prepares for the first person narrative which follows.

Vs. 10 ἐζητήσαμεν first person plural. Note: 1) the naturalness of its sudden appearance; 2) the relation of its appearance and disappearance, Acts 17:1sq., and it reappears at Acts 20:5. Was St. Luke a native of Philippi? See Renan, *St. Paul*, p. 131.

ὅτι . . . εὐαγγελίσασθαι construction confined to St. Luke and St. Paul in the New Testament except 1 Pet 1:12. Alford's note is worth reading however he has passed over one important consideration. The question is between the third plural (e.g. vs. 7) and the first plural. St. Luke would scarcely have been in St. Paul's company at vs. 7 where he was αὐτούς. There is, I think, no instance of the third plural being used by St. Luke where we are sure that he was with St. Paul [investigate]. St. Luke indeed drops the 'we,' but does he use 'they'? In other words, the use of the third person singular 'he (Paul) does so and so' does certainly not exclude e.g. the presence of St. Luke a bit. The use of the third person plural 'They did so and so' certainly does seem to show that he was not present at the time.

16:11-13: Textual Issues

vs. 11 δέ Tischendorf, D adds it as usual.

Vs. 12 τῆς before Macedonia. Lachmann thinks original, included in Byzantine Majority text, omitted by A, C, E, et al.

Vs. 12 αὐτῇ before 'the city'—Tischendorf. Lachmann, A, B, C, D*, E have ταύτῃ.

Vs. 11 εὐθυδρομήσαμεν On St. Luke's nautical terms see Smith, *Voyage and Shipwreck*, pp. 36sq. (new edition). The word also occurs in Acts 21:1. Contrast Acts 20:5 'for days.' The reverse voyage took five days, here only two days, hence εὐθυδρομήσαμεν.

Νέαν Πόλιν See Lightfoot, *Phil.* p. 48. Port of Philippi, probably the ancient Datum, see Smith's Dictionary s.v.

Σαμοθράκην See C+H, p. 331. citing Il. xiii.12sq.

Vs. 12 κἀκεῖθεν i.e. ἐπορευσάμεθα or some such word. Ignatius follows the same route.

On ἥτις see Lightfoot, *Phil.* p. 51 and on κολωνία p. 50.

It seems to be unnatural to make πρώτη 'furthest eastward.' Would it not in this case be ἡ πρώτη? Yet we find the article frequently omitted with numerals in the New Testament where we should expect to find it. No principle however is violated. The numerals are in themselves *definite* and therefore do not require the article, though I believe it is generally found in classical authors. Cf. Acts 12:10; 17:4; 20:18, perhaps however this will not justify πρώτη τῆς μερίδος. The conjunction πρώτης is worth considering if any conjunction were allowable in the New Testament. It would perhaps be easier if we omitted τῆς with Lachmann in which case we might take Μακεδονίας πόλις together, 'a city of Macedonia, first of the district.' μερίδος is peculiar to St. Luke and St. Paul in the New Testament. In short, the words will not bear Alford's translation. They must mean of the district of Macedonia. May not the words πρώτη . . . πόλις mean 'a principal city' or even 'the chief city.' Even if Amphipolis was at the time the capital, still, if Philippi were a more important place it might be called this without reference to its political status, just as Liverpool might be called the chief town in Lancasterhire.

κολωνία is emphatic. The incident turns on this fact.

Vs. 13 παρὰ ποταμὸν see Lightfoot, *Phil.* p. 53sq. The absence of the definite article would perhaps alone be fatal to the the Stryman, and the Stryman was so far off that the distance of the προσευχή would be more than a Sabbath day's journey.

ἐνομίζομεν προσευχὴν εἶναι The reading ἐνομίζομεν—A, B, C, 13, 61, Memph. Eth. This seems also to be the reading of the Harclean Syr. The reading of ἐνομίζεν must be considered a corruption of this. ἐνομίζετο E, 31, Syr. Peshitta.

προσευχήν A2, Aleph, C, 13.61; προσευχὴ A*, B, D ,E, H, L.

The original reading in this verse was altered for several reasons: 1) the proper meaning of προσευχή was not understood; 2) the general purport of the sentence did not seem quite satisfying; 3) προσευχήν got corrupted into προσευχή and some further change seemed to be required. This must be taken in connection with the v.l. in vs. 16 τὴν προσευχήν nearly the same authorities as read προσευχή here omit the definite article there. Obviously, they did not understand the meaning of the word προσευχή which refers to a 'place of prayer.' Hence it cannot imply any building, nor is this necessary. It may simply be a place in the open air where prayer was held. But the words οὗ ἐνομίζομεν seem to decide the issue in favor of the other interpretation. See my notes in *Phil.* p. 52. Comp. Josephus, *Ant.* xiv.10.22 with his *Bell Jud.* iii.296 and his *Vit.* 56; Note, too, Philo, *in Flacc.* 14 and *Leg. Ad Gaius* 21, 43. In Philo it can refer either to a building = synagogue, or to an open-air place. See also le Moyse on Polyc. p. 72sq. and the reference to the *Shep. of Herm.* s.v. The phrase likely means 'where prayer was wont to be held' but in vs. 16 where we have the definite article before προσευχή it seems to be 'place of prayer.'

τῇ τε ἡμέρᾳ τῶν σαββάτων or τὰ σαββάτα is a phrase unique to St. Luke in the New Testament. John 19:31 is an apparent exception and the phrase is found in a v.l. in Mark 6:2 but is wrong.

ταῖς συνελθούσαις γυναιξίν No doubt there were many proselytes like Lydia. On the women in Philippi and Macedonia see Phil 4:2. She is here a noble example of the better spirit of the church to which she belonged and of which she was probably the firstfruits. Cf. Rev 2:19. See Lightfoot, *Phil.* p. 56sq.

Λυδία 1) the name. Probably, she had some other name at home. The form Lydia rather than Lyde suggests part of the Roman population of Philippi. The name occurs in Horace. But note, slave women were called by the name of their country—e.g. the Syrian, the Lydian. Here it is clearly a proper name though perhaps determined by her country of origin cf. Achaius, a native of Corinth. 2) relationship to St. Paul. For Renan's very strange speculations see his *St. Paul*, p. 148 sq. A much more probable hypothesis is to identify her with Euodia or Syntyche. See Claud. *Rescript. Pres.* i.270—'Lydia Sidonis'; Valerius Flacc. iv. 369—'Lyda mursus sparso telas macilaverit ortho.' Proselytes would be more likely to be women than men (cf. Acts 13:50).

Vs. 14 πορφυρόπωλις See Boeckh, for Thyatira 3496, 3497, 3498 and see the note at 3480. For the term πορφυρόπωλις itself see Boeckh, 2519 (a coin inscription). The whole district was famous for its skill in purple-dying. Cf. Ar. Ach. 112. There was a special guild, a company of dyers at Thyatira (the trades seem to have formed themselves into guilds there) οἱ βάφεις. See Boeckh, Corpus Inscrp. ii Part. xiv. Sect. vii. nos. 3496, 3497, 3498 and 3480.

σεβομένη a believing Gentile, a proselyte, see Acts 17:4, especially Acts 17:17; 13:43, 50, and probably Acts 18:7. Perhaps an allusion to this in Acts 18:13. In Acts 19:27 it is used of the worshippers of Artemis at Ephesus. It only occurs in these passages in St. Luke. Outside St. Luke only Mt 15:9; Mark 7:7 (both the LXX of Is.).

διήνοιξεν an 'opened circle.'

Vs. 15 ὁ οἶκος αὐτῆς The argument for infant baptism is not strong from an isolated case, but the referencing of the household strengthens it (see Gloag).

πιστὴν τῷ κυρίῳ This phrase cannot mean, as some would have it, 'believing in the Lord,' but rather 'faithful to the Lord.'

The Church of Thyatira in Revelation. Thyatira was a Macedonian colony (see Trench, Chandler), but when and how evangelized?

Lydia is presented as a type of the church, see Rev 2:19: 1) πιστίς εἰ κεκρίκατε με πιστὴν; 2) διακονία. Perhaps, as Renan suggests, it was through her (Phil 4:15) that the Philippians ministered to Paul's work.

16:16-40: Textual Issues

Vs. 16 τὴν omitted before προσευχήν in Byzantine Majority text with D, G, H, etc.

πύθωνα, probably the right reading, Byzantine Majority text -νος with D, E, G, H, etc.

ὑπαντῆσαι Lachmann, ἀπαντῆσαι A, D, G, H, etc. The two verbs are constantly confused in Greek mss.

Vs. 17 ὑμῖν So B, D, E, vg. The Textus Receptus has ἡμῖν on inferior but fair authority.

Vs. 19 One of the many interpolations of D.

Vs. 24 εἰληφώς, Lachmann. λαβών Tisch. on better authority.

Vs. 30 D adds τούς λοιπης ἀσφαλισάμενος καί.

Vs. 31 Byzantine Majority Text adds Χριστόν after 'Jesus.'

Vs. 35 Another curious addition in D, syr. Marg.—συνελθόν οἱ στρατηγοί etc.

Vs. 39 another long gloss in D.

Vs. 40 πρός A, B, D, G, H, L et al. There is scarce any authority for εἰς which the Textus Receptus has.

Vs. 16 παιδίσκην 13 times in the New Testament comp. Gal 4:31 [and apparently from the LXX here]. Here the sense of the term is determined by τοῖς κυρίοις αὐτῆς. She was a slave.

πορευομένων ἡμῶν Probably on a subsequent occasion.

εἰς τὴν προσευχὴν 'to the place of prayer.' Of these places see Howson, I p. 346.

Πύθωνα See Lightfoot, *Phil.* p. 54; Plutarch, *Moralia* p. 414; *Clemen. Hom.* ix. 16. The term ventriloquist would however convey a wrong idea. Not art, but rather demonical possession is the main idea, a divining spirit that was considered to come from Apollo (Plutarch *de Def. Oracl.* 419E, other passages in Wettstein). The divining spirit seems to be the essential thing and ventriloquism an accidental element in a Πύθων. Is Πύθων ever a name of Apollo? Meyer says, 'Πύθων ist Name des Apollo also das (der?) orakelgottes.' Antholog. Jacobs I p. 55. She was in the popular language Πύθωληπζος. On the nature of this spirit see Baumgar. ii. p.121. In using the word Πύθωνα St. Luke is no doubt accommodating his language to popular belief but this cannot be the case with πνεῦμα; the whole point of the narrative turns on the fact of the girl being possessed by a spirit.

μαντευομένη The only place in the New Testament where this word or its cognates occurs. Contrast προφητεία to μάντις, μανία. See Plotius, and consider the Montanist controversy.

ὑπαντῆσαι 'Came to meet,' whether with friendly or hostile purposes, can also mean 'came up to,' 'confronted.' Not ἀπαντῆσαι (the Textus Receptus) which would simply be 'met' without any idea of direct confrontation. Comp. κατακολουθοῦσα (vs. 17) which is the right reading. The *absolute* distinction between ὑπαντῆσαι (by design) and ἀπαντῆσαι (by chance) however cannot be maintained (see R+P). But still the former is more appropriate here and is more likely to be used where there is design, the other where it seems more a matter of mere chance (comp. Mark 14:13). All the words for ὑπαντῆσαι suggest persistency and importuning.

μαντευομένη, not elsewhere in the New Testament. As for its use in the LXX Deut 18:10, 14; so 2 Kings 17:17; Eccles (31) 34:5. This Greek word almost always represents the Hebrew קסם divination, which always has a bad sense, except Prov 16:10 where it is a sort of figure. Sometimes it is associated with other similar Hebrew words (see Jer 60:36; Ezek 21:23) that can have a good sense but in Ezek 13:8 חָזָה has a negative sense and the root HZH is regularly contrasted with προφήτης. See Micah 3:11 'her prophets divine for money.' The main differences between μαντεία and προφητεία: 1) the former has no moral element in it; 2) it is respective of the will or the consciousness of the speaker. The orthodox writers urged this against Montanism. See especially Auctor., *Ab Catapha*. In Eusebius *H.E.* v.16-17, critiquing that they spoke 'in an ecstasy.' Even with Balaam the case is not so, yet Balaam is the extreme limit of προφητεία and he is called μάντις as a reproach (Josh 13:22).

ἐργασίαν business, trade, hence the proceeds of the trade.

Vs. 17 ἔκραζεν means 'kept crying.'

κατακολουθοῦσα 'following close behind' only here and in Luke 23:5 in the New Testament, 'dogging their steps.'

οἵτινες 'for they'

ὑμῖν more probable than ἡμῖν. 'Arrests this attractions.'

Vs. 18 διαπονηθείς only here and Acts 4:2.

Vs. 19 ἐξῆλθεν ἡ ἐλπὶς Repetition of the same word. Dumb. Not a rational and literate [phenomenon], but the evil spirit had gone out of her. The connection is destroyed in the A.V. where the first ἐξῆλθεν (in vs. 18) is translated 'came out,' the second 'was gone.'

ἐπιλαβόμενοι See the notes on Acts 9:27.

εἰς τὴν ἀγορὰν the marketplace (the Greeks and Romans shut the gate to the Hebrews).

τοὺς ἄρχοντας The special term, defined in vs. 9. This is quasi-oblique. The plaintiffs in expressing their intentions would naturally say 'before the magistrates or authorities.' The historian speaks directly here in his own person and is more precise in vs. 20, τοῖς στρατηγοῖς, 'the mayors.'

Vs. 20 στρατηγοῖ See the article in Smith's Dictionary s.v. Philippi. So Paul and Silas come into the town to the 'agora,' the marketplace, where the magistrates (ἄρχοντας) sat, who turned the matter over to the military authorities (στρατηγοῖ). On these military officials see Lightfoot, *Phil.* p. 51. Observe the Roman characteristics of Philippi throughout the narrative. See Baumgar. ii. p. 123. On στρατηγοῖ see Aust. *Polit.* vi.8 (p. 178 with Bekk.).

ὑπάρχοντες being Ἰουδαῖοι to begin with, there is an a priori assumption of offense. It is obvious that the higher members of the hierarchy here at Philippi are not Jews, as elsewhere, and 'we do not let the Jews take part in it.'

Vs. 21 ἔθη, 'customs.' On the 'Jewish superstition,' see Arrian xiii.32 ('extrema superstitio'). Remembering the political character of ancient religion, especially at Rome, the Jews were viewed as both unpatriotic and inhuman and not surprisingly there was persecution, for example under Domitian (Dur. Cap. lxvii.14). The edict of Claudius must have been issued shortly before this incident in Philippi. See Acts 18:2 (Suetonius, *Claud.* xv), if identified with the Senatus Consultum Mandate (see Tacitus, *Annal.* xii.52) it would be in A.D. 52. It would give the clue to the feeling expressed at Philippi here, a Roman colony. Here again the sentiments are thoroughly Roman. Contrast the instigation of the persecution and consequently the form of the accusation at Thessalonike (17:7). A political imprisonment here, note the parallelism and yet contrast with the account of St. Peter's in Acts 12. See Baumgar. ii, p. 122: 'Among the Jews this ... assumes a religious form; among the Gentiles of the Roman Empire it takes a political shape.'

Vs. 22 συνεπέστη But to whom does the συν refer? Rose up with whom? To the instigators of the persecution? More than likely to translate 'rose up as one man.'

περιήξαντες αὐτῶν τὰ ἱμάτια . . . αὐτῶν i.e. of Paul and Silas. This deduction comes 1) from the Greek, for while αὐτῶν might refer to the thing in itself, but coming before the reference to the ἱμάτια, this is hardly probable; 2) from the requirements of the sense of the sentence. They were not Jews, who would not listen to blasphemy. This was done by means of the lictors. Notice how thoroughly true, thoroughly Roman all this is, though no parade by the author of his knowledge. He does not mention the lictors by name until later, he does not give the fatal word 'summons,' 'despolie verbera.' He is content with giving the narrative in his own style, and it bespeaks a Roman colony because it is faithful.

περιρρήσειν here, the περι conveying the notion of stripping (cf. Mt 26:65; Joel 2:13; Acts 14:14). For the process see Dionysius of Halicarnassus iii.30 (p. 502) and ix.39 (p. 1849). Also Plutarch, *Vita Popl.* 6. The other Greek references in Wettstein need not be consulted. Here the magistrates are said to do what they ordered the military to do. There is no talk of a judge hanging or imprisoning a convict. See Seneca, *de ora.* i.19 and C+H I. p. 357.

ῥαβδίζειν See 2 Cor 11:25 where Paul says he was beaten with Roman rods three times.

Vs. 24 ἠσφαλίσατο a middle. See Mt 27:65-66. This is the first persecution originating with Gentiles. See Baumgar. ii. p. 122.

εἰς . . . φυλακὴν C+H I p. 357sq.

On ξύλον, 'stocks,' see Eusebius *H.E.* vi.39 (also V.I. *Ep. Ner.* no. 27).

Vs. 25 singing—'to boast in tribulations' as St. Paul himself says, see Baumgar. ii. p. 127.

Vs. 27 μάχαιραν, v.l. τὴν μάχαιραν (Lachmann).

Vs. 28 The strangeness of the incident. The Apostles singing Psalms at midnight in a dungeon and the miraculous earthquake, had so affected the prisoners that their minds were too much occupied with what had happened to attempt to make the escape. See the gloss of D on vs. 30 τοὺς λοιποὺς ἀσφαλισάμενος.

Vs. 29 φῶτα, 'lights,' not as in the A.V. 'light.'

Vs. 30 ἵνα σωθῶ Powerfully affected by what had happened, he naturally asked the question—he had heard before of his prisoners professing to show 'the way of salvation.' If he did not know the full import of this word 'salvation,' he at least knew enough to make him eager to secure it.

Vs. 31 καὶ ὁ οἶκός σου Not meaning of course that the belief of the jailor would secure the salvation of his family also, but 'believe on the Lord Jesus Christ and thou shalt be saved,' these terms are offered to him, and to all members of his household no less.

Vs. 33 ἔλουσεν (i.e. 'lavit'), ἐβαπτίσθη ('baptizatus est'). With regard to this incident it may be remarked (Bengel): 1) the arguments drawn from the narrative in favor of infant baptism are very precarious; 2) but it does seem to imply a sanction of baptism by aspersion without immersion, though any such sanction is scarcely needed and the practice as in this case is justified rather by the spirit of the Apostle's teaching.

Vs. 34 ἀναγαγών 'having brought.' A.V. 'And when he had brought them into his house, he set meat before them.' It is perhaps sufficient to remember that they were in a prison that would probably be underground. Cf. e.g. the chamber of the Mamertine in Rome.

παρέθηκεν τράπεζαν the opposite is ἀπαίρειν.

See Pollinx, *Laert.* vi.84, x.81.

πανοικεὶ 'all + house'

Vs. 35 ῥαβδούχους (i.e. the lictors of duumvirs) the first mention of lictors by name, but as for their actions see vs. 22. Plutarch, *Moralia P.* 280A, Cicero *Leg. Cyr.* ii 34 no. 93. But by word ῥαβδούχους seems to be the common translation of 'lictor,' no less of those that carried the 'fisces' than of those who carried the 'bacilla,' οἱ ῥαβδοι being the Greek translation for either the fisces or the bacilla. Cf. Plutarch, *Vit. Rom.* 26.

The earthquake must have been reported to, and perhaps felt by the duumvirs and the accompanying incidents had reached their ears. This with their recollections of the previous day decided their conduct.

ἀπέστειλαν here, ἀπέσταλκαν in vs. 36.

Vss. 36-37 ἀπήγγειλεν 'reported.' Note the threefold approach: 1) δημοσίᾳ (publicly); 2) Ῥωμαίους; 3) ἀκατακρίτους (uncondemned).

Cicero, *Pro Rabri.* 4 (12). An earlier law the Valerian (254 A.U.C.) and the Porcian (506 A.U.C.), had forbidden scourging of Roman citizens, except in certain circumstances. See Cicero, *Verr.* ii.5 nos. 57, 62, 66. See the passages in Alford.

How did St. Paul possess the Roman franchise? It was not as a native of Tarsus, for Tarsus was neither a 'colonia' nor a 'municipium.' Some ancestor must have procured the freedom of the city, either by purchase, or as a reward for services, for St. Paul was himself born free (Acts 22:28). Silas also, from this account, seems to have been a Roman citizen.

οὐ γὰρ 'certainly not.' An expression of indignation. Paul shows a sense of his political rights. Comp. Acts 22:28, 1 Thess 2:2—ὑβρισθέντες (having been insulted). Paul's political sensibilities influences his diction e.g. Phil 3:20—πολίτευμα. The Romans are proud of their citizenship but our true 'familia' is in heaven.

Vs. 38 ἐφοβήθησαν Plutarch, *Pomp.* 24.

Vs. 40 πρὸς τὴν Λυδίαν

Macedonia and On to Athens
(Acts 17)

Acts 17:1-15: Textual Issues

Vs. 1 The Byzantine Majority text has ἡ συναγωγή, the article omitted by Lachmann, A, B, D, et al.

Vs. 3 The best supported reading seems to be ὁ Χριστὸς Ἰησοῦς with Tischendorf.

Vs. 4 Lachmann with but slight authority has καὶ Ἑλλήνων.

Vs. 5 Read with Lachmann Ζηλώσαντες δὲ οἱ Ἰουδαῖοι καὶ προσλαβόμενοι, and also προαγαγεῖν (Lachmann).

Vs. 13 Lachmann adds ταράσσοντες τοὺς ὄχλους with A, B, D, 25.

Vs. 15 See a gloss of D here.

Vs. 1 Διοδεύσαντες They passed through Amphipolis and Apollonia because having founded one Christian community in Macedonia Prima, they were anxious to found another in Macedonia Secunda. Thessalonike is the capital of the 2nd district of Macedonia. From Thessalonike the Apostle goes to Berea which is in the 3rd district of Macedonia. That is indeed separate from Philippi. The evidence of synagogues in Amphipolis etc. is lacking. Even in Philippi there is only a place of prayer. This may have had some influence in dictating the Apostle's steps to Thessalonike.

Vs. 2 We are not of course to assume that the Apostle's preaching was confined to the three Sabbath days and that during the week he did nothing as Mr. Jowett has hastily done. The Sabbath days would be the only days that he could get the Jews together, and speak to them as a body, see Acts 17:17.

κατὰ δὲ τὸ εἰωθὸς τῷ Παύλῳ εἰσῆλθεν As he himself declares (Rom 1:16—'the Jew first').

Vs. 3 διανοίγων a word peculiar to St. Luke in the New Testament, except Mark 7:34 (and v.l. at vs. 35). Cf. Luke 24:32 that shows that the general meaning is 'to expound.'

παρατιθέμενος 'Laying before them.'

καὶ ὅτι οὗτός ἐστιν A change from the oblique to the direct narrative, after the manner of St. Luke cf. 14:22.

Alford's translation is wrong here. It should be 'that this is the Christ—namely Jesus, whom I preach to you.'

Vs. 4 προσεκληρώθησαν, not as E.V. but cf. Acts 2:47. cf. the right reading in Eph 1:11. As God's κλήρος see 1 Pet 5:3.

Vs. 5 Ἰάσονος Possibly a Grecized form of the Jewish name, Jesus or Joshua. In 1 Macc 8:27, 2 Macc 2:24 it is a Jewish name. One Jason is mentioned in Rom 16:21, where he is called a 'kinsmen' of St. Paul, i.e. probably a Jew. They went there after one of their own countrymen who had deserted [to join] the Apostle. So again at Corinth (Acts 18:17).

πονηρούς means lewd.

Vs. 6 ἔσυρον. . . . ἐπὶ See Lucian, *Lex.* 50.

τοὺς πολιτάρχας the municipal authorities at Thessalonike. Sophocles, *Lex.* quotes Sophronius. For this see Migne Patrol. Graecae lxxxvii, 3401D. The magistrates of Thessalonike have an unusual title not mentioned in ancient literature, but it appears from a monument of a different kind that the title is perfectly correct. Thessalonike was a free city, hence the δῆμος. See the paper by W. S.W. Vaux, 'On a Great Inscription of Saloniki,' *Transaction of the Royal Society* Vol. 8 2nd series (1866), pp. 525-30, inscription on politarchs with an honorific list of names (male and female), and see C+H i. p. 359; Boeckh ii. p. 52, remarks: 1) Evidential value: A crucial test of the accuracy of Luke; 2) Secondary illustration of the Apostolic narrative a) the prominence given to women (e.g. Cleopatra in the inscription); b) the coincidence of names, Secundus of Thessalonike (Acts 20:4); Gaius of Macedonia (Acts 19:29); Sosipater (Sopater) of Berea (Acts 20:4); and Demetrius (Demas). See below. The inscription begins 'ΠΟΛΕΙΤΑΡΧΟΝΤΩΝ . . .'

CONCLUSIONS OF VAUX ABOUT THE INSCRIPTION: 'As nothing follows these names upon the stone, we may suppose they were inscribed on the slab to be [displayed], and the erection of the arch itself [took place] during the politarchate. We are not able to state exactly where on the arch the inscription was placed . . . it may be that [the inscription] was on the right side of the road-way, and not, as might have been expected, over the centre of the arch. . . . '

It may be seen that the name Flavius disappears, and with it one criteria of a date. Nicopolia is a woman's name on which see 1957g, 1994d.

Vs. 7 ἀπέναντι τῶν δογμάτων Here the issue is the decrees of Caesar, the crime called 'majestatis' (false claims to kingship). In Philippi it was the issue of religio licita.

βασιλέα ἕτερον see 2 Thess 2:4, 1 Thess 4:6. comp. John 19:12, 15. Neander (Pfl I, p. 157) suggests that perhaps Paul's preaching about the parousia and resurrection and the messianic Kingdom had led to the suggestion of a violation of the decrees. See Meyer. Cf. 2 Thess 2:4 to 1 Thess 4:6.

Vs. 8 πολιτάρχας The word occurs in Oneas, *Poliorcet.* c.26, where it does not denote a special magistracy, but is equivalent to ὁ στρατηγός 'the general in charge of the city.' But should it be πολιτάρχας here? This is only one manuscript of Oneas. See Sophronius, Migne Patrol. Graec. lxxxvii. P. 3401D where we have πολιτάρχας but not in reference to Thessalonike.

Vs. 9 καὶ λαβόντες τὸ ἱκανὸν It is a translation of the Latin phrase 'satis accipere.' See the notes on Plautus. On ἱκανόν, see Diog. Laertius iv.50, comp. Cicero, *Pro Qui* xiii.49; Plautus, *Must.* 1.3.67. Here it could be giving security for their good will, being handed over to keep the peace.

Vs. 10 Παῦλον καὶ τὸν Σιλᾶν. No mention of Timothy. The same at Philippi. Yet it is highly probably that Timothy was with them at Philippi and almost certain (1 Thess 1:1; 2 Thess 1:1) that he was with them at Thessalonike. Still, he was much younger and held an inferior position, and therefore was exempt from persecution.

Βέροιαν not a hiding place. In Macedonia Fortia. See in the Chronicles of Macedonia p. 9.

EXCURSUS: THE HISTORY OF ST. PAUL'S DAYS AT THESSALONIKE
Supplemented by notices from the Epistles: A) his preaching; B) his

means of support; C) his converts in Thessalonike (Intro. to Chapter p. 10, C. p. 14).

The chief additional facts we derive from St. Paul himself regarding this stay at Thessalonike are:

1) That though St. Luke only mentions the preaching on the three Sabbath days and dwells chiefly on his converts from among the Jews, we conclude from his language about the Thessalonians that he was there for a longer period and that he made a large number of Gentile converts (possibly the majority were Gentiles). This fact is not mentioned by St. Luke, but it is not excluded (cf. e.g. 1 Thess 1:9 and Paley *Horae Paulinae*). The principle Thessalonian converts of whom we read are Aristarchus (Acts 19:29; 20:4; 27:2) who was a Jew, who accompanied Paul to Jerusalem and hence to Rome and shared his imprisonment with him there (Col 4:10; Philem 24). He was with St. Luke at Rome (see passages last cited), and from him St. Luke may have derived information (as well as from the Apostle himself) of what happened at Thessalonike.

2) That St. Paul laboured with his own hands while there, 1 Thess 2:9-10 and that contributions were sent to him from Philippi (Phil 4:15-16—possibly it refers to this visit, the expression ἐν ἀρχῇ τοῦ εὐαγγελίου coming close after ὅτε ἐξῆλθον ἀπὸ Μακεδονίας. The phrase refers to the beginnings of the Gospel relative to Macedonia).

Vs. 11 εὐγενέστεροι of qualities of mind. The basic meaning is ingenuous, frank, liberal, as opposed to the normal type of the slave described as cunning, subtle.

Vs. 12 τῶν Ἑλληνίδων γυναίκων Ἑλληνίδων refers grammatically only to γυναίκων but in sense it is carried on to ἀνδρῶν. See Lightfoot, *Philippians*.

εὐσχημόνων comp. Acts 13:50; Mark 15:43. Joseph of Arimathea is εὐσχήμων βουλευτής. These are the only three passages in the New Testament where the term is used of persons.

Vs. 13 σαλεύοντες 'the swaying to and fro like a large wave.'

ταράσσοντες a general disturbance as in a sea buffeted by the winds.

κἀκεῖ goes with ἦλθον probably (not with σαλεύοντες as Meyer says). ἐκεῖ is sometimes used with verbs of motion in the New Testament e.g. Mt 2:22; John 18:3; Rom 15:24.

Vs. 14 ἕως ἐπὶ unquestionably the right reading. The ἕως is not redundant but expresses the purpose or intent or aim of those who escorted St. Paul, without however implying that the purpose was unfulfilled—'for the purpose of conducting him to the sea.'

This text has been strangely neglected. It will not mean a 'feint' [in a particular direction]. Thus there is no question as to whether this journey toward the sea was a feint or not, and there is no reason to suppose that St. Paul went by land. Better rendered 'as far as the sea.' There he would be ready to take ship to any port he preferred as opportunity allowed. The contrast in vs. 14 is not that they took a different way than that which they set out on, but that they went a further distance. This would insure his escape and further his missionary projects. As for the idea of going to Athens, he does not yet seem to be definitely concerned about that.

ἐπὶ τὴν θάλασσαν Probably at D as the words seem to suggest.

Vs. 15 καθιστάνοντες See passages in Winer. They were conducted, brought to this destination. Lit. 'set him down.' Comp. 1 Sam 5:3; 2 Chron 28:15 LXX on this verb. On the movement of Silas and Timothy southward see Acts 18:5. On St. Paul's choice of 'stations' in Macedonia, see Introduction to the *Chronicles of Macedonia*, p. 7.

ACTS 17:16-31: TEXTUAL ISSUES

Vs. 16 θεωροῦντος with the lectionaries, θεωροῦντι Textus Receptus, with D, G, H.

Vs. 18 αὐτῷ by some omitted.

Vs. 23 ὅ . . . τοῦτο Textus Receptus ὅν . . . τοῦτον with E, G, H, Chrysos. Comm. etc.

Vs. 25 ἀνθρωπίνων Textus Receptus ἀνθρώπων. There are various other minor variations of the T.R. in these verses from the probable right readings e.g. in vs. 30 πάντας is changed to πᾶσι in T.R., G, and H.

Vs. 16 παρωξύνετο was provoked, distressed, a keen edge was given to it. Comp. Heb 10:24—παροξυσμόν.

κατείδωλον etc. 'Over run with idols.' All the writers through several centuries bear witness to this character of Athens (for full ref. see C+H I p. 427; Renan, *St. Paul*, p. 173), but comp. Soph. *Od.* 260; in the 4th century B.C.

Xen. *De Rep. Ab.* ii.9, iii.8;[1] in the 4th century A.D. Julian, *Misopagon.* p. 74, calls them 'lovers of gods, all of them' and of the Athenians as excelling even all other Greeks in this. The point is, throughout the whole period, and more writers could be cited to the same effect, they point to this character of Athens. Not far from the date of St Luke we have Josephus, *c. Apion.* ii.11. So the Athenians were called θεοφιλεῖς, φιλόθεοι, and like terms. This is not the impression we would get from the profanity of Aristophanes, but that was only a passing phase. The profusion of images, statues, festivals, sacrifices, is dealt with by writer after writer. See especially the fine chorus in Arist. *Nub.* 701sq. Lucian calls the Athenians 'pius populus.'

There are blunders in Gloag. εἴδωλον—an image i.e. 1) a phantom etc.; 2) a likeness. Hence its appropriate references in Jewish and Christian language—the gods of the heathens.

Vs. 17 μὲν οὖν 'to continue.'

ἐν τῇ συναγωγῇ i.e. on the Sabbaths which is naturally understood as the antithesis to κατὰ πᾶσαν ἡμέραν.

Vs. 18 Why Epicureans and Stoics only? 1) these were the most influential sects at the time. The world had tired of metaphysical speculation, and philosophy had taken an ethical turn. The Stoics and Epicureans were less secluded; 2) the schools of the Stoa. The garden of Epicurus was apparently in the city (see C+H, I p. 402). On the other hand, the Lupercalia and Aea dinners were outside the city.

συνέβαλλον 'encountered' as the A.V. has it. Comp. Acts 20:14. Suggesting a collusion or a deliberate purpose which is also suggested by παρατυγχάνοντας [vs. 17]. Others take this to mean 'conferred' comp. Acts 4:15.

σπερμολόγος an Athenian term of abuse. For its primary sense see Aristoph. *Au.* 233. See also Alexis Athenaeus viii, p. 344 for a play on the word, and Demosthenes, *de Corona* no. 127 (p. 269).

Ξένων δαιμονίων the accusation made against Socrates. See Plato, *Tim.* 378D; Xen. *Mem.* i.1.; Cicero *de Leg.* ii.8.

καταγγελεὺς a rare word, meaning a formal announcement.

τὸν Ἰησοῦν καὶ τὴν ἀνάστασιν The Greek commentators seem to be right

---

[1]Here Lightfoot notes, 'I cannot find where this reference is in Xenophon, though Wettstein and others cite it.' Notice again how he does not simply cite the primary sources as found in secondary sources; he checks them against the originals. (BW3)

in supposing that 'Resurrection' was mistaken for a goddess. There is no other way of accounting for the addition of τὴν ἀνάστασιν by St. Luke as Baumgart. has justly observed. Otherwise, δαιμονία plural must mark the category (as Meyer, and not as Alford). Chrysostom's interpretation seems to be correct. Bentley indeed (*Interp.* iii p. 132) reports the 'concert' of Chrysostom, but the wider context points to it. An erection of an altar to 'anastasis' would be quite in accord with the Athenian precedent. Pausanias i.17 mentions an altar to Pity, Persuasion, etc. In any case, 'resurrection' would sound strange to Athenian ears cf. Aeschylus, *Eum.* 618.

Vs. 19 ἐπὶ τὸν Ἄρειον Πάγον Its position—nearness to the forum and doubtless convenience for a hearing decided the choice of place. There is nothing of a judicial character in this. No judge, no accusation, no verdict. It is quite a stretch to suppose that Paul was tried by the Court of the Areopagus. There was a prudential propriety in the locale as it was the court that did try religious offenses. More particularly, it authorized the erection of statues (see Renan, p. 193). This is a perfectly voluntary act on St. Paul's part. The request is even courteously made by those who would hear him. βουλόμεθα οὖν γνῶναι, e.g. the motive is given in vs. 20. And yet the spot was well chosen where, both on religious and political grounds, religion had so strong a hold on the Athenian mind.

Vs. 20 τίνα θέλει ταῦτα εἶναι What these things purport to be.

ξενίζοντα more than just ξένα, novel and astonishing, we find the middle in the sense of 'to feel strange,' 1 Pet 4:4, 12, not 'strange' but 'innovating.'

Vs. 21 οἱ ἐπιδημοῦντες The ξένοι were always a numerous class of people at Athens. See Theophrastus, *Charact.* 3, and especially Thucydides vi.30.

On καινότερον (the newer folk) see Theophrastus, *Charact.* 8. 'Other cities had their newsmakers; in Athens an official demand produced the news made.' (Zebo [?] p. 239).

Seneca, *Epist.* 94 'Alexander. . . . Athenas facere.'

Vs. 22 ὡς δεισιδαιμονεστέρους Over careful in religious matters. Thus as if Paul had said 'I am not accusing you of being irreligious, if anything your religion is in excess, only it is misdirected.' There is a passage in Arrian (?) *Var. Hist.* v.17 on the δεισιδαιμονία of the Athenians. δεισιδαιμονία occurs in Acts 25:19 where it seems to be said somewhat in scorn. It is said by Agrippa, perhaps it is used in an old philosophic spirit. See Josephus *Ant.*

v.30. Theophrastus takes δεισιδαιμονία in a bad sense and defines it as Δειλία to the δαιμόνιον. See also the passages in Plutarch *de Superstit.* 165B, 168C, and others in Wettstein. And see M. Antonius 1.16. Philo too opposes δεισιδαιμονία to εὐσέβεια. The word appears not to be used by Plato. It seems in itself to be a neutral word and would imply more or less rebuke according to the religious sentiments of the speakers and hearers. It is, I think, impossible to divest it of all blame, especially before an Athenian audience. The shade of censure is of course deepened by the comparatives, yet the E.V. is much too strong. Therefore, in itself the word could be used in a good sense (see Josephus, *Ant.* x.3.2).

θεωρῶ Even from where St. Paul stood, this statement might be a plain fact. W.G.C. informs me however that the Parthenon is hidden from view by a large obstacle (the Propylaea).

Vs. 23 ἀναθεωρῶν τὰ σεβάσματα See Diodorus Sic. xii.15. What he would see as he passed through the city we may gather from Pausanias. σεβάσματα refers to objects of devotion. It is perhaps more than an accident that the only other passage in which this word occurs is 2 Thess 2:4, written within a few months of the time when St. Paul spoke on Mars Hill.

ἀναθεωρῶν reviewing, examining, inspecting.

Ἀγνώστῳ θεῷ Not to 'the' unknown god, but to an unknown god. Note reference to the custom of the Athenians. See Pausanias i.1.4 who mentions unknown gods and also Philostr. vi.3; Diog. Laert. i.110; Aulus Gelius ii.28; Jerome, *ad. Tit.* i.12, Isidor. Pelus., *Ep.* iv.69; Lucian, *Phlg.* 9 and 29. Doutbless there were several such altars.[2] See Renan, p. 174 (and investigate recent discoveries in Athens). Compare the Roman custom *sei deo, sei dea.* Aul. Gellius ii.28. Such an inscription as what he mentions can actually be found at Rome (see Burris, *Rome* p. 158, references in Renan, p. 173). Renan, p. 175 makes a full comment suggesting that in effect Paul's Greek meant he was 's'agissant d'un dieu appele par excellence,' "la Dieu inconnu" and in the note he adds, 'Si tel avait ete le sous l'un script eut offert θεῷ Ἀγνώστῳ et non Ἀγνώστῳ θεῷ.' I can't at all follow him in his view of the Greek and should have said quite the op-

---

[2]There are in fact four such altars to be seen in the Istanbul Archaeology Museum, on the third floor of the old building where biblical items (like the Gezer calendar, the inscription from Hezekiah's tunnel, and the warning sign from the Herodian temple) are to be found. (BW3)

posite. But surely Paul's argument here cannot have the meaning of the Greek attributed to him by M. Renan. St. Paul however does not intend anything of the kind. He appeals to this anonymous altar as evidence of an element of uncertainty in their religious confusion, in what they confessed, and he offered to reveal this to them.

τοῦτο ἐγὼ καταγγέλλω ὑμῖν an answer to the question about 'strange deities.' It means 'This it is that I declare to you.'

ὃ οὖν... τοῦτο Comp. John 4:22. The various readings here are important. St. Paul does not identify here the true God of the Christians with the unknown god of the Athenians as the received text makes him do, but he represents the God of revelation as a real counter to the ways of ignorance.

Vs. 24 ὁ θεὸς (see Chrysostom ad loc, IX, p. 288). The Epicureans made the world independent of God. The Stoics made it identical with God. Paul will insist that His sovereignty is prior to and independent of 'your worship.'

οὐκ ἐν χειροποιήτοις A reminiscence of St. Stephen's speech (Acts 7:48) and this is not singular cf. Gal 3:19 to Acts 7:53. This addressed to the populace. Both Stoics and Epicureans would allow this, and in fact Stoics frequently use such language. See Lightfoot, *Phil.* p. 288. He would be responded to first by the Stoics, then by the Epicureans.

προσδεόμενος τινος Again thoroughly Athenian in feeling and expression. Here again he is on the side of the philosophers. Stoics—Plutarch *Moral. De Stoic* p. 1052E and also Seneca *Epist.* 95. Epicureans—Lucretius ii. 648 and vi. 54. On all this see Lightfoot, *Phil.* p. 292 and more examples in Wettstein.

καὶ τὰ πάντα The correct reading. The corruption κατὰ πάντα (T.R.) may have been aided by the occurrence of the same phrase in vs. 22.

Vs. 26 ἐξ ἑνὸς This is addressed 'ad populus.' To the Greeks generally who cherished the distinction between Greeks and barbarians, slave and free. To the Athenians especially who boasted of a special 'dignitas.' The Stoics with their cosmopolitan ideas would have some sympathy with this declaration. On ἐξ ἑνὸς comp. Heb 2:11; 11:12 and Rom 5:16. The question is—is ἑνός a masculine or a neuter?

κατοικεῖν E.V. seems to be right here, rather than Alford.

παντὸς προσώπου Comp. Eph 2:21. See Winer, no. 18, p. 138 (Moulton).

ὁρίσας A philosophy of history is only possible with the idea of unity and continuity of design, hence the Book of Daniel and the Book of Romans. No parallel in heathen literature. Comp. Deut 32:8-9 LXX.

προστεταγμένους The right reading.

τὰς ὁροθεσίας A late and rare word. May this be its earliest occurrence? τὰ ὁροθεσία likewise late, and a little less rare. The articles show that τῆς . . . καὶ goes with ὁροθεσίας alone.

Vs. 27 ζητεῖν This was the purpose of His creating the human race, and assigning them their seasons and boundaries.

τὸν θεόν is the right reading and this is the word St. Paul so naturally uses, addressing a heathen audience.

Ψηλαφήσειαν

καὶ γε Luke 14:32 v.l., Acts 2:18.

ὑπάρχοντα When all the while he is not far from us.

ἡμῶν Identifying himself with the race.

Vs. 28 St. Paul here recognizes the element of truth on which the pantheistic error is built. This element was deep seated in the consciousness of men and was expressed by some of the Greek Poets. It was that which the Apostle Paul had in common with the Greeks, and which he therefore made his starting point. If he had been speaking to the Jews he would have turned to the other pole of natural theology—the oneness and distinct personality of God. That was an idea that had no distinct place in the Hellenistic mind, and therefore he could not make it the basis of any argument. See Seneca *Epistl.* 41 no. 1. 'Prope est a te deus. . . .'

τινες τῶν καθ' ὑμᾶς ποιητῶν On 'we are God's offspring,' see two Stoic writers Aratus, *Phenom.* 5; Cleanthes, *Hymn.* 5, hence the plural καθ' ὑμᾶς perhaps turning to the Stoic part of the audience.

τινες St. Paul may have studied the Greek poets during the period while he was at Tarsus after his conversion (Acts 9:30, see Baumgar. here) or even under Gamaliel (see C+H, I p. 70).

ζῶμεν the principle of life, ἐνέργεια the energy (cf. Trench, p. 99 and the note on Acts 5:20). Paul is condescending to the Greek conception of ζῶ? Meyer's and Alford's climax seems to be fanciful. Rather compare vs. 25.

Vs. 29 'man's art and device' not as the E.V.

ὑπάρχοντες and comp. the same word in vs. 24 and vs. 29. Even here the Apostle speaks with great courtesy and forbearance (see Baumgar.).

χρυσῷ ἢ ἀργύρῳ See Seneca, *Epist.* 31. On statues made of these materials see Boeckh, *Pall.* p. 626sq. On gold inconsiderable p. 627. Paul might have seen the chrys. statue?

λίθῳ The matter of Hym. and Pel. Comp. Xenephon, *Vetig. ??* i.4.

Seneca xxxi.26. Xenephon ibid., iv speaks of the abundant yield of silver, but Strabo, ix. p. 613A that the yield is failing.

A.V. 'graven by art and man's device' but ἀνθρώπου belongs to both.

τὸ θεῖον in Greek philosophy may be considered as a compromise between the polytheistic mythology, and some higher divine principle. It was sufficiently vague and sufficiently far from implied personality not to come into collision with the established belief in the many gods of Olympus. τὸ θεῖον again is a condescension to the Athenian mode of thought and expression. Cf. Phil 4:8 where perhaps the mention of ἀρετή, the old heathen name for the highest excellence, is a similar condescension. It is a hapax in St. Paul though it occurs in a different sense in St. Peter. τὸ θεῖον is a hapax in the New Testament and the word θεῖος only occurs in 2 Pet 1:3-4, and θειότης Rom 1:20. 'Godhead' of the E.V. is too concrete for the vague τὸ θεῖον of Greek philosophy. θεότης occurs only in Col 2:9. St. Paul appeals to the dignity of human nature, an appeal that was not unlikely to fall dead on Athenian ears.

Vs. 30 ὑπεριδὼν Compare St. Paul's language in Rom 3:25. The signs are overlooked, nothing is said of their remission. The sentiment is strikingly similar.

πάντας The right reading and more expressive than πᾶσιν. He had a multifarious audience before him.

Vs. 31 καθότι The right reading, confined to St. Luke in the New Testament.

ἐν ἀνδρὶ in a man. Middleton's rule does not seem to be founded on any intelligible principle.

ἔστησεν ἡμέραν comp. 1 Macc 4:29; 1 Cor 4:3.

πίστιν παρασχὼν πᾶσιν Giving a pledge, an assurance. Comp. e.g. Arrian, *Hist.* 30 p. 548. A common phrase in classical Greek (see Wettstein). Elsewhere, ἀπαρχή 1 Cor 15:20, 23. Paul does not calculate on the Athenian hearers' understanding of πίστις in any higher sense. Is πίστις ever used by St. Paul in the low sense when addressing believers?

Vs. 32 ἀνάστασιν This could be equally repugnant to both the philosophers and the vulgar. The Epicureans rejected immortality; the Stoics never got beyond the concept of an impersonal unconscious being. All alike were to be repelled by the notion of a *bodily* resurrection. 1 Cor 15.

ἀνάστασιν νεκρῶν a general resurrection of the dead. This is not distinctly mentioned but the reported speech can only be regarded as an abstract. Doutbless Paul elaborated on this topic as he did at Corinth comp. 1 Cor 15:1-2, 12-20. Comp. Arch. Eum. 618. See Alford's note. Yet the term here seems to refer to a general resurrection of the dead such as is at least implied in the close of St. Paul's speech if not distinctly stated (the reference to judging the world). And as we must regard this as not a full report but rather an abridgement of St. Paul's speech, we may well suppose it was explicitly mentioned.

καὶ πάλιν The importance of the speech not to be confused with its effects. See Baumg. ii.

Vs. 34 Διονύσιος [ὁ] Ἀρεοπαγίτης The [ὁ] is suspicious here as it may have been introduced afterwards when the name became famous, and he was called 'the Areopagite' distinguishing him from others. E.g Dionysius in Eusebius *H.E.* iv. 23 in his letter to the Athenians, compared with the St. Diony. of France. And bear in mind the writings attributed to him.

Ἀρεοπαγίτης It was a title and position still coveted by Roman citizens. See Cicero, *pro Bal.* 12. In the inscriptions of the early Imperial times the order of positions is 1) the *boule*, 2) 'from the Ares Pagus.' See C.I. no. 320 (of the reign of Claudius), no. 361 (a statue erected to Berenice), and sometimes the council of 600 is referenced (e.g. 315, 316). See other references in Renan, pp. 193, 209, 505. See also an inscription of the 4th century no. 372, with Ἀρεοπαγίτην. From Aeschylus to Constantine the dignity of this court appears.

Δάμαρις Not Dionysius' wife. The Greek will not allow this. Comp. Acts 18:2 as Chrysostom *Sacerd.* iv.7 and others make clear. The name Δάμαρις appears not to occur (elsewhere), though we have Damalis. Δάμαρης occurs in a Spartan inscription, see Steph. Ins. s.v. Δάμαριον at Paros, Inscrp. 2393, but does Damaris have anything to do with either? Renan, p. 209 suggests that it is a Semitic name, and mentions that several Phoenician inscriptions have been found at Athens. For the possibility of it being a form of Damalis, see Smith's Dictionary s.v on Damaris, and for Damalis comp. Dorcas.

The comparative failure of Paul's preaching at Athens. Reasons for this. St. Luke's reporting. Later church in Athens: First century—Dionysius as its first bishop, Eusebius *H.E.* iii.4, iv.23, on the authority of Dionysius of Corinth. 2nd century—the Apologists, Aristides and Quadratus, Eusebius *H.E.* iv.3, Jerome, *de Ver. Illustr.* 28, 29 on the occasion of Hadrian's visit to Athens. c. A.D. 125. The passages of Quadratus speaks of our Lord's miracle. Martyrdom of Paulin. In Eusebius l.c. but date of the martyrdom uncertain. Succeeded by Quadratus, the same as the Apologist? State of the church at this time. The Edict of Antonius Pius (138–151). Melito in Eusebius *H.E.* iv. 26. Letter of Dionysius to the Athenians, Eusebius *H.E.* iv. 23. Athenagoras, literary character of the Athenian church. For its later history see the references in Renan, pp. 209, 210.

AND SO TO CORINTH
(ACTS 18)

18:1-17: TEXTUAL ISSUES

Vs. 4 Observe a stupid gloss of D.

Vs. 5 τῷ λόγῳ Lachmann, Tischendorf, A, B, E, G, etc. The Textus Receptus' τῷ πνεύματι has very slender support.

Vs. 12 ἀνθυπατεύοντος, Lachmann has ἀνθυπάπου ὄντος [as does] A, B, D, et al.

Vs. 15 ζητήματά, not the T.R. which has ζήτημά.

Vs. 17 Textus Receptus adds οἱ Ἕλληνες after πάντες, others add 'the Jews.' Both are glosses.

Vs. 1 Κόρινθον Corinth contrasts with literary Athens, as the busy commercial and political capital of Achaia.

Vs. 2 Ἀκύλαν Like Aquila, the translator of the Old Testament (LXX), this Aquila also came from Pontus. From this we should conclude it was a common name in Pontus. The church of Pontus. No direct account of the evangelizing of it. It lay outside of St. Paul's route. See Acts 2:9; 1 Pet 1:1. Pliny was in Pontus. Dionysius of Corinth wrote to the diocese of Pontus, Eusebius *H.E.* iv. 23. On the spread of Montanism in Pontus, Eusebius *H.E.* v.16. The Paschal Controversy, Palmas (?) its bishop, v.23.

προσφάτως ἐληλυθότα By calculation of the relative chronology of the Acts itself, we arrive at the conclusion that St. Paul arrived in Corinth in the year A.D. 52. Suetonius *Claud.* xxv, 'Judaeos impulsore Chresto assidue tumul-

tuantes, Roma expulit.' Chrestus = Christus see Lightfoot, *Phil.* p. 16. False
messiahs, or the true Messiah? Probably both. If Priscilla and Aquila had
already been converted, they would be among those for whom the edict was
directly intended. There is no certainty about the date of the edict of Claudius
but so far as probabilities go, it coincides: 1) Agrippa the younger was high
in the favor of Claudius. He resided in Rome until A.D. 50 when he left to
take possession of his dominion. He returned to Rome at the close of A.D.
52, and in A.D. 53 his favor with Claudius added a new district to his
dominion. Claudius died in A.D. 54. 2) Tacitus, *Annal.* xii.52 on the year A.D.
52 speaks about problems with Jews in Italy and elsewhere. This was probably
contemporaneous. Egyptians, Judeans, Chaldeans, all superstitious people
who belong in the same category, in Roman feeling. There were a batch of
edicts against foreign superstitions. The edict against the Jews seems to have
been the first of these decrees. Tacitus describes the other decrees as about
'atrox et irritum.' See Diog. Laertius. The edict referenced by Tacitus as
against Jews was issued early in A.D. 52. See on this subject Cresb. (?) pp.
121-28, Diog. Laert. lx.6. This is placed at the announcement of the reign of
Claudius in A.D. 41 and probably states his earlier policy. The decree of
Claudius against the Jews, like the other decree mentioned by Tacitus seems
to have been 'savage and fruitless' ('atrox et irritum'). It might cause the immediate removal of such folk as Aquila and Priscilla, but a few years after
we find that they had returned and probably the majority of the Jews never
left. Perhaps the reappearance of Agrippa may have caused Claudius to
suspend or rescind the execution of the decree, or his successor may have
abolished it.

Πρίσκιλλαν here and vss. 18, 26 i.e. wherever it occurs in St. Luke [the
name takes this form]. But Prisca, Rom 16:3; 1 Cor 16:19; 2 Tim 4:19. Wherever
it occurs in St. Paul the v.l. Priscilla is fairly supported in the Rom 16 and
2 Tim 4 references but slenderly in 1 Cor 16. On abbreviation of names see
Silas and Silvanus, Sopater and Sosipater, Drusca and Druscilla, Livia and
Livilla. This couple seems to have moved between Rome, Corinth, and
Ephesus, in prosecution of their trade. They are expelled from Rome by
Claudius, visit Corinth and fall in with St. Paul, travel with him to Ephesus
(Acts 18:18), where he leaves them. He finds them there on his return (Acts
18:26), and they are with him when he writes his First Epistle to the Corin-

thians from thence (1 Cor 16:19—see Stanley on that passage). When on the occasion of a subsequent visit to Corinth he wrote Romans, they were once more in Rome (Rom 16:3, and Paley, *Horae Paulinae*). When we last hear of them they are again in the East (2 Tim 4:19). This is during St. Paul's second imprisonment.

προσῆλθεν αὐτοῖς This seems to show that if they were not already Christians, they had shown some pre-disposition toward Christianity.

Vs. 3 ἠργάζετο His earnings were however supplemented by contributions from the Macedonian churches (2 Cor 11:9) and were especially from the Philippians (Phil 4:15). This support was only supplementary τὸ ὑστέρημα (2 Cor 11:9 v.l.) and he subsisted mainly by his own labours.

ἦσαν γὰρ σκηνοποιοί 1) the precepts of the rabbis See C+H, I p. 58; 2) cilicium C+H, pp. 58, 209. Used in Asia Minor (p. 177)—goat's hair tents.

Vs. 4 ἔπειθέν is not necessarily connected with διελέγετο . . . ἐν τῇ συναγωγῇ so that Ἕλληνας need not mean proselytes. Yet it probably does mean this [here]. cf. Acts 14:1.

Vs. 5 Ὡς δὲ κατῆλθον Cf. 1 Thess 3:1-7 and Paley, *Horae Paulinae* iv. Paley seems to have given the right account of the matter though he has over-pressed the narrative in the Acts to get a coincidence (see Jowett's remarks, though he gives more wrong the other way). It is quite possible that St. Luke may have known of Timothy's visit to Athens and return to Thessalonike, and yet have passed it over, just as he passed over the return of Silas from Jerusalem to Antioch (Acts 15), though his account presumes Silas' return, and is unintelligible without it.

Silas and Timothy. See 17:14-16. He is expecting them at Athens, but they come to him in Corinth. But see 1 Thess 3:2. But if 1) εὐδοκήσα<u>μεν</u> ἐπέμψα<u>μεν</u> (1 Thess 3:1-2) can refer to St. Paul alone then it is only reasonable to suppose a mission of Timothy from Berea to Thessalonike and both he and Silas would join St. Paul at Corinth. But if 2) the plural cannot refer to St. Paul alone, and must include Silas, then Silas at least must have found St. Paul at Athens as was expected, and afterwards have started hence on a mission to Macedonia where he picked up Timothy and they together joined St. Paul at Corinth. We have already had a parallel instance of a mission of Silas in Acts 15:33, 40 (where the received text supplies the omission).

συνείχετο τῷ λόγῳ 'was constrained by the Word.' λόγῳ almost = τοῦ εὐαγγελίου, viewed as something concrete and objective. For the construction see Luke 4:38. Comp. 2 Cor 5:14. A.V. adds of St Paul 'was pressed in the Spirit.' The construction συνείχετο τινι is common in St. Luke e.g. Luke 8:37; Acts 28:8.

εἶναι τὸν χριστὸν Ἰησοῦν The omission of the εἶναι in the received text is an attempt to make χριστὸν a part of the proper name.

Vs. 6 ἐκτιναξάμενος comp. 13:51, and Mt 10:14. The fact that St. Paul is borrowing the language of Ezekiel (which applies to him as a preacher) and that he was speaking to Jews, who would understand the meaning of the expression is quite sufficient to explain this 'unPauline speech.' Cf. Acts 20:26; 1 Cor 14:8. In both of these passages he seems to be referring to ancient prophet's imagery.

Vs. 7 The reading ΟΝΟΜΑΤΙΟΥΣΤΟΥ was corrupted into ΟΝΟΜΑΤΙΤΙΤΙΟΥΙΟΥΣΤΟΥ and since such a name would be very strange it was corrected to ΟΝΟΜΑΤΙΤΙΤΟΥΙΟΥΣΤΟΥ.

On the whole Titus or Titius Justus seems the right reading. Perhaps Titius would explain the other readings, but supposing that Titus is the Titus of St. Paul's Epistles (and if not, Titus is not mentioned by St. Luke). Note as to the place: 1) this Titus is a resident of Corinth, the other a resident of Antioch; 2) the other Titus had been converted two or three years before and would hardly be called a proselyte! In Galatians he is a 'Greek,' which suggests he did not pass through the intermediate stage of proselytism. Titus however had some later connection with Corinth. 2 Cor 2:13; 7:6, but Paul does not speak of him as a Corinthian, but rather otherwise. See 2 Cor 8:23. Cf. James who is called 'the just' (ὁ δίκαιος).

Vs. 8 Κρίσπος 1 Cor 1:14. A common Jewish name (comp. Josephus *Vit.* 6, 69).

ἀρχισυνάγωγος See on vs. 17. One of the synagogue officials, and when in the plural it can refer to the elders Acts 13:15 cf. Mark 5:22.

ἐβαπτίζοντο But not necessarily by St. Paul's own hands, cf. 1 Cor 1:14. Silas and Timothy were with St. Paul assisting him. 2 Cor 1:19; 1 Thess 1:1; 2 Thess 1:1. He was one of the few at Corinth Paul was responsible for having baptized. Of the others see Baumgar.

Vs. 9 Comp. 2 Cor 12:8.

Vs. 10 λαός . . . πολὺς

Vs. 11 Ἐκάθισεν δὲ A.V. 'He continued' but it is much more precise a word. Luke 5:3, καθίσας . . . ἐδίδασκεν, or comp. Mt 23:2, καθέδρας ἐκάθισαν—'a professional chair,' ex cathedra.

ἐνιαυτὸν καὶ μῆνας ἓξ So that with the time which elapsed before and after, we may set down the whole length of his stay as about two years.

Vs. 12 Γαλλίωνος It does not follow from the mention of Gallio's name here that he continued on his proconsulate during St. Paul's sojourn at Corinth. See similar constructions in Luke 2:1; 3:1. But the more probable explanation is: 1) The Office—Another instance of St. Luke's accuracy. Achaia was a senatorial province, therefore governed by a proconsul. ἀνθυπάτου ὄντος is the right reading here. It had originally been a senatorial province. Tiberius (see Tacitus *Annal*. i.76) took it from the Senate in A.D. 15. (See Becker and Marquardt, I p. 321). Claudius in A.D. 44 (Suetonius, *Claud*. xxv; Dio Cassius, lx.29) gives it back to the Senate. Thus between A.D. 15–44 the term that Luke uses here, ἀνθυπάτος (cf. Howson, I p. 175) would be inappropriate. 2) The Present Holder of the Office—The elder Seneca had three sons. Lucius Annaeus Novatus is the original name of the man who took the name Junius Annaeus Gallio, from his adoptive father L. Junius Gallio.[1] His proconsulship in Achaia is not directly mentioned, but the notice in St. Luke is a connecting link between two notices in Roman writers. Pliny, *N.H.* xxxi.33, speaking of the advantage of taking a sea voyage, when suffering from a malady, mentions in passing Gallio. Seneca, *Epistle* 104 speaking of taking charge, mentions his brother 'Gallionis, qui cum in Achaia.' Connecting these two passages we see that immediately after his consulship ('proxime post consulatus') he was in Achaia (Seneca). Luke gives the reason for his sojourn in Achaia. He was proconsul. This would naturally come immediately after he was consul, according to the Roman practice.

But when was this? Gallio was not one of the consuls who gave the name to the year. He was only *suffectus*. Hence, we do not know the date. But Seneca was in disgrace and exile until A.D. 49. His brother Gallio is not likely to have been appointed until Seneca's return to imperial favor. Therefore, Gallio was not consul until A.D. 50, and not proconsul until 51, though

---

[1] A noted rhetorician. (BW3)

perhaps a year or more later. This accords with the date [for the Acts account] of A.D. 52–54. This way of putting things is quite after St. Luke's manner cf. Luke 2:2; 3:1.

Vs. 13 παρὰ τὸν νόμον . . . If the accusation had been τοί θεοί and not τον θεόν, Gallio might have accepted it and proceeded against St. Paul, as teaching a 'religio illicita' but as it was the νόμος plainly appealed to was the law of Moses, not the law of Rome. The Jews may have tried to mystify the matter but the real meaning was betrayed in τὸν θεόν. Clearly then, it was νόμου τοῦ καθ' ὑμᾶς.

Vs. 14 μέλλοντος δὲ probably the right reading. 'Well then if . . . ' the reply to something said by the Jews.

ῥᾳδιούργημα See notes on Acts 13:10. A light, thoughtless, reckless deed.

κατὰ λόγον Apparently a hapax legomena in the New Testament. 'In all reason I had borne with you.'

Vs. 15 περὶ λόγου A mere 'logomacchia' [word battle], a contention over statements of doctrine, or form of words.

Vs. 17 πάντες Some few, but insufficient, add οἱ Ἕλληνες others, wholly inadequate, add οἱ Ἰουδαῖοι. Both are glosses, but which is correct [in meaning]? Probably the latter: 1) πάντες would naturally refer to those mentioned before. A Gentile crowd has not been alluded to before. 2) the position of Sosthenes. If he is identified with the Sosthenes in 1 Cor 1:1 which seems probable (the name is not heard of elsewhere, he is attached to St. Paul and Corinth in both cases which strong supports the conclusion that this is the same Sosthenes). If he returned to Corinth (after conversion) he would find himself the mark of the Jews' anger. Compare the case of Jason at Thessalonike. They could not get hold of St. Paul who was still in the magistrate's control and protection and so they wreaked their vengeance on Sosthenes.

τὸν ἀρχισυνάγωγον So Κρίσπος (vs. 8). In all probability Sosthenes was Krispus' successor because he is said to be 'the ἀρχισυνάγωγος,' not 'one of the ἀρχισυνάγωγοι,' a body of men, see the notes above on Acts 13:15 cf. Mark 5:22.

οὐδὲν τούτων . . . Here we see the real character of Gallio's action as related by St. Luke. He indiscriminantly blames and indiscriminantly praises: 1) his rejection of the case. Here he did his duty as a judge, but his manner and language showed his religious indifference; 2) his toleration of tumult, showing indifference to his duty as a magistrate. He was a weak, easy-going person, lacking a high sense of duty or purpose in respect to the public order. This is quite in keeping with his character as portrayed in Seneca, *Quest.* iv, *Prob.* I suppose the expression 'dominus meus Gallio' in *Epistl.* 104 denotes the ascendancy of his [career progress] over his brother and not. . . . his 'official dignity.' See also Statius Sil. ii.7.30sq.

Vs. 18 ἡμέρας ἱκανὰς An indefinite time, Acts 9:23, 43; 27:7. It will vary according to the circumstances.

κειράμενος To what or whom does it refer? No argument can be drawn from the word order. It is in different orders in St. Paul—Aquila and Prisca (1 Cor 15:19), Prisca and Aquila (Rom 16:3; 2 Tim 4:19). It is indifferent also in St. Luke—Aquila and Priscilla in Acts 18:2, and Priscilla and Aquila in Acts 18:26 where the received text has A+P, however every argument internally and externally points to P+A as the right reading. Who then is meant? The immediate connection supports Aquila, but St. Paul is the principal person in the narrative and as the historian would hardly be concerned with a subsidiary act of Aquila, it would seem more probable then that St. Paul himself is meant. Consider: 1) that it would have a significance to him which it cannot have to us; and 2) that it may have been a carrying out of his rule of becoming a 'Jew to the Jew' as e.g. Acts 16:3; 21:20sq.

Κεγχρεαῖς See Rom 16:1. There was already a church there when this Epistle was written.

εὐχήν The cutting of the hair would come at the end of the vow, as in the case of the Nazarites. Num 6:5, 18. This instance was not strictly a Nazaritic vow, but was modified by the circumstances. On the other hand, in Acts 21:24sq. we have a strictly Nazaritic vow.

St. Paul's stay in Corinth is marked by: 1) the writing of his earliest letters, those to the Thessalonians; 2) the foundation of the hitherto most important of the churches planted by him (on his converts see 1 Cor 1:14-16; 16:17; Rom 16:21-23). Of the contrast between St. Paul's preaching at Corinth in contrast with his preaching at Athens see Baumgar. cf. 1 Cor 2:1-2, 8—'I resolved to know nothing but Christ and him crucified.' The manner of Apollos' teaching had been somewhat different.

Vs. 19 κατήντησαν The right reading. Textus Receptus has κατήντησεν. St. Luke disposes of the movement of Priscilla and Aquila so he may give his

whole attention to St. Paul. The visit to the synagogue was probably immediately before his departure.

Vs. 21 δεῖ με πάντως is an interpolation and must be omitted with
Lachmann and Tischendorf so any discussion about the intended Festival
is out of place here. If the words were genuine the Feast would be the Feast
of Pentecost A.D. 54, the year of Nero's accession.

'One of a numerous class.' Perhaps this preserves a true tradition?
Compare however Acts 20:16 from which it may have been derived.

Vss. 22, 23 ἀναβὰς . . . κατέβη—Topographical terms

ἀχηθη . . . κατῆλθον—Nautical terms

ἀναβὰς with εἰς i.e. to Jerusalem. This construction regular in Acts. The
absence of any mention of Jerusalem would be an additional motive for the
interpolation in verse 21.

His fourth visit to Jerusalem A.D. 54, the year of Nero's accession.

Vs. 23 τὴν Γαλατικὴν χώραν καὶ Φρυγίαν See Acts 16:6. On the visit to
Galatia, see Gal 4:13, 16. Contrast the expression here with that of Acts
16:6. Here St. Paul is traveling from East to West and takes Galatia first
and then Phrygia.

Vs. 24 Ἀπολλῶς = Ἀπολλώνιος (which D has here, though it might be
Apollodorus, Apollonides). He falls in with Aquila and Priscilla here, departs to Corinth where he preaches (1 Cor 3:6, Ἀπολλῶς ἐπότισεν) and assumes (Acts 19:1) a very influential position (1 Cor 1:12; 3:4-6; 3:22; 4:6). He
returns to Ephesus. That is where he is when St. Paul writes 1 Corinthians
(1 Cor 16:12—St. Paul had exhorted him to undertake the journey to Corinth).
When St. Paul wrote to Titus (after his release), when he was making his way
westward to Nicopolis, he asked him to bring Apollos on his way (Tit 3:12).
So Apollos may have been journeying from the East to Rome. There is thus
no historical objection to his having written the Epistle to the Hebrews from
Rome after St. Paul's martyrdom, and while Timothy was still in prison.
Probably some confusion of, or some speculation founded on an earlier
notice about, the Epistle to the Hebrews. Clement of Alexandria in Eusebius
H.E. vi.14 mentions Paul. The argument is pressed in Eusebius *H.E.* vi.25
saying some circles ascribed it to Clement (of Rome) and some to St. Luke.
Tertullian ascribed it to Barnabas, hence the summary of Plotius.

λόγιος has two senses: 1) 'learned,' more specifically 'well-informed in history'; 2) eloquent. The former is the cultic and earlier sense, the latter the popular and later sense. See references in Wettstein, especially Phocylides (Lubbeck, p. 198). It will evidently be in the former sense here. Perhaps a reference to the Apollos party in 1 Cor 1:17sq.; 2:1sq; comp. 2 Cor 10:10. St. Paul's oratory was despised in comparison.

ἀνὴρ λόγιος i.e. a rhetorician in a good sense of the term. This would include a vast knowledge acquired by way of training (see Meride, Vol. v, p. 227). For the distinction between the earlier and the later sense of the term see the passage in Wordsworth, of which however, he has not made proper use combining the two senses. Westcott, *Gospel Harm.* p. 33 contends the expression with Herodotus ii.3, but then does not recognize the distinction between the earlier and later sense of the word. Perhaps we may see some traces of ἀνὴρ λόγιος in St. Paul's rebuke to the Corinthians (1 Cor 1:17-26; 2:1-6).

The two points which are noticed then, with respect to Apollos: 1) his eloquence; 2) his handling of Scripture, not improbably pertained to allegorical interpretation such as prevailed at Alexandria. He was to Christianity in fact what Philo was to Judaism. This entirely accords with the Epistle to the Hebrews.

Vs. 25 κατηχημένος Used especially of Christian teaching, cf. Gal 6:6. In the New Testament it is found only in St. Luke (Gospel 1 time, Acts 3) and St. Paul—Rom 2:18; 1 Cor 14:19; Gal 6:6.

ζέων τῷ πνεύματι 'fervent in or by the Spirit.' The article seems to point to the external agency. Comp. Rom 12:11.

ἀκριβῶς τὰ περὶ τοῦ Ἰησοῦ Apparently there is a contradiction of statement here, but obviously the writer did not seem ambivalent (?). He knew accurately certain facts about the life and teaching, and possibly too the passion of Jesus, but in the nature of baptism, he had not gotten beyond the baptism of John. He had not been taught that baptism in Christ was the passport to the Kingdom of heaven.

Vs. 26 Πρίσκιλλα καὶ Ἀκύλας Doubtless the right order: 1) the preponderance of authorities; 2) the temptation to change the order was twofold: a) to put the man's name first; b) to adopt the order to the masculine ἀκούσαντες.

Vs. 27 προτρεψάμενοι Having encouraged, stimulated him. Consider a) the order, and b) the terms. A.V. is wrong here 'exhorting the disciples to receive him.' Compare St. Paul's language of Apollos 1 Cor 16:12. The term seems to refer to Apollos, judging from the order of the words.

διὰ τῆς χάριτος to be attached to συνεβάλετο πολύ. Comp. Acts 6:8; 7:10. Rom 12:3 'through the grace which was given to me.' Comp. Rom 12:6; 15:15. It adds little or nothing if attached to τοῖς πεπιστευκόσιν.

Vs. 28 εὐτόνως with nervous energy. Here and in Luke 23:10 only. 'Die Schilderung das Trikens des Apollos vs. 27f. stimmt ganz mit 1 Kor.iii.6.'

διακατηλέγχετο He held constant, and convincingly disputed with the Jews.

Finally at Ephesus
(Acts 19)

Vs. 1 ἀνωτερικὰ It may derive from ἡ ἄνω Ἀσια, it is not to be taken in as precise a sense as that phrase. It is the parts in both directions. ἡ ἄνω Ἀσια is presumably Asia east of the Halys, which St. Paul would hardly reach, or did he? But from the direction we saw him taking (Acts 18:23), he cannot have been far beyond. It seems to be simply opposed to the seaboard and the coast of Asia.

Vs. 2 The A.V. is wrong here 'Have ye received the Holy Ghost since ye believe?'

ἀλλ' οὐδ' εἰ Comp. John 7:39-40. See Alford. The πνεῦμα ἅγιον here is not the person but the manifestation. They might have heard of the promise, but they had not heard of the fulfillment. On the other hand, the absence of the article may suggest it is a proper name.

Vs. 3 εἰς τὸ Ἰωάννου βάπτισμα The disciples of John are at Ephesus. See John 1:6, 15sq; 3:23sq.; 5:33-36; 10:40-41. See *Sibyl. Oracle* iv.160.

Vs. 4 John's baptism distinguished from Christ's, as the former is a baptism unto repentance, the latter the baptism of the Spirit. So in the Gospels, and also Acts 1:5; 11:16, comp. Acts 13:24, noting τῷ λαῷ is in the emphatic position in that verse. The unexpected clause may be supplied easily from the language of John himself (Mark 1:7-8). The difference between the baptism of John and that of Jesus as given here exactly accords with the distinction in the Gospels (cf. Acts 11:16). St. Paul alludes to John's baptism in Acts 13:24.

The position of ἵνα in this verse very frequent e.g. Gal 2:10; 1 Cor 9:15.

Vs. 6 ἐλάλουν τε γλώσσαις καὶ ἐπροφήτευον The two principal gifts—
1 Cor 13:1; 14:2sq. comp. 1 Cor 10:46. The importance of passages like this one
is it links the incident on the day of Pentecost to the notices in 1 Corinthians.

Vs. 9 τὴν ὁδὸν On this phrase see Acts 9:2; 19:23; 24:22; comp. John 14:5-6.

ἐν τῇ σχολῇ Τυράννου On this use of σχολῇ see Pliny N.H. xxxv.27(10);
xxxvi.5(4), a common term for a heathen philosophy school (see Wettstein).
Perhaps a public building like the Schola Xantia, Schola Octarce (?) in Rome.
Several orators were named Tyrannus, one a Sophist, but without giving a
date or place (See Renan, p. 345sq.). Justin's *Dialogue with Trypho* 1, is held
in the 'walks of Xystus' at Ephesus. See Philostratus, *Vita. Apoll.* viii.26.
Perhaps, however, Tyrannus was some living person and the building was
private. As the correct text omits τινες this on the whole is the more probable
explanation. In any case he is probably a heathen, this verse marking the
transition from the Jews especially to the Gentiles especially in St. Paul's
ministrations at Ephesus (cf. Acts 18:7).

Vs. 10 ἐπὶ ἔτη δύο during the period of three years. 2 Cor 12:14; 13:1 must
be interpolated indicating a visit to Corinth during this period. In Acts 20:31
we read τριετίαν. A.D. 54–57. But the two years here seem intended to exclude: 1) the period before when he preaches to the Jews (Acts 19:1-9), and
2) a period after the tumult of the Greeks (19:21-41). This last period must
have comprised some months.

πάντας τοὺς κατοικοῦντας The evangelization of Laodicea, Hierapolis,
Colossae through Epaphras, see Col 1:7sq; 2:1; 4:12. These were Phrygian
towns, but belonged to pro-consular Asia. On this occasion he would make
the acquaintance of Nymphas of Laodicea, and Philemon and his household
at Colossae. Perhaps at the same time the remaining of the seven churches.

Vs. 12 σουδάρια, σιμικίνθια—'semicinctia.' Comp. Quintus, Quinctius etc.
Martial xiv.153—'semicinctia.' The nature of these miracles? On this we may
remark: 1) although no outward sign was necessary for the working of a
miracle, still such was commonly vouchsafed. There was generally a double
aspect to the miracles during this dispensation. There was the outward
manifestation as well as the inward work and thus Christianity appeals to
the whole nature. This is neither wholly spiritual nor wholly material but
both (consider e.g. the resurrection of the body); 2) that the outward sign

was well adapted to the circumstances of the case. The sick would not visit St. Paul, and so some outward sign of connection was necessary.

Vs. 13 τῶν περιερχομένων As we would say, itinerant. The 'strolling' Jews. Perhaps these were Jews with Essene tendencies. See Josephus, *Bell. Jud.* ii.8.6. This is explained by *Ant.* viii.2.5. He then relates the story of one Eleazar who in the presence of Vespasian and his sons and the crowd expelled demons by this means.

Vs. 14 τινος Σκευᾶ See Corpus Inscrip. 288g and references in Wettstein. ἀρχιερέως Corpus Inscrip. 6363. These references from Renan, p. 347.

Vs. 15 γινώσκω, ἐπίσταμαι 'I recognize, acknowledge in his workings'; 'I am well acquainted with . . . '

Vs. 16 ἀμφοτέρων is the right reading.

Vs. 19 περίεργα occult arts. The idea of praying unto forbidden beings. See the references in Wettstein. See Horace, *Epod.* xvii.76. On the accusation against Socrates see Plato, *Apol.* 19B. The word is used especially of illicit knowledge. See Catullus *Epod.* 7. Cf. Apollonius of Tyana a γόητες 2 Tim 3:13. On 'Ephesian writing' cf. especially Meineke, *Com. Frag.* iii. p. 345, iv. 181; Lobeck, *Aglaspham.* p. 1330.

Ἐφέσια γράμματα became a proverb of those who spoke obscurely and mysteriously.

τὰς βίβλους See Menander, iv.181; Plato, *Symp.* vii.5; Clement of Alexandria, *Strom.* v. (p. 672). 2 Tim 3:13 the meeting point of Judaism and paganism. But does it explain the invocation in vs. 14?

τὰ ἱερὰ γράμματα see 2 Tim 3:15.

These ἐφέστα γράμματα were discussed by several philosophers. See Androcyde the Pythagorean (Clement of Alex. l.c.) and Sextus Africanus. See Becker and Marquardt, iv. p.123.

κατέκαιον They did freely what the Roman law required.

ἀργυρίου μυριάδας πέντε Clearly not Jewish money but Greek or Roman. The drachma or denarius. Slightly short of a franc.

Vs. 20 κατὰ κράτος used especially of taking a city by storm. In a metaphorical sense see 2 Cor 10:4.

The Third Missionary Journey
(Acts 19:21–21:39)

Vs. 21 Vs. 21sq. recapitulation. St. Paul's first intention had been to take Asia first (2 Cor 1:15), but this had been thwarted. Once he got there, not surprisingly the great feature of the third missionary journey is the long residence at Ephesus (τριετίαν Acts 20:31), whereas the great feature of the second had been the long residence at Corinth (two years). These three years [encompassed] the summer of A.D. 54 to the summer of A.D. 57, roughly speaking. At this point, the greater part of that period was already past. There is: 1) the earliest instances—Acts 19:1-7; 2) the three months preceding in the synagogue—Acts 19:8; and 3) the two years preceding in the school of Tyrannus—Acts 19:10, and possibly after the lapse of these two years we are well into the third year, perhaps this last episode comes from the end of 56 and the beginning of 57. At all events the two points to especially note about the sojourn in Ephesus are: 1) the encounter with the disciples of John; and 2) the encounters with the strolling exorcists, and the dabblers in magic, charms etc. Both these illustrate the type of religious feeling at Ephesus and throw light on later history e.g. the henobaptists, the Sibylline oracles, and St. John's Gospel and secondly Essene Judaism (Colossians). See on γόητες, 2 Tim 3:13.

During this period Paul wrote his four great epistles: 1) 1 Corinthians, at Ephesus, Easter 57; 2) 2 Corinthians, Macedonia, later 57; 3) Galatians, Macedonia or Achaia end of 57 or beginning of 58. The date of Galatians is uncertain but this is most probably correct; 4) Romans, Achaia, spring 58.

The date of the missionary journey may be gathered from two considerations: 1) the sequence of his journey. Paul's first intention had been to take Achaia first, so as to pay the Corinthians a *double* visit. See 1 Cor 16:5; 2 Cor 1:16. He had informed the Corinthians of this intention, probably in the lost letter of 1 Cor 5:9. This intention had already been abandoned when he wrote 1 Corinthians (apparently about Easter A.D. 57). The point of time here may be taken therefore as about the very beginning of 57, hardly later. The force of the expression διελθὼν τὴν Μακεδονίαν καὶ Ἀχαΐαν would suit either the one grand intention or the subsequent fact. But it seems framed with a view to the latter, and perhaps the original intention may have been mapped out to St. Luke. It is quite clear from many indications that St. Luke was not acquainted with any of St. Paul's Epistles. 2) The collection of alms and the journey to Jerusalem. εἰς Ἱεροσόλυμα—the object. Acts 24:17. Compare this with the Epistles, 1 Cor 16:3; Rom 15:25sq., 31. When 1 Corinthians was written, he was not yet quite sure. When Romans was written his decision was made and on the point of being carried out.

The collection of alms may have begun some time before 1 Cor 16:1-4, διέταξα, 2 Cor 8:1-4, 10; 9:2sq. It would date from the end of 56 or the beginning of 57. St. Paul's general purpose would take its sense coincidentally with these collections, but it would not take the shape of a definitive decision until later.

ἔθετο ὁ Παῦλος ἐν τῷ πνεύματι Ambiguity of the A.V. decided in different editions by the printing of 'spirit' or 'Spirit.' Comp. Acts 5:4 ἔθου ἐν τῇ καρδίᾳ σου (comp. Luke 1:66; 21:14), comp. Rom 1:9 ἐν τῷ πνεύματι μου, and Rom 1:8. The former rendering ('spirit') seems necessary because τίθεσθαι above could not signify 'to determine.'

καὶ Ῥώμην ἰδεῖν Rom 1:15; 15:24 comp. Acts 23:11. Hence his appeal to Caesar which was his purpose. It is kept consistently in view by St. Luke, Acts 25:10-12, 21; 26:32; 27:24. The trip to Rome and the establishment of the Gospel there is the goal of St. Luke's history. The Acts is not abruptly terminated, but this then [Acts 19:21] is the beginning of the end. In other words, this incidental allusion to Rome here points to the close of the book.

Vs. 22 δύο τῶν διακονούντων αὐτῷ Comp. Acts 13:5 ὑπηρέτην. Mark in the first missionary journey (Acts 13:5), the others in the second missionary journey (Acts 16:3). For baptizing etc. 1 Cor 1:14.

EXCURSUS: TIMOTHY AND ERASTUS

Timothy had been dispatched before the writing of 1 Corinthians was sent—
1 Cor 4:17; 16:10. He was dispatched with the intention that he go as far as
Corinth. Here St. Luke says Macedonia, in 1 Cor 4:17 St. Paul says Corinth
(but with some apprehension that he might not get that far—1 Cor 16:10.
This apprehension seems to have been justified if we may judge from a) the
account here, and b) from the circumstance of St. Paul. He does not mention
Timothy's visit to Corinth in 2 Cor 12:10, 17).

How are the statements to be reconciled? Timothy seems to have been
detained in Macedonia where he was ultimately found by the Apostle. 1) In
the latter passage (Acts 16:10) a doubt is expressed whether he would reach
Corinth; 2) When St. Paul crosses over to Macedonia, we find him in the
company of Timothy (2 Cor 1:1) who goes with him to Corinth (Rom 16:21);
3) In 2 Cor 12:17-18 he is not mentioned, as he almost certainly would be if
he had visited Corinth at this time. Neither is there any mention of relations
between Timothy and the Corinthians; 4) On the contrary, we find St. Paul
at Troas and Macedonia anxiously expecting tidings of his first letter, and
awaiting the return of Titus for that purpose.

Erastus. No mention of him in 1 Cor or 2 Cor but in Rom 16:23 a person
of this name is mentioned. They must be identified. He would go on to
Corinth, and remained there, as his native place. Comp. on a later occasion
where he is mentioned in 2 Tim 4:20. Why Alford refuses to identify this
Erastus with the one in Rom 16 is difficult to say. Alford objects on the basis
of the office mentioned in Rom 16 but this appointment could have been
made after he returned to Corinth. It was probably an annual office. Cf.
2 Tim 4:20.

Geographical sense: 1) local—Asia, meaning the continent of Asia. This
got to be identified, more or less, with the first Asiatic power, the Persian
Kingdom. See Aeschylus, *Pers.* 12; Herodotus i.4, and thus with the Persian
monarchy. 2) After the subjugation of Persia, and the division of Alexander's
possession, the part of his Kingdom which lay on this continent became 3)
the Selucid (Antiochene) monarchy—1 Macc 8:6, Antiochus, King of Asia,
2 Macc 3:3, Seleucus, King of Asia. 4) The Romans conquer Antiochus and
Magnesia. ? ii.38—L Scipio Africanus expels Antiochus. Tacitus xxxvi.4. It
was given over to the Pergamon kings (the Pergamene monarchy). See Sue-

tonius iv.19. The name not disturbed afterwards. On all this see Becker and Marquardt, iii. p. 130 and C+H I. Cicero, *Pro Flacc.* 27. Asia included Phrygia, Mysia, Caria, Lydia. This is only a rough inscription, and moreover we doubt if the province varied from that time. 5) The last king of Pergamon, Attalus, left his possessions to the Romans, who created a province in 129 B.C. The phrase 'Asia Minor' was quite a later expression.

ἐπέσχεν χρόνον First Epistle to Corinthians written, probably about Easter, 1 Cor 5:7, certainly before Pentecost 1 Cor 16:8. Sent by Titus and another brother (cf. 1 Cor 16:11-12 with 2 Cor 12:8), or nearly at the same time as their mission. In it is expressed Paul's intent to come quickly (14:19).

Vs. 23 οὐκ ὀλίγος Comp. Acts 12:18; 14:28sq.; 17:4, B*, etc. Sent by the hands of two brothers. Acts 16:11-12. These were Titus and another (2 Cor 12:18). Apollos was with St. Paul at this time. His previous communications with the Corinthians (1 Cor 16:12) were: 1) the lost letter, 1 Cor 5:9; 2) his second visit, 2 Cor 12:14; 13:1. The sending of the letter would seem to be before the tumult. If so he had suffered previous humiliations (ἐθηριομάχησα 1 Cor 15:32).

περὶ τῆς ὁδοῦ cf. Acts 9:2. See C+H ii. p. 89.

Vs. 24 Δημήτριος Another of the name [appears in] 3 John 12. Perhaps this could be the full name of Demetrius (see above).

ποιῶν ναοὺς [ἀργυροῦς] Ἀρτέμιδος See the explanation in Aristotle, *Rhet.* i.14. Dionysius Hal. ii.22 on the name Artemidoros. Dion Cassius, xxxix.20. These were portable shrines containing inscriptions (on the inscriptions Dura. Cap. xxxix, London-Atla. c. xvi p. 108; Boeckh, C.I. iii, p. 437 on shrines of Isis). Ammon. Macel.(?) xxi.13 on the Asclepiades. See Diod. Sicculus xx.14 of Heracles of Tyre.

Staley, Canterbury, p. 234—'As manner and custom is, shrines there were bright, for men of culture to know charms they had sought. Each man set his silver in such things, and the like.' See Boeckh 3858e. Comp. Plutarch *Brutus* 51. So an ἔπαρχοι τέχν. is mentioned again 4340f, 4340g.

On these shrines see Dionysius of Hal. ii.22. 1) their nature (parallels with other deities); 2) their material—silver (here), wood (see Aristotle), copper (see 2 Tim 4:14? ὁ χαλκεύς, the smith); 3) their purpose—twofold—a) as memorials. Amm. (?) Marc. xxi.13; b) as votive offerings. See Royal Academy, Augst. 1871, p. 371. Parallels, St. Thomas of Canterbury, the virgin of Loretto.

Vs. 25 περὶ τὰ τοιαῦτα ἐργάτας

Vs. 26 σχεδὸν πάσης τῆς Ἀσίας No example cited, see vs. 10. Epaphras and Philemon at Colossae. The evangelization of the Lycus Valley. Other of the seven churches?

Vs. 27 ἦν ὅλη [ἡ] Ἀσία See Boeckh, C.I. no. 2954. This inscription contains a decree of the Ephesians, relative to Artemis (it's a eulogy of Artemis), set up in the reign of Tiberius. Also Strabo iv.1, p. 179 mentions that she was worshipped at Marseilles. Apuleius ii. She dates from the primeval age. Before the settlement of Greeks in Asia Minor (Pausanias, vii.2. no 4). Destroyed and rebuilt many times.

The temple which St. Paul saw was reputed to have been the eighth (Falkener, p. 217). See Guhl, *Ephes.* p. 160sq. Falkener, *Ephesus* etc. p. 220. Built with the offerings of all of Greece and Asia Minor, C+H, ii p. 85. Built by Hierostratos in 357 B.C. coincident with the rule of Alexander. Rebuilt and adorned from time to time, see Pliny *N.H.* xxxvii.21. It was in all its splendor when St. Paul wrote. Renovated to greatness by Gallerius Galba in about 260 A.D. Philo, Byz. *de Spectacl. Mud.* vii. It was 425 feet long and 225 wide—Ionic architecture. Its site a matter of dispute? C+H ii. p. 86. Falkener. It has recently been discovered, see Royal Academy, 1871 p. 371.

Παρείχετο Was the means of bringing. Comp. Acts 16:16 where it is παρεῖχεν. τεχνίταις artisans, craftsmen, see Smith's Diction. of the Bible s.v. Ephesus.

Vs. 27 τοῦτο κινδυνεύει ἡμῖν τὸ μέρος This department, this hand of fate.

ἀπελεγμὸν blatant reproaches and so 'contempt.' I do not find any other examples of the substantive in the lexicons (another form in Sophocles).

τῆς μεγάλης θεᾶς Ἀρτέμιδος See Boeckh, Corp. Inscrip. 2963 for the very same phrase. Also Xenephon, *Ephes.* I p. 15 (quoted by Wettstein). Achilles Tat. viii, p. 501.

καθαιρεῖσθαι τῆς μεγαλειότητος 'deposed from her magnificence.' Not as Grimm takes it 'aligned.' Circ. Nic. Can. 17, Circ. Ant. Can. 3 (?).

Vs. 28 Ἄρτεμις Ἐφεσίων The addition of the place name necessary, for she was not the ordinary Artemis of Greek mythology but a special deity of Ephesus. See Jerome, prof. Epistl. and at Ephes. viii, p. 539. She was publicly seen as a quite independent local deity, not originally identified with the Greek Artemis, but some resemblance in her attributes. Her distinctiveness from the common Artemis is recognized and she was adopted by other cities e.g. Marseilles where her temple is called Ἐφεσίων. See Aristides quote in Wettstein. The city took its name from the goddess, not from colonization accord to Grabe (?) *Ephesus*, pp. 98sq.

Vs. 29 ἡ πόλις τῆς συγχύσεως the confusion spread through the city.

εἰς τὸ θέατρον The local place of assembly for such popular meetings. See the passages in Wettstein. More especially Diodorus Sicc. xvi.84. See Philo, *Flacc.* nos. 10, 11, 20. See Hermann, *Grech. Ant.* III, no. 128, p. 288. Thucydides x. 128; Cicero *pro Flacc.* The theatre on Mt. Pison is 660 feet in diameter and able to hold 56,700 spectators, the largest known of its kind. See the picture in Smith's *Dictionary of the Bible* s.v. Ephesus. See C+H, II p. 83. It was not far from the agora where the tumult would probably arise. Was the temple of Artemis in sight?[1] See Falkener, p. 101, Grabe, *Ephesus*, p. 182.

Γάϊον Not mentioned elsewhere. Two companions of St. Paul have the same name: 1) of Derbe (Acts 20:4); 2) of Corinth (1 Cor 1:14; Rom 16:23). For an interesting inscription about a Gaius see Boeckh no. 1987, and Lightfoot, *Philippians*, p. 61.

Ἀρίσταρχος a Thessalonian, Acts 27:2. He accompanies St. Paul: 1) later in this missionary journey (Acts 20:4, A.D. 58); 2) he is with him in Caesarea and departs with him on the sea voyage (Acts 27:2, A.D. 60); 3) he is with him at Rome (Col 4:10; Philem 24, A.D. 62–63). St. Paul in Col 4:10 may refer to this event, but more probably he refers to the sharing of his captivity at Rome.

Vs. 30 δῆμον the popular assembly see Acts 12:22; 17:5. It is not ὄχλος nor λαός.

Vs. 31 Ἀσιαρχῶν President of Asia, rather than the chief of Asia. See Babington (?) on an imperial coin of Laodicea in Phrygia (London, 1866). Magistrates who represented τό κόινον of Asia. Their functions: 1) super-intendents of games. Thus the games were celebrated on behalf of τό κόινον of Asia; 2) board of works, either erecting monuments or permitting their erection, and lay out gardens; 3) sacerdotal functions; see Tertullian, *de Spect.* 11, who refers to their presiding at sacerdotal functions. Their imperial and judicial functions seem to have been well documented. Were the offices of Asiarch and high priest the same? See Babington, p. 105sq. It is with the

---

[1] We can now answer this question in the negative. It was near neither the theater nor the agora. (BW3)

first of these roles we are concerned. See *Martyrd. of Polycarp* 22, and in Ch. 21 the mention of the Ἀσιαρχῶν. There is a parallel in a reference to a 'Syriarch' in Libanius *Epistl.* 1217. See Babington p. 10 and references there to the word 'munerarius.' The title is common in inscriptions from Ephesus, e.g. 2990, one Dionysios. See Babington, p. 25. See 2464 at Thera, and also 2994. There could be several Asiarchs at a time (Babington, p. 11sq.). It was a highly honorable office.

Vs. 33 συνεβίβασαν must mean persuaded, prevailed upon, convinced (1 Cor 2:16). I do not find any parallel instance of the sense 'constrained.' Is he to be identified with the Alexandros of 1 Tim 1:20; 2 Tim 4:14? Hardly with the first, but possibly with the second. The name occurs (as naturally it would) in an Ephesian inscription.

τῶν Ἰουδαίων Alexander (see Boeckh inscriptions nos. 2961b, 3008) seems to have been thrust forward by the Jews to show that they were not at all implicated in these doings of Christians. Note the use of ἀπολογεῖσθαι. This seems to be the natural account of the matter and if so he may have been and probably was the Alexander of 1 Tim 4:14. For another narrative about the persecution of Christians see Acts 6:27sq.

Vs. 34 ἐπιγνόντες See Winer, lxiii p. 710 (Moulton). Comp. Acts 15:22; 20:3; 24:5.

Vs. 35 καταστείλας. τίς γάρ ἐστιν ἀνθρώπων 'why what mortal man is there?' The mildness (?) of the expression.

ἀνθρώπων, stronger than the common reading, ἀνθρώπως. What's this tumult for—Mt 27:23; John 7:41.

γραμματεὺς Frequent in Ephesian inscriptions. See Grabe, *Ephes.* p. 73. The term notary or clerk. Scribes called τῆς πόλεως in the inscriptions. Boeckh, nos. 2953, 2961b, 2964, 2965, 2966, 2968, 2990, 3001, 3015b. He is a very important functionary and takes the initiative in decrees. See also Royal Academy, Augst. 1rst 1871, p. 370.

νεωκόρος the temple warden (see Boeckh inscription nos. 2965, 2977, 2972, 2988, 2990, 2991, 2993), not as menial, as the Jews come to suggest: 1) of the individual priest see Xenephon, *Anab.* v.3.6; 2) of the people see Josephus, *Bell. Jud.* v.9.4. On the influence of the Emperors, the inscriptions and coins only go so far to indicate the case here, as they show that the term is applied to the whole people, and not exclusively to the priests.

τοῦ διοπετοῦς Important. The Temple existed for it, and not it for the temple. Its material doubtful, whether ebony or something else. It had survived the destruction of seven temples. Around this the service centered. All the later and more prominent statues did not inculcate the same awe. See Falkener, p. 287. It is a βρὲξας.

Vs. 37 οὔτε ἱεροσύλας E.V.

τὴν θεὸν The force of the form of θεὸς—the goddess regnant, goddess in her own right as the Attic writers speak of. She is ἡ θεὸς on the inscriptions—2953b, 2954. The 'great god' in 2963.

ἀγοραῖοι ἄγονται καὶ ἀνθύπατοι Note plurals. See e.g. Euripides, *Iph.* 1359. Mt 2:20—general plural. See Winer no. 27, p. 218, and no. 4, p. 67 (Moulton). See Kühner, II pp. 14, 17. Josephus, *Ant.* xiv.10.21; Strabo, xiii, p. 629. See references in Becker and Marquardt, iii.1, p. 136sq.

ἀνθύπατοι εἰσιν Asia is a proconsular province.

Vs. 38 ἀγοραῖοι (courts), ἀνθύπατοι (proconsuls) cf. *Iph. Taur.* 1359.

Vs. 39 περαιτέρω B, 13 and other good witnesses; περ᾽ ἕτερον E, περὶ ἑτέρων—Aleph, A, D, H, L, P, Philox. (which I have verified), Arm (likewise verified). The first of these is to be adopted as the reading which on the whole best explains the others, and as more likely to be altered, than the converse. This is beyond the reach of scribes, and the common expression περὶ ἑτέρων would come more naturally.

ἐννόμῳ ordinary, regular. ἔννομος is not 'lawful' as opposed to 'unlawful' but rather 'ordered by law' as opposed to 'extraordinary.' On the use of these sort of terms at Athens, see Hermann, *Griech. Ant.* III no. 128, p. 285g with references. Comp. Boeckh, C.I. 1567.

In other words, the matter can afford to wait until one of the stated days for the ἐκκλησία comes. The present meeting was an ἐκκλησία, it would be seen as a lawful gathering, but it was a special gathering and therefore not ἔννομος.

ἐπιλυθήσεται 'It will be solved.' Comp. Mark 4:34; 2 Pet 1:20. He obviously contemplates some question of public interest, which would be discussed in a public assembly, as opposed to a legal trial between Demetrius and the defendants which would go before a law court.

στάσεως περὶ so the preposition ought to be accented (see Chandler, p. 250) though all the versions omit it. It must be neuter comp. Luke 23:4, 14,

22. The Memphis has the negative here. There are two ways of taking it: 1) though no real blame attached, we shall not be able to clear ourselves; 2) seeing that we have no excuse, then we shall not be able to clear ourselves concerning etc. putting a stop after ὑπάρχοντος. The latter is better.

Acts 20: The Tumult, the Trip, the Farewell

Vs. 1 Μετὰ δὲ It does not appear clear whether the tumult hastened St. Paul's departure from Ephesus or not. It could not have done so materially since he intended to leave at Pentecost anyway (see 1 Cor 16:8).

ἐξῆλθεν πορεύεσθαι Sometime in the summer of A.D. 57. He had intended to leave about Pentecost 1 Cor 16:8. Supposing that the letter was written before this tumult (in which case the ἀντικείμενοι πολλοί [1 Cor 16:9] must refer to something previous) this tumult might have hastened his departure, but, if so, it cannot have been very much hastened. In regard to St. Paul's own feelings and his movements at this time, see 2 Cor 2:12-13 (Troas), and then in Macedonia he meets Titus (2 Cor 7:5-6).

There is another indication of the time of the year. The great festival of Artemis was held in May (see Grabe (?), *Ephesus*, p. 116sq.). The incident of this tumult seems to be part of this time—the excitement of the people, the heightening of the traffic, the presence of the Asiarchs. This is quite in accord with the notices in the Corinthian Epistles.

Vss. 2-5 From about Pentecost 57 to about Easter 58, some ten months told by the historian in a few verses with a meager itinerary. Yet when we turn to the Epistles, we find that it was one of the most momentous in the Apostle's life for:

1) The infusion of his energy and the intensity of his feelings, and the severity of his sufferings. See 2 Corinthians espec. 2 Cor 1:5, 8-10; 11:23sq.; 2) his literary activity—three epistles, 2 Corinthians, Galatians, Romans. Letters fill in the details: 1) He leaves Ephesus and goes to Troas. His anxiety there (2 Cor 2:12); 2) he comes over to Macedonia (2 Cor 2:13), and finds Timothy there (2 Cor 1:1). His continued anxiety (2 Cor 7:5). Arrival of Titus (2 Cor 7:6sq., 13sq.). Then he writes the second Epistle to the Corinthians. He dispatches it with Titus and two brothers (2 Cor 8:16sq.). Then is engaged with the collection of alms—2 Cor 9:1sq. The suffering of the Macedonian churches (ἐν πολλῇ δοκιμῇ θλίψεως—2 Cor 9:2). Then writes the Epistle to

the Galatians, here or in Achaia, or while on the journey.

2) He goes to Corinth, writes the letter to the Romans. His intention at this time—Rom 15:23sq. His circumstances, companions etc. Rom 16:21sq.

Vs. 2 Ἑλλάδα The only example of this form in the New Testament. The term of the Roman province is generally used 'Achaia.' St. Paul's third visit to Corinth (the second mentioned in the Acts).

Vs. 3 ὑπὸ τῶν Ἰουδαίων The Jews at Corinth had been his great opponents on the occasion of his first visit. Acts 18:12-17. Writing to the Corinthians first before the visit, he had spoken of κινδύνοις ἐκ γένους (2 Cor 11:26).

ἐγένετο γνώμης 2 Pet 1:20; 1 Cor 14:33 and other references in Winer, no. 30 p. 244 (Moulton). This phrase implies a change of purpose. This accords with the notices in the Epistles. He there incidently considers the possibility of sailing straight through to Palestine. Rom 15:25. 2 Cor 1:16 will stand equally well, independent of the change of purpose indicated in the previous part of the verse.

Vs. 4 ἄχρι τῆς Ἀσίας See on vs. 15. It certainly falls short of the truth with regard to Trophimus. The case of Aristarchus is not so clear.

Σώπατρος A Σώπατρος is mentioned in Rom 16:21, as being: 1) a kinsman of St. Paul, i.e. a Jew by birth; 2) as with St. Paul in Corinth on this occasion. Are we to identify the two? In favor of the identification: 1) the contemporaneousness of the notices; 2) he is there mentioned in connection with Jason, perhaps the Jason of Thessalonians of Acts 17:5sq. and so a Macedonian. In this case he would be one of those Berean Jews who were εὐγενέστεροι among their countryman (Acts 17:11). Against the identification: 1) the slight difference in the form of the name; 2) the addition of the word Πύρρου may be intended to distinguish him from another Sopater or Sosipater. In Josephus *Ant.* xiv.20 is a mention of a Σώπατρος, a Jew and two sentences later a Sosipater, apparently the same person. Another Jew bearing the name is mentioned in 2 Macc 12:19sq. But it represents what Hebrew name? Apparently an uncommon heathen name. See Steph. Tres. s.v.

Ἀρίσταρχος See above Acts 19:29. He accompanied Paul to Rome (Acts 27:2) and is mentioned in Col 4:10, Philem 24.

Σέκουνδος Not mentioned elsewhere in the New Testament. Not a common name at Thessalonike, but one of the politarchs, Inscrip. 1967, 1969, 1988, and 1988b.

Γάϊος Δερβαῖος Not mentioned elsewhere.

Τιμόθεος Mentioned here because he came from the neighboring town of Lystra, Acts 16:1. The Peshito here adds 'of Lystra.' He had been taken by St. Paul to Macedonia on his journey out, and had been with him at Corinth (Rom 16) and had returned with him.

Ἀσιανοὶ The geographical limits, it does not include Lystra and Derbe.

Τυχικὸς καὶ Τρόφιμος Some mss. add 'Ephesoi.' This is probably because it was a fact, though a false reading. Trophimus can certainly be an Ephesian (Acts 21:29), Tychicus was probably so (Eph 6:21; 2 Tim 4:12). They are perhaps the two brethren of 2 Cor 8:18sq.; 9:3 but see below. They were with St. Paul in Greece. Trophimus is with Paul in Jerusalem (e.g. Acts 21:29), and is with St. Paul after his release (2 Tim 4:20). Tychicus appears with St. Paul 1) at Rome (Eph 6:21; Col 4:7); 2) after his release and Paul seems to have left him at Miletus (Tit 3:12; 2 Tim 4:12, 20). He possibly accompanied Paul to Rome. 2 Cor 8–9 sheds great light on these companions of St. Paul. They are apparently bearers of the alms of different churches to Jerusalem.

ἄχρι τῆς Ἀσίας has disappeared from the text (cf. vs. 4).

Vs. 5-6 οὗτοι δὲ How many of those previously named? Tychicus and Trophimus only, or all? The latter only . . . comp. Mt 26:39? The whole number accompanied the Apostle, but how far, St. Luke does not say. If they were bearers of contributions, probably as far as Jerusalem. This was certainly the case with Trophimus. But δέ serves as a sort of corrective, so 'I am anticipating by mentioning these latter, but they only joined us at Troas.' But these two Asiatics could and would be at Troas. Thus προσελθόντες gets its force right and this incident proceeds naturally—'having traveled with us i.e. from Asia.'

προελθόντες the right reading. Whether the intended word or not it must be regarded as of earlier authority so far as regards what was *written*.

ἔμενον ἡμᾶς Observe that 1) the writer is not Timothy or one of the others mentioned by name; 2) the first person plural is resumed at Philippi where it was dropped some years before (see Acts 16:40).

ἡμᾶς, ἡμεῖς Remark: 1) the 'we' is distinguished from Timothy; 2) the 'we' returns at the same place where it was dropped; Acts 16:11, 16. The two places with which the 'we' was connected before were Troas and Philippi. This was *six years earlier.*

Vs. 6 μετὰ τὰς ἡμέρας τῶν ἀζύμων ἀπὸ Φιλίππων He spent this festival season with his beloved Philippian converts. The other instance of St. Paul observing a season is at Acts 20:16. Another example which occurs in the Received Text (Acts 18:21) has disappeared.

ἄχρι ἡμερῶν πέντε On ἄχρι see Heb 3:13. Contrast the character of this journey with Acts 17:11. ἄχρις refers to the end of a period not as in Acts 16:11 εὐθυδρομήσαμεν.

διετρίψαμεν ἡμέρας ἑπτά With the aim of remaining on the Lord's Day. There would be some disciples here. On his first visit he had apparently done nothing (Acts 16:1-11), but on his later visit 'a door was open' (2 Cor 2:12). Thus the notices in the two recent Epistles supplements and explains the notices in the Acts. The Acts does not hint at preaching or making disciples in Troas.

Vs. 7 Ἐν δὲ τῇ μιᾷ τῶν σαββάτων Was it the Sabbath or the Sunday evening? John 20:19; 1 Cor 16:2. See Justin Martyr *Apol.* i.67 (pp. 158, 160). Rev 1:10 is more doubtful.

κλάσαι ἄρτον Comp. 1 Cor 10:16 with Acts 2:42 and Justin, *Apol. I* 98E (p. 160, Otto). It was generally accompanied by the ἀγάπη as in its original constitution, which makes the expression more intelligible, but the heart of the festival was the breaking of the Eucharistic bread.

ἡμῶν . . . αὐτοῖς the disciples of Troas.

Vs. 8 ἦσαν δὲ λαμπάδες ἱκαναὶ a touch of an eyewitness. It accounts for the dramatic description of Eutychus. It has no further motive. It may serve us now, that there is no mistake about the facts, but this evidential value clearly had no place in the narrator's mind.

ἐν τῷ ὑπερῴῳ Apparently, this was an abrupt choice, though they would be less likely to be molested there than in the courtyard of the house comp. Acts 1:13. So he passes over a chamber Mark 14:15; Luke 22:12.

Vs. 9 Εὔτυχος a common name.

ἐπὶ τῆς θυρίδος not by the window, but upon the window-sill. Comp. *Acts of Paul and Thecla*, 7.8.4

τριστέγου As we should say, 'from the second floor.' διστέγον [the floor below it].

Literally 'the chamber with the third roofing' = 'the chamber on the second floor.' Even this was unusual in ancient houses, which did not go beyond two stories. Some houses in Rome however had four stories, see Juvenal, *Sat.* iii. 199.

Vs. 10 ἐπέπεσεν, like Elijah and Elisha. Probably with prayer. Different from our Lord.

Vs. 11 τὸν ἄρτον, the bread, as he had intended, comp. vs. 7.

ὁμιλήσας homiletical sense of the word. Comp. Ignatius, *Polyc.* 5.

ἐξῆλθεν From the chamber or from Troas? Probably the latter, see vs. 7.

The miracle [and] attempts to dispose of it: 1) By interpretation. νεκρός = ὡς νεκρός. He was at least a corpse so far as any external indications appeared to the bystanders; 2) by analysis of the document. But obviously this miracle cannot be separated from the 'we' narrative, the account of the happenings in which it occurred. It is closely interwoven.

γευσάμενος May simply mean 'tastes' cf. Mt 27:34.

Vss. 13-15 On St. Luke's knowledge of seamanship, see Smith, *Voyage and Shipwreck of St. Paul*, p. 36sq. See Josephus, *Ant.* xviii.6.4; Herodotus, vii.179; Thucydides iii.32 and references in Cassius Dio i.12.

Vs. 13 προσελθόντες v.l. προελθόντες.

ἐκεῖθεν μέλλοντες The distance travelled from Troas to Assos, judging from Kiepsart's (?) map must be about twenty miles, not more. The sea voyage around Cape Lectum must be *nearly twice* the distance. Anton (?) Ths. pp. 334-35 makes 36 miles between Troas and Antardus (?). See C+H, II p. 258. The Assos of 27:13 is a variant of some texts.

Vs. 15 καὶ μείναντες ἐν Τρωγυλλίῳ [Byzantine Majority Text]. The preponderance of ancient authorities against it. Trogylium or Trogilium. The Western variation of the New Testament. There was an island of the same name—see Strabo, xiv.1.13, p. 636 in no. 14. C+H, II p. 264 says (e.g. of Trycale) that not more than a mile from Samos is the anchorage of Trogylium. The words however are no part of the original text. This is only one example of several we find in the Acts of the Apostles. Either there was a second recension by St. Luke himself, or later annotations by someone well acquainted with the facts. *Some* of these appear in the Textus Receptus, e.g. Acts 28:16. Others which are not there we find in D and other authorities e.g. Acts 12:10. Under any circumstances it does not affect the reckoning of time. The ἐχομένη starts from τῇ ... ἑτέρᾳ.

Παρεβάλομεν See below.

Vs. 16 τὴν ἡμέραν To arrive at Jerusalem and spend the [Pentecost] day there. Did he succeed? He leaves Philippi immediately after Easter, Acts 20:6. From Easter to Pentecost are 50 days, but one must make allowance for the days of Unleavened Bread themselves, six days. So we have: 1) from Philippi to Troas, 5 days (Acts 20:6); 2) sojourn at Troas, 7 days (Acts 20:6); 3) Troas to Assos, 1 day; 4) Assos to Mitylene and on to Chios, 1 day (Acts 20:15); 5) Chios to Samos, 1 day (Acts 20:16); 6) Samos to Miletus, 1 day (Acts 20:16); 7) sojourn at Miletus, 2 days? The distance from Trogylium to Miletus is about 17.5 nautical miles. If the vessel sailed at 6 in the morning it would arrive in the harbor at 9. All this = 19 days.

Then, 1) Miletus to Cos, 1? day; 2) Cos to Rhodes, 1 day (Acts 21:1); 3) Rhodes to Patara, 1 day; 4) Patara to Tyre, 5? Days; 5) sojurn at Tyre, 7 days (Acts 21:4); 6) Tyre to Ptolemais, 1 day; 7) sojourn at Ptolemais, 1 day; 8) journey to Caesarea, 1 day (Acts 21:8). Total = 18 days. This reckoning is ample. In Acts 27:2 the voyage from Caesarea to Sidon only occupies one day. The reckoning of five days from Patara to Tyre is taken from Chrysostom *Hom. on Acts*, 45 (Op. ix, p. 340). Chrysostom reckons 34 days from Philippi to Ptolemais. Also, this reckoning is quite in accord with the notices of ancient sea voyages (e.g. arrival on the fourth day from Rhodes to Alexandria). See Diodorus iii. 34. With a favorable wind, a vessel from 1,000 to 1,200 stades in 24 hours. See Friedlander, Se. II pp. 14-15. We have thus 43 days. Now when St. Paul arrives in Caesarea he stays ἡμέρας πλείους (Acts 21:10). As it had been his object to arrive at Jerusalem at Pentecost 'if it be possible,' this sojourn at Caesarea might be due to either of two causes: 1) either he found out he would not arrive in Jerusalem in time, and so there was no object in proceeding forward, or 2) there was plenty of time still to spare. The reckoning (above) shows that the latter was the case. According to Jerome, the journey from Caesarea to Jerusalem is sixty-eight miles, but there was a shorter route (see Acts 28 and Smith's *Dictionary of the Bible* s.v. Antipater). At Miletus, he could not finesse the contingencies of the voyage. Therefore, he did not venture χρονοτριβῆσαι ἐν τῇ Ἀσίᾳ (vs. 16). At Tyre he stayed 7 days. There however he might have been delayed owing to the inability to get another vessel (though this is hardly probable). But at Caesarea, he was his own master, and could have proceeded to Jerusalem as soon as he liked. The delay therefore must be explained by the fact that time was no longer an object to him. He had a sufficient number of days to spare. The journey from Caesarea to Jerusalem would take two days at least.

Vs. 17 Ἀπὸ δὲ τῆς Μιλήτου Miletum E.V. of 2 Tim 4:20. Miletus has four harbors. Now a second rate town, see C+H, ii, p. 267. St. Paul probably found out that the vessel would stay a sufficient time in the harbor. According to one reckoning, it took practically three days for summoning the Ephesian elders, for their journey to Miletus, and St. Paul's discourse. The distance from Miletus to Ephesus—some 30 miles?

τοὺς πρεσβυτέρους τῆς ἐκκλησίας To be noted: 1) πρεσβυτέροι = ἐπισκόποι (see vs. 28 and Lightfoot, *Philippians*, p. 94sq.; 2) the statement of Irenaeus iii.14.2 (see Ibid, p. 96) is inconsistent with the direct language here: a) τῆς ἐκκλησίας; b) There would be no time.

Vs. 18 ἀπὸ πρώτης Without the definite article, e.g Mark 15:25; Acts 13:10.

ἐπέβην εἰς τὴν Ἀσίαν Asia in its limited sense. It is thus consistent with: 1) the narrative of the Acts, which only narrates Ephesus as the scene of St. Paul's persona, ministry; 2) the notices in the Epistles, e.g. Colossians, yet this is especially the church which we would have *expected* to have had his personal invitation.

Vs. 19 δακρύων Gionardi's (?) *St. Paul.*

πειρασμῶν τῶν συμβάντων μοι Acts 19:9, 13sq., 33. The notices in 1, 2 Corinthians do not mention Jews by name, but the references to persecution suggest this, e.g. 2 Corinthians 1.

Vs. 20 ὑπεστειλάμην practiced no evasion, kept nothing in the background, did not withdraw or withhold. References in Steph., s.v. p. 431sq.; Demosthenes, *Panton.* p. 980; Plato, *Apol.* 24A. It might mean either: 1) shrink from nothing, or 2) kept back nothing. Probably the latter. Comp. Josephus, *Bell. Jud.* i.20.

δημοσίᾳ In the school of Tyrannus.

Vs. 21 chiasm

Vs. 22 τῷ πνεύματι, in my spirit. Apparently distinguished from 'the Holy Spirit,' as is occasionally interpreted of Acts 19:21.

Vs. 23 λέγον or λέγων. If the latter, compare the ἐκεῖνος of St. John. λέγον however would seem to be correct. This apparently the reading of B. Either by the mouth of the prophets (e.g. Acts 21:11) or directly to St. Paul (e.g. Acts 16:6-7).

Vs. 24 οὐδενὸς λόγου a conferring of instructions publicly, during the course of the report. The common reading can only be regarded as a correct for the sake of the diction. New references on λόγος in Steph. H. s.v. p. 372. τῆς χάριτος τοῦ θεοῦ The Pauline teaching, comp. Acts 15:9, 11.

Vs. 25 ἐγὼ οἶδα Phil 2:24, Philem 22, Clement of Rome. But did he visit Ephesus? Not absolutely certain. See 1 Tim 1:3, but οἶδα need not be pressed.

Vs. 28 1 Pet 5:2.

ἐκκλησίαν τοῦ κυρίου A.V. Similarly in Latin. ἐκκλησίαν τοῦ Θεοῦ E.V.

1) κυρίου A, C, D, 13 Philx. marg., Ital., Sahid., Memph., Peshit., *Apostl. Const.* ii.61, though the original reading had been Θεοῦ.

2) Θεοῦ ℵ, B, Philx. text, Pesch v.l., Cyril, Epiph. et al.

3) Combining 'Lord and God' H, L, P (the majority of cases). There are other minor readings and variants.

The question is between 1) and 2). All the others are secondary readings. Now on external evidence we should decide for 2). But the other reasons perhaps support the reverse decision. Θεοῦ more likely to have been altered than conversely, to meet Patripassionism, Nestorianism, Apollonarianism etc. The latter, more distant reasons in this discussion. On the one hand, it is agreed that ἐκκλησία τοῦ Θεοῦ is the common phrase in St. Paul, whereas he does not use ἐκκλησία τοῦ κυρίου. This is true, but such a fact was not very likely to influence similar use, especially as St. Paul does use the phrase ἐκκλησία τοῦ Χριστοῦ (Rom 16:16) so that there would be nothing unusual in the expression, although this motive is much less potent than the other. But with regard to the probability of the reading in itself, it is to be observed: 1) that it is a different thing from saying τοῦ αἵματος Θεοῦ; 2) that the Christian writers of the earliest age (before Patripassianism) did not shrink from expressions which later would be considered Patripassianist. See e.g. *Clement of Rome* ii 'the suffering of God'; Ignatius, *Ephes.* i; *Rom.* vi; *Test. 12 Patriarch, Lev.* iv.

Vs. 29 ἐγὼ οἶδα Indications in the Epistles to the Ephesians and Colossians. The evil has already broken out in the Pastoral Epistles. 1 Tim 1:6-7, 20; 4:1-3; 6:3; 2 Tim 1:5; 2:16-18; 3:1sq., 13; Tit 2:10-16; 3:9sq. The messages to the seven churches Rev 2:6, 9, 14-15, 20; 3:9.

Vs. 33 ἀργυρίου ἢ χρυσίου Comp. 1 Sam 12:3.

Vs. 34 The punctuation. πάντα in vs. 35 to be attached to what precedes it? 1 Cor 10:25, 33; 11:2 so τὰ πάντα Eph 4:15.

Vs. 35 ὑπέδειξα 'I set up an example.'

Μακάριόν ἐστιν See *Clement of Rome* ii; *Apostl. Constit.* iv.3. Relation to St. Luke's Gospel—there are facts related in the Acts which are not narrated in the Gospel, e.g. the promise of the Comforter.

EXCURSUS: THE SPEECH OF ST. PAUL AT MILETUS

1) It has the appearance of being a short report of the speech. In the Received Text, the abruptnesses are smoothed out, connecting particles added (e.g. προσέχετε οὖν, vs. 28; αὐτοὶ δὲ, vs. 34; ἐγὼ γὰρ οἶδα, vs. 29), contracts are explained (e.g. ἀλλ᾽ οὐδενὸς λόγον ποιοῦμαι οὐδὲ . . . vs. 24), and curtness of expression amplified (e.g. βασιλείαν τοῦ θεοῦ, vs. 25; ἐποικοδομῆσαι, vs. 32).

2) It has quite the character of a speech of St. Paul (after allowance is made for the editing (?) etc. of reporting). **Vs. 18** Ὑμεῖς ἐπίστασθε, the opening appeal to his missionary work among them. 1 Thess 1:10; 2:5 the very expression ἐγενήθημεν. ἀπὸ πρώτης ἡμέρας see Phil 1:5. **Vs. 19** δουλεύων τῷ κυρίῳ Comp. Rom 12:11, and so 'servant of Christ,' 'servant of God' elsewhere in St. Paul. ταπεινοφροσύνης a favorite word of St. Paul. Elsewhere in the New Testament it occurs only once, 1 Pet 5:5. The very expression μετὰ πάσης ταπεινοφροσύνης occurs at Eph 4:2. **Vs. 20** (and vs. 27) ὑπεστειλάμην [Gal 2:12], not elsewhere in the New Testament except Heb 10:38 where it is from the LXX. **Vs. 20** διαμαρτυρόμενος Confined to St. Luke and St. Paul in the New Testament (with one passage in Hebrews). **Vs. 22** ἐν πνεύματι Pauline parallels in Alford, reference to 17:16. **Vs. 23** δεσμά St Paul's frequent allusion to his bonds. The plural in St. Paul is δεσμοί, in St. Luke δεσμά. This is just where the reporter would come in. Phil 1:13; Luke 8:29; Acts 16:26. The passages where we searched as sufficient for an indication. Comp. the dramatic allusions to his bonds in the speeches of St. Paul, Acts 26:29. It was the sense of indignity in a Roman citizen. **Vs. 24** τελειῶσαι τὸν

δρόμον The common metaphor in St. Paul. Esp. 1 Cor 9:24sq.; 2 Tim 4:7. In the latter passage τὸν δρόμον τετέλεκα. τὴν διακονίαν—a very frequent and indeed characteristic expression of St. Paul in speaking of the office (e.g. Rom 11:13; 2 Cor 4:2; 6:3; Eph 4:12 etc. and especially Col 4:17). διαμαρτύρασθαι a common usage in St. Luke, in the correct text of 2 Tim 4:1 we seem to have the construction but not elsewhere, τῆς χάριτος τοῦ θεοῦ, the Pauline doctrine. **Vs. 25** εγὼ οἶδα St. Paul anticipating the future with οἶδα (Rom 16:29; Phil 1:19). In other connections οἶδα common in St. Paul. ὄψεσθε τὸ πρόσωπόν μου Col 2:1; 1 Thess 2:17; 3:10 in all places used of personal relations between St. Paul and his correspondents. The expression only occurs elsewhere in the New Testament at Acts 6:15; Rev 22:4, and there in different senses. **Vs. 26** μαρτύρομαι Gal 5:3; Eph 4:17 (not elsewhere in the New Testament). τῇ σήμερον ἡμέρᾳ 2 Cor 3:14 (the right reading). Rom 11:8 St. Paul is quoting the LXX, but in place of the diction of the LXX he has ἕως τῆς σήμερον ἡμέρας. The expression τῇ σήμερον ἡμέρᾳ does not occur elsewhere in the New Testament. **Vs. 28** ἔθετο 1 Cor 12:28, chiefly Pauline, the verb only in St. Paul (1 Tim 3:13; comp. Eph 1:14). διὰ τοῦ αἵματος Comp. Eph 1:7; Col 1:14, 20; comp. Heb 13:12. **Vs. 29** φειδόμενοι seven times in St. Paul, elsewhere only 2 Pet 2:4-5. **Vs. 31** μνημονεύοντες ὅτι Eph 2:11; 2 Thess 2:5. Only St. Paul in the New Testament. νύκτα καὶ ἡμέραν. Very frequent in St. Paul and only in this order. Elsewhere frequently in Revelation and see Mark 4:27; 5:5; Luke 2:37. Alford is wrong that the accusative does not occur outside of St. Paul. See Luke references. οὐκ ἐπαυσάμην Comp. Eph 1:16; Col 1:9. The expression however occurs in St. Luke. μετὰ δακρύων (as also in vs. 19). Comp. 2 Cor 2:4. On this it may be observed that: 1) the two notices refer to the same crisis in his life; 2) he alludes to his tears in both passages by way of appeal to his concern. νουθετῶν ἕνα ἕκαστον Comp. Col 1:28. The word νουθετεῖν is peculiar to St. Paul in the New Testament. 1 Thess 2:11. **Vs. 32** δοῦναι τὴν κληρονομίαν See Eph 1:18; Col 1:12. **Vs. 33** ἀργυρίου ἢ χρυσίου The appeal to his disinterestedness 1 Cor

9:15sq.; 2 Cor 7:2; 11:9sq.; 12:13sq.; Comp. 1 Thess 2:5. **Vs. 34** αὐτοὶ γινώσκετε St. Paul's mode of appeal. See especially 1 Thess 2:1; 3:3; 2 Thess 3:7 and elsewhere. ταῖς χρείαις μου Comp. especially Phil 2:25; 4:16. On the phrase μετ' ἐμοῦ . . . αἱ χεῖρες, 1 Cor 4:12 (comp. 1 Thess 4:11). ὑπηρέτησαν his own example of manual labor urged upon his converts 2 Thess 3:7. The affection (?) of the example, see 1 Cor 10:31–11:2. ἀντιλαμβάνεσθαι, only in Luke 1:54; 1 Tim 6:2 but see especially 1 Thess 5:14 and for the general idea and expressions see Eph 4:28.

SUMMARY: We have thus shown that: 1) the Pauline doctrine appears; 2) that the practical applications and mode of appeal of St. Paul are strikingly reproduced; 3) that there are very few expressions for which parallels cannot be produced in St. Paul's Epistles and some are singularly characteristic of him. Contrast the speeches at the beginnings of Acts. Evidence of growth.

Vs. 37 ἱκανὸς A very favorite word with St. Luke. This a crucial instance of the sense 'very great,' Acts 5:37; 9:23.

Vs. 38 εἰς τὸ πλοῖον, whether the same vessel or not, we cannot determine. Probably so, as the sojourn had been brief. Comp. prior to Acts 21:6.

ACTS 21: ONCE MORE TO JERUSALEM

Vs. 1 εὐθυδρομήσαντες On the prevailing north-westerly and northern winds, see C+H, ii, p. 274. 'With the wind the vessel would make the passage from Miletus to Cos in six hours' (p. 272). As St. Luke does not say ἑξῆς or the equivalent here, they probably arrived on the same day as they started. On the 'etesia flabra Aquilorum' see Luc. v.742, vi. 715, 730; Drod. i.38.2; Arist. *De Mund.* 4 (p. 395). The whole voyage seems to have been safe and prosperous, as indeed with the prevailing winds it would probably be.

εἰς τὴν Κῶ The connection of words which gives the modern name to the island 'Stanko.' Κῶ is the right reading here. The connection with Judaea—privileges conferred on this island by Herod. Josephus, *Bell. Jud.* i.21.11, as shown in the inscription in Boeckh, no. 2502 i.e. Herod the Great's son, Herod Antipas, tetrarch of Galilee, contrast Mt 2:1 with Acts 14:1. From Cos, the main coast began to bend off in an easterly direction. The travel from Cos to Patara was from NW to SE, from Patara onward from W to E. The south coast, rightly speaking would be said to begin opposite Rhodes. Patara a sort of port town of Xanthus. See Appian, *Bell.* iv. 81. See references in Wettstein. Obviously an important shipping station. Comp. Strabo, xiv.3 (p. 666). The bay now is choked with sand.

Vs. 2 διαπερῶν 'a through passage.' See Winer xlv, p. 429 (Moulton). It would appear that this was not the starting point, however this is not certain. The present only signifies that it may be the point of starting.

Vs. 3 ἀναφάναντες, 'have sighted.' See Winer no. 39 p. 326. A nautical phrase, illustrative of St. Luke's seamanship. See C+H, II p. 282, comp. ἀποκρύπτειν.

εἰς Τύρον They did not coast, but sailed across the open sea leaving Cyprus on their north and obviously at some distance, so that they only sighted it. The distance between Patara and Tyre, 340 geographical miles (C+H ii. p. 281). The rig of a (?) peculiarly favored, a quick run? The voyage is said to be accomplished in 48 hours. I have allowed five days, following Chrysostom.

ἐκεῖσε γὰρ Whether the vessel was already full of cargo, i.e. whether the vessel was bound on the errand of unloading her cargo. See Winer no. 45, pp. 439, 592. Two points to be observed: 1) the abridgement of the sentence— whither it was bound and there it would unload; 2) the use of the present for the future, as if to say 'And there I unload my cargo' because it is a part of the present intention. The process had in some sense begun.

Vs. 4 ἀνευρόντες 'Having found out the disciples.' The natural language of one who was present. The A.V. obliterates this sense, 'having found disciples' as if εὑρόντες μαθητὰς τινὰς. The fact of there being disciples is assumed. How came there to be disciples at Tyre? 1) Our Lord's personal ministry. He visited these parts, Mt 15:21; Mark 7:24. 2) Persons from these parts seek this ministry, Mark 3:8; Luke 6:17, see the Συροφοινίκισσα; 3) the Apostles, Phoenica—Acts 11:19; 15:3 in connection with St. Paul himself; 4) the *Clementine Hom.* vii.5 and elsewhere.

ἐπιβαίνειν Not to set foot in Jerusalem, comp. Acts 20:18. This word much more vivid and forceful than ἀναβαίνειν of the Received Text.

Vs. 5 ἐξαρτίσαι 'completed.' See Hippocrates ii.180 and elsewhere, passages quoted in Lubeck, *Phyrg.* p. 447. The other meaning given to ἐξαρτίσαι here 'we had spent the days in making our preparations.'

ἐπὶ τὸν αἰγιαλὸν the sandy or pebbly beach. See references in Steph. Ther. s.v. p. 895. This would be reported for the incident, and this is the character of the coast at Tyre.

Vs. 6 ἀπησπασάμεθα Hiner, *Phot. Bill.* 243 p. 369, instances of the word are given. Different from what is in the Received Text ἀσπασάμενοι.

τὰ ἴδια Luke 18:28 v.l.; John 1:11; 16:32; 19:27.

Vs. 7 τὸν πλοῦν διανύσαντες ἀπὸ Τύρου 'having accomplished the voyage from Tyre.' This cannot be forced to mean that they finally left the ship at Ptolemais and performed the rest of the journey by land. In order to make it mean that: 1) the ἀπὸ Τύρου is taken with what follows, but why this emphatic position of this phrase? 2) the order would imply that they had finished the voyage *before* they went from Tyre to Ptolemais. Ptolemais was one of the best harbors in the whole area. No other mention of Ptolemais in the New Testament. There is an exactly parallel passage from Xenephon, *Ephes.* showing the force of this expression, see C+H and Gloag—meaning 'having ended the whole voyage.' There is a bishop of Ptolemais in the latter half of the second century, see Eusebius, *H.E.* v.25.

Vs. 8 ἐξελθόντες does not necessarily imply a land journey. In C+H, ii. p. 287—'ἐξ is far more suitable for a departure by land than by sea.' See e.g. vs. 5.

Vs. 9 Philip the Evangelist, carefully distinguished by St. Luke from Philip the Apostle. There was confusion in later ages. A certain Philip lived in Hierapolis. Which Philip can it be? See Papias (*H.E.* iii.39), Polycrates (*H.E.* iii.29, 31), Clement of Alexandria (*H.E.* iii.30). Hitherto no trace of confusion. Dialogue of Ca. and Proculus (*H.E.* iii. 31) followed by Eusebius.

Vs. 10 προφήτης ὀνόματι Ἄγαβος comp. Acts 11:27-28 (and see the reading of D).

Vs. 11 δήσας ἑαυτοῦ the right reading, and indeed he would. Τὸν ἄνδρα οὗ ἐστιν shows that it was not Paul himself who was bound.

τοὺς πόδας καὶ τὰς χεῖρας The better authenticated reading, preferable in itself because it gives the only possible order. On the symbolical action see 1 Kings 22:11, Zedekiah; Is 20:2, Israel in sackcloth; Jer. 13:1sq., Jeremiah's girdle; Acts 27:2, the bonds and yoke. Ezek 4:1; 12:3; 24:3; and Amos 8:1.

Vs. 14 Τοῦ Κυρίου τὸ θέλημα The emphatic position important. The Lord's will, not ours etc.

Vs. 15 ἐπισκευασάμενοι The word is used of packing the luggage, or the wagon, or the beast of burden. Generally used in the active sense, see Xenephon, *Cyr.* vii.3.1. Sometimes in the middle. Xenephon, *Hell.* vii.2.8. See more references in Wettstein, and on one who accompanied the wagon or the beast of burden.

Vs. 16 ἄγοντες The A.V. is right: 1) the order favors it; and 2) it supplies the sense and the attraction is more natural. See Rom 6:17. Kühner, II p. 913; Winer, no. 24, p. 205, no. 31, p. 268.

Μνάσωνί For the name see Shep. Herm. s.v. and the recent (?) inscription from Cyprus. It is an adaptation of the Hebrew name Manassah comp. e.g. Jason. He would be a Jewish Christian going up to Jerusalem for the Feast.

ἀρχαίῳ μαθητῇ For ἀρχαίῳ comp. Acts 15:7, for Cyprus Acts 11:19; 13:4.

Vs. 18 πρὸς Ἰάκωβον Acts 12:17—A.D. 44, Acts 15:13—A.D. 51; Gal 1:19, 2:9 sq. πρεσβύτεροι Acts 11:30; 14:23; 15:2sq.; 16:4.

Vs. 20 πόσαι μυριάδες not to be interpreted literally, e.g. Plato, *Leg.* vii (p. 804). It is quite possible at this time however, that the Jewish and even Hebrew Christians associated the terms of (?).

πάντες 'It is quite certain that,' comp. 1 Cor 9:10; Luke 4:23. The alarm is vividly expressed in the abruptness of the correct text.

Vs. 23 εὐχὴν ἔχοντες Nazarite vow, Num 6. Its length uncertain, but at this time it possibly lasted 30 days—Josephus, *Bell. Jud.* ii.15, so the Mishnah, *Nazir* i.3 (Surent., III p. 148). The main act, an offering at the end of the period.

Vs. 24 ἁγνίσθητι, not that St. Paul himself undertook a Nazarite vow. There was no time for this, and obviously the ἁγνίσθητι excludes the supposition that he had one already, for in that case we would have here ἡγίσμένος already. But a temporary abstinence from defilement would serve the necessity of a condition of his taking his part.

δαπάνησον Josephus *Ant.* xix.6.1 of Agrippa I. So too, Alexander Janneus pays the expenses for 300 Nazarites. See Smith's *Dictionary of the Bible*, s.v. Nazarite, p. 472.

ξυρήσονται seems to be correct (though there would be a tendency to conform to γνώσονται). A future is possible with ἵνα e.g. Rev 3:9 and Winer no. 41, p. 360sq. (Moulton). If ξυρήσονται is correct then γνώσονται is a change to direct construction as in Luke 22:30 (the correct reading), and Eph 6:3.

Relation of the Proceeding to: 1) St. James—See Hegisippus in Eusebius *H.E.* ii.23; 2) St. Paul 1 Cor 7:17-19; 9:20; 8:13; Rom 14:21. In Acts comp. the circumcision of Timothy and the vow at Cenchreae. St. Paul persistently maintained the freedom of the Gentile Christians. He did not interfere with the observance of the law by Jewish Christians, probably recommended it. Time—the destruction of Jerusalem, 'the coming of the Lord,' would complete the work. But what did he do in his own person? We may suppose that he would practice that course which would be ἀπρόσκοποι . . . Ἰουδαίοις (1 Cor 10:32), i.e. he would generally observe the law, *for the sake of the Jews*, though in very exceptional cases a departure from it might be necessary *for the sake of the Gentiles*. This view is quite consistent with Gal 2:11sq. where it is the question of *eating with the Gentiles*.

Vs. 25 See Acts 15:20, 29; 16:4.

Vs. 26 ἕως οὗ προσηνέχθη 'until . . . *had* been fulfilled.' Is this connected with declaring the fulfillment of the days or the days of purification? If with the former then it would seem to simply [indicate] that he was not interrupted. With the latter we might expect προσηνέχθειν. But the statement here is made without counting on the contingency that it might be aborted. The instances of the indicative in Alford (following de Wette) are not to the point here. See Kühner, II no. 567, p. 950; Winer no. 41, p. 371.

Vs. 27 οἱ ἀπὸ τῆς Ἀσίας Ἰουδαῖοι who were there for the Festival. Comp. Acts 2:9.

αἱ ἑπτὰ ἡμέραι This raises the question of the chronology of this visit to Jerusalem:

Table 2. Paul's Visit to Jerusalem

	Days
21:17 arrival in Jerusalem	
v. 18	1
v. 26 he enters into the temple [the seven days—v. 27]	1
22:30 Paul addresses the Sanhedrin	1
23:11, 12-31 conspiracy against Paul, he is recognized by sight	1
v. 32 he is taken to Caesarea	1
24:1 arrival of Tertullas and others and the speech of St. Paul (it is not absolutely clear from what point these five days are reckoned)	5

St. Paul says (Acts 24:11) οὐ πλείους εἰσίν μοι ἡμέραι δώδεκα ἀφ' ἧς ἀνέβην προσκυνήσων εἰς Ἰερουσαλήμ. There are therefore ten (supposing that the five days are reckoned from his removal from Jerusalem) or nine days after his arrival in Jerusalem. We cannot therefore add to this seven whole days. What then are the seven days?:

1) They refer to the Pentecostal Festival, but according to the law it was only a single day (Lev 23:15; Num 28:26sq.). At this time however, there is good reason for thinking that Pentecost, as indeed all the great Festivals, was preceded by a week of solemn preparation, and so was a seven days' Festival, the great day being the last of the Festival. Comp. Josephus *Ant.* xviii.4.3, the discussion about the high priest, and see also Mishnah, *Hagg.* ii.4; *Mo'ed Ka.* iii.5 (Sur., II pp. 419,420), with the commentary of Mamonides, hence Acts 2:1 συμπληροῦσθαι. In this case, the period of the days has nothing to do with the reckoning. The twelve days would be made up then by interposing a day or two between Acts 21:26 and Acts 21:27 i.e. between St. Paul's first appearance in the temple and the tumult, not by reckoning in the two day journey from Jerusalem to Caesarea, because the events of vs. 26 and vs. 27 can hardly have taken place on the same day.

2) The seven days are the days of St. Paul's purification, i.e. the days of purification of vs. 26 = the seven days of vs. 27. And so far this interpretation is plausible. But, there is no evidence of such seven days of purification, though it might be founded on the analogy of Num 6:9. Also, it leads to a slightly forced interpretation of ἔμελλον αἱ ἑπτὰ for only three of the days could have passed.

Vs. 28 βοηθεῖτε 'to the rescue!'

ἔτι τε καὶ See Josephus, *Bell. Jud.* v.5.2; *Ant.* xv.11.5. On the famous warning inscription in the temple, see M. Ganneau's discussion Palestinian Exploration Fund. Aug. 1871 p. 132 (see also Oct. 1871, p. 172). M. Ganneau has apparently overlooked the second passage from Josephus. Comp. Philo, *Leg. ad Gaius* 31 (p. 571).

Vs. 29 Τρόφιμον τὸν Ἐφέσιον

Vs. 30 ἔξω τοῦ ἱεροῦ, not the whole of the enclosure, but the court of the Israelites for: 1) it must be defined by the ἱερόν in vs. 28; Gentiles were admitted within the outer court; 2) the subsequent scene evidently takes place within the enclosure. The θύραι then are the gates that shut off the Court of the Israelites. This in fact is what Josephus, *Bell. Jud.* v.5.2 calls 'the second temple.'

Vs. 31 τῷ χιλιάρχῳ, the tribune. His name is Claudius Lysias (Acts 23:26). Lysias indicates of Greek extraction, Claudius indicates connection with the imperial household.

τῆς σπείρης 'cohort.' Polybius xi.23.1. See *Shep. Herm.* s.v. p. 669. On the presence of the soldiers at Feasts see Josephus, *Bell. Jud.* ii.12.1, sometimes more than one σπείρα (ii.15.3).

Vs. 32 ἐξαυτῆς they were kept in arms, ready for any consequences.

Χιλίαρχον A tribune and his soldiers.

Vs. 33 ἁλύσεσι δυσί Comp. Acts 13:7. Where the confinement was not so strict, one chain was enough. Acts 28:20; Eph 6:20; 2 Tim 1:16. τίς εἴη (who he was) καὶ τί ἐστιν πεποιηκώς (and what he has done), a change of construction from the oblique to the direct. The correct reading is τίς εἴη not τίς ἂν εἴη (Majority Text). The A.V. however, reading the latter has translated it as if it were the former.

Vs. 34 παρεμβολήν, see vs. 31 ἀνέβη, vs. 32 κατέδραμεν, vs. 35 ἀναβαθμούς (the stairs). On the Antonia Fortress see Josephus *Bell. Jud.* i.5.4 on its name and position, also v.5.8, vi.2.9, and *Ant.* xv.11.4. See Robinson, I 292sq. and III p. 230sq. On the παρεμβολήν or barracks Lubbeck, *Phryg.* p. 377 on Macedonians.

Vs. 37 Ἑλληνιστὶ γινώσκεις Xenephon *Ap.* vii.5.31. See Luke 22:23. It cannot have been St. Paul's knowledge of Greek, but rather something in the manner of his address [that led to the question].

Vs. 38 ὁ Αἰγύπτιος Josephus gives an account of this imposter in *Ant.* xx.8.6 and *Bell. Jud.* ii.13.5. In the former passage he calls him 'a certain one from Egpyt, claiming to be a prophet,' in the latter he calls him a pseudo-prophet. He collected a large number of followers, situated himself on the Mt. of Olives, claimed that at his bidding the walls of Jerusalem would fall down, persuaded his followers to advance and attack the city, was anticipated and thwarted by Felix. The point of coincidence between Josephus and St. Luke being the general description of the man, and his proceedings, more or less: 1) the date, St. Luke πρὸ τούτων τῶν ἡμερῶν, the words are spoken in 58. The account of Josephus however requires us to place it at the commencement of Nero's reign i.e. 55; 2) the place, St. Luke says 'in the desert'; Josephus that he came out of the desert [to Jerusalem]; 3) the pretensions of the man, claimed to be able to do miracles, called by Josephus a false prophet.

4) character of his followers, St. Luke mentions the sicarri, dagger men; 5) attitude of the inhabitants, for once we find them taking the side of the Roman governor, against the rebel; 6) fate of the Egyptian himself, Josephus *Bell. Jud.* ii.13.5 says he escaped Felix's army with a few followers, St. Luke's tribune contemplates his turning up again.

And yet the accounts are plainly independent. This will have appeared in the parallels already noticed. In the account of the numbers of followers it is not quite clear. In *Bell. Jud.* it is said he gathered around him 30,000, but these are only a part of his whole force. Again Josephus says nothing specific about placing the sicarii in connection with the Egyptian, but it is highly probable that they would take part in the attack on Jerusalem. It was a golden opportunity for them. At this point their ingenuities were at their height. They are mentioned by Josephus for disturbing the peace of Jerusalem and making life insecure, but immediately before and immediately after this attempt by the Egyptian, see *Bell. Jud.* ii.13.2, 3, 6; *Ant.* xx.8, 4, 5, 6.

εἰς τὴν ἔρημον Perhaps the wilderness of Judah, Comp. Josephus *Bell. Jud.* ii.13.5.

τῶν σικαρίων Described in Josephus *Bell. Jud.* ii.13.3, they carried daggers and secretly assassinated their enemies. So too *Ant.* xx.8.5. This then was just the time when the Romans were likely to assert their presence.

Vs. 39 ἄνθρωπος μέν This μέν is not answered, I think, by the following δέομαι δέ. We may suppose he was giving 'and I was brought up in Jerusalem,' as in vs. 3. He backs off suddenly however. It occurs to him that he had better reserve his fuller explanations for the whole people; and he therefore requests permission to do so.

τῆς Κιλικίας Generally taken with what follows, but there is much to be said for the A.V. reading.

οὐκ ἀσήμου πόλεως See Dion Chrysos. *Oracle* xxxviii, p. 399A on the Tarsians.; Comp. Ammuan. iv.8. Wettstein questions where this phrase occurs—see Eury. *Ion* 8, and later citations.

CONCLUSION

I have here taken some pains to trace the historical character of this scene, and for the following reasons: The Tübingen theory represents the St. Paul of Acts as inconsistent with the St. Paul of his own Epistles. The most signal instance of this inconsistency is in his approach on this occasion. The history therefore is discredited by the notice. I have already shown that his conduct here was the result of his carrying out his principles as enunciated in his Epistles and their natural consequences. But apart from this, let us look at the narrative itself. It possesses in this part the care of an eyewitness. It is preceded by a careful itinerary, which we can follow from place to place, and almost from day to day. When we get to Jerusalem we find: 1) that a thorough knowledge of local customs is exhibited—the Nazarites, the seven days (the very difficulty in defining its meaning is in its favor), the prohibition in the Temple, the relation of the Romans and the Jews, the Festivals, the guard; 2) that it shows an exact knowledge of local topography—the temple, the Antonia Fortress, and yet the relative position of the two is only indicated accidentally [by the verbs predicated of the guard], the mention of the steps; 3) Incidentally too it exhibits a knowledge of contemporary history. The Egyptian, the allusive not forced [description] yet perfectly in accord with facts, and even minute facts. All is artless, natural, and connected, what you feel might have occurred, nay what must have occurred. You cannot separate the Nazarite vow from the rest.

Conclusions on the Rest of Acts

Though we do not have Lightfoot's exegesis of Acts 24–28 we do know a good deal of what he would say about this material in the light of the fact that (1) he believes Acts was written by Luke, a sometime companion of Paul, including on his third missionary journey; (2) he thinks the record of Paul's journey to Rome and shipwreck is accurately told (and he relies on that nineteenth-century staple that indicates the account is accurate in detail—Smith's *The Voyage and Shipwreck of St. Paul*); (3) he tends to think that Paul was exonerated when he got to Rome, and went on to do further ministry;[1] and (4) he does not see the ending of Acts 28 as abrupt.

Perhaps equally importantly, Lightfoot sees Acts as integrating well with the Pauline chronology, including the chronology of his letters, and he would not agree with the notion that the Paul of Acts is somehow a different or even divergent Paul from the one we recognize in the Pauline corpus. He believes Acts is a historically serious work like other ancient historical monographs (e.g. those by Thucydides), though he also is firmly committed to the idea that Luke relied on and edited sources in ways that accorded with his own style and purposes. The fact that he would defend at length a speech from Acts, namely the Stephen speech, tells us that he thinks that the speeches, no less than the narrative, are historically substantive, though of course they are not mere verbatim transcripts of all a person said on the occasion. (BW3)

---

[1]See the discussions below in appendixes A and C.

Appendix A

Lightfoot's Article on Acts for Smith's *Dictionary of the Bible*[1]

Acts of the Apostles *1. The Title.* The title of this Book, as given in the oldest authorities is either 'Acts' or 'Acts of Apostles.' The former (πράξεις) appears at the commencement and in the headings of the pages in א; the latter (πράξεις ἀποστόλων) in B, D (but with the itacism πράξις in D), and in the subscription of א. Accordingly, the Book is quoted indifferently by the early Fathers as 'Acts,' 'The Acts' (Origen, *Op. I* p. 434, iv. pp. 6,25; comp. Eusebius *H.E.* vi.25; Tertullian *c. Marc.* v.3, *de Praescr.* 22, and elsewhere), or 'Acts of Apostles,' 'The Acts of the Apostles' (Irenaeus iii.13,3; Clement of Alexandria *Strom.* v.12, p. 696; Tertullian, *c. Marc* v. 1,2, and elsewhere; Origen, *Op.* I p. 22, ii. p.538 & c.). Longer titles, such as 'Acts of the Holy Apostles' (πράξεις τῶν ἁγίων ἀποστόλων), found in the subcription of E, G, H may be dismissed at once from our consideration. The

---

[1]This article by Lightfoot appears to be one of the last pieces he ever wrote on the New Testament itself. While some have conjectured that the piece was written before he became bishop of Durham in 1879, this can hardly be the case since Lightfoot interacts with works within the text itself (not just references in a bibliography that could have been added later by an editor) that were *not written* before the mid-1880s or so. Lightfoot died in 1889. This article then becomes important not only in itself but also for comparing what we have presented in the commentary, culled from his Cambridge lecture notes from the period from 1855 to 1879. It is a great pity that this article was replaced in the American edition of the second edition of Smith's work by a much inferior piece and disappears altogether in subsequent editions of the dictionary in the twentieth century, as this article shows in detail Lightfoot's capacity to argue his case about Acts, dealing with all, or almost all, of the introductory matters that needed to be covered. (BW3)

author of the *Muratorian Canon* (c. A.D. 180?) refers to the Book as containing 'acta omnium apostolorum' (p. 18, ed. Tregelles); but he does not give this definitely as a title, and by inserting 'omnium' which however is not a correct description, he obviously desires to distinguish it from apocryphal histories of individual Apostles, such as the 'Acta Petri' etc. Whether we should consider the larger title a later expansion of the shorter, or whether on the other hand 'Acts' is an abridgement of 'Acts of Apostles' for convenience, may be a matter of question. On the whole, perhaps the latter view is the more probable; since the long and short forms are found in the same writers, and moreover whenever the title of the Book is distinctly recorded as such—for instance by Eusebius (*H.E.* iii.25) and by Athanasius (*Op.* ii. p. 767) and by Chrysostom (*Op.* iii. p. 54) and by Euthalius and by Photius (*Amphil. Qu.* 123)—the word ἀποστόλων is never wanting. We gather also from the evidence, that in the original form the definite article was absent. Thus for instance, Chrysostom (in the passage just referred to), having distinctly given the title without the articles (πράξεις ἀποστόλων) nevertheless in the same context writes τῶν πράξεις τῶν ἀποστόλων. This example shows that no stress can be laid on the fact that elsewhere the Book is quoted in early writers as 'The Acts of the Apostles.' In Wycliffe's Version which was translated from the Vulgate it is headed 'Deeds of the Apostles'; but in the Authorized Version (1611) the heading is 'The Acts of the Apostles' as also in the previous English Versions of the 16th century generally, which were made from the Greek. But, though it seems clear that the earlier title was 'Acts of Apostles' (πράξεις ἀποστόλων) without the definite article, the value of the fact in its bearing on the contents is diminished by the consideration that in titles and headings the omission of the article was common in ancient times, as it is with ourselves. Thus in Mt 1:1 the words are 'book of generation (or genealogy) of Jesus Christ' (Βίβλος γενέσεως κ.τ.λ.). Moreover, we have no ground for assuming that this title, whether πράξεις ἀποστόλων or πράξεις simply, was given to the Book by the writer himself. In other cases in the New Testament we find indications that the earliest existing headings are somewhat later than the writings themselves (Lightfoot, *Colossians*, p. 16). The later word πράξαποστόλος is not a title of this individual Book; but, being compounded of πράξεις and ἀποστόλος, designates lectionaries which contained lessons from the Acts and Apostolic Epistles (Scrivner's *Intro-duction,* pp. 71, 279, 301).

2. *The Scope and Contents.* The Acts of the Apostles, like the Third Gospel, is addressed to one Theophilus. Was he an actual person, a disciple or friend of the writer? Or have we here a fictitious name, a representative of the Christian reader generally? The former is the view commonly taken by modern writers. He has been made a native of Antioch, of Alexandria, of Rome, etc. by different critics, all without any shadow of authority that deserves consideration. If he were a real person, we might with greater probability place him at Philippi, for the writer of Acts apparently had close relations with this place. Yet the other opinion is not to be hastily rejected; for it is at least consonant with the literary character of St. Luke's two trea-tises, and more especially of the prefaces. This view is thrown out as a sug-gestion by Epiphanius (*Haer.* li.7). It seems also to be present to the mind of Origen, though he does not express himself very clearly (*Hom. In Luc. 1, Op.* iii. p. 933 Delarus). So also St. Ambrose, 'Scriptum est evangelium ad Theophilum hoc est ad eum quem Deus diligit' (*Exp. Evang. Luc.* 1.12, *Op.* i. p. 1270, ed. Bened.). In modern times it has found some rather lukewarm supporters (e.g. Renan, *L'Eglise Chretienne,* p. 256). As the Greek equivalent to the Hebrew Jedidiah, Theophilus is not uncommon as a Jewish name. Thus it is borne by the Jewish high-priest (A.D. 37–41) the son of Annas (Josephus, *Ant.* xviii.5.3; xix.6.2), who has been identified—an extremely improbable identification—with the persons here addressed by St. Luke. Again, we find two persons so called in an inscription in a Jewish cemetery at Rome (Schürer, *Gemeindeverf. Der Juden in Rom,* p. 39). It was a frequent heathen name likewise (Pape, *Worterb. Griech. Eigennamen,* s.v., Fabric, *Bibl. Graec.* vii. p. 106 sq. ed Harles; compare Tacitus, *Ann.* ii.55). Naturally also it was common among the Christians e.g. the apologist Theophilus, Bishop of Antioch (c. A.D. 180). A reminiscence of this later Theophilus combined with the tradition that St. Luke himself was an Antiochene, may have given rise to the Clementine statement that Theophilus was a person of importance in Antioch (*Recogn.* x.71, 'Theophilus qui erat cunctis po-tentibus in civitate sublimior'), who consecrated his house as a basilica, where the chair of St. Peter was established. In *Apost. Const.* vii.46, a Theophilus is represented as the third Bishop of Caesarea of Palestine, and

appointed to the see by the Apostles themselves, his predecessors being Zacchaeus and Cornelius. Probably our Theophilus is meant, as it is the practice of this writer to find an episcopal see for every worthy whose name is mentioned in the New Testament. In the Armenian *Epistle of the Corinthians to St. Paul* (Aucher, *Armen. Gramm.* p. 177) one Theophilus is represented as a joint writer of the letter.

The adoption of the name Theophilus or Philotheus as a representative godly Christian, has parallels in both ancient and modern times. Thus the treatise of Hippolytus, *de Antichristo* (pp. 1, 36, Lagarde), is addressed to his 'beloved brother Theophilus,' evidently a fictitious name; and in the *Symposium* of Methodius (ii. 1, p. 14, Jahn) one of the divine maidens bears the name Theophila. So likewise Law's *Atonement* is a *Dialogue between Eusebius and Theophilus*, and Wordsworth's treatise on the Church is designated *Theophilus Anglicanus*; while in Ken's *Manual of Prayer* for the Winchester scholars he addresses his reader as Philotheus.

If this view be correct, this second treatise is drawn up, like the first for the instruction of the godly reader who seeks information respecting the foundation of the Church (here addressed under the imaginary name Theophilus). It is no objection that he is designated κράτιστος (Luke 1:3), a title given to those in high position (Acts 23:26; 24:3; 26:25); for there is no reason why the writer should not have wished to commend the faith of Christ to persons of this class.

Its aim, purport, and contents are set forth in the preface (Acts 1:1-8). The first treatise is there described as an account of 'all things which Jesus began both to do and to teach (ἤρξατο ὁ Ἰησοῦς ποιεῖν τε καὶ διδάσκειν) until the day on which, having given the commandment through the Holy Ghost to the Apostles whom He had chosen, He was taken up (into heaven).' This language suggests: 1) that, if the writer had given any title to the work, he might well have styled it 'Second Treatise' (δεύτερος λόγος); and 2) that he regards it as strictly a continuation of the first, for this is implied in ἤρξατο, 'began.' But here a question arises. Is the 'doer and teacher' the same person in the second part as in the first? In other words, is Jesus Himself here regarded as continuing in the history of the Church the work that He began in His personal ministry? This is Baumgarten's view, and it has been followed by some later critics. In its favor are the facts: a) that the form of the sentence suggests the same agent, and b) that our Lord is again and again represented as interposing in person in the course of the narrative. If so, the title πράξεις ἀποστόλων is misleading, and obscures the author's main conception. But this view is not altogether free from the charge of artificiality. At all events we might expect that, if this had been the writer's leading idea, he would have emphasized it more plainly. It seems on the whole therefore more probable that the Apostles are represented as *continuing* the work which Jesus inaugurated in person. If so, the common title of the Book is fairly adequate, and Photius (*Amphil.* 123, p. 716, Migne) is right when he speaks of the Gospel as 'comprising the Acts of the Lord.' Similarly Irenaeus (iii.15.1) describes the second treastise as 'sequens testificatio ejus (Lucae), quam habet de *actibus et doctrina apostolorum*,' with an obvious reference to the 'doing and teaching' of our Lord as contained in the first. In this case the ἤρξατο may be answered by ἄχρι ἧς ἡμέρας κ.τ.λ., i.e. 'the whole history of the doings and teachings of Jesus from the beginning until the final day of the Ascension,' as it is taken by Chrysostom (*Op.* ix. p. 5). This view also accords with the fact that special stress is laid on the selection of and charge to the Apostles, that their names are given again (though previously mentioned in the Gospel), and that the completion of their number is recorded. Bengel, following Chrysostom, describes the relation of the two treatises somewhat differently 'non tam Apostolorum quam Spiritus Sancti describens, sicut prior liber Acta Jesu Christi habet'; but this is not the antithesis present to the mind of the writer himself.

Thus the two treatises are regarded respectively as the ministry of Jesus and the ministry of the Apostles, or (if we take the other view) the ministry of Jesus in his own person and the ministry of Jesus through the Apostles. The first has been given in full by St. Luke (περὶ πάντων κ.τ.λ.); the second, not being yet concluded, could not be so given. The contents of the first have been directly described. This description is expressed in such language (μὲν πρῶτον κ.τ.λ.) as to lead the reader to expect an antithetical clause . . . describing the contents of the second. But this antithetical clause never appears, and in place of it the sentence runs off into a narrative of facts. In this narrative of facts therefore we look for the explanation; and we are not disappointed. The Lord is represented as conversing with the disciples after the Resurrection and preparing them for their mission. His words are prophetic of the future, and thus implicitly involve a table of contents:

'Ye shall receive power when the Holy Ghost,' etc. (Acts 2:1-13)
'And ye shall be witnesses unto Me,

    1. Both in Jerusalem (2:14–8:1)

    2. And in all Judaea and Samaria (8:2–11:18)

    3. And to the uttermost parts of the earth' (11:19–28:31).

The first two sections are complete; the fulfillment of the third is given not actually but potentially. Such an earnest of it is afforded as to leave no doubt of its ultimate accomplishment. St. Paul travels to the far West; he preaches the faith in Rome without hindrance; and thus Christianity has obtained a firm footing in the metropolis of the human race, the stronghold of heathendom.

After this anticipatory abstract of the history of the Christian Church, our thoughts are led forward to the great and terrible day, the consummation of all things, when this history shall be wound up. But again this is effected, not by his own words, but by the narrative of the sayings and doings of others (Acts 1:8-11). The departure of Jesus by the Ascension is thus linked with His return in the Second Advent. The narrative of the Acts spans over this interval potentially.

These considerations will explain the close of the Book. Whatever apparent abruptness there may be in the ending, the writer was clearly not interrupted so as to leave his work unfinished. He closes with the event that his aim required. The occupation of Rome, the capital of the world, was the one eventful crisis that closed an epoch. Nor did he contemplate a 'third treatise,' as some have imagined. There is indeed no conceivable plea for any third treatise if our view of his main design be correct. Nor again can any chronological argument be drawn from his stopping at this particular point; as, for instance, that he was unacquainted with St. Paul's visit to Spain or with the martyrdom of the two Apostles. He was not writing the biography of either Apostle.

It will be observed also that the close of the second treatise is strictly analogous to the close of the first:

| Fufillment of prophecies | Luke 24:44-49/Acts 28:23-29 |
| Joyful termination | Luke 24:50-53/Acts 28:30, 31 |

The following then is the table of contents:

INTRODUCTORY

(i.)	Connection with the previous narrative	1:1-2
(ii.)	Christ's final commands and prophecies respecting the Kingdom of God	1:3-8
(iii.)	The resurrection, and announcement of the Second Advent	1:9-11
(iv.)	The names and attitude of the Apostles	1:12-14
(v.)	The vacant place in the apostolate filled	1:15-26

THE MAIN NARRATIVE

A. *The Hebraic Period* (2–5).

(1)	Consecration of the Apostles and first disciples by the out-pouring of the Holy Ghost	2:1-13
(2)	The ingathering of the first-fruits on the day of Pentecost	2:14-41
(3)	The inner life and the extension of the infant Church	2:42-47
(4)	The first miracle (of mercy and Restoration). The address of Peter and the conflict with the rulers consequent thereupon	3:1–4:31
(5)	The unity and communion of goods of the early Church	4:32-37
(6)	The sin of Ananias and Sapphira. The second Miracle (of retribution of judgment)	5:1-11
(7)	The miraculous working of the Apostles. Their imprisonment, their appearance before the priests and rulers and their dismissal.	5:12-41
(8)	This period closes with a notice of their energetic and incessant preaching of Jesus as the Christ.	5:42

B. *The Transitional Period* (6–12).

(1)	Appointment of a diaconate (chiefly or wholly Hellenist) to meet complaints of Hellenists as to the distribution of alms.	6:1-7

(2) The labors, apprehension, speech and mar-   6:8–7:60
tyrdom of Stephen

(3) The consequences of martyrdom:

(4) Scattering of the disciples in Judaea and
Samaria;

(5) Antagonism of Saul   8:1-4

(6) Samaria evangelized through Philip, whose   8:5-25
work is confirmed by the Apostles Peter and
John. First conflict with a false form of religion
(outside Judaism) in the person of Simon
Magus

(7) Conversion of the Ethopian eunuch, a pros-   8:26-40
elyte

(8) Conversion of Saul and vision of Ananias. Saul   9:1-30
is healed and disputes with the Hellenists at
Jerusalem.

(9) Peace in the churches 'throughout the whole   9:31
of Judaea and Galilee and Samaria'

(10) Peter's miracles at Lydda (Aeneas) and at   9:32-43
Joppa (Dorcas)

(11) Visions of Cornelius and of Peter. Peter visits,   10:1-48
converts, and baptizes Cornelius and his
companions. Their Baptism is anticipated by
an out-pouring of the Holy Ghost.

(12) Peter reports the case to Church at Jerusalem   11:1-18
and obtains its approval

(13) Disciples scattered at the persecution of   11:19-24
Stephen preach in Phoencia, at Cyprus, and at
Antioch, the Greeks (v.l. Hellenists). Their
action confirmed by the Apostles through
Barnabas.

(14) Saul preaches at Antioch, where the disciples   11:25, 26
are first called Christians.

(15) The Christians of Jerusalem relieved by the   11:27-30,
Gentiles churches.   12:25

(16) Herod's persecution of the Church. Martyrdom of James imprisonment of Peter. Release of Peter who goes *elsewhere,* and punishment of Herod.	12:1-23
At the close is a notice of the triumphant progress of the Word of God.	12:24

C. *The Gentile Period* (13–28).

I. Consecration of Barnabas and Saul to the apostolate	13:1-3

II. First missionary journey of Paul (accompanied by Barnabas)

1)	Preaching in Cyprus and conversion of Sergius Paulus	13:4-12
2)	Journey through Pamphylia (desertion of John Mark)	13:13
3)	Paul in the synagogue at Antioch of Pisidia Rejection by the Jews and acceptance by the Gentiles.	13:14-52
4)	Preaching at Iconium (stoning of Paul)	14:1-7
5)	Healing of the impotent man at Lystra	14:8-18
6)	Subsequent preaching and return to Antioch	14:19-28
7)	Apostolic Council at Jerusalem (liberation of the Gentile Christians from the obligation of the Law)	15:1-35

III. Second missionary journey of Paul (accompanied by Silas)

1)	Separation of Paul and Barnabas	15:36-39
2)	Paul confirms the church already founded on the previous journey, and, after visiting the district of Phrygia and Galatia, is summoned by a vision into Macedonia.	16:1-11
3)	Preaching at Philippi. Imprisonment and release.	16:12-40

3) Subsequent Journey and arrival at   28:11-16
   Rome
4) Conference with the chief Jews ends   28:17-29
   unsatisfactorily and he turns to the
   Gentiles
5) Success of his preaching   28:30, 31

The Book had begun with the discourses of Christ relating to the career of 'the Kingdom of God' (λέγων τὰ περὶ τῆς βασιλείας τοῦ θεοῦ). These discourses elicit the question from the disciples 'Dost thou at this time restore the Kingdom (τὴν βασιλείαν) to Israel?' We are told at the close that the chief Apostle of the Gentiles 'proclaims the Kingdom of God' (κηρύσσων τὴν βασιλείαν τοῦ θεοῦ) in the chief city of the Gentiles. Here is the indirect answer to the Apostles' question, so far as any answer could be given. The subject of the Book then is the history of the Kingdom of God, with more special reference to the relaxation of the terms of admission, the ingathering of the Gentiles, and the transference of the centre of gravity of Christendom from Jerusalem elsewhere.

This history comprises three periods. Of these, the second, the epoch of transition is the most instructive; and indeed the narrative of Acts hinges on it. This period itself may be divided into two parts: *First* (1–7), that which deals with the Hellenists, Samaritans, and proselytes of the gate, persons of mixed nation or religion, neither wholly Hebraic nor wholly Gentile; and *secondly* (8–14), that which treats of the extension of the Church among the Gentile proper at the end of these two divisions, as if he had arrived at a fresh landing-place, the author after his manner inserts an encouraging notice of the progress of the Gospel. Obviously he has paid special attention to the transitional period, gathering together every notice that seemed to illustrate either the principles, the agents, or the recipients, in this gradual enlargement of the bounds of Christendom.

3. *External Testimony.* The external authority in favour of this Book is full and unanimous. Only at a comparatively late date do we find any exception to the testimonies that assign it to St. Luke, and even then its canonical authority is not questioned. If we place ourselves in the later decades of the second century, we are confronted with witnesses from all parts of the

Church, and the evidence leaves nothing to be desired. 1) Irenaeus who represents three Churches—Asia Minor, Rome, and Gaul—quotes or refers to it between fifty and sixty times. The quotations range over nearly the whole Book. He gives St. Peter's speech at Pentecost (Acts 2:22-36), St. Peter's speech at the Beautiful Gate (Acts 3:12-26), St. Paul's speech on the Areopagus (Acts 17:24-31), and the speeches of St. Peter and St. James at the apostolic council together with the apostolic letter (Acts 15:7-11, 13-21, 23-29) in full or nearly so (iii.12.3,9,14). As this third book was published during the Roman episcopate of Eleutherus (A.D. 175–189), we know the latest possible date of the testimony. He several times distinctly ascribes it to St. Luke, and argues from this fact (i.23.1; iii.13.3; iii.14.1sq.; iv.15.1). He attributes scriptural authority to it (e.g. iii.12.5,9). He not only argues from its Lucan authorship himself, but assumes this as common ground with his adversaries. In fact he quotes it just as any strictly orthodox divine would do in the present day. It is difficult therefore to understand the statement that 'it is undeniable that no distinct and unequivocal reference to Acts of the Apostles, and to Luke as their author, occurs in the writings of the Fathers before one by Irenaeus about the end of the second century' (*Supernatural Religion*, iii. p.2).

2) Clement of Alexandria (c. A.D. 190–200) represents more especially the Church whose name he bears; but he mentions obligations to six different teachers—in Greece, in Egypt, in Palestine, Assyria, and the East—who had received the 'tradition handed down direct from father to son from the holy Apostles Peter and James, John and Paul' (*Strom.* i.1, p. 322). He quotes the Acts repeatedly, and in one passage (*Strom.* v.12, p. 696) gives the name of the writer Luke.

3) The *Muratorian Canon* probably represents Rome, and is generally placed about A.D. 170–80 (since the author speaks of the episcopate of Pius, c. A.D. 140–55, as 'nuperrime temporibus nostris'), but may be a few years later. This writer (ed. Tregelles, p. 18), in a passage which is somewhat corrupt, but of which the general tenor seems clear, after the four Gospels mentions 'Acta omnium apostolorum' as written by Luke and addressed to Theophilus, adding that he wrote down the events of which he had personal knowledge ('corprindit quia [l. quae] sub praesentia ejus singular gerebantur'), and that evidently he was not an eye-witness of the martyrdom of Peter and the journey of Paul to Spain.

4) Tertullian is the chief representative of the African Church. His literary activity covers the last years of the second and the early years of the third centuries. He quotes the Acts many times. About 150 references or quotations are given by Ronsch (*Das Neue Testament Tertullians*, p. 291sq.), but a certain percentage of these may be doubtful. He quotes it generally as *Acta* or *Acta Apostolorum* and ascribes it to St. Luke (*de Jejun.* 10). He cites it too as Scripture (see e.g. *Praescr. Haer.* 22), and designates it *Apostolicium Instrumentum* (*Pudic.* 12) or *Scriptura Apostolicorum* (*Marc.* v.2).

5) Polycrates of Ephesus (A.D. 189–198) represents Asia Minor at the close of this century. He lays great stress on the primitive tradition, which he had inherited through several relatives who were Bishops (Eusebius, *H.E.* v. 24). He quotes Acts 5:29 *verbatim*, though not by name, in the words 'They that are greater than I have said, *It is right to serve God rather than men*' (πειθαρχεῖν δεῖ θεῷ μᾶλλον ἢ ἀνθρώποις), a saying ascribed in the Acts to 'Peter and the Apostles.'

We find then that in the last decades of the second century the Book is quoted profusely and without any sign of misgiving as authoritative Scripture and as the work of St. Luke. The testimony comes from all quarters of the Church; and the witnesses are persons who were mixed up in various religious controversies and bad alliances far and wide, striking (in some instances) deep into the past. There can be no doubt therefore about the universal verdict of the Church at this time. Thus at the earliest moment when we have sufficient materials for a judgment, the evidence in favor of the Book is overwhelming. The earliest testimony is of the same kind as for most of those Canonical Books of which the authenticity has never been questioned.

The Apostolic Fathers do not directly quote Romans or 2 Corinthians or Galatians, nor are these Epistles named by any Church writer before Irenaeus. Of Acts 20:35 'To remember (μνημονεύειν) the words of the Lord Jesus, how He said, It is blessed rather to give than to receive' (μᾶλλον διδόναι ἢ λαμβάνειν), we have reminiscences in *Clement of Rome* 13 'especially remembering . . . the words of the Lord Jesus which he spake' (comp. 46) and 2 'more gladly giving than receiving' . . . for in the context of this latter passage the Corinthians are praised for 'giving heed to the words' of Christ. Again in 18, 'What shall we say of David, to whom witness is borne . . . unto whom God said, I have found a man after My heart, David the son of Jesse with oil.' Clement is compounding the original passage in the Psalms 88 (89):20 with the quotation in Acts 13:22, 'To whom also He said, bearing witness . . . I have found David the son of Jesse a man after my heart, who will do,' where the features borrowed from the Acts are: 1) the mention of the 'witness'; 2) the addition of 'a man after My heart' (comp. 1 Sam 13:14); and 3) the further addition of 'the son of Jesse'—none of these being found in the original passage of the Psalms. This threefold coincidence is not easily explained away.

The coincidences in Ignatius are somewhat less close, but not insignificant. *Magn.* 5, 'to go to his own place' recalls Acts 1:25 'to go . . . to his own place.'[2] In *Philad.* 11 we have the phrase 'a man bearing witness' which occurs also in Acts. 6:3 (ἄνδρας ἐξ ὑμῶν μαρτυρουμένους). In *Smyrn.* 3, 'After His Resurrection He ate and drank with them,' there is an allusion to Acts 10:41 συνεφάγομεν καὶ συνεπίομεν αὐτῷ μετὰ τὸ ἀναστῆναι κ.τ.λ.

In Polycarp the coincidences are of the same kind, but stronger. No. 1 'Whom God raised . . . loosing the pangs of Hades' closely follows Acts 2:24 'whom God raised up, having loosed the pangs of death' (ἀνέστησεν λύσας τὰς ὠδῖνας τοῦ θανάτου)[3] where there is a v.l. ᾅδου (Hades) which is shown from the authorities (D, E, Vulg., Memph., Iren.) to have been current at least as early as the 2nd century. Though the individual expressions (e.g 'pangs of Hades') may be found elsewhere, there is nothing approaching to the parallelism throughout the sentence, so that it cannot be regarded as accidental. Again in no. 2 we have an expression 'judge of the quick and the dead' as in Acts 10:42. There are also other coincidences (no. 2 to Acts 20:35, no. 6 to Acts 7:52, no. 12 to Acts 8:21), on which however no stress can be laid.

Of Papias (Eusebius *H.E.* iii.39) we can only say that his anecdotes deal with personages mentioned in Acts—Judas Barsabbas and the daughters of Philip (if he be the same Philip), and that his story of Judas the traitor is used by Apollinaris of Laodicea in the fourth century to reconcile the accounts of his death in St. Matthew and in the Acts, and may have had some such reference as told by himself.

In Hermas who gives not a single quotation from the Old or from the New Testament, we stumble on coincidences with the Acts, which however

---

[2] Using a different verb for *go*.
[3] A different word for *raised* is used by Polycarp.

would have no great value in themselves. Thus Hermas uses the word καρδιογνώστης, 'heart-knower' of God, which occurs twice in the Acts (Acts 1:24; 15:8) but is found nowhere else in the LXX or the New Testament. Again he speaks of being thought 'worthy of bearing the Name' and of 'being healed' or 'saved by the Name' (*Vis.* iv.2, *Sim.* ix.28), expressions which are close parallels to Acts 4:12; 5:41.

In the Apologists there are similar coincidences. Thus in Justin Martyr we have in two passages (*Dial.* 36,76) a reference to prophecy as announcing παθητὸς [ὁ] χριστός, 'the Messiah would be passible,' as in Acts 26:23. Here the coincidence consists not in the idea, but in the manner of expressing it, the word παθητός not occurring elsewhere in the LXX or the New Testament. So again the summary of events after the Crucifixion in *Apol.* i. 50 seems to be taken from Acts 1:8sq. (comp. Acts 2:33), the expression 'to receive power' (λαμβάνειν δύναμιν) being common to both, besides other coincidences. Again, *Dial.* 68 'How saith the Word unto David that God would take a son for Himself from his loins (ἀπο τῆς ὀσφύος αὐτοῦ) and would seat (καθίσει) him on the throne of His glory' is best explained as a reminiscence of Acts 2:30 'God sware unto him by an oath that he would set (καθίσαι) of the fruit of his loins (τῆς ὀσφύος αὐτοῦ) upon his throne'; for in both passages 'loins' (ὀσφύος) is substituted for 'body' (κοιλία) and 'set' (καθίξειν) for 'place' (τίθεσθαι) of the LXX of Psalm 131:11 (132:11), though in neither case does the Hebrew suggest such a substitution. Again in *Dial.* 16 we read 'Ye slew the Just One and before Him the prophets,' which has a close parallel in Acts 7:52 (comp. Is 57:1). Again the connection of 'common or unclean things' with 'refraining to eat' is matched by Acts 10:14, 28; 11:8; and there are other coincidences likewise. It seems difficult with these facts before us, to resist the inference that Justin was acquainted with the Acts.

The coincidences in the other Apologists are much slighter. Thus Tatian (*Orat. Ad Graec.* 6) writes, 'Though you consider us . . . babblers' (σπερμολόγους) the word used of St. Paul by the Athenians in Acts 17:18. In Theophilus again (*ad. Autol.* ii.1) there is the same play on γινώσκειν, ἀναγινώσκειν which appears in Acts 8:30.

Of other writers in the 2nd century Dionysius of Corinth is reported by Eusebius (*H.E.* iv.23) as recording . . . that 'Dionysius the Areopagite, when turned (προτραπείς) to the faith by the Apostle Paul in accordance with the records . . . in the Acts was the first to be entrusted with the bishopric of the diocese . . . of Athens.' From this passage indeed it does not necessarily follow that Dionysius actually mentioned the Acts; but if the language of Eusebius may be interpreted strictly, Dionysius of Corinth must have said that his early namesake was converted by St. Paul (not ὁ προτραπείς but προτραπείς) as therein stated.

In the Epistle of Vienne and Lyons (Eusebius *H.E.* v.1) the last prayer of 'Stephen the perfect martyr' is given from Acts 7:60, just as elsewhere in this same document the language used of Zacharias (the father of the Baptist) is taken from Luke 1:6. These obligations to the two treatises of St. Luke can only be evaded by postulating doubles of both writings (see *Supernatural Religion*, iii. p. 25), but this is an alternative that need not be seriously discussed.

It should be added also that in all the versions of the second century (the Syriac, Latin, and Egyptian), so far as our information goes, this Book formed a part.

Moreover the early Apocryphal Acts and other historical romances show an acquaintance with this work, to which they are frequently indebted for their personal and geographical notices, where they cross the historical path of the canonical Acts. Such are the Acts of Peter and Paul, and those of Paul and Thecla. So too Cornelius (*Hom.* xx.13) and others are mentioned in the Clementine *Homilies*, while Theophilus also appears in the *Recognitions*. The *Homilies* moreover contain several expressions found in the Acts such as 'heart-knower,' *Hom.* x.13 πρὸς καρδιογνώστην θεόν (comp. Acts 1:24; 15:8); 'What purporteth this to be?' *Hom.* xiii.6, xiv.9 τί θέλει τοῦτο εἶναι (comp. Acts 2:12; 17:20); 'What hindereth me to be baptized?' *Hom. xiii.* 5 (see also xiii.11; comp. Acts 8:36). Similar resemblances also appear in the *Recognitions*.

It was indeed rejected by several heretics of the second century, not however in a single instance (so far as we can discover) because they questioned its authorship, but in many cases obviously on this very account. Those who, like the Ebionites, denied the apostleship of St. Paul, were forced to repudiate the authority of his disciple. Those on the other hand who, like the Marcionites, maintained a direct antagonism between St. Paul and the Apostles of the circumcision, could not do otherwise than reject a work which represented them as meeting each other on friendly terms. For the Ebionites see Irenaeus iii.15.1. Again as regards the Marcionites, Irenaeus argued with them throughout on the hypothesis of its Lucan authorship, as if this were common ground (iii.12.12, iii.14.1sq.). When dealing with the Valentinians and other Gnostics, he distinctly states that they accept the Book as authoritative, but try to get round it by false interpretations, or by a distinction between an esoteric and exoteric doctrine (iii.12.12, iii.14.4, iii.15.1,2). Thus these Valentinians are valuable witnesses—all the more valuable because the acceptance of the Book that involved them in great difficulty.

It should be added also that, as the Third Gospel and Acts were evidently the work of one man—and the admission of this fact may now be regarded as practically universal—all the evidence which testifies to the authorship of the former is available also for the latter, and conversely. But the testimony in favor of St. Luke as the author of the Third Gospel is absolutely unbroken, and no shadow of suspicion overclouds it for nearly eighteen centuries.

The unanimity and directness of testimony which we have observed at the close of the second century continue in the succeeding ages. At the close of the fourth century however, we find Chrysostom saying that he is induced to explain the Book because many are ignorant of its existence and its authorship (*Comm. in Acts. Apostl* i.1; *Op.* ix. p. 1). As it is freely quoted without any suspicion cast on its authorship by all the great fathers of his own generation, as well as before and after this can only mean that it was more or less neglected by the general reader. This neglect may be accounted for by the fact that it would not be read regularly in churches like the Gospels or the Apostolic Epistles, and copies would not be multiplied to the same extent as in the case of these other Scriptures. As it did not bear its author's name in the title (in this respect differing from the other Books of the New Testament), ignorance on this point becomes more inexplicable.

Still more perplexing, and still less reconcilable with the facts, is a notice in Photius (*Amph. Qu.* 123) at the close of the ninth century: 'Some say that the author of Acts was Clement of Rome, others Barnabas, and others again Luke the Evangelist; but Luke himself settles the question (ἐπικρίνει).' As there is not the faintest trace of any difference of opinion in all the preceding eight centuries, I am disposed to think that Photius is here guilty of a con-

fusion with the Epistle to the Hebrews, these three persons being named by
ancient Fathers as claimants for the authorship of this letter (Origen, in
Eusebius *H.E.* vi.25; Tetullian *de Pudic.* 20; Eusebius *H.E.* iii.38; Hieronymus
Vir. Ill. 5).

4. *The Authorship.* We have seen that the universal tradition of the first
eight centuries ascribes the Book with no faltering voice to St. Luke; and that
this evidence is further fortified by a still greater mass of testimony—equally
unanimous—which independently ascribes the Third Gospel to this same
person. How far is this assumption supported by internal evidence?

The first person plural 'we' is used in certain parts of the narrative,
where the writer is describing the journeys of St. Paul. He therefore professes to be a companion of St. Paul. This first person appears in the ordinary text for the first time at Troas (Acts 16:10), during the second missionary journey (c. A.D. 51 or 52), and continues to Philippi, where it is
dropped (Acts 16:17) as suddenly as it had appeared. It is taken up again
after several years (A.D. 58) during the third missionary journey at this
same place Philippi (Acts 20:5), and continues till St. Paul arrives at Jerusalem and confers with James and the elders (Acts 20:18). When again he
set sail for Italy (Acts 27:1) it accompanies him and remains in his company
during the voyage and shipwreck and until his arrival in Rome (Acts
28:15-16, for in ver. 16 the best supported reading is εἰσήλθαμεν). But besides these occurrences in the ordinary text, it is found likewise in D at a
much earlier point (Acts 11:28), where the prophecy of Agabus is mentioned at Antioch. Though the variations in D seem in many passages to
give contemporary traditions, yet the capriciousness of this MS. elsewhere
forbids us to regard this as the original reading.

Who then is this writer who uses the first person? The obvious answer is
that which identifies him with the traditional author of the work, St. Luke.
This person was certainly a trusty companion of the Apostle (Col 4:14;
Philem 24; 2 Tim 4:11); and though the notices in St. Paul's Epistles refer to
a somewhat later date, he might very well have been with the Apostle at this
time. Not a single Epistle of St. Paul was written during the precise periods
covered by 'we' in the Acts, and therefore the absence of Luke's name in the
Epistles prior to the Roman captivity is not even a *prima facie* objection.
Moreover, Luke is described as 'the beloved physician' (Col 4:14), and a ten-

dency to the use of medical terms has been observed both in the Third Gospel and the Acts. If many of the examples adduced must be set aside as proving nothing, the residuum is quite sufficient to establish the main point (see esp. Hobart's *Medical Language of St. Luke,* Dublin, 1882).

But though the natural inference from the use of the first person plural seems plain enough, it has given rise to various opinions. These may be divided into four classes: 1) That which regards it as a mere literary fiction to give an air of credibility to the narrative. This view has been held by two or three critics, of whom Schrader (*Der Apostel Paulus,* 1836) may be taken as the type. As no one now upholds this view, I need not take the trouble to refute it; 2) That which identifies it with St. Luke, who is regarded as also the ultimate author of the work. This is the vastly preponderating opinion even in the present day, and until quite recent times it was the sole possessor of the field. Its consistency and verisimilitude have been already shown; 3) That which identifies it with St. Luke as the original authority for this portion of the narrative, but maintains that the Book, as a whole, was compiled by some later person. This is the view of Baur and Zeller, with several subsequent critics, of whom the latest is Holtzmann (*Zeitsch. F. Wiss. Theol.* 1881, p. 408sq.; *Einl.* p. 385, 1885);[4] 4) That which identifies it with some one else besides St. Luke. The persons selected for this distinction are: a) Timothy. This is the view of Schleiermacher, De Wette, and others, notably Bleek (see esp. *Introd. To New Test,* i. p. 355sq. Engl. Transl.). It appears to have been first suggested by Konigssmann, *De Fontibus Comm. Sacr. Qui Lucae nomen praefereunt,* &c., 1798; b) Silas. This hypothesis is vigorously maintained by Schwanbeck (*Ueber die Quellen der Schriften des Lukas,* i. p. 168 sq. 265 sq.), though he was not the first to suggest it. It is sometimes connected with the identification of Silvanus (Silas) with Lucanus (Lucas), as e.g by Hennell (*Untersuchung uber den Urspring des Christenthum,* 1840). This identification is put forward by Van Vloten (*Zeitschr. F. Wiss. Theil.* 1867, p. 223 sq.; comp. ibid., 1871, p. 431 sq.) as if he were the originator of the theory. He is answered by Cropp (ibid., 1868, p. 353 sq.). c) Titus. This view seems to have been suggested first by Horst (*Sur les Sources de la deuxieme partie des Actes,* &c., 1849; see Holtzmann, *Einl.* p. 385), and has been adopted by Krenkel,

---

[4]Noting the date of this article is a further clue of when this Lightfoot article was written. (BW3)

Jacobsen, and others, notably by Hooykaas (*Bible for Young People*, v. 33; see Salmon, *Introd.* p. 312 sq.). In connection with this theory should be mentioned the identification of Titus with Silvanus (or Silas) maintained by Zimmer (*Zeitschr. F. kirchl. Wiss. U. kirchl. Leben*, 1881, 4 p. 169 sq.; *Jahrb. F. Protest. Theol.* 1881, p. 721 sq.), who supposes Silas the prophet of Antioch to be a different person from the Titus Silas the companion of St. Paul. His theory is discussed by Jülicher (*Jahrb. F. Protest. Theol.* 1882, p. 538 sq.).

The two solutions b) and c) may be quickly dismissed. The identification of Silvanus with Lucanus on the ground that *silva* and *lucus* are synonyms is about as reasonable as would be the identification of persons bearing the names Wood and Forest and Grove, or Lea and Field and Meadows, or Mountain and Hill, or Rock and Cliff and Stone. The objection to the other identification is of a different kind. Everything points to the separation of Titus and Silvanus. Thus the two are mentioned by their respective names in one and the same Epistle by St. Paul (2 Cor 1:19; 2:13; 7:6 &c.). Moreover, Titus was a Gentile (Gal 2:3), while Silas (Silvanus) was plainly a Jew (Acts 15:22); for it is altogether arbitrary to distinguish the Silas of Acts 15:22, 27, 32, [34], from the Silas of Acts 15:40, &c. Having thus cleared the way, we may deal generally with the hypotheses which belong to the third and fourth classes.

Of the third we may remark: 1) that the 'we' sections are absolutely identical in style with the rest of the Acts, and indeed with the Third Gospel also, so that they can only have been written by the ultimate compiler of both narratives; 2) that accordingly these 'we' sections contain numerous cross references to other parts of the narrative; 3) that the ultimate compiler (whoever he was) shows not only literary ability, but literary care. This point is strongly insisted upon (among others) by Renan, who speaks of the Third Gospel and Acts as forming one work excellently put together (*tres bien redige*) composed with reflection and even with art &c. (*Les Apotres*, p. xi.). But it is incredible that an author evincing this literary capacity and aim should commit the school-boy blunder of inserting paragraphs written by another without even taking the trouble to alter the personal pronouns. It is not sufficient to point to such carelessness in medieval chroniclers as Schwanbeck does. The examples are not parallel. We have in the Acts 'not one of those low organizations which do not resent being pulled asunder' but 'a highly organized structure, showing evident marks that the whole proceeds from a single author' (Salmon, *Introd.* p. 316); 4) Lastly, the hypotheses belonging to this class have not a shadow of evidence in their favor. On what grounds then should they claim to displace the traditional view? Is the strongest historical attestation to count for nothing?

It will be seen at once that some of these objections apply equally to the fourth class. But the individual hypotheses again, which belong to this class, present additional difficulties of their own—a) The assignment to Timothy is irreconcilable with Acts 20:5-6 where the writer, having mentioned him among the others who accompanied St. Paul, adds, 'But these (οὗτοι δὲ) had gone before and were waiting for us (προσελθόντες ἔμενον ἡμᾶς) in Troas'; where οὗτοι naturally refers to all those previously mentioned, and the restriction to the last two, Tychicus and Trophimus, is not justified by the form of the sentence; b) The attribution to Silas has nothing to recommend it. Silas or Silvanus is a prominent figure during the Apostle's second missionary journey in the Acts; and this prominence is borne out by the notices in St. Paul's Epistles relating to this period (1 Thess 1:1; 2 Thess 1:1; 2 Cor 1:19). On the contrary, he nowhere appears during the third missionary journey either in the history or in the letters, whereas the 'we' occurs frequently during this period; c) The only ground for suggesting Titus is the negative fact that he is not mentioned by name in the narrative,[5] though he is known to have been with St. Paul during part of this period, (2 Cor 2:13; 7:6sq.; 12:18), and is a prominent person among the Apostle's companions. But what is the value of this negative fact? What advantage has the Titus guess over the Luke tradition? Unless indeed it be 'thought a disadvantage to an hypothesis that it should have some amount of historical testimony' (Salmon, p. 313). Moreover, of these attributions generally we may remark that the propriety

---

[5]In Acts 18:7 the reading is most probably Τιτίου Ἰούστου, though some read Τίτου Ἰούστου, some Τίτου simply, and some Ἰούστου simply (the received reading). At all events the alternative lies between the first and the last, as the variation must have arisen from the addition or omission of the same recurring letters (ΟΝΟΜΑΤΙΤΙΤΙΟΥΙΟΥΣΤΟΥ). But even if 'Titus' were read here, he could hardly be the same person; for he is mentioned here as a Jewish proselyte, and his surname Justus implies that he was an observer of the Mosaic law; whereas the Apostle's companion Titus had been converted to Christianity before this (Gal 2:1) and is called a 'Gentile' without any qualification. Moreover this Justus was a resident of Corinth, whereas St. Paul writing to the Corinthians (2 Cor. *l.c.*), mentions Titus in such a way as to preclude the supposition that he was one of themselves.

in the change from the first to the third person, and conversely, as pointed out previously, ceases, and the use of the pronouns from being orderly and consistent, becomes a chaos.

Nor is it easy to understand how St. Luke's name should have thus been persistently assigned to the work, if had had nothing to do with it. As Salmon has pointed out (p. 372), it is not attached to this second treatise in any uncial MS. But the Third Gospel had the name of St. Luke prefixed, and the Acts bore evidence on the face of it that it was written by the same author. Hence the attribution. Indeed the sequence of facts is a most powerful argument in favor of the genuineness of the work. These are as follows: 1) The Gospel bears the name of Luke; but Luke was a companion of St. Paul; 2) When we examine the Gospel, we find not only that it brings into special prominence certain points in Christ's teaching which illustrate the cardinal doctrines of St. Paul, the universality and the freedom of the Gospel, justification not by works of law but by faith, and the like; but also that, where St. Paul refers to incidents in our Lord's life, as for instance to the Last Supper (1 Cor 11:23sq.; comp. Luke 22:19sq.) or to the appearances after the Resurrection (e.g. 1 Cor 15:5, ὤφθη Κηφᾷ: comp. Luke 24:34, ὤφθη Σίμωνι), his references present striking resemblances to this Gospel rather than to the others. Yet there is not a word nor a hint of any connection with any knowledge of the Apostle; 3) The Acts professes to be written by the same person as the Third Gospel, of which it is a later continuation; and this profession is fully borne out by its style and character; 4) We read over more than half this second treatise without any indication that the writer was a companion of St. Paul; 5) Then at length the token of companionship occurs. Yet even now it is not distinctly stated, but the fact is inferred from the incidental occurrence of the first person plural, which makes its first appearance quite unsuspiciously. And not only so, but in its subsequent disappearance and re-appearance it shows a congruity that cannot fail to strike the mind. Who will be bold enough to explain these harmonies as a fortuitous concourse of pseudo-historical atoms? Yet it would require greater hardihood still to ascribe them to a sustained and elaborate artifice.

Apart from the hypotheses that we have hitherto considered, stands the view propounded in H. H. Evans, *St. Paul the Author of the Acts of the Apostles and of the Third Gospel* (London, 1884). The Pauline authorship is maintained by this writer on the ground of certain resemblances of diction. He does not attempt to deal with the first person plural or to grapple with the difficulties that beset his theory on all sides.

5. *Authenticity and Genuineness.* In discussing the authenticity of any work, two main divisions of the subject present themselves: 1) The internal characteristics, as indication of verisimilitude or the contrary; 2) The external tests as evidences of veracity or the contrary.

1) In treating of the internal characteristics, I must satisfy myself with pointing out a few heads, giving here and there an example, but without any attempt to do more than indicate the lines of investigation which the reader may carry out for himself.

(i.) There is first of all *the change of moral and spiritual atmosphere.* As we pass from the beginning to the end of the Book, we find that the religious climate, so to speak, is quite changed, and we are breathing a different air. In short we have passed from the Hebraic to the Hellenic. This change manifests itself throughout, in the speeches, in the actions, in the modes of feeling and in the local customs and institutions. Yet the transition is not sudden. It is a gradual growth, as the Church emancipates itself, both locally and morally, from the tutelage of its Hebrew infancy. Between the two extremes the intermediate Hellenistic territory is duly traversed. In short, the work, regarded from this point of view, betokens a writer who either had witnessed the progressive career himself, or made use of successive contemporary documents; but such a narrative would be quite impossible from one who some generations later attempted to furnish a story of the apostolic doings, trusting mainly or solely to his own faculty of invention.

(ii.) Not unconnected with this feature is the *sequence and connection of events.* We may take as an example the incidents that prepared the way for the extension of the Church to the Gentiles. What could be more natural, and yet what more unlike the work of a forger than these fragmented disconnected notices, that, as we see after the fact, must inevitably have led to the result, but which no one could have foreseen or devised, and which required careful piecing together before we can trace their bearing and direction. These are: 1) The murmuring of the Hellenistic widows, Acts 6:1; 2) the creation of the diaconate, Acts 6:2sq.; 3) the composition of this diaconate, comprising especially Stephen and Philip, Acts 6:5sq.; 4) Stephen's

disputations, speech, and martyrdom, Acts 6:8–7:60; 5) Saul's appearance
on the scene, Acts 7:58; 8:1, 6) the scattering abroad of the disciples and the
consequence of this persecution, Acts 8:1, 7) the preaching of Philip in Samaria and elsewhere, as the result of this scattering, Acts 8:5-40; 8) the wider
dissemination of the word and the first preaching to the Gentiles through
the outlying members of this scattered band, Acts 11:19-20. A little reflection
will show that all this is inconceivable, except as an account of facts that
actually occurred.

(iii.) Another point is the *disproportion and inequality* of the narrative.
This argument is strongly insisted upon by Renan (p. xv.) among others: 'Ce
qui distingue l'histoire composee d'apres des documents de l'histoire ecrite
en tour ou en partie d'original, *c'est justement la disproportion.*' A narrator
who allows himself *carte blanche* to invent will take care that the different
parts of his narrative bear some proportion to each other. On the other hand,
a recorder of facts is limited by the historical knowledge at his disposal. At
some points he has very ample information; at others it entirely fails him.
Now nothing is more striking than the want of proportion in the Acts. In
some parts the history of a few months occupies several chapters; in others
the history of many years is disposed of in two or three verses. Sometimes
we have a diary of a journey or voyage; elsewhere a bald statement of the
main fact is given. But nowhere is this disproportion more striking than in
some of the speeches, notably in that of Stephen. This is by far the longest
record of a speech in the Book, extending over 52 verses. Having all this
space at his disposal, a forger would have made it both pertinent and complete. He would have provided a well-reasoned defense against the twofold
crime with which Stephen is charged. But here we have nothing of the kind.
There is a long and at first sight irrelevant account of the early history of the
Jewish people, which occupies 49 verses, and the last three are taken up in
a denunciation of his accusers. Direct answer to the charges there is none.
Only when we examine it more carefully, we discover two things: first that
the incidents in the long historical narrative illustrate the transitory character of the present dispensation and of the local sanctuary; and secondly
that the latter part of the speech (Acts 7:48-53) is interrupted and hurried.
Thus the whole speech, as we have it, is a preamble, and the argumentative
application which should have formed the main part of his defense does not

appear at all, or at least is confined to two or three short sentences, doubtless because the clamors of the bystanders bring the speaker prematurely to a close. But until we discover the key to its meaning, this rambling discourse is quite unintelligible under the circumstances, and such as no forger would or could have invented. It is only conceivable as the substantially true record of what was actually said. Another instance of similar disproportion is the speech on the Areopagus (Acts 17:22-31), where there is no distinctive Christian teaching till the last verse, and here only one point is touched upon. In this case however the probable explanation is that it was not so much the speech itself, as the report of the speech accessible to the historian, which was fuller at the commencement and hurried at the end. But the bearing on the point at issue—the truthfulness of the narrator—is the same.

(iv.) We have also another indication of genuineness in the *minor discrepancies and errors*, or what appear to be such in the account. Thus we have three separate accounts of St. Paul's conversion (Acts 9:3sq.; 22:6sq.; 26:12sq.). The divergences may not be irreconcilable, but they do not reconcile themselves. The reasonable explanation is not that the writer himself invented the three accounts, but that he obtained them as he found them. Again the inaccuracies in the reference to the Old Testament history in St. Stephen's speech are probably due to the strict reproduction of a report taken under necessarily unfavorable circumstances. In some cases at all events (e.g. Acts 7:43, the substitution of 'Babylon' for 'Damascus') we seem to see that they are due to hurried condensation.

(v.) The *naturalness* of the language, as indicating direct knowledge of facts, should also be noticed. The incidental appearance and disappearance of the 'we,' to which attention has been directed already, is a good illustration. Another example appears in the order of the names Barnabas and Paul (or Saul). Barnabas is the earlier disciple (Acts 4:36), and the mediator between Saul and the elder Apostles (Acts 9:27; 11:22-26). Accordingly, in the earlier part of the history the order is always 'Barnabas and Saul' (Acts 11:30; 13:2). But when their missionary journeys commence, and they stand on Gentile ground, St. Paul's supremacy of character asserts itself, and the order is tacitly changed to 'Paul and Barnabas' (Acts 13:43, 46, 50; 15:2, 22, 35). There are indeed exceptions in this latter part, but they only 'prove the rule.' At the apostolic council and in the apostolic letter the old sequence 'Barnabas and Paul' is again resumed (Acts 15:12, 25); and so too at Lystra, where Barnabas is identified with Zeus and Paul with Hermes, the former naturally takes the precedence for the moment (Acts 14:14). As instances of naturalness in the language represented to have been used by the speakers, we may allege the distortions of facts by Claudius Lysias (Acts 23:27) to save his own credit, or the exaggerated compliments paid to Felix by Tertullus (Acts 24:2sq.), which are explained but not justified by his career as governor.

Altogether, it may be affirmed that if there had been no miraculous element in the narrative, and if it had had no bearing on religious controversy, the form and contents of this work would have placed it beyond all suspicion, as regards genuineness and authenticity.

2) From the consideration of the internal characteristics we turn to the external tests, as evidence of truthfulness.

(i.) In the earlier part of the narrative we have rarely an opportunity of testing the incidents by reference to other Christian documents; but in the latter portion, giving the history of St. Paul, may be compared with and checked by the Apostle's own letters. This work has been done admirably by Paley in his *Horae Paulinae*; and the main result is conclusive. He has elicited a mass of 'undesigned coincidences' that renders the hypothesis of a fictitious history impossible. The comparison of the four greater Epistles, more especially (Romans, 1 Corinthians, 2 Corinthians, Galatians), belonging to the years 57–58 elicits striking examples. Any reader, for instance, who will take the pains to go carefully over Paley's discussion of the passages relating to the contributions for the Christian poor at Jerusalem, observing how they dovetail into one another, may satisfy himself of the validity of the argument. Yet it is plain that the writer of the Acts was unacquainted with these Epistles, or at all events that, if he had ever seen them, he made no use of them in compiling his history. Otherwise, we are wholly unable to explain the omission of any reference to the incidents and persons mentioned: for example, in Rom 15:19, 28; 16:1sq., 23; 1 Cor 1:11sq.; 16:15sq.; 2 Cor 2:12; 7:5; 11:24; 12:3sq.; Gal 1:17; 2:11sq.; to say nothing of the absence of any allusion to Titus in connection with Corinth or of the different aspects which the third visit to Jerusalem bears in the Acts (Acts 15:1sq.) and in St. Paul's Epistle (Gal 2:1sq.).

(ii) Another point of comparison with external documents related to the language ascribed to the different Apostles in the Acts. St. James, St. Peter, and St. Paul, all have speeches assigned to them. Is their language such as might be expected from the writers of the Epistles bearing their several names? The very few sentences ascribed to James do not afford much scope for comparison. Yet the sentiments attributed to him are what might have been expected from one who was the recognized head of the Church of Jerusalem as well as from the writer of the Epistle that bears his name. It has been observed also that of the canonical writers James alone uses the common formula χαίρειν as the heading of his Epistle (James 1:1), which appears likewise at the beginning of the apostolic letter, evidently represented in the Acts as dictated by him.

The speeches and sayings of St. Peter afford considerably more material for comparison. In the diction and still more in the ideas, they exhibit such parallels with the Epistles bearing the name of this Apostle as to suggest identity of authorship, notwithstanding the alterations in form that they have necessarily undergone by transmission. On this subject see Weiss, *Der Petrinische Lehrbegriff*, p. 6sq. and *passim*; Kahler, *Der Reden des Petrus in der Apostelgeschichte, Stud. U. Krit.*, 1873, p. 492sq.; Salmon, *Introd.* p. 335sq. ed. 2, as well as the commentaries on this Book, especially Nosgren, p. 47sq.

For St. Paul the material is much more ample, and the resulting correspondingly more conclusive. The speech at Miletus (Acts 20:18, sq.) more especially has been carefully analyzed, and exhibits throughout both Pauline matter and Pauline diction. Moreover, it is not fanciful to trace more special correspondences with the letters belonging to the several periods at which the speeches are represented as being delivered. Thus the one Christian doctrine which is mentioned in the speech on the Areopagus (17:31)—the Second Advent and the Judgment—is the one prominent topic of the Epistles to the Thessalonians, written at this time. Again, the speech at Miletus, already mentioned, exhibits resemblances to the Epistles of the third missionary journey which preceded this epoch, and with the Epistles to the Philippians and Ephesians which succeeded it.

(iii) The geographical and historical tests which the subject-matter of the Acts invites us to apply, are exceptionally wide and various. If, for instance, we confine ourselves to geography, we accompany the Apostle by land and sea; we follow him about in Jerusalem, in Palestine and Syria, in Asia Minor, in Greece, in Italy. The topographical details are scattered over this wide expanse of continent, island, and ocean; and they are both minute and incidental. Yet the writer is never betrayed into an error. The account of the Apostle's journey to Rome (for example) is so accurate and consistent, that a modern writer has been enabled almost to reproduce a log-book of the voyage (James Smith's *Voyage and Shipwreck of St. Paul*). The amount of geographical and topographical illustrations which the narrative of the Acts admits may be seen from such books as Conybeare and Howson's *Life and Epistles of St. Paul* and Lewin's *Life and Epistles of St. Paul*; and these works will afford a measure of strength to the argument to be derived from such considerations.

When we turn from geography to history, the tests are still more numerous, and lead to still more decisive results. The laws, institutions, the manners, the religious rites, the magisterial records of Syria and Palestine, of Asia Minor, of Macedonia and Greece, all live in the pages of this narrative. It will suffice to mention one or two of the more striking facts. When St. Paul first visits Europe, he sojourns at two important Macedonian cities in succession, Philippi and Thessalonike. In neither case does the political constitution follow the normal type of a Greek city; yet in both the local government is correctly and significantly indicated. Philippi was a Roman colony (Acts 16:12). Accordingly, here we find all the apparatus and coloring of a colony, which was a miniature reproduction of Rome herself (see Lightfoot, *Philippians* p. 51sq.). There are the local magistrates, the duumvirs, who, after the way of such colonial magnates, arrogate to themselves the title of praetors (στρατηγοί, Acts 16:20, 22, 35-36). There are the attendant lictors (ῥαβδοῦχοι, Acts 16:35). The majesty of Rome is appealed to again and again (Acts 16:21, 37-38). But when we turn from Philippi to Thessalonike, all is changed. Thessalonike was a free city, with a magistracy of its own. A collision occurs here, as at Philippi, and the alleged offenders are again brought before the magistrates. These magistrates mentioned, though quite incidentally as politarchs (πολιτάρχας, Acts 17:6, 8). It so happens that this word (πολιτάρχης) has not hitherto been found anywhere in Greek literature, though πολιτάρχος appears in a general sense, in an obscure passage of Aeneas Tacitus, c. 26 (p. 81, Schweigh). From inscriptions however, found at Thessalonike itself (Boeckh, *C.I.G.* no. 1967; see *Greek Inscriptions in the*

British Museum, II clxxi. p. 32, with the notes) we learn that this was the local name of the chief magistrates of Thessalonike, who were seven in number. It should be added also that at Thessalonike mention is made (Acts 17:5) of a popular assembly (δῆμος) which is likewise in keeping. Again, at Corinth, the notice of the chief magistrate is in strict accordance with history though the chances of error were very great. The province of Achaia at this epoch was bandied about between the senate and the emperor, being transferred and retransferred from one to the other, and was governed by a proconsul (ἀνθύπατος) or proprietor (ἀντιστρατηγός) accordingly. At this moment (A.D. 52 or 53) it was in the hands of the senate, and the designation of the chief magistrate as ἀνθυπατεύων in the Acts (Acts 18:12) is therefore correct. But it had only been retransferred to the senate a few years earlier (A.D. 44) by Claudius (Suetonius *Claud.* 25; Dion Cassius lx.24), after being in the emperor's hands for some thirty years (since A.D. 15); and somewhat later under Nero (A.D. 67) it ceased to be a Roman province (Pliny *N.H.* iv. 6; Suetonius *Nero*, 24, &c.: see Clinton, *Fast. Rom.* i. p. 50), and remained autonomous till Vespasian again restored the provincial government. Moreover, the person represented as holding the proconsulate at this, Gallio, is mentioned by his brother Seneca (*Epist.* 104.1) as residing in Achaia, though his office is not named. In this passage however Seneca mentions an illness and consequent sea-voyage of Gallio during his residence in Achaia, and Pliny (*N.H.* xxxi.33) refers to this same incident in Gallio's life as taking place *post consulatum*, but without any mention of Achaia. Thus the notice in the Acts links together the statements of the two profane writers, for the proconsulship of Achaia would be a natural sequel to the consulship. Moreover, the time harmonizes; for as Seneca was not restored to favor till A.D. 49, after eight years' banishment, his brother's promotion to office would naturally take place after that year, and probably not long after. Gallio's character also, as here given, accords with the description of him by his brother Seneca (*Quaest. Nat. iv. Praef.*), and his friend Statius (*Silv.* ii.7.30sq.), who both use the same epithet 'dulcis.' The easy-going magistrate was the amiable sweet-tempered companion. Similarly, the description of Sergius Paulus as *proconsul* of Crete, is confirmed by notices and inscriptions, though here again any one but a contemporary would be very liable to error, owing to the transference and retransference of the province (see *Contemporary Review*,

May 1878, p. 290). Not only do the inscriptions show that at this time it was governed by proconsuls, but one discovered a few years ago by Cesnola (*Cyprus,* p. 425) mentions 'the proconsulship of Paulus' (ΕΠΙ ΠΑΥΛΟΥ [ΑΝΘ]ΠΑΤΟΥ). On the probability that this is Sergius Paulus mentioned by Pliny, see *Contemp. Rev.* l.c.

Among other Greek cities which St. Paul is represented as visiting, comparatively full accounts are given of his sojourns at two especially, Athens and Ephesus. It is instructive to study the narratives of his residence at these two places, in themselves and in comparison one with another. Athens is the most Hellenic of all cities, the heart and citadel of Greece; whereas at Ephesus there is a very strong intermingling of the Oriental spirit and institutions with the main stream of Hellenism. The diverse tone of these two typical cities of heathendom comes to life in the Apostle's conflicts with his audiences on either occasion. The one is inquisitive, philosophical, courteous, and refined; the other fanatical, superstitious, and impulsive. Nor does the truthfulness of the narrative manifest itself only in the moral and religious atmosphere of the two places. It descends even to the details. At Athens (Acts 17:16sq.) we are confronted with some of the main topographical features of the city—the Areopagus and the agora. There are the representatives of the two dominant philosophical schools, the Stoics and the Epicureans. There is the predominant attitude of inquiry in this metropolis of newsmongers and here even the characteristic Athenian term of abuse (σπερμολόγος) finds its proper place. There is the large number of foreign residents, which was always a distinguishing feature of Athens. There is the reference to the numerous images and temples which 'thronged the city' to the boastful pride of the citizens in their religious devotion to the gods consistent as it was with no small amount of theological skepticism; to their jealousy of the introduction of strange deities, as manifested in the case of Socrates and at various points in their history; to their practice of propitiating the offended powers after any plague or other infection, by erecting an altar to 'an unknown god' or 'unknown gods'; to their custom of deifying attributes of character, frames of mind, and conditions of body, so that 'Resurrection' (Anastasis) would seem to them to be only another addition to their pantheon, which already included 'Pity,' 'Modesty,' 'Rumor,' 'Persuasion,' 'Impulse,' &c. (Pausanias i.17). Lastly, there is an appropriate allusion to τὸν θεόν, an expression which would commend itself to his philosophical audience, but which occurs nowhere else in the New Testament; and an equally appropriate appeal to the sentiments of the Stoic poets Aratus and Cleanthes (τῶν καθ᾽ ὑμᾶς ποιητῶν), who had proclaimed the universal fatherhood of Zeus. The amount of illustration which has been gathered together from classical sources by such writers as Wettstein, Conybeare and Howson, and Renan (not to mention the numerous commentators on the Acts), is sufficient evidence how true to the local coloring is this description of St. Paul's visit to Athens, even in the finest touches. When we turn from Athens to Ephesus (Acts 19:1 sq.), the indication of the truthfulness of the narrative is equally complete. Here however the verification is found more in ancient inscriptions than in extant literature. The recent excavations at Ephesus more especially have added largely to our stores of illustrations. On this subject see a paper by the writer of this article in the *Contemporary Review* May 1878, p. 292 sq. We have mentioned, in St. Luke's account of the magical books, of which we read elsewhere under the name Ἐφέσια γράμματα, of the chief buildings of the city, not only the Temple of Artemis but the Greek Theatre, with which the recent excavations have made us familiar; of the great officials of the city and province—the proconsul as the chief imperial magistrate, the town-clerk as the chief municipal authority, and the Asiarchs as the principal religious functionaries; of the court days, by implication divided into two, the regular and the special, as we know to have been the case; above all, of the prevailing cultus of the place 'Artemis of the Ephesians' dominates everywhere. The characteristic religious phraseology of her worshippers is reproduced—the city is the 'temple-sweeper', the 'verger', of the 'great goddess'; the silver models of her shrine which were carried away as keepsakes by pilgrims to Ephesus appear in the narrative; the image which 'fell down from Zeus' has its place there; everything is strictly in keeping.

These instances of geographical and historical propriety are taken from Greece and Asia Minor, and the illustrations are drawn from the classical writers and inscriptions. But the pictures relating to Jerusalem and Palestine are found to be drawn with equal fidelity, where we can test them. Of topographical accuracy an example will be given presently in the vivid description of a scene that takes place in the Temple area. The historical fidelity

of the narrative may be illustrated by the part assigned to the Sadducees. It
is not among the high-priests and leaders of the hierarchy that we should
have expected to find a Sadducean predominance. Yet the author of the Acts
boldly represents the high-priestly circle as members of this sect (Acts 4:1;
5:17), and this representation is confirmed by the direct testimony of Josephus (*Ant.* xx.9.1). Moreover it has been more than once observed that,
whereas the Pharisees are the chief opponents of Christ and His disciples in
the Gospels, the Sadducees take the lead in Acts, and that this change is
explained from the fact of the Apostles making the Resurrection the foundation of their preaching, and thus striking at the root of Sadducean doctrine. From this point of view, it is noticeable that in the Fourth Gospel,
though the sect of the Sadducees is not mentioned by name by St. John, the
most virulent opposition of the high-priestly party led by Caiaphas begins
first at the point where we should expect it to begin, after the miracle of the
raising of Lazarus (John 11:47sq.), and that it was a main object with them
to put Lazarus to death (John 12:9-11) and thus get rid of the evidence for a
resurrection. Accordingly, the course of events as related on a subsequent
occasion, when St. Paul pleads before the Sanhedrin at Jerusalem (Acts
23:1sq.), is perfectly consistent and evidently historical. The Apostle had offended the Sadducean high-priest Ananias, who presided; and he recovered
his position with his audience by declaring that he and his forefathers were
Pharisees, and that the main subject of his contention was the doctrine of
the Resurrection, which the Pharisees held in common with him, thus di-
viding the assembly and securing (as it would appear) the support of the
majority. Whether this declaration was strictly defensible (as it was certainly
true), I need not stop to inquire; but it is what a sagacious man would naturally do under the circumstances, and the fact that it is frankly recorded is
a token of the narrator's veracity.

The evidence then in favor of the authenticity of the narrative is far fuller
and more varied than we had any right to expect. But certain *objections* have
been taken, which it is necessary to remove.

(i) Thus it is asserted that the *diction* is the same throughout, and therefore
the speeches ascribed to the principal characters are unhistorical. It is not
Stephen or Peter or Paul who speaks, but Luke or pseudo-Luke himself.
Long lists of words and modes of expression have been drawn up, which

regarded as characteristic of the writer's style. These extend over the whole of the Gospel as well as Acts. There is frequently very great exaggeration in these lists (e.g. *Supernatural Religion*, iii. pp. 72 sq.; 146sq. &c.). Irrelevant expressions are included; Septuagint quotations are treated as if they were the narrator's own language; words used in wholly different senses (e.g. βῆμα, 'footstep' and βῆμα, 'tribunal') are treated as parallels; terms which are necessitated by the subject-matter are regarded as characteristic of the author; the commonest words in the language are invested with a special value. Thus an entirely false impression is conveyed. But after all these spurious examples are set aside, there is a certain *residuum* of resemblance in the diction (see e.g. Lekebusch, p. 35 sq.). Characteristic words and phrases of the author appear in the speeches, as well as in the narrative portion. But this was inevitable. It was impossible that the speeches could be reported word for word. Sometimes they must have been spoken in Aramaic; in other cases only shorthand and fragmentary reports were in the author's hands; in others again he may have heard them by word of mouth; in all probably they were much abridged. A certain infusion of his own phraseology was a natural consequence, and it does not affect their substantial accuracy. It appears even in the example which I have already given of an evidently Pauline utterance—the speech to the Ephesian elders at Miletus. The measure of the *extent* to which it would affect the language is seen by the example of the Third Gospel. Here we are able to compare St. Luke's account with the parallel narratives of the two other Synoptists; and the historical character remains, notwithstanding the literary editing of the third Evangelist. There is no reason to suppose that he dealt more freely with his materials in the Acts, where we have no such means of testing them. Indeed, as he was nearer to the events and more familiar with the persons, we should expect, if anything, a closer adherence to the form in which he received the reports.

   (ii) A second objection, or rather a second class of objections, is based on the representation here given of the principal agents in the planting of the Church, more especially of the relations between St. Peter and St. Paul and their respective followers. These objections start from the assumption that there was an irreconcilable opposition between the Apostle of the Circumcision and the Apostle of the Gentiles; that their views of Christianity were diametrically opposed; and that the former never emancipated himself from

a strictly Judaic and national conception of the Christ's Kingdom, whereas
the idea of the latter was cosmopolitan and universal. The author of the Acts,
it is assumed living at a later date, was desirous of finding a meeting point
for the conflicting parties, and thus invented positions, words, and actions
for the chief Apostles, so as to bring them into accord. His aim was *conciliation*, and he twisted or forged history accordingly. This is too wide a
question for discussion here. The objection indicated involves a *petition
principii*. Our chief authority for the relations existing between the leading
Apostles is this very Book itself. We can only say that to ourselves such passages as 1 Cor 1:12sq., 23; Gal 1:18; 2:6sq., 14sq. seem to indicate a substantial
harmony in principle between the two supposed antagonists;[6] that they are
placed on the same level by the two earliest of the Apostolic Fathers (Clement
of Rome 5; Ignatius *Rom.* 4), and are quoted as of equal authority by the
third (Polycarp, *Phil.* 2, 5, 6, &c.); that the mainstream of Christian history
betrays no evidence of this fundamental antagonism as the substratum of
the Catholic Church; and that the first distinct mention of it occurs in an
obviously fictitious narrative, which cannot date before the second half of
the second century, though doubtless even from the apostolic times there
were some extreme men who used the names of the two Apostles as party
watchwords.

According to this conception of early Christianity, it would be impossible
that St. Peter should have seen the vision obliterating the distinction of
meats clean and unclean, which led to the conversion of Cornelius, or that
St. Paul should have taken part in the Nazarite vows, and so have been guilty
of complicity with Jewish customs, on his last visit to Jerusalem. Above all
the representation of the attitudes of the respective leaders at the so-called
apostolic council is called in question, both as impossible in itself and as
irreconcilable with the notices of what is apparently the same occasion in
Gal 2:1-10.

As regards the apostolic council, I may perhaps be allowed to refer to a
full consideration of the question in my *Galatians* p. 123sq. The subject is

---

[6]So far as regards St. Peter's attitude towards the Pauline doctrine of faith and grace, we can only
say that the Acts represents him as adopting it (Acts 15:9, 11), just as the Epistle bearing his name
(1 Peter 1:5, 9, 13, &c.) adopts it, though not giving it the same special prominence, and as indeed
it is distinctly implied that he adopted it in St. Paul's argument in Gal 2:14.

too long for discussion here. It has been treated from various ponts of view, not only in Introductions, Apostolic Histories, and Commentaries but also in separate articles and monographs. Among the latter are Grimm, *Stud. U. Krit.* 1880, Hft. 3; Hilgenfeld, *Zeitschr. f. Wiss. Theol.* 1858, p. 74 sq., p. 317 sq.; Holsten, *Zum Evangelium des Paulus f. Wiss. Theol.* 1882, p. 436 sq., p. 129 sq.; Keim, *Aud dem Urchistenthum,* p. 64 sq.; Pfleiderer, *Jahrb. F. Protest Theol.* 1883, p. 78 sq. p. 241 sq.; Reuss, *Revue de Theologie,* 1858, 1859; K. Schmidt in Herzog-Plitt. *Real Encykl.* i. p. 575, 1877; Schneckenberger, *Stud. U. Krit.* 1855, p. 554 sq.; Volkmar, *Theol. Zeitschr. aus d. Schweiz.* 1885, p. 33 sq.; Weizacker, *Jahrb. F. Deutsch Theol.* 1873, p. 191 sq.; Wittichen, *Jahrb. F. Protest. Theol.* 1877, p. 653 sq. See also other reference in Holtzmann l.c. p. 436 sq. The opinions of Baur, Lechler, Neander, Ritschl, Schwegler, Zeller, and others, will be found in their several works mentioned at the end of this article; and the question is discussed at length in some of the Commentaries (e.g. Overbeck and Nosgen).

But it so happens that at the very two points in the narrative where St. Paul is represented as making the largest concessions to the Judaic Christians, and where therefore the author is supposed to diverge most widely from historical truth in order to gratify this assumed motive, we find in the character of the context indications which, in any case, would be regarded as striking evidences of veracity in an ancient narrator. These are the account of the third visit to Jerusalem, including this apostolic council in the 15th chapter and the conduct of the Apostle on his last visit to this same place in the 21st chapter.

(1) The account of the apostolic council is preceded by one avowal of weakness in the factions and quarrels in the Church (Acts 15:1-2sq.), and succeeded by another in the contention and separation of Paul and Barnabas (Acts 15:36 sq.). These frank confessions at all events afford a strong presumption of truthfulness. The whole narrative is essentially simple, straightforward, and natural as a record of events. The principal speakers, Peter and James, express opinions and use language as we have seen, which at all events presents resemblances to the Epistles extant in their names. The 'apostolic decree' bears such manifest traces of genuineness, and would have been so impossible at a late date, that few even of those who impugn the representation of St. Paul's actions have ventured to question it. The relative

positions of Peter and James harmonize with the circumstances, the official superiority of James at Jerusalem being recognized. The relative positions of Paul and Barnabas show still more subtle traces of authenticity, as I have already pointed out. Where the author is narrating in his own person, the order 'Paul and Barnabas' which would be natural to him, is adopted (Acts 15:2, 22, 35); but where the Church of Jerusalem is interested, as in the order of hearing accorded to the two (Acts 15:12) and again in the apostolic letter itself (Acts 15:25), the order is reversed—Barnabas being the older disciple, and better known to the Christians in Jerusalem. As a minor indication of truthfulness again, we may mention that Peter here, and here only in the Acts (in the speech of James) is called by his Hebraic name in its Hebraic form 'Symeon' (comp. 2 Pet 1:1). Indeed, the whole narrative is such that no one would have hesitated to accept it as a genuine record, if this pre-possession as to the mutual relations of the Apostles at this crisis had not stood in the way.

(2) The same is true of the later incident, the concession of the Apostle to the Jewish Christians in the matter of the Nazarite vows, on the occasions of his last visit to Jerusalem. The account is preceded by a diary of a voyage to Caesarea (Acts 21:1-8) and the sojourn in Caesarea (Acts 21:9-14) which is singularly plain, straightforward, and lifelike, which satisfies every test of truthfulness, and which in the purposeless-ness of the incidental touches is only explicable as a narrative of an eye-witness. This is especially true likewise of the verse immediately preceding the visit (Acts 21:16), which records the journey from Caesarea to Jerusalem, 'taking with us one Mnason of Cyprus, a primitive disciple, with whom we were to lodge.' There is no reason for this mention of Mnason, of whom we never hear again, except that the fact struck the narrator. The whole account again belongs to the 'we' sections, and manifests the life-like character which pervades these sections, moreover, it is allusive. It omits to explain certain points to the reader, be-cause they were obvious to the writer. Such for instance is the reference to 'the seven days' (Acts 21:27), which has puzzled the commentators. Again, the narrative of the tumult in the Temple, which follows, is not only full of life but (what is more important) saturated with local coloring. The alarm that the Apostle had introduced the Gentile Trophimus, the Ephesian, into the Temple is illustrated by M. Ganneau's discovery (*Palestine Exploration*

Fund, 1871, pp. 132sq., 172sq.) of the inscription on the stone barrier (δρύφακτος) which divided off the Court of the Israelites, forbidding any foreigner to pass it on pain of death, as correctly recorded by Josephus (*Ant.* xv.11.5; comp. *Bell. Jud.* v.5.2, vi.2.4); and hence doubtless St. Paul drew his illustration of the middle wall of partition (τὸ μεσότοιχον τοῦ φραγμοῦ) separating the Jew and Gentile in Eph 2:14, not without a remembrance (we may well suppose) of this incident of Trophimus the Ephesian, which was the beginning of his captivity. Again, in the tumult that follows, the same characteristics are still more prominent. The 'tribune,' the 'cohort', the 'descent' (v. 12) the 'steps', the 'fortress'—what is the meaning of all this? A minute topographical knowledge underlies the narrative. The tower of Antonia, dominating the Temple area and ascended thence by a long flight of stairs, with the armed cohort stationed there to keep order during the Festivals (Josephus, *Bell. Jud.* i.12.1) are the facts familiar to the writer which explain and vivify the incidents. But they are assumed, not stated. Upon this follows immediately the reference to the Egyptian pretender, who as we learn from Josephus (*Ant.* xx.8.6; *Bell. Jud.* ii.13.5), some three years before this time had threatened Jerusalem. He had disappeared and nothing more was heard from him. What more likely than that the Roman captain should suppose that he had started up again to disturb the peace? The manner in which he is mentioned is altogether natural and unstudied. On the other hand, is it at all probable that a writer in the second century would be capable of the very subtle and ingenious artifice that would be involved in this reference, if the narrative were not genuine? In fact the whole of this passage before and after the account of the Nazarite vows hangs together; and it is marked throughout with many and various tokens of authenticity.

Not unconnected with the objection based on the conciliatory tendency of the Book, is the supposed parallelism between the careers of the two Apostles in the former and latter parts of the narrative respectively. Paul is miraculously released from prison at Philippi (Acts 16:26 sq.), as Peter at Jerusalem (Acts 12:6 sq.). Paul strikes the sorcerer Elymas blind (Acts 13:6 sq.), as Peter struck the liars Ananias and Sapphira dead (Acts 5:1sq.). Sick persons are healed by handkerchiefs and aprons brought from the body of Paul (Acts 19:11sq.), as they are healed by the shadow of Peter falling upon them (Acts 5:15). And so forth. When the incidents are extracted from their context and marshaled in pairs, they produce a great impression and it is not surprising that many able critics of different schools have laid stress on this parallelism. On nearer examination, however, it is difficult to find any indication that this design was present to the mind of the writer, though he could hardly have concealed the fact, if he had entertained it. Nor, except in the miraculous release from prison, is there any close correspondence; and in this case the effect of the parallelism, as an indication of any such purpose, is destroyed by the fact that a third miraculous release from prison, earlier than either, is recorded (Acts 5:19), in which 'the Apostles' generally are involved. But in fact parallelisms far more close are common in history.

(iii) But a whole different objection had been urged to the genuineness of the Book. Several persons and incidents mentioned in the Acts have a place likewise in Josephus. As the two writers were treating of the history of the same country during the same period, we should hardly have expected it to be otherwise. But it is urged that the writer of Acts borrowed from Josephus, and therefore cannot have been St. Luke. This objection was started by Holtzmann (*Zeitschr. f. Wiss. Theol.* xvi. [1873], p. 85 sq.), and followed up by Krenkel (ibid., p. 441 sq.), by the author of *Supernatural Religion* (*Fortnightly Review* [1877], p. 502 sq.), and by Keim (*Urchristenthum* [1878] p. 1 sq.). Holtzmann was answered by Schürer (*Zeitschr. f. Wiss. Theol.* xix. [1876], p. 574 sq.), to whom he made a counter-reply (ibid., xx. [1877], p. 535 sq.).

As regards the narrative of facts, the divergences between the two are a sufficient answer to the charge of plagiarism. Indeed, the genuineness of the narrative in the Acts has been assailed on two wholly different and irreconcilable grounds. On the one hand its coincidences with Josephus are taken to prove that it is a work of a later pretender; on the other hand, its divergences from this same historian are regarded as evidence that the narrative is inauthentic. The attempt to reconcile these two contradictory grounds of attack by the supposition that when the author followed Josephus, he trusted his memory and was betrayed by it, will hardly carry conviction to anyone. We may remark in passing that it is an unproved assumption that, wherever there are divergences between the two, Josephus is right and St. Luke is wrong. Probabilities are often the other way. When, for instance, Josephus (*Bell. Jud.* ii.13, 15) gives the number of the sicarii who followed the Egyptian as 30,000 and the author of Acts as 4,000 we can have no hesitation in pre-ferring the smaller number to the larger. Moreover, Josephus is not always consistent with himself in his different works, and is full of inaccuracies when dealing with Old Testament history (*Dictionary of Christ. Biogr.* s.v. Josephus, iii. pp. 445, 455). As regards resemblances of diction, no coinci-dences have been alleged which make out even a *prima facie* case of pla-giarism. Thus when Holtzmann compares *Ant.* xx.5.1 with Luke 3:1 (ἡγεμονεύοντος Ποντίου Πιλάτου τῆς Ἰουδαίας) or when Krenkel sets side by side Josephus' account of his own boyhood (*Vit.* 2) with St. Luke's account of Christ's childhood (Luke 2:42sq.), laying stress on the occurrence of such words as 'intelligence' and 'progress' and on the fact that the one was fourteen years old and the other twelve, or when the author of *Supernatural Religion* calls attention to the dedication of Josephus' treatise to Epaphro-ditus, whom he designates 'κράτιστε' as Theophilus is designated κράτιστε by St. Luke, and then ransacks the preface of Josephus, which extends over several pages to find words such as . . . αὐτόπτης . . . ἀκριβῶς . . . we are able to measure the value of this objection. To take the last case, the epithet κράτιστε is very common as applied to persons in high position; it occurs many times, for instance, in the inscriptions in Wood's *Ephesus*. In one single inscription (*Great Theatre*, no. 17) it is found twice within six lines, applied to two different persons . . . ; and in another (*City and Suburbs*, no. 5), twice within four lines, applied to four different persons, three of them being women. . . . Again, in every case the words used by both these writers in common are obvious words to express the things signified, as any lexicon will show; and where two authors are dwelling on similar topics (e.g. the authorities for contemporary or nearly contemporary history), they cannot fail to employ similar language; nor is it easy to explain how any one who could write the Third Gospel and the Acts should be driven to Josephus to replenish his vocabulary with such ordinary words as 'attempt,' 'accurately,' 'eye-witness,' 'observe,' and the like.

(iv) Another objection to the genuineness and authenticity of the nar-rative is the alleged fact that it contains certain unhistorical statements. For the most part however, the errors adduced do not affect the veracity of the historian himself. Thus, for instance, it is affirmed that St. Stephen's speech, as tested by the Old Testament, contains several inaccuracies. These would doubtless require consideration, if we were discussing the nature and limits of inspiration; but for the question of the veracity of the author they have no value at all. We have no ground for supposing that he was in any degree responsible for them. Nearly all the alleged historical errors are of this kind. The speakers are to blame, not the author who records their speeches. One or two examples, however, do not belong to this class. The chief and most formidable of such historical difficulties is connected with Theudas, the religious insurgent or pretender, whose name is mentioned in the speech of Gamaliel (Acts 5:36) as having been put to death 'aforetime' (πρὸ τούτων τῶν ἡμέρων), and his followers, about four hundred in number, dispersed. A person of this name appears likewise in Josephus (*Ant.* xx. 5.1), where he is described as a 'wizard' (γόης), who pretended that he was a prophet; undertook to divide the waters of the Jordan, so that it might be traversed dryshod; and was followed by a great mass of common people. . . . The procurator Fadus promptly sent a detachment of cavalry after him. The leader himself was beheaded, and of his followers some were slain and others captured alive. It is assumed that the Theudas of Josephus is the same with the Theudas of St. Luke; and if so, there is an insuperable chronological discrepancy. The procurator Fadus entered upon his office A.D. 44, but the Theudas of St. Luke must be placed long before this time: for 1) the speech of Gamaliel itself is supposed to be spoken some years earlier, and 2) Gamaliel describes the insurrection of Judas the Galilean, as subsequent to that of Theudas (vs. 37 μετὰ τοῦτον), and the insurrection of Judas certainly took place 'in the days of the taxing' i.e. soon after the birth of Christ (see Josephus, *Ant.* xviii.1.1, xx.5.2; *Bell. Jud.* ii.17,18). Though the narrative of Josephus is disfigured by demonstrable errors and inaccuracies, yet it is hardly possible that he can have been mistaken here. We must therefore suppose the Theudas of Gamaliel to be a different person as Origen does (*c. Celsus* i. 57 . . .). Beyond the name there is no close resemblance; and Theudas contracted from Theodorus, Theodotus, Theodosius (frequently written Theudorus, Theudotus, Theudosius, as the Greek equivalent to several Hebrew names—Jonathan, Mattaniah, Matthias, Nathanael, &c.—would be commonly affected by the Jews). On these names, Theodorus &c. among the Jews, see Zunz, *Gesamm. Schriften,* ii. pp. 6, 7, 10, 22. Josephus himself mentions four pretenders named Simon, and three named Judas—these last all within ten years (see Gloag, i. p. 197). The Theudas of Gamaliel, therefore, will probably have been one of the many pretenders of whom Josephus speaks as troubling the peace of the nation about this time (Josephus, *Ant.* xvii.10.8; *Bell. Jud.* ii.4.1), without however giving their names. There is something to be said for the solution of Wieseler (*Synopsis*, p. 90 sq. Eng. Trans.), who, on the ground of the name, would identify him with Matthias the son of Margalothus, an insurgent in the time of Herod; for this person has a prominent place in Josephus (*Ant.* xvii.6.2 sq.). In connection with this charge of the falsification the language respecting Judas of Galilee attributed to Gamaliel in the context deserves notice. He speaks of Judas' rebellion as coming to nothing. This was natural enough on the lips of Gamaliel before the sequel had revealed itself, but would be out of place at a later date; for two sons of this rebel leader, James and Simon, broke out in rebellion under Claudius, and were crucified by the procurator Tiberius Alexander (*Ant.* xx.5.2); while a third son Menahem headed a formidable rebellion shortly before the commencement of the Jewish war, and he too was put to death (*Bell. Jud.* ii.17.8sq. See Nosgen, p. 146sq.).

6. *The Time and Place of Writing.* What was the date of the Acts? To this we can give no certain answer. It has been shown that the conclusion of the history is intentional, that there is no abruptness in it and that therefore we cannot draw any inference from it, as though the book were written at the point of time when the narrative closes. This indication of date having failed us, no clue remains. The fancy of Hig and others that αὕτη ἐστὶν ἔρημος ('this is desert') in Acts 8:26 refers to the destruction of Gaza immediately before the fall of Jerusalem (Josephus *Bell. Jud.* ii.18.1), and therefore points to a date not earlier than about A.D. 80, is based on a misconception. The words are perhaps not the author's own, but the Angel's, and they certainly refer not to the city, but to the road. They would thus be an instruction to Philip to take this route, because it passed through an uninhabited and un-frequented country, where he would be unmolested in his interview with the Ethiopian. The Book itself contains no reference to any event later than the close of the narrative itself.[7] It must however have been written later than the Gospel, and we are thus led to investigate the date of this 'former

---

[7]Except of course for the second advent, final judgment, and restoration of Israel. (BW3)

treatise.' Here it is confidently assumed that the turn given to our Lord's predictions of the coming troubles (Luke 21:20-24), as compared with the parallel passages in the other Evangelists, show that this Gospel was written after the destruction of Jerusalem. I am unable to see the force of this argument. The destruction of Jerusalem seems clearly to be indicated in Christ's prophecies in the other Evangelists likewise, and the difference of language does not seriously affect the case. Yet, though the reason given may not be valid, the date assigned is perhaps not far wrong. It would at all events be a probable date for a writer who was a younger disciple and a personal follower of St. Paul. Not a few of those who recognize St. Luke as the author of the work have accepted this date as approximately correct.

The *place* of writing is altogether indeterminable. Something may be said in favor of Philippi. At all events the writer seems to have spent some time there (see above), and the use of the first person at this point, without any explanation, may suggest some corresponding local knowledge on the part of the recipient. Again Antioch is far from improbable, since St. Luke according to an old tradition was born at Antioch, and some details connected with this city are given with exceptional particularity (Acts 6:5; 11:26; 13:1sq.; 15:22sq.). Again Rome has a certain claim to be considered, since the writer accompanied St. Paul on the visit with which the narrative closes. Other places which have been suggested, such as Alexandria or Ephesus, have nothing to recommend them.

7. *Sources of Information.* The authorities of which the writer made use must remain a matter of speculation. It has been inferred from the preface to the Gospel, that St. Luke discarded all written sources of information, such as any memoirs of Christ's life and teaching which others before him may have published, and depended entirely on oral tradition, as received directly from eye-witnesses. It does not seem to me that his language suggests this strict limitation. The 'tradition' of which he there speaks might be written as well as oral. Nor again, even supposing that he had confined himself to oral communications of eye-witnesses in the first treatise, are we justified in assuming him to have acted precisely the same way in composing the second? As a question of probability, the life and words of Christ, being the subject-matter of Christian teaching, would form a more or less definite body of oral tradition; but the doings of the Apostles had no such impor-

tance that they should assume this form. The question as regards the Acts resolves itself into one of internal evidence and probability. So regarding it we are forced to the conclusions that, for some parts at least (the speech of Stephen will serve as an example), he must have used written notes taken down at the time; for this speech is inconceivable as a fiction and almost equally so as an oral tradition. When we take into account the common use of shorthand among the ancients, there is no improbability in this supposition; since the gravity and interest of the defense on such a critical occasion must have impressed itself on all, more especially on the disciples.

The materials then would be partly oral, partly written. The written materials would be here and there a document, such as the letter of the apostolic council (Acts 15:23sq.); here and there notes of speeches taken down at the time or immediately afterwards; and occasionally also diaries or memoranda of facts. Besides these, he would receive a large amount of oral information; and for some portions of his narrative he was himself an eye-witness. His chief authority would naturally be St. Paul, with whom at different epochs he spent large portions of time. But he likewise lodged a considerable time (ἡμέρας πλείους) with Philip the Evangelist (Acts 21:10), and from him he may have received written or oral information respecting the earliest history of the Church, more especially the doings of the deacons, in which Philip himself 'pars magna fuit' (Acts 8:5-40). From this source he might have derived his information respecting the conversion of Cornelius, for Caesarea seems to have been Philip's permanent home before as well as after this event (Acts 8:40; 21:8). For portions of this earlier history also he may have been indebted to John Mark, in whose company we find him at a later date (Col 4:10, 14; Philem 24; 2 Tim 4:11). For all that related to Barnabas (Col 4:10) and to St. Peter (1 Pet 5:13), Mark would be a competent authority. His intercourse with men like Timothy and Tychicus also must have been considerable; and they may have supplied information for the latter part of his narrative, where Paul failed him. How close may have been St. Luke's intimacy with any of the Twelve, we cannot say. To any such intimacy we find no reference within the compass of his own narrative; but an acquaintance with St. Peter afterwards, at Rome, is consistent with the notices.

8. *The Motive and Design of the Work.* The motive and design of the work have been considered already, when its contents were under discussion. Ad-

dressing one Theophilus, either an actual person or an imaginary representative of the Christian student, St. Luke merely purposes to give for the edi-
fication of his readers a history of the Christian Church from its foundation
to its establishment in the metropolis of the world. If there were sufficient
grounds for postulating a theological principle as the basis of the narrative,
it would be the continued working and presence of Jesus, no longer in the
flesh, but in the Church.

But a large number of recent critics have seen in this work a motive of a
wholly different kind. They have regarded it as written with an *apologetic* or
conciliatory purpose. In the present case these two epithets come to the same
thing. For if *apologetic*, it was intended either to defend St. Paul from the
charge of hostility to the Jews, or St. Peter from the charge of opposition to
the free admission of the Gentiles; if *conciliatory*, its motive was to bring
together and amalgamate two parties in the Christian Church—the Judaic,
which clung to the name of St. Peter, and the Gentile, whose watchword was
the liberalism of St. Paul.

It will be seen at once, that such a view of the purpose is consistent with
a frank recognition of the genuineness of the work and of the truthfulness
of the narrative. Its aim would then be the correction of prevailing mis-
understandings. Such was the position of Schneckenburger (1841), who was
the first to emphasize the real or supposed parallelism between St. Peter and
St. Paul as showing the apologetic design of the author;[8] but he himself
herewith maintains the substantial credibility of the account. This same idea
however was adopted by the critics of the Tübingen school, who occupied
another platform, and to whom it was a convenient weapon for their destructive warfare. Baur (*Paulus*, p. 1sq. 1845), Schwegler (*Das Nachapos-
toliche Zeitalter*, ii. p. 73sq. 1846), and Zeller (*Die Apostelgeschichte*, p. 316sq.
1854), all took this parallelism as the basis of their theories and regarded the
Book as the work of a Pauline Christian in the second century, whose object
was to reconcile parties, and who freely invented his story accordingly. Not
very different is the position of Hilgenfeld (*Einleitung*, p. 576sq.), who takes
it to represent 'Unionist Paulinism' not earlier than the close of the first
century. Several other critics, also without going to these extremes, have

---

[8]Baur had previously suggested the idea of this 'tendency' in the *Tubing. Zeitschr. f. Theol.* iii. p.
38sq. 1836.

regarded the narrative as colored by this 'conciliatory' motive. Thus Renan (*Les Apotres*, pp. 13sq., 28sq.), though confidently ascribing the work to a companion of St. Paul, and therefore presumably to St. Luke, and employing its statements as generally credible yet holds that the representations of the chief Apostles are highly colored, so as to produce an impression of harmony which was not justified by the facts.

In answer to such allegations it is sufficient to say that St. Paul's own practical maxim of 'becoming all things to all men' and therefore of 'becoming a Jew to the Jews' covers all the actions ascribed to him in St. Luke's narrative; that the very context, in which these particular actions are related, manifests, as I have already shown (above), unmistakeable tokens of authenticity; that St. Paul's language and conduct in dealing with Gentile converts like the Galatians is no standard at all for measuring his intercourse with the Church of Jerusalem; and that generally the tone and character of the narrative ought to place it above the suspicion of any conscious distortion of facts. For the rest, if any false impressions were abroad about the relations of the two chief Apostles, St. Peter and St. Paul, it is not unnatural that the writer should wish to correct them.

9. *The Chronology.* There are two fixed points in the chonology of the Acts, as determined by contact with secular history. The first of these is St. Paul's second visit to Jerusalem (Acts 11:30; 12:25), which is obviously synchronous, or nearly so, with the death of Herod Agrippa (Acts 12:23); but this latter event is known to have happened in A.D. 44 (Josephus, *Ant.* xix.8.2). The second is St. Paul's appearance before Festus and consequent voyage to Rome (Acts 26:32; 27:1). This occurred immediately after Festus had arrived in the province. But from various considerations it appears that the deposition of Felix and the accession of Festus most probably happened in A.D. 60, and must certainly have happened close upon that year; see Wieseler, *Chronol.* p. 66 sq.

Besides these two fixed dates, there are other references to events in secular history of which the date indeed is not definitely determined, but that serve as rough verifications. Such are the great famine (Acts 11:28), the banishment of the Jews from Rome (Acts 18:2), the reign of Aretas at Damascus (Acts 9:25; 2 Cor 11:32), and the proconsulship of Gallio in Achaia (Acts 18:12).

Of the two fixed dates—the death of Herod Agrippa—is isolated and renders no assistance in the general scheme of chronology. But the second is of the highest value. The notice of the intervals of time in the Acts are fairly continuous from the apostolic council (Acts 15) to the end of the Book. Thus by working backwards from the accession of Festus and the journey to Rome (A.D. 60), we are able to frame a skeleton of the chronology for the latter half of the Book, and we arrive at about A.D. 51 for the apostolic council. From this point, still working backwards, the chronological notices in Gal 1:18; 2:1, enable us to fix some of the early dates. The whole system is worked out most thoroughly by Wieseler. The results will be found in any of the common books related to the apostolic history or the life of St. Paul. The special books on the chronology of St. Paul and of the Acts are Anger, *De temporum in Act. Apostl. Ratione* (Lipsiae, 1833), and Wieseler, *Chronologie des apostolischen Zeitalters* (Göttingen, 1848). Lewin's *Fasti Sacri* (London, 1865) is a useful work, and is not as well-known as it deserves to be.

10. *The Text.* Accounts will be found of the authorities for the text of Acts in their proper place in the well-known Introductions and Prolegomena of Tregelles (1856), Scrivener (ed. 3, 1883), Tischendorf (ed. Greogry, 1884), and Westcott and Hort. Special works relating to this particular book are J. D. Michaelis, *Curae in Versionem Syriacam Actuum Apostolicorum* (Göttingen, 1755); Belsheim, *Die Apostelgeschichte u. die Offenbarung Johannis in einer alten lateinischen* Uebersetzung (Christiania, 1879); and F. A. Bornemann, *Act Apostolorum ad Cod. Cantabrigiensis fidem recensuit* (Grossenhainae, 1848). In the last, as the title suggests, the Ms. D is taken as the standard of the text—*a conclusion which is not adopted by any sound textual critic.* But the text of D and of a few other authorities that coincide with it in greater or lesser degrees, presents a difficult problem. The variations from the normal text are greater than are found in any other portion of the New Testament. They are of two kinds—partly paraphrases and amplification, and partly insertions of additional incidents or particulars. As examples of this latter class may be mentioned such passages as Acts 12:10, where the number of steps is given in the account of St. Peter's release from prison, or Acts 28:16, where the delivering of Paul and his fellow-prisoners to the prefect of the praetorium is mentioned. In this latter passage, however, D is wanting. Such additions belong to the same class of which the pericope related to the

woman taken in adultery (John 8:3sq.) is the most prominent example. The editor or transcriber seems to have had access to some very early and genuine tradition; and the fact that the incident in the pericope in St. John was related likewise by Papias (Eusebius *H.E.* iii.39) suggests that the source of these traditions is to be sought ultimately in the disciples who gathered about St. John and his successors in Asia Minor.

11. *The Literature.* The literature which has accumulated about the Acts is so vast that an exhaustive catalogue is quite impracticable. In the following list all works which are directly homiletic or are intended for school purposes are omitted; nor have I for the most part included monographs and articles which treat special points. Many of these have been noticed in their respective places. After these deductions the following books may be mentioned:

A. *General Commentaries*, including the whole or a great part of the New Testament. Of the older commentaries those of Calvin, Grotius, and Bengel deserve to be specially named. Among recent works Alford, Wordsworth, the *Speaker's Commentary* (Cook and Jacobsen), Ellicott's *New Testament Commentary for English Readers* (Plumptre), in England; and Olshausen (ed. 4, 1862, re-edited by Ebrard), De Wette (ed. 4, 1870, re-edited by Overbeck), Meyer (ed. 5, 1880, re-edited by Wendt), Lechler (in Lange's *Bibelwerk* ed. 4, 1881), in Germany, may be mentioned.

B. *General Introductions to the New Testament.* Bleek (Eng. Trans.), 1869; Davidson vol. ii, 1842; Guericke, 1868 (ed. 3); Hilgenfeld, 1875; Holtzmann, 1885; Hug (Eng. Trans.), 1827; Marsh's Michaelis, 1802 (ed. 2); Reuss, 1860; Salmon, 1886 (ed. 2); Weiss, 1886.

C. *Special Commentaries on the Acts.* The Homilies of St. Chrysostom are the only patristic commentary of real importance on this Book. Passing to recent times, we have Baumgarten, Braunschweig, 1852, 1854 (Eng. Trans.); Gloag, Edinburgh 1870; Hackett, Boston 1863 (new ed.); Humphrey, London 1854 (ed. 2); Nosgen, Leipzig 1882. A complete list of commentaries, special and general up to the date (1859), will be found in Darling's *Cycl. Bibl.* 1167 sq.

D. *Special Works on the Acts.* Biscoe, *Hist. of the Acts, &c. confirmed from other Authors.* &c. 1742, reprinted 1840; Klostermann, *Vindiciae Lucanae sive de Itinerarii in libro Actorum asservati auctore*, 1866; Klostermann, *Probleme im Aposteltexte*, 1883; Konig, *Die Echtheit der Apostelgeschichte*, 1867; Lekebusch, *Composition u. Enstehung der. A.-G.*, 1854; Lightfoot, *Hebrew and Talmudic Exercitations on the Acts of the Apostles*; Oertel, *Paulus in der A.G.*, 1868; Paley, *Orae Paulinae* (edited by J. Tate, 1840; by Birks 1850); Schmidt, K. *Die Apostelgeschichte*, Band i. 1882; Schneckenberger, *Ueber den Zweck der A.-G.*, 1841; Schwanbeck, *Ueber die Quellen der A.-G.*, 1847; *Supernatural Religion*, vol. iii, 1877; Stier, *Die Reden der Apostel* (ed. 2) 1861; S.P.C.K. *The Heathen World and St. Paul* (no date), Rawlinson, Plumptre, Davies, Merivale; Zeller, *Die Apostelgeschichte*, 1854.

F. *Apostolic Histories, Lives of St. Paul, &c.* Baur, *Paulus*, 1845; Coneybeare and Howson, *Life and Epistles of St. Paul*, 1856 (2nd ed.); Ewald, *Geschichte des apostolischen Zeitalter*, 1858 (2nd ed.) being vol. vi. of *Geschichte des Volkes Israel*; Farrar, *Early Days of Christianity*, 1882 (1st ed.); Farrar, *Life and Work of St. Paul*, 1879 (1st ed.); Lechler, *Das Apostolische u. das Nachapostolische Zeitalter* (1st ed. 1857; 2nd ed. 1885); Lewin, *Life and Epistles of St. Paul*, 1872; Neander, *Pflanzung und Leitung*, 1862 (5th ed.); Pfleiderer, *Urchistenthum*, 1887; Renan, *Les Apotres*, 1866 (1st ed.); *Saint Paul*, 1869 (1st ed.); Ritschl, *Die Entstehung der altkatholischen Kirche*, 1857 (1st ed.); Schaff, *Hist. of the Christian Church—Apostolic Christianity*, 1882; Schwelger, *Das Nachapostolische Zeitalter*, 1846; Thiersch, *Die Kirche in apostolischen Zeitalter*, 1886. This list might be considerably increased, if there is any object in increasing it. [J.B.L.]

Appendix B

'Illustrations of the Acts from Recent Discoveries'[1]

In a former volume M. Renan declared his opinion that 'the author of the Third Gospel and the Acts was verily and indeed (*bien réellement*) Luke, a disciple of Saint Paul.'[2] In the last installment of his work he condemns as untenable the view that the first person plural of the later chapters is derived from some earlier document inserted by the author, on the ground that these portions are identical in style with the rest of the work.[3] Such an expression of opinion, proceeding from a not too conservative critic, is significant; and this view of the authorship, I cannot doubt, will be the final verdict of the future, as it has been the unbroken tradition of the past. But at a time when attacks on the genuineness of the work have been renewed, it may not be out of place to call attention to some illustrations of the narrative which recent discoveries have brought to light. No ancient work affords so many tests of veracity; for no other has such numerous points of contact in all directions with contemporary history, politics, and topography, whether Jewish or Greek or Roman. In the publications of the year 1877 Cyprus and Ephesus have made important contributions to the large mass of evidence already existing.

---

[1] This article first appeared in the now-defunct journal *Contemporary Review* 32 (May 1878): 288–96.

[2] *Les Apotres*, p. xviii.

[3] *Les Evangiles*, p. 436.

(1) The government of the Roman province at this time was peculiarly dangerous ground for the romance-writer to venture upon. When Augustus assumed the supreme power he divided the province under the Roman dominion with the Senate. From that time forward there were two sets of provincial governors. The ruler of a senatorial province was styled a proconsul (ἀνθύπατος) while the officer to whom a senatorial province was entrusted bore the name of proprietor (ἀντιστράτηγος) or legate (πρεσβεύτης). Thus the use of the terms 'proconsul' and 'propraetor' was changed; for whereas in republican times they signified that the provincial governors bearing them had previously held the offices of consul and praetor respectively at home, they were now employed to distinguish the superior power under which the provinces were administered without regard to the previous rank of the governors administering them. Moreover, the original subdivision of the provinces between the Emperor and Senate underwent constant modifications. If disturbances broke out in a senatorial province and military rule was necessary to restore order, it would be transferred to the Emperor as the head of the army, and the Senate would receive an imperatorial province in exchange. Hence at any given time it would be impossible to say without contemporary, or at least very exact historical knowledge, whether a particular province was governed by a proconsul or a proprietor. The province of Achaia is a familiar illustration of this point. A very few years before St. Paul's visit to Corinth, and some years later, Achaia was governed by a proprietor. Just at this time however it was in the hands of the Senate, and its ruler therefore was a proconsul, as represented by St. Luke.

Cyprus is a less familiar, but not less instructive, example of the same accuracy. Older critics, even when writing on the apologetic side, had charged St. Luke with an incorrect use of terms; and the origin of their mistake is a significant comment on the perplexities in which a later forger would find himself entangled in dealing with these official designations. They fell upon a passage in Strabo[4] where this writer, after mentioning the division of the provinces between the Emperor and the Senate, states that the Senate sent consuls to the two provinces of Asia and Africa but praetors to the rest on their list—

---

[4]xvii. p. 840.

among which he mentions Cyprus; and they jumped at the conclusion—very natural in itself—that the governor of Cyprus would be called a proprietor. Accordingly Baronio[5] suggested that Cyprus, though a praetorian province, was often handed over *honoris causa* to be administered by the proconsul of Cilicia, and he assumed therefore that Sergius Paulus held this latter office; while Grotius found a solution in the hypothesis that proconsul was a title bestowed by flatterers on an official whose proper designation was proprietor. The error illustrates the danger of a little learning, not the less dangerous when it is in the hands of really learned men. Asia and Africa, the two great prizes of the profession, exhausted the normal two consuls of the preceding year; and the Senate therefore were obliged to send ex-praetors and other magistrates to govern the remaining provinces under their jurisdiction. But it is now an unquestioned and unquestionable fact that all the provincial governors who represented the Senate in imperial times, whatever magistracy they might have held previously, were styled officially proconsuls.[6]

The circumstances indeed, so far as regards Cyprus, are distinctly stated by Dion Cassius. At the original distribution of the provinces (B.C. 27) this island had fallen to the Emperor's share; but the historian, while describing the assignment of the several countries in the first instance, adds that the Emperor subsequently gave back Cyprus and Gallia Narbonensis to the Senate, himself taking Dalmatia in exchange;[7] and at a later point, when he arrives at the time in question (B.C. 22), he repeats the information respecting the transfer. 'And so,' he adds, 'proconsuls began to be sent to those nations also.'[8] Of the continuance of Cyprus under the jurisdiction of the Senate, about the time to which St. Luke's narrative refers, we have ample evidence. Contemporary records bear testimony to the existence of proconsuls in Cyprus not only before and after but during the reign of Claudius. The inscriptions mention by name two proconsuls who governed the province in this Emperor's time (A.D. 51, 52),[9] while a third and perhaps a

---

[5]Sub ann. 46.

[6]See Becker and Marquardt *Rom. Alterth.* III.i.p. 294sq. Even De Wette has not escaped the pitfall, for he states that 'according to Strabo, Cyprus was governed by propraetors,' and he therefore supposes that Strabo and Dion Cassius are at variance. De Wette's error stands uncorrected by his editor, Overbeck.

[7]Dion Cassius liii.12.

[8]Dion Cassius liv.4.

[9]Q. Julius Cordus and L. Anninus Bassus in Boeckh *Corp. Inscr. Graec.* 2631, 2632.

fourth are recorded on the coins.[10] At a later date, under Hadrian, we come across a proprietor of Cyprus.[11] The change would probably be owing to the disturbed state of the province consequent on the insurrections of the Jews. But at the close of the same century (A.D. 198)—under Severus—it is again governed by a proconsul;[12] and this was its normal condition.

Thus the accuracy of St. Luke's designation is abundantly established; but hitherto no record had been found of the particular proconsul mentioned by him. This defect is supplied by one of General Cesnola's inscriptions. It is somewhat mutilated indeed, so that the meaning of parts is doubtful; but for our purpose it is adequate. A date is given as ΕΠΙ. ΠΑΥΛΟΥ.[ΑΝΘ] ΥΠΑΤΟΥ 'in the proconsulship of Paulus.' On this Cesnola remarks: 'The proconsul Paulus may be the Sergius Paulus of the Acts of the Apostles (chap. xiii), as instances of the suppression of one of two names are not rare.'[13] An example of the suppression in this very name Sergius Paulus will be given presently, thus justifying the identification of the proconsul of the Acts with the proconsul of this inscription.

Of this Sergius Paulus, the proconsul of Cyprus, Dean Alford says that 'nothing more is known.' But is it certain that he is not mentioned elsewhere? In the index of contents and authorities that forms the first book of Pliny's *Natural History*, this writer twice names one Sergius Paulus among the Latin authors to whom he is indebted. May not this have been the same person? The name is not common. So far as I have observed, there is only one other person bearing it[14]—probably a descendant of this Cyprian pro-

---

[10]Cominius Proclus and perhaps Quadratus; see Akerman's *Numismatic Illustrations of the New Testament*, p. 39.

[11]*Corp. Inscr. Lat.* iii.6072, an Ephesian inscription discovered by Mr. Wood.

[12]*Corp. Insc. Lat.* iii.218.

[13]Cessnola's, *Cyprus*, p. 425. [As a side note from one of the editors (BW3), there is an inscription on stone in Pisidian Antioch, now in its museum, which several of us discovered gathering mold and moss in the courtyard of the little museum there, and had the curator move inside. What it shows is a connection between Sergius Paulus on Cyprus and Pisidian Antioch, which may suggest that Paul got a letter of reference from the governor when he went there. On this stone the full name of the Paulii family is found. What this find shows, as does this article by Lightfoot, is that so far as Luke can be checked against the archaeological record he appears to be very accurate indeed, knowing first-century conditions, which must surely count against a second-century date for Acts when things had changed considerably in the provinces of Asia, Galatia and elsewhere.]

[14]Dean Alford indeed (on Acts 13:7) following some previous writers, mentions a Sergius Paulus, intermediate in date between the two others—the authority of Pliny and the friend of Galen— whom he describes as 'one of the consules suffecti in A.D. 94.' This however is a mistake. A

consul—is mentioned, of whom I shall have something to say hereafter; and he flourished more than a century later. Only one test of identity suggests itself. The Sergius Paulus of Pliny is named as an authority for the second and eighteenth book of that writer. Now on the hypothesis that the proconsul of Cyprus is meant, it would be a natural supposition that, like Sir J. Emerson Tennent or Sir Rutherford Alcock, this Sergius Paulus would avail himself of the opportunities afforded by his official residence in the East to tell his Roman fellow-countrymen something about the region in which he had resided.

We therefore look with interest to see whether these two books of Pliny contain any notices respecting Cyprus, which might reasonably be explained in this way; and our curiosity is not disappointed. In the second book, besides two other brief notices (cc. 90, 112) relating to the situation of Cyprus, Pliny mentions (c. 97) an area in the temple of Venus at Paphos on which the rain never falls. In the eighteenth book again, besides an incidental mention of this island (c. 57) he gives some curious information (c. 12) with respect to the Cyprian corn, and the bread made therefrom. It should be added for the second book, in which the references to Cyprus come late, Sergius Paulus is the last-mentioned Latin authority; whereas for the eighteenth, where they are early, he occupies an earlier, though not very early, place in the list. These facts may be taken for what they are worth. In a work which contains such a multiplicity of details as Pliny's *Natural History* we should not be justified in laying too much stress on coincidences of this kind.

From the Sergius Paulus of Luke the physician we turn to the Sergius Paulus of Galen the physician. Soon after the accession of M. Aurelius (A.D. 161) Galen paid his first visit to Rome where he stayed for three or four years. Among other persons whom he met there was L. Sergius Paulus, who had been already consul suffectus about A.D. 150, and was hereafter to be consul for the second time in A.D. 168 (on this latter occasion as the regular consul of the year), after which time he held the Prefecture of the City.[15] He is

---

certain inscription mentioning L. Sergius Paullus as consul, is placed by Muratori (p. cccxiv.3) and others under the year 94; but there is good reason to believe that it refers to the friend of Galen, and must be assigned to the year when he was consul for the first time as suffectus, i.e. about about 150. See Marini, *Atti e Monumenti de' Fratelli Arvali*, p. 198; Waddington, *Fastes des Provinces Asiatiques*, p. 731.

[15]This person is twice mentioned by Galen *de Anat. Admin.* i.1 (*Op.* ii. p. 218 ed. Kuhn) and *Op.*

probably also the same person who is mentioned elsewhere as proconsul of
Asia in connection with a Christian martyrdom.[16] This later Sergius Paulus
reproduces many features of his earlier namesake. Both alike are public men;
both alike are proconsuls; both alike show an inquisitive and acquisitive
disposition. The Sergius Paulus of Acts, dissatisfied (as we may suppose)
alike with the coarse mythology of popular religion and with the lifeless
precepts of abstract philosophies, has recourse first to the magic of the sorcerer Elymas, and then to the theology of the Apostles Barnabas and Saul,
for satisfaction. The Sergius Paulus of Galen is described as 'holding the
foremost place in practical life as well as in philosophical studies'; he is especially mentioned as a student of Aristotelean philosophy; and he takes
very keen interest in medical and anatomical learning. Moreover, if we may
trust the reading, there is another striking coincidence between the two accounts. The same expression 'who is also Paul' (ὁ καὶ Παῦλος), is used to
describe Saul of Tarsus in the context of the Acts, and L. Sergius in the account of Galen. Not the wildest venture of criticism could so trample on
chronology as to maintain that the author of the Acts borrowed from these
treatises of Galen; and conversely I have no desire to suggest that Galen
borrowed from St. Luke. But if so, the facts are a warning against certain
methods of criticism that find favor in this age. To sober critics, the coincidence will merely furnish an additional illustration of the permanence of
type that forms so striking a feature in the great Roman families. One other
remark is suggested by Galen's notices of his friend. Having introduced him
to us as 'Sergius who is also Paulus,' he drops the former name altogether in
the subsequent narrative and speaks of him again and again as Paulus simply.
This illustrates the newly-published Cyprian inscription, in which the proconsul of that province is designated by the one name Paulus only.

  2) The transition from General Cesnola's *Cyprus* to Mr. Woods *Ephesus*

---

ii. p. 612. In this latter passage the words stand 'Σέργιός τε καὶ ὁ Παῦλος' in Kuhn and other
earlier printed editions that I have consulted, but they are quoted Σέργιός τε ὁ καὶ Παῦλος by
Wettstein and others. I do not know on what authority this latter reading rests, but the change in
order is absolutely necessary for the sense; for 1) in this passage nothing more is said about Sergius
as distinct from Paulus, whereas Paulus is again and again mentioned, so that plainly one person
alone is intended. 2) In the parallel passage Sergius Paulus is mentioned, and the same description
is given of him as of Paulus here. The alternative would be to omit καὶ ὁ altogether, as the passage
is tacitly quoted in Borghesi (*Euures* viii p. 504).

[16]Melito in Eusebius *H.E.* iv.26: see Waddington, *Fastes des Provinces Asiatiques*, p. 731.

carries us forward from the first to the third missionary journey of St. Paul. Here, again, we have illustrative matter of some importance. The main feature in the narrative of the Acts is the manner in which the cultus of the Ephesian Artemis dominates the incidents of the Apostle's sojourn in that city. As an illustration of this feature, it would hardly be possible to surpass one of the inscriptions in the existing collection.[17] We seem to be reading a running commentary on the excited appeal of Demetrius the silversmith, when we are informed that 'not only in the city but everywhere temples are dedicated to the goddess, and statues erected and altars consecrated to her, on account of the manifest epiphanies which she vouchsafes . . . '; that 'the greatest proof of the reverence paid to her is the fact that a month bears her name, being called Artemision among ourselves, and Artemisius among the Macedonians and other nations of Greece and their respective cities'; that during this month 'solemn assemblies and religious festivals are held, and more especially in this our city, which is the nurse of its own Ephesian goddess'; and that therefore 'the people of the Ephesians, considering it meet that the whole of this month which bears the divine name . . . should be kept holy, and dedicated to the goddess,' has decreed accordingly. 'For so,' concludes this remarkable document, 'the cultus being set on a better footing, our city will continue to grow in glory and to be prosperous to all time.' The sense of special proprietorship in this goddess of world-wide fame, which pervades the narrative in the Acts, could not be better illustrated than by this decree. But still the newly-published inscriptions greatly enhance the effect. The patron deity not only appears in these as 'the great goddess Artemis' as in the Acts, but sometimes she is styled 'the supremely great goddess . . . Artemis.' To her favor all men are indebted for all their choicest possessions. She has not only her priestesses, but her temple-curators, her essenes, her divines (θεολόγοι), her choristers . . . her vergers . . . her tire-women or dressers . . . and even her 'acrobats' whatever may be meant by some of these terms. Fines are allocated to provide adornments for her; endowments are given for the cleaning and custody of her images; decrees are issued for the public exhibition of her treasures. Her birthday is again

---

[17]Boeckh, *Corp. Inscr. Graec.* 2954. The first sentence which I have quoted is slightly mutilated; but the sense is clear. The document bears only too close a resemblance to the utterances of Lourdes in our day.

and again mentioned. She is seen and heard everywhere. She is hardly more at home in her own sanctuary than in the Great Theatre. This last-mentioned place—the scene of the tumult in the Acts—is brought vividly before our eyes in Mr. Wood's inscriptions. The theatre appears as the recognized place of public assembly. Here edicts are proclaimed, and decrees are recorded, and benefactors crowned. When the mob, under the leadership of Demetrius gathered here for their demonstration against St. Paul and his companions, they would find themselves surrounded by memorials which might stimulate their zeal for the goddess. If the 'town-clerk' had desired to make good his assertion. 'What man is there that knoweth not that the city of the Ephesians is the sacristan of the great goddess Artemis?' he had only to point to the inscriptions which lined the theatre for confirmation. The very stones would have cried out from the walls in response to his appeal.

Nor is the illustration of the magistracies that are named by St. Luke less complete. Three distinct officers are mentioned in the narrative—the Roman proconsul (ἀνθύπατος), the governor of the province and the supreme administrator of the law, translated 'deputy' in our version; the recorder (γραμματεύς) or chief magistrate of the city itself, translated 'town-clerk'; and the Asiarchs (Ἀσιαρχαί) or presidents of the games and of other religious ceremonials translated 'the chief of Asia.' All these appear again and again in the newly-discovered inscriptions. Sometimes two of the three magistracies will be mentioned on the same stone. Sometimes the same person will unite in himself the two offices of recorder and Asiarch either simultaneously or not. The mention of the recorder is especially frequent. His name is employed to authenticate every decree and to fix every date.

But besides these more general illustrations of the account in Acts, the newly-discovered inscriptions throw light on some special points in the narrative. Thus where the chief magistrate pronounces St. Paul and his companions to be 'neither sacrilegious (ἱεροσύλους) nor blasphemers of our goddess,'[18] we discover a special emphasis in the term on finding from these inscriptions that certain offences (owing to the mutilation of the stone we are unable to determine the special offences) were treated as destructive sacrilege against the goddess. 'Let it be regarded as sacrilege and

---

[18]Acts 19:37 where ἱεροσύλους is oddly translated 'robbers of churches.'

impiety'... says an inscription found in this very theatre,[19] though not yet set up at the time when the 'town-clerk' spoke. So again, where the same speaker describes the city of Ephesus as the 'neocoros', the 'temple sweeper' or 'sacristan of the great goddess Artemis,' we find in these terms inscriptions for the first time a direct example of this term so applied. Though the term 'neocoros' in itself is capable of general application, yet as a matter of fact, when used of Ephesus on coins and inscriptions (as commonly is the case of other Asiatic cities), it has reference to the cultus not of the patron deity, but of the Roman emperors. In this sense Ephesus is described as 'twice' or 'thrice sacristan' as the case may be, the term being used absolutely. There was indeed every probability that the same term would be employed also to describe the relation of the city to Artemis. By a plausible but highly precarious conjecture it had been introduced into the lacuna of a mutilated inscription.[20] By a highly probable but not certain interpretation it had been elicited from the legend on a coin.[21] There were analogies too which supported it. Thus the Magnesians are styled on the coins 'sacristans of Artemis,'[22] and at Ephesus itself an individual priest is designated by the term 'sacristan of Artemis.'[23] Nor did it seem unlikely that a city which styled itself 'the nurse of Artemis' should also claim the less audacious title of 'sacristan' to this same goddess. Still probability is not certainty; and (so far as I am aware) no direct example was forthcoming. Mr. Wood's inscriptions supply this defect. On one of these 'the city of the Ephesians' is described as 'twice sacristan of the Augusti according to the decrees of the Senate and sacristan of Artemis.'[24]

One other special coincidence deserves notice. The recorder, desirous of pacifying the tumult, appeals to the recognized forms of law. 'If Demetrius and his fellow-craftsmen,' he says, 'have a matter against any one, assizes are held, and there are proconsuls.'[25] 'Let them indict one another. But if you

---

[19]*Inscr.* vi.1 p. 14.

[20]Boeckh, *Corp. Inscr.* 2972.

[21]Eckhel, *Doctr. Num.* ii. p. 520. The legend is ΕΦΕΣΙΩΝ.ΤΡΙΣ.ΝΕΩΚΟΡΩΝ.ΚΑΙ.ΤΗΕ.ΑΡΤΕΜΙΔΟΣ.

[22]Mionnet, iii. p. 153, *Suppl.* vi. pp. 245, 247, 250, 253.

[23]Xenephon, *Anab.* v.3, 6.

[24]*Inscr.* vi.6 p. 50.

[25]Acts 19:38: ἀγόραιοι ἄγονται καὶ ἀνθύπατοί εἰσιν, translated 'the law is open, and there are deputies' in the Authorized Version, but the margin, 'the court days are kept,' gives the right sense of the first clause. In the second clause 'proconsuls' is a rhetorical plural just as e.g. in Euripides

have any further question (i.e. one which does not fall within the province of the courts of justice), it shall be settled in the lawful (regular) assembly.' By a 'lawful (regular) assembly' (ἔννομος ἐκκλησία) he means one of those that were held on stated days already predetermined by the law, as opposed to those that were called together on special emergencies out of the ordinary course, though in another sense these latter might be equally 'lawful.' An inscription found in this very theatre in which the words were uttered, illustrates this technical sense of 'lawful.' It provides that a certain silver image of Athene shall be brought and 'set at every lawful (regular) assembly (κατὰ πᾶσαν νόμιμον ἐκκλησίαν) above the bench where the boys sit.'[26]

With these facts in view, we are justified in saying that ancient literature has preserved no picture of Ephesus of imperial times—the Ephesus which has been unearthed by the sagacity and perseverance of Mr. Wood—comparable for its life-like truthfulness to the narrative of St. Paul's sojourn there in the Acts.

I am tempted to add one other illustration of an ancient Christian writer, which these inscriptions furnish. Ignatius, writing to the Ephesians from Smyrna in the early years of the second century, borrows an image from the sacred pageant of some heathen deity, where the statues, sacred vessels, and other treasures, of the temple are borne in solemn procession. He tells his Christian readers that they all are marching in festive pomp along the Via Sacra—the way of love—which leads to God; they all are bearers of treasures committed to them—for they carry their God, their Christ, their shrine, their sacred things in their heart.[27] The image was not new. It is found in the Stoic writers. It underlies the surname Theophorus, the 'God-bearer,' which Ignatius himself adopts. But he had in his company several Ephesian delegates when he wrote; and the newly discovered inscriptions inform us that the practice that supplies the metaphor had received a fresh impulse at Ephesus shortly before this letter was written. The most important inscriptions in Mr. Wood's collection relate to a gift of numerous valuable statues, images, and other treasures to the temple of Artemis, by one C. Vibius Salu-

---

(*Iph. Taur.* 139). Orestes and Pylades are upbraided for 'stealing from the land its images and priestesses' . . . though there was only one image and one priestess.

[26]*Inscr.* vi.1 p. 38.

[27]Ignatius, *Eph.* 9.

taris with an endowment for their custody. In one of these (dated A.D. 104) it is ordained that the treasures so given shall be carried in solemn procession from the temple to the theatre and back 'at every meeting of the assembly, and at the gymnastic contests, and on any other days that may be directed by the Council and the People.' Orders are given respecting its route. It must pass through the length of the city, entering by the Magnesian Gate and leaving by the Coressian.[28]

---

[28]*Inscr.* vi. 1 p. 42.

Appendix C

St. Paul's History After the Close of the Acts[1]

THE CONCLUSION, AT WHICH WE HAVE ARRIVED in the last section, assumes St. Paul's release from his captivity at Rome.[2] We must suppose that he resumed his active missionary labors, and these were terminated by a second captivity ending in his martyrdom, of which the Second Epistle to Timothy sounds the knell. In the present section it will be my business *first*, to show that there are sufficient grounds independently for assuming this release, and *secondly*, considering this as established, to sketch out his movements by the help of the record in the Pastoral Epistles.

I. Of this release with the subsequent events, there is no intimation in the New Testament beyond the notices in the Pastoral Epistles that seem to demand it. In the memoir of St. Luke there is not the slightest intimation of the future. The Epistles of the First Roman Captivity hover between hope and fear, between anticipation of release and forebodings of condemnation.

---

[1]This lecture was originally published posthumously in a collection of biblical essays, which Baker reprinted in 1979 with a fresh introduction by Philip Edgecumbe Hughes, though now long out of print. We are happy to re-present this lecture here as a fitting conclusion to this volume's presentation of Lightfoot's direct discussion on Acts. (BW3)

[2]Lightfoot is referring to his previous lecture on the authenticity of the Pastoral Epistles, which suggested to him a setting considerably later than the Captivity Epistles—Philippians, Colossians, Ephesians, Philemon. Having concluded that these documents are from a later period in Paul's life, the inference he drew was that Paul must have been set free in around A.D. 62 or so. (BW3)

They contain nothing that leads directly to the result we are seeking.

One passage indeed has been adduced as conclusive against a subsequent visit of St. Paul to Ephesus; and as, by surrendering this visit, we should be surrendering all the advantages gained by the assumption of his release, and should be thrown back upon our difficulties with respect to the Pastoral Epistles, it is important to consider what is the value of this argument. St. Paul in his farewell address to the Ephesian Elders on the eve of the First Captivity says (Acts 20:25), 'and now, behold, I know that ye all, among whom I have gone preaching the kingdom of God, shall see my face no more.' This is supposed to be inconsistent with a later visit to Ephesus and *pro tanto* with his release from captivity. But in no other province of history would it be allowable to convert a presentiment, however strongly expressed, into a fact; and as this is purely a personal matter, inspiration does not enter into the question. A presumption might indeed have been founded on this expression, if no intimation existed of a release; but the notices in the Pastoral Epistles to the contrary are in themselves more than sufficient to set this presumption aside. Then again, in what infinite difficulties does this supposition involve us! To the Romans he says 'I will pass by you into Spain' (Rom 15:28). This however, it may be said, was before the conviction (or the revelation) declared to the Ephesian Elders had seized him. What are we to say of the expressions scattered through the Epistles of the First Captivity? Why does he waver between hope and fear, if the fatal result was certain? Why does he entreat prayers of his converts for his release, if he knew that release to be absolutely impossible?

Writing to the Philippians he says that he trusts in the Lord, that he himself also will come shortly (Phil 2:24). Nay, he even affirms positively that he will be released. 'Having this confidence,' he says, 'I know (τοῦτο πεποιθὼς οἶδα) that I shall abide and continue with you all (Phil 1:25)'. Why is the οἶδα to be regarded as decisive in the one case, and disregarded in the other? But it may be urged that the supposed revelation did not negate his release *in toto*, that it is limited, that it referred only to his revisiting these Churches of Asia Minor. To this too St. Paul's own language furnishes a reply. He bids Philemon 'prepare him a lodging' at Colossae, he 'trusts through their prayers he shall be given unto them' (Philemon 22)—language which he could not have held, if he had had a revelation to the contrary. And if here again it be urged that he might have gone to Colossae without revisiting the neighboring Church of Ephesus, to this we should reply, *firstly*, that when the inference from οἶδα is paired down to these dimensions, we have obtained such a concession as will explain the notices in the Pastoral Epistles, for, though a visit to Ephesus is much more probable, a visit to the neighborhood would suffice; and *secondly*, that it will be felt that so limited an inference is meaningless, and of course valueless to those who refuse to allow the release of St. Paul.

But though the New Testament, with single exception of the Pastoral Epistles, is silent about this release, it is most satisfactorily established from external tradition.

1) CLEMENT OF ROME [died c. A.D. 96], a contemporary of the Apostles, after mentioning several incidents in St. Paul's life, and saying that he had preached in the East and the West, adds that he was 'a teacher of righteousness unto the whole world' and before his decease 'reached the furthest bounds of the West and bore testimony before the ruling powers' (ἐπὶ τὸ τέρμα τῆς δύσεως ἐλθὼν καὶ μαρτυρήσας ἐπὶ τῶν ἡγουμένων). Considering that Clement was writing from Rome, and bearing in mind the common significance of the expression 'the extreme West'[3] at the time, as referring to the Pillars of Hercules,[4] we can scarcely be wrong in concluding that St. Paul was released from captivity and fulfilled his purpose, expressed years before, of visiting Spain.[5]

---

[3]For the expression, referring to the western extremity of Spain, the pillars of Hercules, comp. Strabo ii.1 (p. 67) . . . ii.4 (p. 106) . . . iii.1 (p. 137) . . . iii.5 (pp. 169-70) . . . and see Strabo's whole account of the western boundaries of the world and of this coast of Spain. Similarly *Veil. Patere* 1.2, 'In ultimo Hispaniae tractu, in extreme nostril orbis termino.'

[4]It is instructive to mention some interpretations by which the force of these words has been evaded: 1) 'to his extreme limit towards the west' (Baur, *Paulus der Apost.* p. 230, Schenkel, *Studien und Kriitken*, p. 71, Otto, *Pastoralbr.*), 2) 'the sunset of his labors' (Reuss, *Gesch. Des N.T. Schrift*, p. 124) explained metaphorically, 3) 'to the boundary between the East and the West' (Hilgenfeld, *Ap. Vot.* p. 109, Schrader, *Paulus*) 4) 'to the goal or centre of the west' (Matthies *Pastoralbr.*), 5) 'before (ὑπὸ for ἐπὶ) the supreme power of the west' (Wieseler *Chron. Der ap. Zeitalt.* p. 533 followed by Schaff, *History of Apostl. Ch.*, I p. 400). Such attempts are a strong testimony to the plain inference that follows from the passage simply interpreted. Had the expression been ἐπὶ τὰ τέρματα τοῦ κόσμου, it might be explained (as Meyer proposes) as a rhetorical exaggeration, but not as it stands. [See the notes on the passage in Lightfoot, *Apostolic Fathers Pt. 1*, Vol. II p. 30 ed. 2, from which the above are expanded.]

[5]It has been urged (e.g. by Davidson *Introd.* II p. 101 ed. 1), that Clement cannot have meant this, because in that case Eusebius (*H.E.* iii.4) would certainly have adduced the passage which he does not. To this the reply is twofold: 1) that all arguments drawn from silence of a writer are in

It might be urged indeed that Clement has here the passage in the Epistle to the Romans in his mind, and that he assumes the intention was carried out. But seeing that at least one of the facts mentioned in the context—the Apostle's seven captivities (ἑπτάκις δεσμὰ φορέσας)—is not recorded in the New Testament, he must be deriving his information from independent sources, as indeed, living in Rome and having perhaps known the Apostle personally, he was very competent to do. And it may be argued further that this fact obliges us to prolong the Apostle's labors beyond the captivity with which the Acts closes.

2) Two generations later (c. A.D. 180), the anonymous writer of the MURATORIAN CANON gives the following account of the Acts of the Apostles. 'Luke comprises in detail in his treatise addressed to the most excellent Theophilus the incidents in the lives of the Apostles of which he was an eyewitness. As he does not mention either the martyrdom of Peter, or the journey of Paul to Spain, it is clear that these took place in his absence.'[6]

3) EUSEBIUS speaks of St. Paul's release and second visit to Rome, which ended in his martyrdom, as a common report (λόγος ἔχει).[7] It is true he goes on to confirm this report by a false interpretation of 2 Tim 4:16, explaining the two apologies there mentioned of the Apostle's two captivities; but the worthlessness of his own comment does not affect the value of the tradition on which it is founded, and which must be held quite distinct.[8]

4) In his Epistle to Dracontius ATHANASIUS holds up for imitation the earnestness of the Apostle to the Gentiles whose zeal prompted him 'to preach as far as Illyricum, and not to hesitate to go even to Rome, nor to

---

the highest degree precarious; and 2) that we are quite as competent to judge what Clement meant as Eusebius was.

[6]'Lucas obtime Theofile (l. optimo Theophilo) comprindit, quia (l. quae) sub presentia wius singular gerebantur sicuti et semote passsionem Petri evidenter declarat, sed et profecrionem Pauli ab urbe ad Spaniam proficiscentis' *Frag. Murat.* (pp. 19, 40 ed. Tregelles Oxon. 1867; Westcott, *Hist. of Canon*, pp. 517, 528 ed. 4). The drift of the latter part of the sentence seems to have been generally misunderstood. I take 'semote' to be opposed to 'sub praesentis eius' in the sense 'at a distance' 'in his absence.' Other solutions, either in the way of interpretation or of correction of the text, may be found in Routh, *R.S.* p. 394, Bensen, *Anal. Antenic.* I, p. 125, Westcott, p. 528, Credner, *Kanon*, p. 141 (ed. 1860), and Wieseler, *Chron.* p. 536.

[7]Eusebius, *H.E.* ii.22.

[8]Meyer's inference (on Romans *Einl.* 1 p. 15) from Origen's silence that he was ignorant of this release is quite arbitrary. At least it did not strike Eusebius so, who quotes Origen . . . *H.E.* iii.1 [approvingly].

take ship for Spain, so that the more he labored the greater the reward he might receive for his labor.'[9]

5) CYRIL OF JERUSALEM in his second catechetical lecture upon the Holy Spirit, adduces as a witness of the power of the Spirit St. Paul's conversion, and his missionary labors, which he names in the following significant order, Jerusalem, Illyricum, Rome, Spain.[10]

6) EPIPHANIUS in the account which he gives of the succession of the episcopate at Rome, explains his theory of the appointment of Linus, Cletus, and Clement as bishops in the lifetime of Apostles Peter and Paul by the frequent journeys which the Apostles had to take from Rome, and the impossibility of leaving the city without a bishop. 'For Paul,' he says, 'even went as far away as Spain, and Peter was frequently superintending Pontus and Bithynia.'[11]

7) JEROME appeals to the testimony of older writers in support of his statement of St. Paul's release from his first imprisonment, which was arranged in God's providence 'that so he might preach the gospel of Christ in the West also.'[12]

8) THEODORE OF MOPSUESTIA speaks in the plainest way of St. Paul's two visits to Rome in the reign of Nero. After relating how he was sent as a prisoner there on his appeal from Festus, he goes on to say that he was 'set free by the judgment of Nero and ordered to depart in safety. But after stopping two years at Rome, he departed thence and appears to have preached to many the teaching of godliness. However coming a second time to Rome, while still stopping there, it happened that by the sentence of Nero he was punished with death for his preaching of godliness.'[13]

9) When we come down to the time of PELAGIUS, we find the release from the first imprisonment generally maintained. Commenting on the Apostle's request to Philemon 'to prepare him a lodging,' he says, 'Here it is shown that on the first occasion he was sent away from the city,' though of the journey to Spain he speaks more doubtfully.[14]

---

[9]Athanasius, *Ep. Ad Dracont.* 4, I. p. 265 ed. Bened.

[10]Cyril, *Hier. Catech.* xvii pp. 276-7.

[11]Epiphan. *Haer.* xxvii, p. 107 ed. Pet.

[12]Hieron. *De Eccles. Script 5,* Vol II p. 823 ed. Vallarsi . . . cf. *Comm. in Amos* v.8, 9 Vol. vi. p. 291.

[13]Theod. Mops. *Argum. in Eph.* I, p. 116 ed. Swete.

[14]Pelagius *Comm. in Philemon,* v. 22; in *Rom.* 15.24 'utrum in Hispania fuerit incertum habetur.'

10) THEODORET, commenting on the Apostle's expression of confidence addressed to his Philippian converts that he would abide and continue with them, remarks: 'and the prediction was fulfilled; For at first he escaped the wrath of Nero.' Then, after quoting the passage in 2 Tim 4:16-17, and appealing to the last verses in Acts, he continues: 'Thence (i.e. from Rome) he departed to Spain, and carried the divine gospel to the inhabitants of that part also, and so he returned and was then beheaded.'[15] Other references to his release and visit to Spain are given below.

On the statements of Eusebius and later writers however no stress should be laid. Even if it were clear that they relied on some independent testimony, and did not found their belief on deductions—in some case erroneous deductions—from St. Paul's own language, they are too far removed from the time of the events to be of any real value as guides. With Clement and the author of the Muratorian fragment the case is different. The former wrote from Rome, at a place where and at a time when the memory of the Apostle's labors was fresh, and his testimony is explicit, so far as it relates to St. Paul preaching in the West. The latter, though living at a later period, is a witness of some importance, for he too was probably a Roman,[16] and he distinctly attests the journey to Spain. Indeed, so irresistible has this evidence appeared to impartial critics, that the release has been accepted as a fact by many writers who cannot be suspected of a bias towards this result—by Hug, for instance, who places the Pastoral Epistles earlier in St. Paul's life, and by Ewald, who denies their genuineness entirely.

But it has been urged that, though there is evidence for the journey to Spain after the Apostle's release, there is none for another visit to the East. This is true, if the notices in the Pastorals themselves are not to be put in evidence; but even then, how does the case stand? St. Paul, while still a prisoner but anticipating his release, expresses his intention of visiting the Philippians again, and writes to Philemon at Colossae to prepare him a lodging. He does obtain his release. In the absence of evidence either way, is it not more probable that he did fulfill his intention of visiting Macedonia and Asia than the contrary?

---

[15]Theodoret *Comm. in Phil.* i.25 vol. iii. p. 451 ed. Schulze, in Ps 116, Vol. I p. 1425, in 2 Tim 4:17.

[16]His use of the phrase 'ab urbe' referring to Rome, shows this.

II. Assuming then that St. Paul was released from his first captivity at Rome and resumed his missionary labors, we shall have to sketch in the events which took place between this date and his final imprisonment, from the notices in the Pastoral Epistles, aided by such probabilities as circumstances suggest. If an intelligible and reasonable account of St. Paul's doings during this interval can thus be given, we shall have found a possible place for the Pastoral Epistles, and shall have furnished an answer to objections raised from the point of view of historical unaccountability; and in the absence of full and direct information, nothing more than this hypothetical solution can be expected.

Before entering into details, however, we must clear the way by settling two main questions; *first*, what was the probable length of this interval; and *secondly*, supposing that St. Paul visited both East and West, in what order did he make these journeys.

1) According to the chronology I have adopted, St. Paul arrived in Rome early in the year 61. The closing verses of the Acts speak of his remaining there without any change in the circumstances of his captivity for two whole years (Acts 28:30-31). This brings us to the beginning of the year 63 at least. Here St. Luke's narrative ends abruptly, so that we are without information as to what occurred afterwards, but the natural inference is that at the end of the two years there was a change in the prisoner's condition—a change either for the better or for the worse, but a change of some sort. Perhaps the most probable supposition is that his trial came on then. If so, we may place his release not later than the summer of 63, at all events it must have taken place between that date and the summer of the following year, for the great fire which broke out in July 64 was a signal for a fierce persecution of the Christians in Rome, and a teacher of the hated religion so zealous and so distinguished could not have escaped the general fate, had he still remained a prisoner.

The data for determining the close of the period are still more vague. Ecclesiastical tradition fixes the martyrdom of St. Paul in Nero's reign, and this is probable in itself, for, after the tyrant's death, the Romans were too much occupied with their own political troubles to pay any attention to the Christians, even supposing the succeeding emperors were animated by the same bitter spirit. It cannot therefore have been later than June 68, the date of Nero's death. Now, when we examine the Pastoral Epistles with a view to obtaining some result, opposing considerations present themselves. On the one hand, their marked difference in style leads us to prolong the interval between them and the earlier Epistles so far as possible, while on the other hand the mention of Timothy's youth is an ever-increasing difficulty as we postpone the date the letters addressed to him. On the whole, perhaps, the latter consideration must give place to the former. The death of the Apostle will then be placed at the very close of Nero's reign, and the Pastoral Epistles will have been written in the year 67 or 68.

Next as to order in which St. Paul visited the East and the West. On the whole, it is probable that he went eastward immediately after his release. It is true that he had intended when he first thought of visiting Rome, to proceed thence westward to Spain (Rom 15:24, 28). But circumstances might have occurred in the intervening period of about five years to alter his purpose and determine him to revisit the troubled Churches of Asia, before he entered on a new mission field in the far West. Such is the impression left by his language to the Philippians and to Philemon.[17]

But if it is probable that St. Paul was in the East immediately after his release, it is certain that he was there towards the close of his life. The notices of his transactions in the East scattered through the Pastoral Epistles reach continuously to the time of his second imprisonment at Rome, which ended in his death. If this be so the visit to Spain and the West must have intervened between the two visits to the East. For these incidents there is ample time in the four or five years which elapsed before his martyrdom.

We obtain then: 1) A visit to the East, probably brief, according with his intention expressed to the Philippians and to Philemon. 2) The fulfillment of his long-cherished purpose of preaching in Spain and the West; 3) A return to the East. Eastward then the Apostle hastens after his release. First of all perhaps he revisited the Macedonian Churches, fulfilling his promise

---

[17]Phil 1:24; Philemon 22. This conclusion however must not be regarded as absolultely certain. It may be that we should not press the ταχέως of Phil 2:24. And the injunction to Philemon to prepare him a lodging may point rather to the certainty than to the nearness of the visit. It is as if the Apostle had said 'You may certainly expect to see me. I shall myself observe what treatment Onesimus has received from you.' With delicate tact, the Apostle's language, suggested by some slight misgiving, assumes the form of an appeal to Philemon's hospitality and kindly feeling towards himself.

to the Philippians. We may imagine him next directing his steps towards the Churches of Asia and Phrygia. The unhealthy tone of religious speculation in these districts needed correction. And to Colossae moreover he was drawn by a personal motive. He was anxious to assure himself that Ones-imus was fully restored to his master's favor, and to carry out his under-taking of staying with Philemon. We can scarcely suppose that he left these regions without a brief visit to the Church of Ephesus, which had occupied so much of his time and thoughts; and it is possible that some of the notices in the Pastoral Epistles refer to incidents which occurred on this occasion, though it is on the whole more probable that they took place on a later visit.

We may conjecture also that, before he left the neighborhood of the Aegean he laid the first foundation of a Church in Crete. There was in this island a large Jewish population[18]—a circumstance that would press itself on the Apostle's attention. Possibly also St. Paul's anchorage there (Acts 27:7-12 esp. v. 9 Ἱκανοῦ δὲ χρόνου διαγενομένου) on his voyage to Rome may have been accompanied by incidents which dwelt on his mind, and stimu-lated his desire to preach the Gospel in Crete. At all events a few years later we find a Christian Church established here, and, if its foundation is to be attributed to St. Paul, no occasion is more probable than this of his first visit to the East after his release.

2) Having thus taken a rapid review of Churches of the East, the Apostle hastened to fulfill his long-postponed intention of visiting the hitherto un-explored region of Spain. There was a considerable Jewish population settled in many of the towns on the Spanish coast[19] and the Apostle would make this his starting-point. This course had many advantages in itself, but a deeper principle of obligation commended it to the mind of the Apostle, who seems to have held sacred the maxim 'to the Jew first, and then to the Gentile.' Whether St. Paul extended his labors in the West beyond the limits of Spain must remain a matter of speculation. At the close of his life we find him sending Crescens on a mission to Gaul—for so we may perhaps under-stand by 'Galatia,'[20] and if this interpretation is correct, it would seem to

---

[18]Philo, *Leg. Ad. Gaium* ii p. 587 (ed. Mangey).

[19]See Remond, *Ausbrietung des Judenthums*, no. 31.

[20]2 Tim 4:10; see Lightfoot, *Galatians*, pp. 3, 31. On Crescens see esp. Gerarius, *Mogunt. Resp.* p. 225 and on the early Church in Gaul, Neander, *Ch. Hist.* I p. 116 (Eng. trans. by Torrey).

imply some previous communication with this region. It is highly probable indeed that either on his way to or from Rome, he should have visited the famous port of Marseilles,[21] and having once set foot in Gaul, he would naturally avail himself of the opportunity of furthering his Master's cause. At all events, the Churches of Spain and Gaul were founded at a very early date, so that Irenaeus appeals to them[22] along with others, as witnesses of the primitive tradition in matters of doctrine. On the other hand, had he remained long either in Spain or Gaul, we should have expected to find in those parts a more direct tradition of his visit.[23]

3) Moving eastward, perhaps passing through Rome, the Apostle may possibly have visited Dalmatia, for with this region again we find him in communication at the close of his life (2 Tim 4:10). If so, he may have continued his journey along the Adriatic coast to Epirus, so that, by wintering at Nicopolis on a subsequent occasion (Tit 3:12), he purposed renewing an intimacy already formed, thus following out his general practice of confirming the Churches of his founding.

We find the Apostle then in the East once more. The slight fragmentary notices in the Pastoral Epistles may be pieced together variously, so that any particular plan of his journey must be more or less arbitrary. The object of framing such a plan is to show that it is possible to give a consistent and intelligible account of his movements, on the supposition of his release; and under the circumstances no more than this can reasonably be demanded. The scheme which I shall give differs from those generally adopted in assuming that the winter which he purposed spending in Nicopolis was in fact spent in Rome.[24] We may suppose that his abrupt arrest and imprisonment frustrated his previous plans. In this way the events are gathered within narrower limits of time; and, the Pastoral Epistles being thus brought into closer chronological connection, the striking coincidences of thought and language between them are the more easily explained. This arrangement of the incidents seems to me slightly more probable than any other, but I lay no stress on it.

---

[21]See the interesting speculations of Blunt, *The First Three Centuries*, p. 184sq. (1861).

[22]Irenaeus, *Haer.* i.10.2.

[23]The journey to Britain must be abandoned as highly improbable, though maintained with a patriotic urgency by many able advocates (Stillingfleet, Burgess, etc.); see the references in Soames, *Anglo-Saxon Church*, p. 21 sq. (1844).

[24]Thus the winter of Titus 3:12 becomes identical with that of 2 Tim 4:21.

Once in the East, then, he would naturally revisit the Churches of Phrygia and Asia, which had caused him so much anxiety. There he found that his gloomiest anticipations had been realized. Grievous wolves had indeed entered the fold, as he had predicted years before. His personal influence had gone. 'All in Asia turned away from him' (2 Tim 1:15 sq.). Phygellus and Hermogenes are especially named among these timid or recreant Christians. There was one bright exception however in Onesiphorus whose attentions—repeated afterwards when the Apostle was prisoner in Rome—are gratefully recorded (2 Tim 1:15-17; cf. 2 Tim 4:19). It was probably at Ephesus too and on this occasion that St. Paul encountered the opposition of Alexander the coppersmith (2 Tim 4:14). And this is perhaps the same Alexander whom, together with Hymenaeus, the Apostle 'delivered unto Satan, that they might learn not to blaspheme' (1 Tim 1:20). If we are right in assigning all these notices to this one occasion, it would seem that the Apostle's residence was more or less prolonged. Altogether the visit was one of bitter trial. It was evident that the clouds were gathering about the Church, and that a period of storm and tempest was imminent.

From Ephesus the Apostle turned northward into Macedonia. At the same time he left Timothy behind to preside over the Church there in his absence (1 Tim 1:3). He would gladly seek consolation after these sad experiences in the affection of that Philippian Church, of which he entertained the most tender remembrance, and which more than once had relieved his wants.

What country St. Paul visited next, we cannot say; it is not unnatural to suppose that following his old route, he would turn towards the Churches of Achaia. Somewhere about this time we may perhaps place the writing of the *First Epistle to Timothy*. Its exact time and place cannot be ascertained, but the following data should be observed: 1) It cannot have been written very long after St. Paul left Ephesus, as the whole tenor of the Epistle shows. It betrays a nervous anxiety such as might be expected from one who had recently delegated a very arduous task to a young and inexperienced successor. Such advice to have any value must be given at once, and indeed the Apostle's ardent temperament would admit of no delay in a matter so important; 2) It would seem to have been written before the incidents occurred which St. Paul relates to Timothy in the Second Epistle (e.g 2 Tim 4:9-13, 20).

When the letter was written, St. Paul hoped to revisit Ephesus soon, but foresaw that he might possibly meet with some delays (1 Tim 3:15).

About this time he also visited Crete. A hypothetical account of the origin of this Church I have already given (see above). Having been recently founded, its organization was still very imperfect; and, as St. Paul himself could not stay to do all that was needful, he left Titus behind him to complete his arrangements there (Tit 1:5).

From Crete we may suppose that he went to Asia Minor, and somewhere about this time he directed a letter of advice and exhortation to Titus. For ascertaining the time of writing of the *Epistle to Titus* we have the following data: 1) As in the case of the First Epistle to Timothy, it cannot have been written long after St. Paul left Crete; 2) Tychicus was still with him when he wrote; and therefore it is before the point of the time noted in 2 Tim 4:12; 3) He has no forebodings of his coming fate for he purposes wintering at Nicopolis, not expecting to have his movement constrained (Tit 3:12); 4) On the supposition that this winter is identical with that mentioned in his Second Epistle, the year cannot have been far advanced now. There is time for him to dispatch a messenger to Titus, for Titus to join him (at Corinth or Nicopolis) and to leave him again for Dalmatia, for him to reach Rome himself, for several incidents at Rome, e.g. his trial etc. for him to dispatch a messenger from Rome to Timothy, for Timothy to join him in Rome; all this before the winter.

In this letter he tells Titus that he will send Artemas or Tychicus—perhaps to act as his deputy—and bids him hasten to join him at Nicopolis. He asks him to provide Zenas the lawyer and Apollos with the necessaries for their journey (Tit 3:12-13).

From this point onwards we can trace the Apostle's course westward with some degree of continuity, for the journey is the reverse of that in Acts 20:13 sq. We find him at Miletus, where he dropped Trophimus on account of illness (2 Tim 4:20). Hence, perhaps he dispatched Tychicus to Ephesus.[25] Miletus was a convenient point from which to communicate with Ephesus as he had found it on a former occasion (Acts 20:17), and we may conjecture that, having abandoned his purpose of revisiting Ephesus, he sent Tychichus

---

[25]2 Tim 4:12. Tychicus and Trophimus were Άσιανοί cf. Acts 20:4; 21:29.

to Timothy to inform him of this (1 Tim 3:14). From Miletus he sails northward to Troas, where he lodges with Carpus (2 Tim 4:13). What were the intermediate stages, we do not know, but we next find him at Corinth, where he leaves Erastus behind (2 Tim 4:20). He was now on his way to Nicopolis—probably the city of that name in Epirus, where he purposed passing the winter. Whether he reached Nicopolis or not must remain uncertain. A probable, though a conjectural, account seems to me this. While he was at Corinth, his old enemies, the Jews, informed against him, as the leader of the hated sect of malefactors, who had roused the indignation of Rome; and on this information he was seized and imprisoned and ultimately carried to the Metropolis to await his trial.[26]

Meanwhile, finding his plan of wintering at Nicopolis frustrated, he dispatches his messenger—probably Artemas (Tit 3:12), since he had left Tychicus behind (2 Tim 4:12)—to Titus in Crete to join him, not in Nicopolis, as he had intended, but either in Corinth or in Rome itself, whither he was soon to be conveyed. At all events Titus did join him at some point in his route (2 Tim 4:10).

Arrived at Rome, the Apostle found himself almost deserted. Onesiphorus, who lived in Ephesus (2 Tim 4:19), and whose kind services the Apostle had experienced during his stay there, coming to Rome sought him out and with some difficulty found him (2 Tim 1:17). But these friendly offices ceased with the departure of Onesiphorus. Of all his more intimate friends and companions in travel Luke alone remained with him (2 Tim 4:9 sq.). Titus had gone to Dalmatia, Crescens to Gaul, probably dispatched thither by the Apostle on some missionary errand. Demas had forsaken him, and gone to Thessalonica, probably his native place. Certain Christians of Rome, Eubulus, Pudens, Linus, and Claudia, join in the salutation, but these must have been comparative strangers.[27] In this forlorn condition he writes his *Second Epistle to Timothy.* He urges Timothy to join him as soon as possible (2 Tim 4:9), at all events to come before the winter sets in and while the sea is yet navigable (2 Tim 4:21). At the same time he charges

---

[26]We know that Nero was in Greece at this time and that he was still there in August 67, though he was recalled to Rome towards the close of the year by Helius (see Clinton, *Fasti Romani* I. p. 50). Perhaps the Emperor himself sent the Apostle to the capital.

[27]On the supposed connection of Pudens and Claudia with Britain see Lightfoot, *Apostolic Fathers* Pt. I; *Clement of Rome,* I. p. 76 (1890).

him to perform a commission at Troas; he had left his cloak with some books and parchments, and he requests Timothy, as he passes, to fetch these (2 Tim 4:13). He evidently contemplates that Timothy will follow the coast to Macedonia, and then take the great Egnatian Road from Philippi to Dyrrachium and cross over the straits thence to Italy. It was perhaps already late in the season and a voyage on the high seas was hazardous. Timothy is to pick up Mark on the way and bring him with him (2 Tim 4:11). Timothy appears to be still at Ephesus, for the Apostle in this letter salutes the household of Onesiphorus, doubtless resident there.[28] He also salutes Aquila and Priscilla (2 Tim 4:19), and they too seem to have had connection with Ephesus (1 Cor 16:19).

The legal proceedings have already commenced when the Apostle writes. He had had his first hearing, and has a respite for a time (2 Tim 4:16). But he is full of gloomy forebodings, or rather he foresees but one termination to the trial. And here, with the notes of his dying strain ringing in our ears, we take leave of the great Apostle.[29]

---

[28] 2 Tim 4:19; 1:16. Onesiphorus himself seems to be absent (2 Tim 1:17).

[29] The essay ends with a note that it was written in 1862, that is, in the midst of his commentary-writing period in Cambridge. (BW3)

Appendix D

THE OBITUARY/HOMAGE
TO LIGHTFOOT

PREFATORY NOTE[1]

ALL the friends of Bishop Lightfoot must be grateful to Mr. Murray for allowing the striking sketch of the Bishop's character and work which appeared in the *Quarterly Review* in January, 1893, to be republished separately. Though the writer has not thought fit to reveal himself, it is clear that he had exceptional advantages for fulfilling the task that he undertook; and the description of the life in Durham shows throughout personal and intimate knowledge. Though my own intercourse with the Bishop during this period was necessarily less close and continuous than during earlier years, I recognise the student, the colleague, the friend whom I knew at Cambridge in every trait, but presented, so to speak, on a larger scale; and I can well believe that while Dr. Lightfoot loved his College and his University with perfect devotion, the busy episcopate, full of great designs and great achievements, was his happiest time. Cambridge, as I often said to him, seemed to be forgotten, and wisely for-

---

[1]This piece first appeared in the *Contemporary Review* in 1893, and was reprinted in 1894 with a new preface by B. F. Wescott and some emendations from certain others. Long out of print, it can now be found at the Project Canterbury website (http://anglicanhistory.org/lightfoot/west cott1894/). Westcott is B. F. Dunelm, the regular abbreviation for a Durham man, just as Lightfoot's was J. B. Dunelm. As to who actually wrote this long tribute, it seems likely to have been either Harmer or Hort. (BW3)

gotten, in the new interests of Durham; and even I, who was the chief loser, felt that I could rejoice in a greater gain.

In Bishop Lightfoot's case the works were the man. What he did was a true expression of himself; and if I may venture to speak from my experience during the last three years, I believe that his greatest work was the brotherhood of clergy whom he called to labour with him in the Diocese, and bear his spirit to another generation—greater than his masterpieces of interpretation and criticism, greater than his masterpieces of masculine and yet passionate eloquence. I could wish indeed that there was some adequate record of his part in University affairs. When I returned to Cambridge in 1870 I found him possessed of commanding influence, trusted and revered alike by all. But from that time he withdrew more and more from public business, though his authority was never found to be less when he was pleased to use it. If he could persuade another to take up what he had prepared, that seemed to be his chief delight.

I have often spoken of the circumstances that attended my own recall to Cambridge; and perhaps I may repeat the story here, for I think that it reveals the man. As soon as it was known that the Regius Professorship of Divinity would shortly become vacant, he bade me lose no time in arranging for my candidature. I naturally replied that the office was his by right: that his past work led up to it by universal consent: that I might then aspire to be his successor as Hulsean Professor. He acknowledged the force of what I said, 'But,' he added, 'I could not retain my fellowship with it, and that consideration is decisive: I must not give up my place on the Governing Body of the College.' I could not resist the argument, so in due time I was appointed. About three months after Dr. Lightfoot came to my rooms and put in my hands a very remarkable letter from Mr. Gladstone containing the offer of the Canonry at St. Paul's. 'What could be better,' I said, 'if it were possible? But, unhappily you cannot hold your fellowship with it.' 'Ah,' he replied, and I can see now his merry smile at my discomfiture, 'I have done all I can for the College.'

Bishop Lightfoot's works, I have said, show what he was, and this sketch seems to me to add just those touches of life that give to his writings a personal interest. It tells a stranger how he grew and moved among his fellows and won them, and, from a stranger, makes him also in some sense a friend.

B. F. DUNELM,
AUCKLAND CASTLE,
October 11, 1893

Joseph Barber Lightfoot was the younger son of Mr. John Jackson Lightfoot, a Liverpool accountant, and was born at his father's house, 84 Duke Street, in that city, on April 13th, 1828. His mother was a sister of Mr. Joseph Vincent Barber, a Birmingham artist of considerable repute, who had married the only daughter of Zaccheus Walker, eldest son of the 'wonderful' Walker of Seathwaite, who is immortalised in Wordsworth's *Excursion*. Of the three other children an elder brother became a good Cambridge scholar, and was for many years Master of the Grammar School at Basingstoke. The younger brother was indebted to him for many acts of kindness that removed difficulties from his early course. One sister was married to the Rev. William Harrison, of Pontesbury, and left an only son, who is a curate in the Diocese of Durham. The other survives, and is the only Lightfoot of this branch now remaining. It has been not unnatural to seek to establish a connexion between this family and that of Dr. John Lightfoot, the seventeenth-century theologian and Hebraist, but there is, we believe, no true ground for doing so.

The young 'Joe,' as he was familiarly called at home and at school, was a delicate lad, and was privately educated until he was about thirteen. His first year of school life was under the care of Dr. Iliff, at the Royal Institution in Liverpool, which claims also among its distinguished pupils Dr. Sylvester the mathematician and the present Bishop of Ripon. He soon found his way to the 'First Class,' which consisted of boys far beyond his own years, and among the more or less legendary stories that have gathered around the early boyhood—such as 'How is Joe getting on with his German?' 'Oh! he has finished German! He is now doing Anglo-Saxon.'[2] The boy's health gave way, and under medical advice the anxious and now widowed mother had all books removed from his room. The little patient grew rapidly worse,

---

[2]*Contemporary Review*, Feb. 1890, p. 174.

and pleaded so earnestly for his books that the mother's heart could not refuse to grant them. They naturally proved the best tonic for the restless mind, and the lad grew rapidly better.

But the chief step in the boy's education was taken in 1844, when the mother, attracted by the advantages of the Birmingham Grammar School, determined to move to the neighbourhood of her relatives in that town. The picture of the great High Master, Dr. Prince Lee, afterwards first Bishop of Manchester, surrounded by his group of brilliant pupils, has often been drawn, and we must look at it only in connexion with our immediate subject. The streams of influence which have flowed from this centre have, however, been so important in their effect upon our subject and upon the history of religious thought and action during the last and the present generations, that we must for a while place ourselves at the feet of this great teacher. 'Three boys,' it has been said, 'Prince Lee loved more than any one else in the world,' and of one of them of whom we are now writing, he is reported to have said, in the winter of 1869, a few days before his own death, 'I should like to live to lay my hands on Lightfoot's head once more.' Each of the three became a great teacher, and each has given a record of the way in which he was himself taught, which has all the strength of the experience of minds that have had not many equals either as learners or as teachers.[3]

Among the words in which the late Bishop of Durham has himself testified to the influence of Dr. Prince Lee are the following:

> I have sometimes thought that, if I were allowed to live one hour only of my past life over again, I would choose a Butler lesson under Lee. His rare eloquence was never more remarkable than during these lessons. I have heard many great speakers and preachers since, but I do not recollect anything comparable in its kind to his oratory, when, leaning back in his chair and folding his gown about him, he would break off at some idea suggested by the text, and pour forth an uninterrupted flood of eloquence for half an hour or more, the thought keeping pace with the expression all the while, and the whole marked by a sustained elevation of tone which entranced even the idlest and most careless among us. I suppose that it was this singular combination of intellectual vigour and devotional feeling which created his influence over the character of his pupils.

---

[3] Cf. 'Memorial Sermon on the Right Rev. James Prince Lee,' by Edward White Benson (1870).

Hesitation in all its forms was alien alike to his nature and to his principles. When I wrote to him, stating my intention of taking orders, but representing myself as undecided what branch of the ministry to follow out, he replied characteristically, 'beseeching' me 'to decide *at once*: *at once* to seek a curacy or a mastership,' if I looked to practical work in either line; '*at once* to begin to read and edit or write,' if I looked to theology; 'for' he added, '*Virtus in agendo constat*.'[4]

Such was the master who sent from a school small and undistinguished as compared with our present great public schools, five Senior Classics and eight Fellows of his own beloved Trinity in a period of nine years, and of whose thirteen First Classmen twelve became clergymen. Such were the powers which in master and in pupil moulded and throughout his life influenced the character and the work of Joseph Barber Lightfoot.

The Cambridge life commenced in October 1847, when Lightfoot went up to Trinity and was placed on Thompson's side. From the end of his first year he read with his old schoolfellow Westcott, who had preceded him to Trinity, and was Senior Classic in 1848. He obtained a Trinity scholarship in 1849, and though he is said to have been some way behind in the University scholarship examinations, his steady devotion to work and his great development of power placed him easily first in the Tripos, and men talked commonly of papers which had not been equalled and were absolutely free from mistake. In addition to being Senior Classic of his year (1851) he was thirtieth wrangler and first Chancellor's medallist. A Fellowship of Trinity came naturally in the following year, and the Norrisian Prize was gained in 1853. It was gained but not claimed, for with characteristic modesty he was dissatisfied with an essay which the examiners had decided to be first, and he never fulfilled the condition of publishing it. In 1854 the young Fellow was ordained by his old master, Dr. Prince Lee, who had now become Bishop of Manchester, at St. John's Church, Heaton Mersey. In February 1857, when only twenty-eight years of age, he became Tutor of the College. The impression left upon his pupils is told by such words as these, which some of them have furnished:

As a tutor, he was very shy, but gave assurance by his ways of readiness to help. One was certain of strong and kind assistance if one needed it.

---

[4]*Ibid. Memorial Notes*, pp. 40, 41.

Lightfoot never made any one ashamed of asking him questions.

He looked round at his pupils, longing for one of them to give him a chance of being kind to him, helping him out in an effort at conversation or advising him. But his temperament did not let him often take the initiative in seeking out and seizing hold of those who wanted help, restraint, or encouragement. He did not thrust his arms out to them, but stood with open arms for those who would come to him.

As a private tutor he had a singular power of inspiring us with a belief in the duty and the pleasure of hard work, not so much by his brilliance, but by letting us know that his great attainments had been won by sheer diligence. At the same time he was full of humour, and ready to join in any excursion; and he never lost sight of a pupil.

To have known him in those lighter moods [of reading parties] is a possession for a lifetime.[5]

During the early years of the Trinity Fellowship the four volumes of the *Journal of Classical and Sacred Philology* appeared (1854–9), and they contained frequent contributions from the pen of Mr. Lightfoot, who was one of the founders and editors. Now he writes a minute criticism of the editions of Hyperides;[6] now short notices of Schaff's *History of the Apostolic Church* and of Falkener's 'A Description of some important Theatres and other Remains in Crete';[7] now an article on 'The Mission of Titus to the Corinthians';[8] now notes on Müller's *Denkmäler der Alten Kunst* or Webster and Wilkinson's Greek Testament,[9] or the translations of the American Bible Union;[10] and in immediate contiguity with these last, a notice of Mr. Blew's *Agamemnon*.[11] To the third volume he contributes, two months before his election to the Tutorship, the remarkable article on 'Recent Editions of St. Paul's Epistles,'[12] a review of Paley's edition of *Aeschylus*,[13] and another article 'On the Style and Character of the Epistle to the Galatians.'[14] The fourth

---

[5]See *Cambridge Review*, Jan. 16th, 1890, p. 135.
[6]Vol. i. pp. 109–124.
[7]Vol. ii. pp. 119, 120.
[8]*Ibid.* pp. 194–205.
[9]*Ibid.* pp. 360 *seq.*
[10]*Ibid.* pp. 361–363.
[11]*Ibid.* 363, 364.
[12]Vol. iii. pp. 81–121, *cf. infra*, pp. 24 *seq.*
[13]*Ibid.* p. 238.
[14]*Ibid.* pp. 289–327.

volume contains articles from the same hand on 'They that are of Cæsar's household,'[15] 'On some corrupt and obscure passages in the Helena of Euripides,'[16] 'On the Long Walls at Athens,'[17] and a review of Conybeare and Howson's *Life and Epistles of St. Paul*.[18]

These exercises of the young giant in the first freshness of his full and free strength are in some respects of permanent value as contributions to their subjects; and they are of special interest both as a harvest of the seed sown by Dr. Prince Lee's teaching, and as themselves seeds to bear a more abundant harvest of developed fruitfulness in Dr. Lightfoot's later work. The un-wearied but concealed labour, the investigation of all available sources of information—inscriptions, MSS., topography—the minute acquaintance with the literature of the subjects, foreign as well as English, the exact schol-arship present everywhere and felt especially in emendations of texts, the firm grasp of the laws of language and the laws of mind, the wide outlook on the whole field, the very choice of the subjects, at once recall the schoolroom at Birmingham, and foreshadow the *magna opera* of the life. He is already entering on the field in which he is to gain such marked eminence. *Qualis fuerit antiquitatis investigator, evangelii interpret*—even these works do testify.

The ease with which the writer passes in these articles from one subject to another, from a review of commentaries on St. Paul's Epistles to an emen-dation of the text of Euripides, from an investigation of the meaning of 'Cæsar's household' to the position of the 'Long Walls at Athens,' represents the work of the Senior Classic and Private Tutor, who at the same time, in the spirit of his own early lessons, regards the New Testament as the goal of all his studies. These articles created so profound an impression in the Uni-versity that when a vacancy occurred in the Hulsean Professorship of Di-vinity in 1860, many of Mr. Lightfoot's friends earnestly hoped that he might be appointed to the Chair. He consented at their entreaty to become a can-didate, but he felt it was natural that one who, as he modestly said, had done much more for the interpretation of the New Testament than himself should

---

[15]Vol. iv. pp. 57–79.
[16]*Ibid.* pp. 153–186.
[17]*Ibid.* pp. 294–302.
[18]*Ibid.* pp. 107–109.

be selected. At the same time the decision seemed to him to bring with it another decision. The time had come for his studies to concentrate and shape themselves in a definite form. The Orestean trilogy of Aeschylus had fascinated him as it has fascinated many great minds. He resolved that night to edit it. Some progress was made in this work, when in 1861 the Hulsean Chair was again vacated, and Mr. Lightfoot was chosen to fill it.

We regard this selection as one of the turning-points not only in the history of the University of Cambridge, but also in the wider history of Christianity in this country, and from this country throughout the world. Few persons with competent knowledge will be disposed, we think, to challenge this opinion. If any are, we invite them to compare the attendance on the Divinity Professor's Lectures before and after this appointment; to consider the influence on Cambridge life and work of the movements initiated by the young Professor himself, developed later on in union with his friends Dr. Westcott (who returned to Cambridge in 1870) and Dr. Hort (who joined them in 1872),[19] and carried into their present state of progress by the band of younger men whom they gathered round themselves; to estimate the effect on English thought of the works enumerated at the head of this article, and of the band of men who have gone forth year by year touched by the spirit and power of the living man who wrote them; to think of this Cambridge movement having its true source in the constant appeal to the Biblical writings as the correlative of the Oxford movement of an earlier generation, and of its sobering effect upon the agitated state of theological thought.

'When he became a Professor at Cambridge,' writes one of Dr. Lightfoot's pupils, 'his greatness was immediately established. The immense range of his acquisitions, the earnest efforts to do his work as well as lay in his power, were at once recognized by the Undergraduates. The frequent failure of Professors to win an audience is a matter of common complaint, and men as learned in their own domain as Dr. Lightfoot have not succeeded. But there was something electric in his quick sympathy with the young, in his masculine independence in his strong practical good sense, in his matchless

---

[19]Since this article was in type, a sketch of Bishop Lighfoot's life from the pen of Dr. Hort, has appeared in the *Dictionary of National Biography*; and, alas! obituary notices of Dr. Hort himself have appeared in the current magazines.

lucidity of exposition; and these gifts caused his lecture-room to be thronged by eager listeners. The late Master of Trinity was not given to enthusiasm, but once he did wax enthusiastic, as he described to me the passage between the Senate House and Caius College "black with the fluttering gowns of students" hurrying to imbibe, in the Professor's class-room, a knowledge of the New Testament such as was not open to their less happy predecessors, and such as would last many of them all their lives as a fountain of valuable exegesis in many a parish and many a pulpit.'[20]

Among the subjects of the earlier courses of the Professor's lectures was the Gospel according to St. John, and he for some time thought of publishing an edition of this Gospel, an intention which he abandoned only when he found it was entertained by one whom he considered more competent to carry it into effect [i.e. Westcott].

But in the beginning of the year 1865, that is, within four years of his appointment to the Professorship, Dr. Lightfoot published his edition of *St. Paul's Epistle to the Galatians*. Eight years before he had intimated in the article on 'Recent Editions of St. Paul's Epistles,'[21] not only where previous editors had signally failed, both in design and in execution, but also where they had succeeded, and he thus incidentally discloses what in his own view an edition of St. Paul's Epistles should be.

When the man who had sketched this ideal of a Commentary, and had been afterwards appointed to the Hulsean Professorship, and had delivered courses of lectures which filled the lecture-rooms to overflowing, announced his intention to publish 'a complete edition of St. Paul's Epistles,' and issued the first instalment of the work, the attention of Biblical students was naturally aroused, and very high expectations were widely formed. We venture to think that no expectation was raised which has not been more than fully realized. The complete plan of the edition has not, indeed, been carried out. It was from the first stated conditionally,—'If my plan is ever carried out,'— and it was so arranged that each part should be complete in itself. We are glad to be able to hope, from hints which have from time to time reached the public ear, that a large portion of the whole field was covered by Dr. Lightfoot's labours, and that some of the MSS. which are in the care of his

---

[20]*Contemporary Review*, Feb. 1890, p. 175.
[21]*Journal of Philology, ut supra*, vol. iii, pp. 81-121.

literary executors will in due course be published; for even if they are only posthumous fragments, the student of St. Paul's Epistles will thankfully welcome them. But the editor's final preparation for the press was given to three volumes only,—the *Galatians*, which appeared in 1865, the *Philippians* in 1868, the *Colossians and Philemon* in 1875; and thus upon these volumes that any claim to have filled the ideal standard which he had himself set for the critic and commentator on St. Paul's Epistles must ultimately rest. The verdict has been given, after most thorough examination, by the most competent judges, and in the most definite form. As each of these volumes appeared it at once took, and has ever since maintained, a recognized position as the standard work on the subject. Grammatical criticism, philological exegesis, historical presentation, philosophical perception, are combined in them as they were never before combined, as they have not been since combined. They have furnished models for others, but they have themselves remained models.

With the growth of knowledge in the future they may become obsolete, and some pupil may arise to excel his master; but the present shows no signs of this, and we may safely predict that any greater commentary on these Epistles of St. Paul will owe part of its greatness to the volumes now before us. It is moreover remarkable as showing the fulness of the editor's early knowledge, and the fixity of his principles, that while edition after edition of these volumes have appeared in quick succession for now many years, they have undergone no material change. The essays reprinted since the author's death, in the volume entitled *Dissertations on the Apostolic Age*, are the essays of the early editions.

In one respect important change is here noted. In the earlier editions of the *Philippians* it was assumed in the essay on 'The Christian Ministry,' that the Syriac version, edited by Cureton, represented the original form of the Epistles of Ignatius. Later and more complete investigations of the writings of this Father, led to the conviction that the shorter Greek form is genuine, and that the Syriac is only an abridgment. An extract from the edition of *The Apostolic Fathers*, to which we shall presently refer, is now added, giving full reasons for the change of opinion. A full note on another subject does not, indeed, express any change of opinion, but protests against imputations of opinion that Dr. Lightfoot never held, and which are inconsistent with a fair interpretation of his essay as a whole. It is not easy to see how an essay which contained from the first such passages as these,

> The evidence for the early and wide extension of episcopacy throughout pro-consular Asia, the scene of St. John's latest labours, may be considered irrefra-gable.[22]
>
> If the preceding investigation be substantially correct, the three-fold ministry can be traced to Apostolic direction; and short of an express statement we can possess no better assurance of a Divine appointment or at least a Divine sanction.[23]

It could be interpreted as in favour of the Presbyterian as opposed to the Episcopal view of the Christian ministry. But it was natural that controversialists should endeavour to support their arguments by the authority of so great a man; and as advocates will always select their facts, we cannot think it is a matter of surprise that some of the statements have been used, perhaps even understood, in a sense which is opposed to that of the author. A great writer on such a subject is sure to be misunderstood if to be misunderstood is possible, and he should take care to make it impossible. When the sixth edition of the *Philippians* was published, in 1881, the Preface contained the following explanation:

> But on the other hand, while disclaiming any change in my opinions, I desire equally to disclaim the representations of those opinions which have been put forward in some quarters. The object of the Essay was an investigation into the origin of the Christian Ministry. The result has been a confirmation of the statement in the English Ordinal, 'It is evident unto all men diligently reading the Holy Scripture and ancient authors that from the Apostles' time there have been these orders of Ministers in Christ's Church, Bishops, Priests, and Deacons.' But I was scrupulously anxious not to overstate the evidence in any case; and it would seem that partial and qualifying statements, prompted by this anxiety, have assumed undue proportions in the minds of some readers, who have emphasized them to the neglect of the general drift of the Essay.

Even after this statement the misrepresentations continued, and soon after the close of the Lambeth Conference of 1888, Bishop Lightfoot felt it to

---

[22]*Philippians*, p. 212, first edition; p. 214, later edition.
[23]*Ibid.* p. 265, first edition; p. 267, later edition. Cf. *Dissertations on the Apostolic Age*, pp. 239-246.

be his duty to collect and print a series of extracts from his published writings bearing on this subject. There is nothing new in them. Their value is that they show distinctly what the author's opinion was and had been throughout; and that they were collected by himself. His trustees have done good service in reprinting them together with the Essay and the following note: 'It is felt by those who have the best means of knowing that he would himself have wished the collection to stand together simply as his reply to the constant imputation to him of opinions for which writers wished to claim his support without any justification.'[24] It is perhaps hardly to be expected that such misrepresentations will cease, but every vestige of justification, if any ever existed, is now removed.

We have been led by the fact that these editions of the *Epistles of St. Paul* could be regarded only as part of one whole to anticipate some of the events of Dr. Lightfoot's life, and it will be convenient to depart further from chronological order so that we may have such a connected view of his literary work as is possible within the scope of this article.

Between the date of the *Philippians* (1868) and the *Colossians* (1875) are to be placed the first editions of the *St. Clement* in 1869, and the *Revision of the New Testament* in 1871. Each of these volumes represents the beginning of a stream which flowed on and gathered force until it became an important river.

The *Clement* was the first-fruits of Dr. Lightfoot's studies of the sub-apostolic age, which were afterwards to yield such an abundant harvest. In 1877 followed an Appendix, giving the chief results of the discoveries by Bryennios and Prof. Bensly. Meanwhile much of the editor's attention had been given to a contemplated edition of *Ignatius*, for some portions of this work were already in print, and the 'whole of the commentary on the genuine epistles of Ignatius, and the introduction and texts of the Ignatian Acts of Martyrdom . . . were passed through the press before the end of 1878.' Dr. Lightfoot was called early in 1879 to undertake the manifold responsibilities of the See of Durham. 'For weeks, and sometimes for months together,' he tells us, 'I have not found time to write a single line.' But he snatched minutes from his days of work and travel, and hours from his days and nights of rest,

---

[24]*Dissertations on the Apostolic Age*, 1892, pp. 21-246.

and it was at length published in 1885.

We invited the attention of the readers of this Review to the importance of this great work at the time,[25] and we must now limit ourselves to a few words of comment. These shall be the words of Professor Harnack of Berlin, which are of the greater interest as he writes in part from an opposite camp:

> . . . his [Dr. Lightfoot's] edition of the Epistles of Ignatius and Polycarp, for the appearance of which we have been earnestly looking, and which we now hail with delight. We may say, without exaggeration, that this work is the most learned and careful Patristic monograph which has appeared in the nineteenth century; that it has been elaborated with a diligence and knowledge of the subject which show that Lightfoot has made himself master of this department, and placed himself beyond the reach of any rival.[26]

These three bulky volumes were no sooner out of hand than the editor returned to the *Clement* with the intention of supplying introductions and essays which should place it in form and matter on a level with what were intended to be the companion volumes of *Ignatius*. He devoted to this work hours that many of his friends felt were robbing the Church of his life, but as with the early days, so with the last, his books were really his strength, and up to and during his final illness, as long as consciousness lasted, the *Clement* was constantly in his hands. The second edition of the work was published after his death. It is not as complete as he would have made it, but, to use the language of another great teacher, who, if he writes from the same camp, writes also with fulness of knowledge and exactitude of balanced judgment:

> . . . in spite of some gaps, the book was substantially finished before the end came. He was happily allowed to treat of 'Clement the Doctor,' 'Ignatius the Martyr,' 'Polycarp the Elder,' in a manner answering to his own noble ideal; and the 'Complete Edition of the Apostolic Fathers,' such as he had designed more than thirty years before, was ready at his death to be a monument of learning, sagacity, and judgment unsurpassed in the present age. . . . and in breadth and thoroughness of treatment, in vigour and independence, in sug-

---

[25]*Quarterly Review*, April, 1886, pp. 467-500.
[26]*Expositor*, December, 1885, p. 1. Cf. Harnack's still more remarkable testimony to Dr. Lightfoot's absolute fairness as distinguished from the tendency of German writers, in *Theologische Literaturzeitung*, No. 12, 1890, col. 298.

gestiveness and fertility of resource, this new edition of Clement will justly rank beside the 'monumental edition' of 'Ignatius.'[27]

The Bishop had also made considerable progress with an edition of the *Apostolic Fathers*, in one volume, which was intended for the use of students. He had himself studied some of them in his own school-days in the edition of Jacobson, and he wished to leave as a legacy to the young an edition which should be more complete than any which had yet appeared. This he was enabled to do by the assistance of his friend and chaplain, Mr. Harmer, whose services as general editor the trustees have been fortunate enough to secure since the Bishop's death.

But in the opinion of Dr. Lightfoot the *Ignatius* was the *magnum opus* of his patristic studies, and indeed of his life. This he tells us, 'was the motive, and is the core, of the whole.'[28] He was not unaware that in the prosecution of this work he was necessarily breaking through another, and, as many thought, a still more important plan.

'I have been reproached,' he writes, 'by my friends for allowing myself to be diverted from the more congenial task of commenting on St. Paul's Epistles; but the importance of the position seemed to me to justify the expenditure of much time and labour in "repairing a breach" not indeed in "the House of the Lord" itself, but in the immediately outlying buildings.'[29]

Nor did he overrate the importance of the position. It was nothing less than the chief foundation of the Tübingen school. 'To the disciples of Baur,' as he expresses it in terms which are not too strong, 'the rejection of the Ignatian Epistles is an absolute necessity of their theological position. The ground would otherwise be withdrawn from under them, and their reconstruction of early Christian history would fall in ruins on their heads.'[30]

There are probably many of the Bishop's friends who still hold the opinion that nothing can compensate for the interruption of the cherished plan of a complete edition of St. Paul's Epistles. What would they not give for a commentary on the 'Romans' and the 'Ephesians,' on a scale commensurate with those on the 'Galatians' and the 'Colossians'? With much of this feeling all

---

[27]Bishop Westcott, in *Clement*, prefatory note, p. vi.
[28]*Ignatius*, Preface, p. ix.
[29]*Ibid.* p. xv.
[30]Preface, pp. xi. xii.

students of the New Testament will have the deepest sympathy, but we are nevertheless of the opinion that the obligations which the Bishop has conferred upon the Church are still greater than they would have been if he had confined himself to a narrower course which he might have completed. It is now with the Pauline Epistles as with the works of the writers of the second century, as with a wished-for opportunity of writing the history of the fourth century, as with many a line of thought, and with many a course of action— if he has not done all he intended, he has at least shown how it should be done.[31] He has left the legacy of an ideal greater even than the actual which he made so great.

The *Fresh Revision of the English New Testament* had its origin in a paper read before a clerical meeting just before the Company appointed for the Revision held its first sitting, and it had beyond question a considerable effect both upon the work of the Revisers and upon the attitude of the public towards that work. Among the criticisms which it drew forth was one by Mr. Earle, afterwards Professor of Anglo-Saxon in the University of Oxford, which attacked what Dr. Lightfoot considered to be the impregnable position of his book. He had 'laid it down as a rule (subject of course to special exceptions) that, when the same word occurs in the same context in the original, it should be rendered by the same equivalent in the Version.' He had indeed laid down the same rule in one of his early criticisms.[32]

Mr. Earle in opposing this principle, cleverly described it as substituting the 'fidelity of a lexicon' for the 'faithfulness of a translation,' and Dr. Lightfoot, while regarding this as a misinterpretation of his principle, replied, 'My objection to the variety of rendering which Mr. Earle advocates is that it does depart from "the faithfulness of a translation," and substitutes, not indeed the fidelity of a lexicon, but the caprice of a translator.'[33] Dr. Lightfoot's reply was generally admitted to have established the principle— and indeed, as stated by him, it can hardly be questioned, and yet the Revised Version must have often recalled Mr. Earle's phrase, 'the fidelity of a lexicon,' which is said, we know not how truly, to have been varied by a learned scholar, who retired from the work of revision on the ground that

---

[31]*Cf.* Bishop Westcott, *From Strength to Strength,* p. 47.
[32]*Journal of Philology,* vol. ii. p. 362.
[33]Preface to the second edition, 1891, p. xii.

he had been invited to 'translate,' and was expected to 'construe.'

To discuss the merits or demerits of the Revised Version is no part of our present subject, and the readers of this Review are not likely to have forgotten the very full and plain-speaking criticism that has already occupied its pages.[34] Nor have we any available means of determining the extent of Dr. Lightfoot's influence on the work. The history of the deliberations of the Revisers has not been written, and will probably never be fully known, but the glimpses afforded by Dr. Newth and others of the method of voting are not very encouraging when we think of the inequality of the voters. Surely here, if anywhere, was there place for the principle that votes should be weighed and not counted. It does not appear that Dr. Lightfoot was immediately concerned in the formation of the Company of Revisers, nor was he at the time a member of the Convocation of either Province; but it is clear that from the first nomination of the Company he was among its chief leaders; that he was consistently loyal to his colleagues, and that he was always ready to defend their common work. Perhaps indeed the most uncertain of his contests was that in which he undertook to defend against Canon Cook the rendering, 'Deliver us from the evil one.' The fresh investigations of Mr. Chase[35] go far in our opinion to confirm the view which Dr. Lightfoot championed, but our readers will remember that there is much to be said on the other side,[36] and we can but regret that Dr. Lightfoot himself did not supply a further reply to Canon Cook's arguments.

But while the advocates of the Revised Version are fully justified in claiming Dr. Lightfoot's strong support, we cannot help thinking that if he and a small body of men of like gifts and like knowledge of English as well as of Greek had formed the Company of Revisers, we should have now had a version practically accepted by the English-speaking peoples. It is impossible to read the notes in Dr. Lightfoot's editions of the *Epistles of St. Paul* without feeling that we are in a different atmosphere from that of the Revised Version, and we believe that if the Version is to gain general acceptance it will have to be again revised on the more conservative model of the work of the Revisers of the Old Testament. If that task is ever attempted, the new

---

[34]*Quarterly Review*, vol. 152, pp. 307 *seq.*; and vol. 153, pp. 1 *seq.*, and pp. 309 *seq.*
[35]*Cambridge Texts and Studies*, No. 3: 'Lord's Prayer in the early Church.'
[36]*Quarterly Review*, vol. 154, p. 338.

Revisers will find no more fitting words to express their principle than these which Mr. Lightfoot wrote as early as 1857:

> If, then, the English of former times speaks more plainly to the heart than the English of the present day, and at least as plainly to the understanding, surely we should do well to retain it, only lopping off a very few archaisms, not because they are not à la mode, but because they would not be generally understood.[37]

Except indeed in the third of 'The Fundamental Resolutions adopted by the Convocation of Canterbury on the third and fifth days of May, 1870':

> That in the above resolutions we do not contemplate any new translation of the Bible, or any alteration of the language, except where in the judgement of the most competent scholars such change is necessary.[38]

During the early years of the work of revision Dr. Lightfoot was engaged also upon literary work of another kind. In 1874 a writer, whose name has never been authoritatively disclosed, but is widely known, published a work entitled *Supernatural Religion: an Inquiry into the reality of Divine Revelation.* He professed to show that there is no miraculous element in Christianity; that miracles are indeed antecedently incredible; that the evidence which is obtainable from the apostolic period is not trustworthy; and that the Four Gospels have no sufficient warrant for their date and authorship. Many reasons combined to give the work an unmerited notoriety, the chief of them being its anonymity and the widely circulated but wholly unwarranted rumour that the author was one of the most learned and venerable of the English prelates. Dr. Lightfoot was led to examine the work publicly, not because of its merits or importance—he thought indeed 'that its criticisms were too loose and pretentious, and too full of errors, to produce any permanent effect'—but because he 'found that a cruel and unjustifiable assault was made on a very dear friend to whom "he" was attached by the most sacred personal and theological ties.' This accounts for a certain tone of severity that is never undeserved, but is present here only in the course of Dr. Lightfoot's writings.

The first part of the examination appeared in the *Contemporary Review*

---

[37]*Journal of Philology*, vol. iv. p. 108.
[38]*Cf.* Preface of Revised Version of the New Testament.

in December, 1874; the last in the same periodical in May, 1877. The whole covers to a considerable extent—and the author had intended that it should completely cover—'the testimony of the first two centuries to the New Testament Scriptures'; and it is in our opinion not too much to assert that if the author of *Supernatural Religion* had been the cause of no other investigation than the remarkable articles by Dr. Lightfoot, he would have been the indirect means of contributing the most valuable addition to apologetic literature which has been made during this generation. There was naturally a strong desire in many quarters that the articles should be collected and published in a permanent form. Year after year this was postponed because the writer designed further additions to them, and it was only in 1889, when 'life was hanging on a slender thread,' that the collection was issued. We could wish indeed that the designed completion had been made, we could wish that the author had been able to abandon the polemical form and to recast the whole; but no course remained but that which has been followed. The work is a legacy as from a death-bed, and it is a legacy of permanent value.

The limits of our space forbid us to refer at greater length to Bishop Lightfoot's literary work, the extent and variety and quality of which would have been remarkable even in a life of learned leisure. Here we have an article or rather the most complete treatise which is known to us on 'Eusebius' in the *Dictionary of Christian Biography*; here a similar treatise on the 'Acts of the Apostles' in the recently published edition of the *Dictionary of the Bible*; here, courses of lectures on 'Christian Life in the Second and Third Centuries' and 'Christianity and Paganism' delivered at St. Paul's Cathedral; here, a speech at a meeting of the Society for the Propagation of the Gospel, which has become a standard authority on 'The Comparative Progress of Ancient and Modern Missions'; here, an edition of Dean Mansel's treatise on *The Gnostic Heresies*; here, lectures delivered to artisans at Rochdale or students at Edinburgh on 'Simon de Montfort and Edward I' or 'The Architecture of the Period and the University life, with special reference to Roger Bacon'; now it is the Inaugural Address to the British Archæological Association; now it is that of the President of the Co-operative Society. Here there is the formal 'Charge' delivered to his Clergy; here, the address on some public or diocesan question which formed part of his daily work. All are marked by the same characteristic features. The matter is everywhere that of the painful investigator, the principle is that of the Christian philosopher, the form is that of the artist in words.

We have not space to attempt to form a complete bibliography, but reference may also be made to articles in the *Dictionary of the Bible*, 1863; on Romans and Thessalonians; in the *Journal of Philology*, 1868, i. 98, ii. 47, 157, 1869 ii. 204, 1871, iii. 193; in the *Academy*, 1869, Oct. 9th and Nov. 19th; on Renan's *St. Paul*, 1889, May 21st; on *The Lost Catalogue of Hegesippus*, 1889, Sept. 21st; *The Muratorian Fragment*; also notes to the posthumous fragment 'Antioch' in Neale's *Holy Eastern Church*, 1873; a contribution to Scrivener's *Introduction to the Criticism of the New Testament*, 1873; on *The Egyptian or Coptic Versions*; and a lecture on 'Donne, the Poet-Preacher' in *Classic Preachers of the English Church*, 1877.

But the four volumes of sermons mentioned at the head of this article claim at least some words of notice. Archbishop Tait, when walking with a friend one morning, said, 'We have made Lightfoot a preacher'; and when asked to explain the process by which such preachers were made, added, 'We have given the finest pulpit in the world to a man to whom God has given the power to use it,' and expressed his conviction that better use of it had never been made. What Canon Lightfoot himself thought of the opportunity may be read in the dedication of his *Ignatius*: 'To Henry Parry Liddon, D.D., to whom God has given special gifts as a Christian Preacher and matched the gifts with the opportunities, assigning to him his place, beneath the great dome of St. Paul's, the centre of the world's concourse.' And what use he made of it is to be seen in part in the volumes before us. We confess that they have taken us by surprise, and we think that our surprise will be shared by many who often heard Dr. Lightfoot preach and were fully impressed by his sermons. Very rarely have we known sermons that were so good to hear prove so much better to read. We shall not quote from them, because no quotations could adequately represent them. We commend them to any of our readers into whose hands they have not fallen, as models of what sermons should be. They are learned, they are philosophical, they are wide in grasp and firm in tread; but from first to last of these four volumes there is not a passage which is technical and not a sentence which the ordinary reader cannot understand. Their logical clearness satisfies the highest intellect, their deep pathos moves the humblest soul.

It was of course obvious that a man of Dr. Lightfoot's remarkable gifts, and still more remarkable devotion in the use of those gifts, should appear to many persons to be specially qualified to hold many offices, and from time to time offers of preferment were made to him; but his heart was in the work of his professorship, and no suggested honour was acceptable to him which would in any way interfere with the most complete discharge of the duties of that office.

He became naturally a select preacher at his own University, and also at Oxford and at Whitehall. He was appointed Chaplain to the Prince Consort, Honorary Chaplain to the Queen, and Deputy Clerk of the Closet. He was for seventeen years Examining Chaplain to Dr. Tait as Bishop of London and Archbishop of Canterbury. But the canonry of St. Paul's was accepted with much hesitation, and only when it was seen that arrangements could be made for his London 'residence' which would not break in upon the Cambridge terms. When the Regius Professorship of Divinity fell vacant, in 1870, he practically declined it, in order that he might bring Mr. Westcott back to Cambridge, 'He called me to Cambridge to occupy a place which was his own by right; and having done this he spared no pains to secure for his colleague favourable opportunities for action while he himself withdrew in some sense from the position which he had long virtually occupied.'[39] But in 1875 he was elected to the Lady Margaret Chair. More than one Deanery, more than one Bishopric, were offered to him on the advice of more than one Prime Minister.

In 1879 came the offer of the See of Durham, which, after much hesitation and much pressure from friends, he at length, and with great diffidence, accepted. He was trembling beneath the conviction that he was not fitted for the work to which nevertheless, after prayer and counsel, he felt that he was called of God; the Church was giving thanks for a decision which all men felt to be the dawn of a bright day. For more than two centuries there had been no direct nomination to the throne of the Prince Bishops of Durham, and yet such was the public estimation in which Dr. Lightfoot was held that there was probably no Churchman who did not rejoice in this nomination,

---

[39]B. F. Dunelm, in prefatory note to *Clement*.

except Dr. Lightfoot himself, and a band of Cambridge friends, who thought the loss to the University would be irreparable. There have always been men who thought their own circle was greater than the world.

We now enter upon the last period of Dr. Lightfoot's work, and it is a period in which we trace the signs of an eminence that is higher even than that of his earlier course. Great he was as *antiquitatis investigator*, great he was as *evangelii interpres*, and yet greater when he united and applied the principles and continued the studies of his earlier life in the practical work of the *ecclesiæ rector*. And here, too, *qualis fuerit . . . testantur opera ut æqualibus ita posteris profutura.*

Dr. Lightfoot was consecrated in Westminster Abbey on St. Mark's Day, 1879, and one sentence in the sermon, which was preached by Dr. Westcott, at once linked together the three old schoolfellows and re-stated for the Bishop then to be consecrated, the principle which his own heart had dictated for the third of the friends exactly two years before. *Who is sufficient for these things?* was the preacher's and yet more the listener's question. The answer now given at Westminster had been given at St. Paul's when Dr. Lightfoot occupied the pulpit, and Dr. Benson was consecrated to be the first Bishop of Truro: 'He who lays down at the footstool of God his successes and his failures, his hopes and his fears, his knowledge and his ignorance, his weakness and his strength, his misgivings and his confidences—all that he is and all that he might be—content to take up thence just that which God shall give him.'[40]

The new Bishop was enthroned, the first instance of this ceremony being performed in the person of any Bishop of Durham since the enthronement of Bishop Trevor in 1752, and preached in his Cathedral Church on the 15th day of May. The first words strike at once the dominant note of his life:

And what more seasonable prayer can you offer for him who addresses you now, at this the most momentous crisis of his life, than that he—the latest successor of Butler—may enter upon the duties of his high and responsible office in the same spirit; that the realization of this great idea, the realization of this great fact, may be the constant effort of his life; that glimpses of the invisible Righteousness, of the invisible Grace, of the invisible Glory, may be

---

[40]*From Strength to Strength*, pp. 17, 18.

vouchsafed to him; and that the Eternal Presence, thus haunting him night and day, may rebuke, may deter, may guide, may strengthen, may comfort, may illumine, may consecrate and subdue the feeble and wayward impulses of his own heart to God's holy will and purpose!

The same sermon indicates two of the immediate objects which the preacher set before himself. One is the division of the Diocese, the other is the duty of the Church in social and industrial questions.[41]

In such devotion, such resolves, such stating and strengthening of principles, passed the first day in the Diocese. The succeeding days were forthwith devoted to carrying these principles into practice. The Bishop lived at first in the Castle at Durham, the ancient home of the Prince Bishops, which had become part of the University through the munificence and foresight of Van Mildert, but in which a suite of rooms had been reserved in perpetuity for the Bishop's use. Here the Visitor of the University was heartily welcomed alike by graduates and students, and these early weeks strengthened the attachment which he brought with him, and laid the foundations of a warm and never broken affection for what he was wont to call the University of his adoption.

It is said that among Dr. Lightfoot's last words to some of his Cambridge friends when he took leave of them was the charge, 'Send me up men to the North.' As soon as Auckland Castle was ready to receive him, he carried out his cherished project of forming a clergy-house under his own roof. Here a band of University men, seven or eight in number, were trained under his own immediate guidance for their future work in the Diocese. They were instructed by himself, by his archdeacons, and by his chaplains. The intellectual work followed the lines of a college course in theology, the practical work in Auckland itself and the pit villages which encircle the castle-grounds enabled the students to test their theories by the realities of life; but their chief lesson was the constant influence of their true Father in God.

We have referred to Dr. Prince Lee's affection for his pupils, and those who know best assert that it is at least equally true that Bishop Lightfoot loved nothing on earth more devotedly than those who were in a special sense his spiritual sons. His strong love strengthened theirs, and men in the

---

[41]*Leaders in the Northern Church*, pp. 164, 165.

vigour of their young manhood learned to love him, and through him to love afresh their God. To love him was to learn from him, to assimilate him, to reproduce him; and not the least of the permanent influences for good which the Bishop left to his Diocese and his Church, was the band of young men numbering more than seventy who had looked upon a life which in the power of its intellect, the devotion of its soul, the humility and self-sacrifice of its whole being was to them a daily ascension into heaven; and who, as they looked upon it had caught something at least of its spirit. Loving them and knowing them as he did, he expected them and always found them to be ready to work with entire singleness of aim and entire devotion to duty. They knew they had no claim to preferment unless to a post of unusual poverty or unusual difficulty, and to such a post only when prepared for it. Some words from an 'In Memoriam' sketch in a college magazine and signed J. B. D., will show how the Bishop looked upon his sons and their work, and what manner of men they were:

> A new district was to be formed in a much-neglected neighbourhood in——. There was neither church nor endowment nor parochial appliances of any kind. Everything must be built up from the foundation. Only a modest stipend for a single curate-in-charge had been guaranteed. It was necessary to rely on youthful zeal, even at the cost of some inexperience I asked C——, who was still curate at——, to undertake the task of building up this new parish, and he accepted the call. To my great joy, B——offered to accompany his friend as a volunteer without remuneration, though he might have had an adequate stipend elsewhere. . . .
>
> I spoke of this offer then as an inspiration, and so I regard it now. Though doubtless the work there hastened his death, who shall regret his decision? Certainly not those who loved him best. . . .
>
> I cannot but regard this splendid unselfishness as a chief corner-stone, on which the edifice of the new parish was raised. . . . Excellent congregations were gathered together; generous donors came forward with liberal offerings; and within two years and a few months from the time when they commenced their work in the district, a large and seemly church was finished and consecrated.
>
> I have had placed in my hands some extracts from a private diary which he kept. . . . I give this relating to the night before his ordination: 'He devoted himself to prayer.' If He, how much more I needed. So in the end I remained

praying in my own room till daylight, about 3.15. It was broad day, and I went to bed.

Of the day itself he writes:

Sunday, Matins at 8.15. I felt calm and at peace. . . . Just broke fast and nothing more. I had no fixed idea about fasting, but thought it better to err in too literal a following of the Apostles than too free a departure from them.

The service at South Church was full of a depth of peace and love to me, such as I have never known. The *Veni Creator* began the climax. My heart was full of an overpowering sense of my own unworthiness and Christ's deep love and trust in one who had done nothing but what deserved the withdrawal of love and trust; and at the actual imposition of hands the surge of mingled regrets and hopes, joys and fears, the sense of being at once infinitely humbled and exalted, broke out *in lacrimas super ora surgentes* [*et*] *defluentes. Gaudebam, quia contristabar; contristabar, quia gaudebam.*

The Bishop adds, 'A ministry' [may we not add, 'an episcopacy'?] 'so supported, could not be otherwise than fruitful.'

With this sketch drawn from the sanctuary of the home life at Auckland Castle, it will be interesting to compare a *pendant* drawn from without. Among the guests entertained by the Bishop in 1882 was the Rev. Robert W. Barbour, a gifted young Free Church Minister. From a memorial volume printed for private circulation after his early death, which shows what a loss this brought to his church and his friends, we are permitted to print the following extracts:

April 28, 1882

10.45. The evening worship was very uniting. The servants came in, and we sang the psalms and hymns, and Dr. Lightfoot and a chaplain read and prayed (from the new version and the prayer book) in his own voice and with his own devout, simple soul uttering itself in all. His after talk in the drawing-room was even more charming [than that in the afternoon]. You know how a mastiff will lie down (out of sheer love for the canine race) and let a crowd of small dogs jump and tumble over him, and put them off, and egg them on with great pawings and immense 'laps' of his broad tongue. Even so did Dr. Lightfoot. . . . It is good for me to be in the midst of so much informal earnestness and Christian manliness.

April 29, 1882

Then I suppose it is not taking her past out of the hands of time, to say that Butler's seat is now filled by his nearest successor; a man as great in his work and in his day, as his great namesake (for they both are written 'Joseph Dunelm'). I know not if there be any better test of true lastingness in any man who is yet living, than when, knowing his written works, one is able to compare them with his person, and to say that these correspond. The same judgment which you admire in Dr. Lightfoot's commentaries meets you in his conversation.

He seems, like justice in her statues, always to give his sentences, holding meantime a pair of other scales. Indeed, the analogy might be extended. Justice is but badly described in stone as being blind-folded in her decisions. But there is in the Bishop a strong cast of eye which enables him, when he speaks, to address himself to nobody in particular; although immediately after speaking, he turns on you a glance that conveys an impression of the most absolute impartiality. . . . He calls these lads (and I can imagine worse things than to feel myself, for the nonce, one of them) his family, and they treat him as frank, ingenuous English gentlemen's sons would treat their father. He is accessible to their difficulties and their doubts, if they have any; but, a thing more remarkable, he is open to all their kittenhood of mirth and fun. To hear him alone with them is to feel you are on the edge of a circle, which tempts you almost to stand on tiptoe and look over and wish you were inside. It is a searching trial of true homeliness, to observe how it comports itself when there are strangers present. But I assert my coming in has not bated one jot of all this family joy. Last evening, after prayers, they were poking fun at the bishop. One man was asked how he was getting on with Hebrew. The fellow boldly turned the weapon round by inquiring whether his lordship was prepared to teach him. Dr. Lightfoot was gently demurring, when somebody else burst in, as if with a child's impatience and fear of some older imcompleted promise: 'No, not before we have had these lectures on botany.'

Then, assuming the air of someone to whom that study was even as his necessary food, he went on to report his observations, taken daily on his walks to and from the district, of two *interesting weeds*. It sounded like a clever parody upon Darwin and his climbing plants trained up the bed-post. I have written all this in order to show—if it is within the power of words to show a thing which lies more in the feeling of the whole, than in any enumeration, however complete, of the details—how happy an example one has here of the spirit and the action of the English Church. Within, you have a home and a beehive both in one; without everything is plain, and simple, and strenuous. The Bishop preaches such sermons as the one I sent you. His chaplains teach, and visit, and preach. The students an earnest, and healthy set of men. Nothing is allowed in the Castle that speaks of pomp or pretension.

You go down morning and evening to prayers in the chapel; I suppose it is about the finest palace chapel in Britain. A simple service is held. The Bishop and a chaplain read the lessons and lead the prayers. Another chaplain has trained a choir of boys from the neighbouring town. Behind these choristers sit the students; the bishop and servants (eight I counted) are in the back seats. One or two from the outside also seem to attend. The psalms and hymns are simply but sweetly sung. So anxious is Dr. Lightfoot that nothing should be unused, nothing rest in an empty name, that I believe he is fitting up the chapel with seats, so as to have a service every Sabbath. Much of what I have seen here, the earnestness and the manliness of the men, the order of the household, the thoroughness of the instruction, the devoutness of the prayers, the sweetness of the singing, the beauty, the learning, the goodness, the simplicity, make me hang my head for shame, both as a man and as a minister; for my whole heart consents to these things that they are right.[42]

Some of the Bishop's friends were also disappointed, and perhaps with more show of reason, that his voice was seldom heard in the House of Lords. But here, too, he was guided by the same principle. He never forgot that he was a lord of Parliament, but he always remembered that he was primarily Bishop of Durham. He was indeed never absent from the House of Lords at a critical division, though his presence involved the sacrifice of an important Diocesan engagement and two nights in a railway carriage; his counsel was always at the command of the leaders of the Episcopal Bench; no man was more in touch with every movement for the social as well as spiritual welfare of his countrymen; but he naturally did not attach to his own utterances the weight which others did, and he felt that the interests of the Church and the

---

[42]There is a long section here enumerating in great detail the churches Lightfoot helped build in the Durham and Newcastle area and the money he raised to accomplish this end. I have deleted this because the point has already been made and is made later of his great work as churchman. (BW3)

people were most safely guided by the great Archbishops, upon whom this burden naturally fell.

Nor did he shrink, when it came clearly in the path of his own duty, from expressing his opinion or offering his counsel on questions that were of universal interest. In 1881 he presided over the twenty-first meeting—the coming of age—of the Church Congress at Newcastle-on-Tyne. The British Association had just kept its jubilee in the metropolis of the Northern Province. Here is the Bishop's happy and characteristically hopeful reference to the coincidence:

> The President availed himself of the occasion to sum up the achievements of the half-century past—untrodden fields opened out, fresh sciences created, a whole world of fact and theory discovered, of which men had hardly a suspicion at the beginning of this period. In this commemoration we are reminded of the revolution in the intellectual world that has taken place in our own time, as in the other,[43] our attention was directed to the revolution in the social and industrial world. Here again we are confronted with a giant force, of which the Church of Christ must give an account. If we are wise we shall endeavour to understand and to absorb these truths. They are our proper heritage as Christians, for they are manifestations of the Eternal Word, who is also the Head of the Church. They will add breadth and strength and depth to our theology. Before all things we shall learn by the lessons of the past to keep ourselves free from any distrust or dismay. Astronomy once menaced, or was thought to menace, Christianity. Long before we were born the menace had passed away. We found astronomy the sworn ally of religion. The heresy of the fifteenth and sixteenth centuries had become the orthodoxy of the nineteenth. When some years ago an eminent man of science, himself a firm believer, wrote a work throwing doubt on the plurality of worlds, it was received with a storm of adverse criticism, chiefly from Christian teachers, because he ventured to question a theory which three centuries earlier it would have been a shocking heresy to maintain. Geology next entered the lists. We are old enough, many of us, to remember the anxiety and distrust with which its startling announcements were received. This scare, like the other, has passed away. We admire the providential design that through myriads of years prepared the earth by successive gradations of animal and vegetable life for its ultimate destination as the abode of man. Nowhere else do we find more

---

[43]The George Stephenson Centenary, which had been recently observed at Newcastle.

vivid and striking illustrations of the increasing purpose which runs through the ages. . . .

Our theological conceptions have been corrected and enlarged by its teaching, but the work of the Church of Christ goes on as before. Geology, like astronomy, is fast becoming our faithful ally. And now, in turn, Biology concentrates the same interests, and excites the same distrusts. Will not history repeat itself? If the time should come when evolution is translated from the region of suggestive theory to the region of acknowledged fact, what then? Will it not carry still further the idea of providential design and order? Will it not reinforce with new and splendid illustrations the magnificent lesson of modern science—complexity of results traced back to simplicity of principles—variety of phenomena issuing from unity of order—the gathering up, as it were, of the threads that connect the universe, in the right hand of the One Eternal Word? Thus we are reminded by these two celebrations of the twin giants, the creation of our age, with which the Church of Christ has to reckon—foes only if they are treated as such, but capable of being won as trusty allies, by appreciation, by sympathy, by conciliation and respect.

In 1885 the Bishop presided at a meeting of the Diocesan Conference at Durham. Disestablishment was in the air and to many persons seemed nearer then than it does now. He was led to speak at some length upon it. We extract a few sentences:

But I cannot blink facts. The question is not sleeping; it has been definitely raised; and I should hold it culpable in anyone in my position not to express, and express definitely, his opinion on the issues involved. . . . The only schemes which are before us involve a wholesale alienation of property, a disregard of personal and corporate rights, and a violation of all the most sacred associations and feelings, such as, in the words of an eminent living statesman, would leave England 'a lacerated and bleeding mass.' Of any such scheme of disestablishment I say deliberately, having carefully weighed these words and feeling the tremendous responsibility of over-statement, that it would be not only a national disaster, but also a national crime, to which it would be difficult to find a parallel in the history of England since England became a nation. I believe that a moral blow would be inflicted on this country, under which it would reel and stagger for many generations to come, even if it ever recovered.

In October, 1889, just two months before his death, the Bishop presided

over the Conference of his Diocese in Sunderland. He addressed it on many
subjects, and especially on the Lambeth Conference, Christian Socialism,
the White Cross Movement, the Brotherhood of the Poor. How touching in
the light of what followed, how firm in the strength of faith, is this reference
to himself:

> While I was suffering from overwork, and before I understood the true nature
> of my complaint, it was the strain, both in London and at home, in connexion
> with this Pan-Anglican gathering, which broke me down hopelessly. I did not
> regret it then, and I do not regret it now. I should not have wished to recall
> the past, even if my illness had been fatal. For what after all is the individual
> life in the history of the Church? Men may come and men may go—indi-
> vidual lives float down like straws on the surface of the waters till they are lost
> in the ocean of eternity; but the broad, mighty, rolling stream of the Church
> itself—the cleansing, purifying, fertilising tide of the River of God—flows on
> for ever and ever. A gathering of Bishops, so numerous and so representative,
> collected from all parts of the globe, is an incident quite unique in the history
> of this Diocese. . . . For to those who have eyes to see and ears to hear, what
> does it all mean? What activities does it not suggest in the Anglican Church
> of the present? What capacities and hopes for the Anglican Church of the
> future? What evidences of present catholicity? What visions of future dif-
> fusion? . . . I hold that God has vouchsafed a signal blessing to our generation
> in this demonstration of the catholicity of the English Church, and I consider
> myself happy that in my chapel at Auckland will be preserved for future gen-
> erations a memorial of this chief event of my episcopate.

How full of wisdom is this comment on the work of the Lambeth Conference:

> But it may be said: this was a very important and very suggestive gathering,
> but what was the outcome? Did it leave behind any result at all proportionate
> to the imposing spectacle? What questions did it settle, disposing forever of
> the relations between Christianity and science, or between religion and pol-
> itics or social life—questions of infinite perplexity, which are troubling the
> minds of men in our own generation?
>
> Heaven be thanked, it did not lay down any formal dogma or infallible
> decree on any of these points. There is such a thing as hastening to be wise,
> even in Church Councils and Conferences. Of all the manifold blessings that
> God has showered on our English Church, none surely is greater than the
> providence that has shielded her from premature and authoritative state-
> ments, which soon or late must be repudiated or explained away, however

great may have been the temptation from time to time. The Church of England is nowhere directly or indirectly committed to the position that the sun goes round the earth; or that this world has only existed for six or seven thousand years; or that the days of creation are days of twenty-four hours each; or that the scriptural genealogies must always be accepted as strict and continuous records of the descent from father to son; or that the sacred books were written in every case by those whose names they bear; or that there is nowhere allegory, which men have commonly mistaken for history. On these and similar points, our Church has been silent; though individuals, even men of high authority, have written hastily and incautiously.[44]

The above extracts are all taken from addresses that the Bishop delivered within the limits of his own Diocese, but it would entirely misrepresent him if the impression should be formed that his sympathies and work were confined to these limits. If space were at our command, we should like to quote other passages, which show how fully he was in touch with the work of the Church far and near.[45]

Nor was it in public only that this help was given. Auckland Castle was almost constantly filled, as with the sons of the house who were being prepared for their future work, so with the clergy and laity from the Diocese, and from afar, who were welcomed to his hospitality and to his counsel. Few perhaps realize what the burden is which the post-bag adds to a Bishop's daily life, and in his case it brought the scholar's burden too; but even this was cheerfully borne, and no letter remained unanswered, whether it was that of the Southern farmer who wished to know if the Bishop could supply him with Durham cows, or that of a lady who felt sure he could find time to read a theological work in MS. before she sent it to the press—and 'may she say in her preface that it had his approval'?—or that of the student in the far West who had just begun the Greek Testament, and would like a solution of his many difficulties, and had 'heard that the Bishop was a good scholar.' In small matters, as in great, no one asked for anything that he felt that he could give, and asked in vain. And so, year after year, the hard work was done, and the noble life was lived. The mental and physical strength seemed equal to every strain.

---

[44]Diocesan Conference, 1889.
[45]He goes on to list various places where Lightfoot spoke or preached. (BW3)

No engagement ever fell through, no weariness was ever apparent. *Ignatius* was refreshment from the work of the Diocese; the work of the Diocese was refreshment from *Ignatius*. The face was always bright; the heart was always glad. The happiest years of his life he thought these Durham years to be; and he thought that he had never been so strong. It was towards the close of the spring confirmations in 1888, when the pressure of work had been unusually heavy, and falls of snow had more than once blocked the roads by which he tried to travel, that this strength seemed for the first time to be strained.

He thought, and his friends thought, that a short summer holiday would completely restore him; but the Lambeth Conference came and the visit of the Bishops to Durham came. Both brought to him great happiness, but both brought much work. The autumn holiday was too late, and the Bishop returned to his Diocese only to leave it again, under positive medical orders, for a winter in Bournemouth. He at once thought of resigning the Bishopric. It was foreign to his whole thought to have personal interests distinct from his office. He could not conceive that any man could accept an office in the Church of Christ without identifying himself with it, or would hold it a day longer than he could fully discharge its duties. One of the burdens that weighed on his soul was that instances to the contrary were not wholly wanting in his Diocese. He at least would do the one thing that was right. But he was still comparatively young; hopes of restoration to health, and strength, and work, seemed to be well grounded; and those to whom he was bound by every tie of allegiance absolutely forbade the step he wished to take.

An Assistant Bishop, first welcomed and soon beloved by himself and by his Diocese, was found in the person of Bishop Sandford, and he somewhat doubtingly acquiesced in a course about which others had no doubt. The spring of 1889 seemed to bring a fulfilment of the hopes that had been formed. The Bishop was able to return to his Diocese, and on Ascension Day the Cathedral Church was crowded by a vast assembly who joined with him in a special Service of Thanksgiving. He was able to fulfil the ordinary Diocesan duties, and to devote a large amount of time to literary work during the months of the summer and autumn; and he took part in three public events of special interest.

On July 2nd he consecrated the Church of S. Ignatius the Martyr, Sunderland, his own noble gift of thanksgiving; on October 17th he presided over the Diocesan Conference, and delivered the remarkable address to which we have referred [above]; on October the 29th he received in a public meeting, at the hands of the Lord-Lieutenant, the beautiful Pastoral Staff, which, together with a portrait by Mr. Richmond, it was determined to present to him on the completion of the tenth year of his episcopate. He thanked the donors in his usual happy, cheerful, tone, and took his farewell with tender words of blessing. It was for the last time. He left for the purpose of wintering again in Bournemouth a few days afterwards. For a time he continued to make progress. He was able to work regularly at the *Clement* up to Tuesday, December 17th. The local papers of the following Saturday morning contained a note from Archdeacon Watkins, 'asking the clergy and other ministers of religion to make special supplication for our beloved Bishop on Sunday and other days.' The evening papers of the same day contained a telegram from Bournemouth, 'The Bishop of Durham passed peacefully away this afternoon, at a quarter to four o'clock.'

The sorrow of the Church and of the nation, and the expression of that sorrow in the pulpit and in the press, is still fresh in the memory. The death and burial were the natural sequence to the life. True goodness and true greatness are honoured by men of every opinion and by men of every rank.[46]

Some estimates of the work of Bishop Lightfoot which were uttered under the influence of strong feeling immediately after death, contained perhaps some expressions and some comparisons which history will not justify. We are writing from the vantage-ground of three years' distance, and with access to many papers and references which have been kindly placed at our disposal, and have endeavoured at every point to follow in the spirit of the inscription which has formed our motto: *Qualis fuerit . . . testantur opera.* For this reason we have largely quoted the Bishop's own words, and if we try to express our own estimate of his work we shall still have recourse to words which he used of another, and which with little change may be as truly said of himself:

But after making all allowance for the fond partiality of a recent regret, we may fairly say that as a Bishop of Durham he stands out preeminent in the

---

[46]See a full account in the *Guardian* of Jan. 1st, 1890.

long list of twelve centuries; as a man of letters, greatest of all save De Bury; as a restorer of the fabric and order of churches, greatest of all save Cosin; as a profound thinker, greatest of all save Butler; as a munificent and patriotic ruler, greatest of all save Barrington; but as uniting in himself many and varied qualifications which combined go far towards realizing the ideal head of a religious and learned foundation, the just representative of a famous academic body, greater than these or any of his predecessors. Vast and varied mental powers, untiring energy and extensive knowledge, integrity of character and strictness of example, a wide and generous munificence, a keen interest in the progress of the Church and the University, an intense devotion to his own Diocese, a strong sense of duty, a true largeness of heart, a simple Christian faith; the union of these qualities fairly entitles him to the foremost place among the Bishops of Durham.[47]

It is natural that men should have attempted not only to portray this great life, but to analyse it; and the Church and the nation would owe a deep debt of gratitude to the writer who could show us how in any degree other men can learn the principles, of which the life and character of Joseph Barber Lightfoot were the product. Two statements among the many that lie before us are of special value in themselves, and derive a special interest from the widely-different sources from which they come.

Canon Westcott, preaching in Westminster Abbey two days after the funeral, said:

What then, you will ask me, is the secret of the life of him to whom we look this afternoon with reverent regard? It is, in a word, the secret of strength. He was strong by singleness of aim, by resolution, by judgment, by enthusiasm, by sympathy, by devotion. In old days it was strength to be with him: and for the future it will be strength to remember him.[48]

Lord Durham, speaking on two occasions separated by three years, said:

I venture to attribute the success of the Bishop to the strong personal feeling he inspires in all those who know him. It is impossible to have been connected with him or to have come in contact with him, without appreciating his strong sympathy and his generous regard for the welfare of the people surrounding him. . . . I think that no prelate in the proud and old princely days of the Pa-

---

[47]*Cambridge Sermons*, p. 119 (of Dr. Whewell).
[48]*From Strength to Strength*, p. 44.

latinate of Durham, with all his pomp and with all his circumstance, ever commanded more true respect than our present Bishop with his simple, kindly life, and his generous and unostentatious charity.[49]

In every town and parish in this county you will find visible and tangible evidence of his untiring zeal, and of the impetus which his genius gave to all those who served under him. But what you will not see, and what no hand can probe, is the impress he made upon the hearts of all with whom he came into contact, and the softening influence of his genial presence upon all sorts and conditions of men. . . . I venture to think that the chief factor in his paramount influence amongst us was his true and genial sympathy—sympathy with our joys and our sorrows, sympathy with our aspirations and with our failures; with our pursuits and with our recreations; and, above all, boundless sympathy with the shortcomings of feeble human nature. He was no proud Pharisee, who thanked God that he was not as other men are, but a true-hearted Christian gentleman, conscious of the trials and temptations of the world, striving with his pure life, and humble, modest ways, to raise mankind to a higher and better level by his example of Christian charity and loving sympathy.[50]

It seems to be certain that the two great secrets of the Bishop's power are here—strength and sympathy. And yet they were veiled in a modesty which men thought amounted to shyness. They were held in reserve; they were ready for fullest use whenever occasion demanded. But his very sympathy was strong, and he could not understand some forms of weakness. One of his early pupils has told us ' . . . he was kindness itself. . . . I once offended him . . . by telling him, when I got my Fellowship that he might have saved me many gloomy misgivings as an Undergraduate, if the Cambridge system had dealt a little more freely in words of encouragement.'[51] One of his clergy, whom he had placed in several difficult posts, said to another after some years of service, 'It would remove a burden from my mind if I felt sure that my work was being done as he wished it, but he has never said to me a single word of encouragement.' The second replied, 'I have had a larger experience, but I should never look for such words from him. He expects strong men to do their work, and would as soon think of encouraging such men as of

---

[49]Presentation of Pastoral Staff, October 29th, 1889.
[50]Unveiling of Monument, October 20th, 1892.
[51]*Contemporary Review*, Feb. 1890, p. 174.

seeking encouragement in words for himself. They must do all and bear all in the light of the Divine Presence, as he himself does.' And yet this second speaker received from the Bishop, not long before his death, a note which contained the following words: 'I have never ceased to be thankful for the inspiration which led me to invite you to assist me in the work of the Diocese. May God give you every blessing. . . . '

Did boys at school wonder that Lightfoot never spoke an ignoble word, or did an ignoble deed? The secret finds its explanation in the spirit that led him and a younger schoolfellow, afterwards not less eminent than himself, to arrange a form of prayer for the hours of the day for their common use. Did men marvel at the influence of the young Fellow and Tutor of Trinity? They would have marvelled less had they known that his life was strengthened by the following among other prayers:

> Since it hath pleased Thee, O Lord, that I should be called to take my part in the teaching of this College, grant that I may not assume the same lightly, or without a due sense of the importance of my trust; but, considering it a stewardship, whereof I shall have to render an account hereafter, may faithfully fulfil the same to Thy honour and glory. Grant, O Lord, that neither by word nor deed I may do aught that may weaken the faith, or slacken the practice of those committed to my charge; but rather grant to me such measure of Thy Holy Spirit, that my duties may be discharged to Thy honour and glory, and to the welfare of both the teacher and the taught. Grant this, O Lord, through Thy son, Jesus Christ, who is the Way, and the Truth, and the Life. Amen.

Among the last words which the Bishop addressed to the public from the very brink of the grave were these:

> I believe from my heart that the truth which this Gospel [of St. John] more especially enshrines—the truth that Jesus Christ is the very Word incarnate, the manifestation of the Father to mankind—is the one lesson which, duly apprehended, will do more than all our feeble efforts to purify and elevate human life here by imparting to it hope and light and strength, the one study which alone can fitly prepare us for a joyful immortality hereafter.[52]

---

[52]Published after his death in the *Expositor*, March, 1890, p. 188. With this remark we may take our leave of Lightfoot in this volume, but we shall return to this note in the future volume that provides Lightfoot's discussions on the Gospel of St. John and early Judaism. (BW3)

Author Index

SCRIPTURE INDEX

Finding the Textbook You Need

The IVP Academic Textbook Selector
is an online tool for instantly finding the IVP books
suitable for over 250 courses across 24 disciplines.

ivpacademic.com